Studies in
Free Russia

Franco Venturi

Studies in
Free Russia

Translated by Fausta Segre Walsby
and Margaret O'Dell

The University of Chicago Press
Chicago and London

Franco Venturi is professor of modern history at the
University of Turin and the director of *Rivista Storica
Italiana*. He is the author of numerous publications,
including *Utopia and the Enlightenment, Italy and the
Enlightenment, Settecento Riformatio*, and *Il Populismo
Russo:*

Sources
Rossija/Russia, ed. by Vittorio Strada (Turin: Einaudi, 1974), vol. 1.
Travel from S. Petersburg to Moscow, by A. Radiščev (Bari: Di Donato, 1972),
Preface reprinted by permission of Editori Riuniti, Rome.
Rivista storica italiana 2 (1972): 451–84.
Il movimento decabrista e i fratelli Poggio (Turin: Einaudi, 1958), © 1956.
Esuli russi in Piemonte dopo il '48 (Turin: Einaudi, 1959), © 1959.
Rivista storica italiana 2 (1972): 485–513.
Populismo russo, 2d ed. (Turin and Paris: Einaudi and Gallimard, 1972),
Preface © 1972 by Editions Gallimard.
Rivista storica italiana 2 (1973): 497–502.

The University of Chicago Press, Chicago 60637
The University of Chicago Press, Ltd., London

5 4 3 2 1   82   83   84   85   86   87   88

Library of Congress Cataloging in Publication Data

Venturi, Franco.
    Studies in free Russia.

    Includes bibliographical references and index.
    1. Soviet Union—Politics and government—Collected
works.   2. Populism—Soviet Union—Collected works.
I. Title.
DK43.V43   947.08   81-23149
ISBN 0-226-85272-5   AACR2

Contents

Preface

During the winter of 1890/91, Sergei Michaelovich Kravcinskii, one of the creators of revolutionary populism, made his "first appearance in America." Going under the pseudonym of Sergius Stepniak—Sergei of the Steppes—he completed a lecture tour of Washington, New York, Boston, and Chicago. In his lectures he returned to the themes of the books he had published during his years of exile: *Underground Russia, Russian Peasants, Russia and the Tzars.* He spoke of "Nihilism," of "Siberian exile," and of "Count Tolstoi." From his speeches, and from his patient organizing efforts, was born the Society of American Friends of Russian Freedom. Francis J. Garrison and George Kennan became the most active and influential members.

An American edition of *Free Russia,* the monthly publication of the movement Stepniak founded, took its place alongside the English- and German-language editions that were already being publisehd in London and Zurich. Through speeches and through the press, Stepniak wished to make the ever worsening situation of the Russian peasants and the increasingly insupportable weight of absolutism there known from one side of the country to the other. At the beginning of the nineties, he saw only one possible outcome of the social and political crises, that is, the conquest, in Russia, of "that political freedom and self-government" that her "Western neighbors have enjoyed for generations." He did not at all repudiate his experiences in organizing revolution. On the contrary, he affirmed—with as much energy and tenacity, as much engagement, as he had placed in the armed, clandestine struggle against czarism—that only political freedom would be able to bring about a profound, authentic transformation of his country. The revolutionaries had eliminated Alexander II, but Russia had not changed. Autocracy was more burdensome than ever. A complete change of direction was therefore necessary. In Russia, as in any other country, political freedom should become the measure against which each action, each rebellion, is measured. Stepniak reminded his American audience that as early as 1881, *Narodnaya Volya,* the same organization that had carried out the assassination of Alexander II, publicly expressed "deep regret" at the death of James Garfield, the American president who was killed by an assassin's bullet. "In a country where the citizens enjoy the right of freely expressing their opinions, and where the will of the people not only makes the laws, but chooses the people who are to execute them—in such a country, political assassinations are the manifestations of despotic tendencies identical to those to the destruction of which we are devoting our lives in Russia." When then, in 1894, the president of the French republic, Sadi Carnot, was assassinated by the Italian anarchist Santo Caserio, Stepniak's monthly, *Free Russia,* declared in an article entitled "Anarchy versus Freedom" that this was a "monstrous act" which could only provoke censure. In Russia, it added, an "anarchist party" did not exist. Revolutionaries and reformers were united in condemning any violence directed against an elected official. The very image of the whole Russian revolutionary movement emerged from this reorientation transformed. Stepniak's journal lost no opportunity to remind its readers how deep were the roots of freedom in Russia and how one generation after another had sacrificed itself in the struggle against autocracy. In October 1892, a new column was inaugurated, "History of Russian Liberalism." The first article was dedicated to Radishchev, "the first Russian liberal." These exiles felt very close to the author of the *Journey from St. Petersburg to Moscow,* not only because of the ideas he expressed and the persecutions that he suffered, but because the weight of imperial despotism still lay on him. One hundred years after the publication of the *Journey,* it was still not possible to reprint it in Russia. The more immutable and perpetual czarist censorship was, the more necessary it became to open the way to political free- dom in Russia.

Early in 1901, when Stepniak had been dead for some years—he died in De- cember 1895 in an ordinary and tragic accident, under the wheels of a train— *Free Russia,* now run by F. Rolchovskii, celebrated the seventy-fifth anniversary of the Decembrist revolt, "that historical event to which the pedigree of the whole Russian revolutionary movement of modern times may in a way be traced." A meeting was organized in London. There Kropotkin emphasized the international character of the Decembrists' attempt. "Indeed their revolution inaugurated a whole era of revolutions in Europe," he said, obviously straining reality and trans- forming this episode from the past into an exhortation for the future. Herzen, Kropotkin added, had known how to gather up their legacy and had become their "lineal descendant." In Geneva and Berne, two more famous Russian Marxists, G. Plekhanov and P. Akselrod, also emphasized the intergenerational continuity of the struggle against autocracy. In Paris, the populist L. Shishko spoke at another gathering of the "enormous influence" the Decembrist movement had had "on the minds of the subsequent generations, the inspiring part it played for the best Russians of the thirties and forties, and later periods of the 19th century." The Russian revolution had not really been crushed on December 27, 1825, in the Senate square, despite appearances. "On the contrary it has been widening and developing since. That is why we celebrate with pride the seventy-fifth anniversary of that great event, while the 'victors' of that year 1825 never have, nor ever will, dare to celebrate their victory!" At the dawn of the new century it could seem indeed that political freedom could become the solid core of the Russian revolution. All the past attempts seemed to flow together in a single "liberation movement"—as the by now ancient struggle against the absolutism of the czar had come to be called. The first volume of the work that Richard Pipes devoted to the biography of P. Struve laid out all the importance of this new vision of the past and present of Russia. The country stood on the threshold of the great decade that preceded the First World War—one of the most creative periods that her history had ever known, animated by a tempestuous desire for liberty, in all areas, from the political to the artistic. The past, too—from Radishchev to the Decembrists, from Herzen to the populists—was discussed again and restudied, in the search for the deep, intricate, and twisted roots of freedom in Russia. Stepniak had been right: a "free Russia" had always existed, ready each time to resume its interrupted path. The experiences of the past could and should be remade by transforming the czar's empire into a country that could stand alongside the free nations of the world.

The war, the defeat, the revolutions of 1917 called into question such certainty, paralleling the loss of faith in freedom in other nations of Europe. Just as there were those in Italy who dared to say that it was predestined to fascism, so there was no lack of those who asserted that a despotic destiny had always been ordained for Russia. While liberty was being uprooted in the Soviet Union, there were those who held that in reality it had never existed there. Certainly, from the thirties on, the study there of the liberal, revolutionary, reform movement became ever more difficult, often impossible. The peasant revolts and those of the military were ignored or transformed into more or less patriotic official myths. In the Stalinist era, the entire populist movement was buried in silence. The very origins of socialism in Russia were veiled or obliterated in the land of real socialism. The passion, the desperation of the *intelligentsia* were masked with the optimistic smile of the successful revolution.

But history cannot be undone. Events in Russia were too closely linked to those in other nations, making it impossible to obliterate so many who had thought, suffered, wished, and striven in Moscow and St. Petersburg one or two centuries earlier. Some of the personalities were too forceful and original (Herzen is an example) for it to be possible to distort their image. The political consequences of certain ideas—this was certainly true of populism—were too relevant for it to be possible to fossilize them entirely.

The essays published here constitute a series of attempts to reach the historical reality, discarding myths and legends, along the often hidden, buried, but always present, vein of free Russia. Theories on feudalism, often of Marxist origin, have obscured the specific characteristics of Russia in the first centuries of the modern age. Some light can be shed on these intricate problems by an inquiry into the formation, in 18th-century Scotland, of the very concept of feudal system, as well as by following the reflection of a similar idea on those who knew directly and from close at hand the empire of Catherine II. Juridical and social problems thus took the form of a debate on despotism versus freedom, West versus East. These themes have recently been reexamined—from a point of view rather more social than political—by Eric Hobsbawm in an important article entitled, "Scottish Reformers of the Eighteenth Century and Capitalist Agriculture," published in the miscellany in honor of Daniel Thorner.

Radishchev could not be omitted, on his journey along the narrow paths of free Russia. Nor could we overlook an attempt to define with precision the ideological origins of the Decembrist movement. Destutt de Tracy, to whom one of the essays collected here was devoted, stands at the crossroads of the ideas of liberty at the beginning of the 20th century in America, Western Europe, and Russia. The recent book by Emmet Kennedy, which appeared in 1978, added several important elements to the reconstruction of this too-neglected thinker. But the cosmopolitan horizon that extends around the "*philosophe* in the age of revolution" is vast indeed. I have sought to enlarge its contours, especially for what may concern Italy, Russia, and Spain. The recent studies of Alberto Gil Novales, concerning the latter country, are a valuable addition to what I have written. In a book published in Turin in 1956, I followed the traces of an Italian family, the Poggios, from their emigration to Russia at the end of the eighteenth century and subsequent involvement in the war against Russia. Through them I reached the very heart of the liberal conspiracy that occurred in the south of Russia during the early twenties. In this collection I have included the pages that seemed to me most significant in understanding how at that time, between the reigns of Alexander I and Nicholas I, Russia tried in vain to choose the path of constitutionalism and freedom for the serfs.

A generation later—a short generation, as happens in times of disturbance—the cities of the kingdom of Sardinia, Nice, Genoa, and Turin, became for a moment after the revolution of 1848 the meeting place of a few, but very active, Russian exiles, survivors of the hopes and delusions of revolutionary Europe. Preeminent among them was Herzen, whose genius illuminated the darkest and most desperate situations, but also Sazonoff, Golovin, and Engelson, minor figures but characteristic of the Russian *intelligentsia,* which by the middle of the 19th century was becoming socialist and rebellious.

From Herzen to the *Narodnaya Volya,* from 1848 to 1881, is the most intense period of the Russian revolutionary movement, to which it is difficult—I believe almost impossible—not to attribute the traditional name of "populist." My book on the subject was published in Turin in 1952. Some years later, in 1960, thanks to the patience and mastery of my friend Francis Haskell, it saw the light in English under the title, *The Roots of Revolution.* The accompanying preface by Isaiah Berlin (which can be read in his volume, *Russian Thinkers,* which appeared

in 1978), opened a wide discussion on populism, which took place in the following years in all countries interested in the Russian past, including the Soviet Union,
which was then in a phase of intellectual openness. I sought to make the debate
known in the introduction to the new edition of my book, which appeared in
Turin in 1972; in Paris in the same year, under the title *Les Intellectuels, le peuple
et la révolution: Histoire du populisme russe au XIXe siècle;* and then, in 1975, in
Madrid, with the title that I frankly prefer to any other, perhaps because it is my
own—*El populismo ruso.* Readers will find this introduction in the pages that
follow. A decade has passed since this work appeared for the first time. But the
historiographical discussion does not seem to me to have revealed any really new
facts and interpretations on the diverse aspects of the Russian revolutionary movement of the 19th century. In the Soviet Union the silence has become even heavier, and once again eyes are averted from the grand hopes—even the grand illusions
—of the sixties and seventies of the past century and of our own. Excellent studies
have appeared—especially in America and in Holland—on some themes examined
by my book, but it does not appear to me that the general perspective has been
substantially altered. Once again, as happens in moments of disillusion and discouragement, some people have come to a point where at times they doubt the
very existence of a free Russia. Those who fought against autocracy have often
been judged negatively. The last volume of A. Ulam constitutes a typical example
of this. However, the very studies of recent times on the 19th century in Russia,
striving to understand its society and the state rather than to explore more deeply
this or that aspect of the revolutionary movement, have ended up by placing the
latter in a better historical perspective, so as to understand better its scope, value,
and importance. Economic history—and here I think with renewed admiration of
Alexander Gerschenkron—has shown us what were the realities that the revolutionaries sought to understand and overcome. Political history—above all in the
works of P. Zayonchkovskii and his students—told us, from the inside, what the
absolutism was that the populists fought against, as well as revealing at last the
exact point at which the edifice of czarism was shaken by the actions of those
who wished to overthrow it. Legal history—here I refer especially to the works of
Richard Wortman in America and N. Troickii in the USSR—has reconstructed the
first phases of the tragic duel between those who wanted change to occur from
above and those who wished it to come from below, a duel which ended in 1917
with the suppression of the freedom that alone would have been able to give an
authentic political value to the transformation that Russia needed. The history
of political ideas—I refer especially to the Polish historian A. Walicki—also contributed to showing the importance of the ideas of the Russian revolutionaries
before Marxism, an importance which was unjustly negated and diminished during the Stalinist era. I marveled, I confess, on reading Isaiah Berlin's review of
Walicki's most recent book, *A History of Russian Thought (From the Enlightenment to Marxism),* in the October 1981 issue of *Slavonic and East European*

Review. Is it true that in my book on the Russian populists I made them give birth to their ideas "out of nothing, as if Herder or Fichte or Novalis had not lived"? In reality, I continue to believe that Novalis had nothing to do with revolutionary populism. As for Herder and Fichte, they are naturally mentioned in my book, as are many other Western thinkers and writers, even more important, in my opinion, to understanding the idea of *Zemlya i Volya* and *Narodnaya Volya.* I am certain that Isaiah Berlin will pardon me, seeing that among those Westerners whom I mentioned I have especially managed to mention Italians such as Mazzini and Pisacane. I have never doubted the truth of what I wrote in the opening of my book, that Russian populism was "a page in the European socialist movement." I have always been true to this position. The essays collected in these pages contain, as the reader will see, many other variations on the theme of relations between Russia and the West.

Cosmopolitanism and freedom have often been tightly connected in the history of modern Russia—and, of course, not only there. The road to freedom often crosses the frontiers of empires, in search of a new and livelier inspiration. In witness of this search, even in the worst of times, even in the Stalin era, I have ended this collection with the too brief words that I wrote in memory of Lev Gordon, a Soviet student of Voltaire and of the French Enlightenment. All his life, Lev Semenovich sought the roots of modern freedom, and to this he kept faith in the midst of the worst tribulations.

F. V.

Turin
January 1982

Works Mentioned in the Preface

Berlin, Isaiah. *Russian Thinkers.* Edited by Henry Hardy and Eileen Kelly. London: Hogarth Press, 1978.

Gerschenkron, Alexander. *Continuity in History and Other Essays.* Cambridge, Mass.: Harvard University Press, Belknap Press, 1968.

———. *Economic Backwardness in Historical Perspective.* Cambridge, Mass.: Harvard University Press, Belknap Press, 1962.

Gil Novales, Alberto. *Las Societades patrioticas (1820–1823). Las libertades de expressión y de reunión en el origen de los partidos politicos.* 2 volumes. Madrid: Editorial Tecnos, 1975.

———. *El trienio liberal.* Madrid: Siglo XXI de España editores, 1980.

Hobsbawm, E. J.; Kula, W.; Mitra, A.; Raj, K. N.; and Sacks, I., eds. *Peasants in History: Essays in Honour of Daniel Thorner.* Calcutta and London: Oxford University Press, 1980.

Kennedy, Emmet. *A Philosophe in the Age of Revolution: Destutt de Tracy and the Origins of Ideology.* Philadelphia: American Philosophical Society, 1978.

Pipes, Richard. *Struve: Liberal on the Left, 1870-1905.* Russian Research Center Studies, no. 64. Cambridge, Mass.: Harvard University Press, 1970.

Troickii, N. A. *Carism post sudom progressivnoj obshchestvennosti. 1866-1895 gg.* [Czarism judged by the progressive society. 1866-1895]. Moscow: Mysl, 1979.

—————. *Carskie sudy protiv revoljucionnoj Rossii. Politicheskie processy 1871-1880 gg.* [The tribunals of the czar against revolutionary Russia. Political trials, 1871-1880]. Saratov: Editions of the University of Saratov, 1976.

Ulam, Adam B. *Russia's Failed Revolutions: From the Decembrists to the Dissidents.* New York: Basic Books, 1981.

Walicki, Andrzei. *A History of Russian Thought: From the Enlightenment to Marxism.* Translated by Hilda Andrews-Rusiecka. Stanford, Calif: Stanford University Press, 1979.

Wortman, Richard S. *The Development of a Russian Legal Consciousness.* Chicago: University of Chicago Press, 1976.

Zaionchkovsky, P. A. *The Abolition of Serfdom in Russia.* Russian Series, vol. 20. Gulf Breeze, Fla.: Academic International Press, 1978.

—————. *The Russian Autocracy in Crisis, 1878-1882.* Translated by Gary M. Hamburg. Russian Series, vol. 33. Gulf Breeze, Fla.: Academic International Press, 1979.

—————. *The Russian Autocracy under Alexander III.* Edited and translated by David R. Jones. Russian Series, vol. 22. Gulf Breeze, Fla.: Academic International Press, 1978.

One   Was Russia a Feudal Country? An Eighteenth-Century Discussion

Many generations of historians have asked themselves whether feudalism existed in Russia, and if so, when and in what form. The needs that drove them to ask this question decade after decade were so varied—as were their answers—that each time it seemed necessary to begin again, rejecting and occasionally forgetting the findings of previous generations. Thus, from Pushkin to the present, the debate on Russian feudalism has proceeded at a tortuous and broken pace through the 19th and 20th centuries.

At the beginning of this century, the discussion seemed to acquire a more scientific approach with Pavlov-Silvansky and Kareev.[1] Forgotten was the dedicated research that had moved the early 19th-century liberals to seek the roots of liberty in the Russian middle ages, and forgotten was the research that in the end had caused the disillusioned Pushkin to write, "Feudalism never existed here, and we're all the worse for that." The preoccupations of the next generation, of Chicherin and Kavelin in the 1850s and 1860s—their desire for legal guarantees, their interest in the origin and development of law—were also overshadowed. What counted for the first Russian historians who considered themselves Marxists in the 20th century was the confirmation of a fundamental uniformity in the development of human society, the proof that a feudal phase was not lacking even in the history of Russia. The following generation (that of Grekov, for example) established Russian feudalism as dogma and devoted its energies to making this unassailable model ever more complicated and detailed.

In the past thirty years, the debate has been reopened, if for no other reason than the inevitable confrontation between what has been written and thought in the West (the name of Marc Bloch suffices to indicate what has been done) and the now closed and hardened historical formula of the Stalin era.[2] There are various options: a healthy return to the sources, setting aside empty generalizations; an attempt, like that of Porshnev and, in Poland, of Kula, to rethink feudalism in economic terms; and, last but not least, a more penetrating historiographical concern, with a strong will to retrace the steps of previous scholars and discover what moved them to study feudalism and to investigate the relationship between Western Europe and Russia.

1

Prior to Pavlov-Silvansky, and except for the generation of the sixties, contemporary Russian scholars thus refer back to the era of the Decembrists, of Pushkin, of the historical debates of Karamzin, Thierry, and Guizot. The sentence quoted from Pushkin, on the disadvantage of Russia's lack of a feudal past, becomes a point of departure for one of the most recent investigations in this field.[3] The article is rich in quotations, known and previously unknown, taken from the writers of the 1820s and 1830s. Here Karamzin accepts, albeit with some uncertainty and with an uncompromising *kazhetsia,* the parallel between "the *feodalnaya,* the *pomestnaya,* and the *udelnaya* systems," thus equating the very foundations of feudal societies in Western Europe and Russia.[4] Here Pogodin divides Russia's past into a first feudal period, begun by Rurik, and a second despotic period under Ivan III. The transition from one form to the other occurred in stages, from *feodalizm* to the *udelnaya sistema.* "The latter was substantially different from the former, even if the *udelnaya* system maintained similar aspects, leaving the power in the hands of one family divided into various branches."[5] In his *Historical Reflections on the Relations between Poland and Russia,* written at the same time, Pogodin rebukes Guizot for not having noted, "in his Slavic lectures on European history," that Eastern Europe "represents a very instructive variety of all the Western institutions, feudalism, monarchy, cities, the middle class, nobility, and peasantry."[6] And, finally, there are the Slavophiles, seeking roots for Russian feudalism that are very different from Western ones. For them, Russian feudalism is based on a willing acceptance of the Normans, whereas the Western type is based on conquest.[7] "This, I would say," wrote Shevyrev in his diary in 1831, "must have been the main source of differences between our feudalism and that of the West."[8] According to him, family, *gens, rodstvo,* finally prevailed over the dominant bonds of dependence found outside Russia. On the other hand, Thierry's reading had shown how difficult it was to compare the history of Russian cities with that of towns in France, and how differently the third estate developed in the respective countries.

But Pushkin's contemporaries were not unaware of how Western historians had traced and rediscovered the germ of liberty in feudalism, bringing to light the voluntary contractual aspect of vassalage. This was the origin of courts and parliaments, charters and constitutions. In Europe, as Madame de Staël had said, liberty was ancient and despotism was new. To what extent could the same be said of Russia? Thus, I. M. Toybin is absolutely right to first clear the slate of the mistaken ideas born in the Stalin era. He must explain the absurdity of Yushkov's comment on Pushkin's statement that "feudalism did not exist here." In 1937, Yushkov remarked that Pushkin "considered the historical development of Russia from a visual angle, recognizing the existence of feudalism in Russia."[9] Less patently absurd but equally erroneous was the approach of many Soviet scholars who attributed to Pushkin the hope that a bourgeoisie would develop in Russia as it had in France, just when he was becoming more critical and doubtful of the results of the July revolution in Paris in 1830 (see the keen observations in V. V. Pugachev's article on Pushkin and Chaadaev, published in the same collection in honor of Blagoy).[10]

Thus Pushkin did not equate the medieval history of Western Europe with that of Russia. Feudalism was a phenomenon in the former and not the latter. But why had he added, "We're all the worse for that"? Toybin believes that the poet was thinking of the lack of a structured military system, which alone would have permitted an effective defense against Tartar invasions. The lack of feudalism was paid for by the fall of Russia. Pushkin's thoughts were certainly inclined that way, but above all he saw in feudalism a system of liberty, a legal and political defense against the aristocracy and despotism. Toybin quotes one of his notes of May 30, 1831: "Feudal government is a strong and simple system in which everything is determined and known—rights and duties, royal power *(le domaine)*, the power of noblemen, and the feudal hierarchy from the lords to the lowest vassal."[11] Elsewhere, Pushkin stresses the independence, the liberty of the barons once their military duties were fulfilled.[12] He follows the origins of parliaments particularly closely. The estates general, he said, were a "fundamental right of the French people."[13] Instead, Russia had known only a "monstrous" form of feudalism that bore a germ, not of liberty, but of aristocratic domination, contained and repressed by the czars, but always resurrected. It was not based on the people, like Western feudalism, but on the minor nobility, the *pomeshchiky*. Pushkin often refers to the "baseness of the high nobility." "The high nobility is not hereditary . . . ," we read in a note from 1830, "it is thus a nobility for life: a means of surrounding despotism with devoted mercenaries and of stifling all opposition and all independence—the opposite is necessarily the means of tyranny, or rather of a base and lax despotism. Despotism: cruel laws, gentle customs."[14] In other words, "Feudalism never existed here, and we're all the worse for that."

These problems and ideas had already been put forward in enlightened Europe, though in different forms. They were considered with special interest in Scotland, where history and the significance of feudalism were studied and felt with particular intensity. In the latter part of the 18th century, both in courts of law and among scholars of the Universities of Glasgow and Edinburgh, there developed what is probably the first discussion on feudalism both in the West and in Russia. It was not without contributions from young Russians who went to Scotland to complete their studies, nor without traces in British political discussions of the times. One of the highlights of the discussion came in a letter by William Richardson, written in 1772 and edited and published in 1784, "concerning the progress of the feudal system in Russia," as he phrased it. All this can be looked upon as a marginal note to the splendid historical debate that took place in those years, among jurists such as Lord Kames, historians like David Hume and William Robertson, economists like Adam Smith, and philosophers such as John Millar and Adam Ferguson. Even the marginal notes of such authors as these are revealing.

Perhaps the first discussion on feudalism in Russia does not deserve the oblivion it has known until now.

The political reason that drove the men of the Scottish Enlightenment to refer back to the medieval past is given by Henry Home, Lord Kames, the man who, in Adam Smith's words, "was after all the master of us all."[15] He observed the Jacobite insurrection of 1745, the harsh repression that followed the English victory, the dismantling of the Highland clans, and the ensuing rapid transformations in Scottish society and government. For this man of law, with his encyclopedic cultural background and enlightened principles, these changes marked a profound breaking point, as much personal as political.[16] He suffered many "disconsolate hours" in 1745 before finding the courage to resume his work and studies. He became convinced that he could restore strength and a voice to his fellow countrymen, persuading them to consider the "antiquities" of their country, "those especially which regard the law and the constitution."[17] Nothing could have been more appropriate in those circumstances than to reconsider the "Introduction of the Feudal Law into Scotland," "The Constitution of Parliament," "Honour, Dignity," and the "Indefeasible Right" which formed the basis of all inheritance.[18] The events had also guided Lord Kames toward the history of comparative law. The rapid legal transformations that were taking place before his very eyes led him to consider the different rhythm of development of Scottish and English law, past and present. He became more and more convinced that legal forms could only be understood if they were related to social and economic causes. About ten years later, in presenting another series of his essays to the public, he did not hide his enthusiasm for his new views. "The history of mankind is a delightful subject." What could be more interesting than the "gradual progress of manners, of laws, of arts, from their birth to their present maturity?" The historical perspective transformed the study of law. "Law in particular becomes then only a rational study when it is traced historically." It was sterile to accumulate fact after fact, as had been generally done. It was futile to indulge the public taste for "the history of wars and conquests." The only subject worthy of study was "the constitution of a state, its government, its laws, the manners of its people." Thus "reason is exercised [only] in discovering causes and tracing effects through a long train of dependencies."

Indisputable evidence of the validity and fruitfulness of this method is found in the study of the feudal past. The method reveals, not just myriad laws and facts, but a true "feudal system" to those wishing to understand "the history of the modern European nations." The "system" allowed a comparison between the various forms feudalism had taken in different countries, that is, "a careful and judicious comparison of the laws of different countries." This was the only means of finding "the true spirit of law." England and Scotland could serve as examples. In England, the "feudal system" had by now been reduced "to a shadow" while in Scotland it survived in a great variety of forms. Viewed in a historical light, the two countries nevertheless had much in common. The similarities and differences seemed to be made especially for a useful comparison. "They have such resemblance as to bear a comparison almost in every branch, and they so far differ as to illustrate each other by their opposition." Politically, too, the same kind of comparison was essential. Scotland had given up its political independence, and Lord Kames had long since abandoned his youthful Jacobite sympathies, stating openly that he favored the union, but he certainly had no intention of renouncing the laws and legal traditions of his own country. He asked, "What nation will tamely surrender its laws more than its liberties?" Thus it was the duty of the English to study Scottish laws, and vice versa. The method proposed was an instrument of political peace as well as of lucid, rational legal interpretations.[19]

In 1757, the year before these *Historical Law-Tracts* were published, John Dalrymple, one of Lord Kames's followers, dedicated his first essay to his master. In it he compared Lord Kames's ideas with those of Montesquieu and Voltaire. A motto taken from the *Esprit des loix,* which had come out about ten years previously, embellished the title page of Dalrymple's *Essay.*[20] "The feudal laws form a very beautiful prospect. A venerable old oak raises its lofty head..." The branches reached toward the sky, and as for the roots, "the ground must be dug up to discover them." As Virgil had written,

...Quantum vertice ad oras
Aethereas, tantum radice ad Tartara tendit.[21]

A deeper historical investigation led scholars to search for the origins of the feudal system in old German traditions, in the customs of the barbarians who invaded the Roman Empire, and in an obscure, mythical historical past. "A system of laws and politics, the most peculiar that ever appeared in the history of mankind, had arisen there." Nor was it the product of the "most consummate political prudence and refinement" but rather the "very natural consequence of very natural causes."[22] The system had been generated by the "situation of the Germans...a band of independent clans...with a spirit of oligarchy, not of equality."[23] It had not spread from one population to another by imitation. The same causes had produced similar effects in "all the northern nations of the continent...however different in their dialects, separated by seas and mountains, unconnected by alliances and often at enmity with each other."[24] Dalrymple did not explicitly pose the problem of how far geographically the area of the germination of feudalism extended among northern populations. Traditional names spring spontaneously from his pen: Saxons, Normans, Langobards, Franks, and Goths. But why limit himself to these? As the "feudal system" gradually lost specific traits, such as English or Scottish characteristics, and tended to become a model of political and social relations that could appear wherever the prerequisites for its development existed, it was natural that the question of geographical limits

should arise. Montesquieu had provided Dalrymple with an image of feudalism
as an organic form, like a tree. Voltaire had suggested to him that it could exist
"among the Timarriots in the Turkish empire and among other nations."[25] After
all, it was "an exceeding simple system." Its essential elements were conquest, the
destruction of existing relationships, the distribution of land, and "annexing to
the gift a condition of military service."

Dalrymple soon abandoned these sociological suggestions about a universal
feudalism, though he did try to include them in a brief scheme of the development of mankind, from the hunters and fishermen through the wandering shep-
herds to the agricultural and commercial populations. His attention focused on
the extraordinary feudal tree that was capable of surviving for long periods, even
when its branches had been cut and its trunk severed. "It still takes a very long
time before roots...can decay."[26] This could be verified in "the whole feudal
world." (Here he was also thinking of France, the Low Countries, and Germany.)[27]
Feudalism was at the very root of the constitutions of England and Scotland.
Like Lord Kames, Dalrymple favored their union. Through union, Scotland, a
country where "a mixture of monarchy and oligarchy" dominated, took part in
the mixed constitution—monarchic, oligarchic, and democratic—that was "the
wonder of mankind." It was England, free from Scottish feudal laws, that had
permitted the development of cities and towns. The comparison favored England
in all areas. "In the declensions of almost every part of the feudal system," he
concluded, "the English have gone before us: at the distance sometimes of one
and sometimes of many centuries, we follow."[28]

For the famous historian William Robertson, the idea of the "feudal system"
is central to his interpretation of the origins of modern Europe. The long and
detailed introduction to his *History of Scotland* is an attempt to identify the
specific characteristics of Scottish feudalism, to explain why the nobles were
more powerful and independent there than elsewhere and the kings were weaker
and poorer. The mountainous nature of the country, the scarcity of cities, the
existence of clans, the small number of nobles and their ability to unite in solid
unions and alliances, the frequent wars with England, and the many minor periods
of sovereignty explained why the struggle to weaken the aristocracy was less
successful in Scotland than in England and France.[29] About ten years later, in
his famous preface to the history of Charles V, Robertson extended these problems to all Europe.[30] "Though the barbarous nations which framed the feudal
system settled in their new territories at different times, came from different
countries, spoke various languages and were under the command of separate
leaders, the feudal policy and laws were established with little variation, in every
kingdom of Europe." This "amazing uniformity" could be explained "with greater
probability" by a "similar state of society and of manners to which they were
accustomed in their native countries and to the similar situations in which they
found themselves on taking possession of their new domains."[31] Robertson does

not admire the feudal tree, nor does he find it a subject of interest through which to understand the secrets of its origins and development. He sides with the monarchs and mainly shows the gaps in the feudal system which the kings used to restrain the nobles' independence and to keep the system free of anarchy.[32] After half a century he comes forth as the new Du Bos. (The comparison tells us what strides were made in the meantime in historical understanding, thanks especially to Voltaire.) He concentrates on cities, on commerce, on emancipation, and on the new modes of life which led to the dismantling of feudalism. He says that in many places this was the only means of progressing beyond that unstable compromise between monarchy and aristocracy which for centuries had made most life in Europe poor and uncertain. "The inhabitants of Europe during these centuries were strangers to the arts which embellish a polished age, they were destitute of the vertues which abound among people who continue in a simple state. . . . The spirit of domination corrupted the nobles, the yoke of servitude depressed the people, the generous sentiments inspired by a sense of equality were extinguished and nothing remained to be a check on ferocity and violence."[33] In other words, feudalism had existed during that hard and cruel phase, during the passage from primitive to civilized society, from Tacitus's German world to the beginning of the 11th century, when "government and manners began to improve."[34]

Nor could David Hume draw near the problem of feudalism without stopping. In his majestic narration of the history of England from the invasion of Julius Caesar to Henry VII, he pauses to give an ample and important dissertation entitled, "The Feudal and Anglo-Norman Government and Manners." He refers back to Montesquieu, to Robertson, and to Dalrymple, but he cannot refrain from giving his own interpretation of "that prodigious fabric, which, for several centuries, preserved such a mixture of liberty and oppression, order and anarchy, stability and revolution as was never experienced in any other age in any other part of the world."[35] Hume's analysis is political rather than legal or social. Even when he discusses economics, he is referring mainly to the finances of the king. He does not present "feudal law" or the "feudal system," but rather the "feudal constitution." He sees the typical feudal military bond manifest itself not only in war but in baronial assemblies, in parliaments, and in the institutions that created the "consent" and provided the "advice" that a sovereign needed. Thus, an essential stage in the history of feudalism was the concession of the Magna Carta.[36] The logic of feudalism tended to favor aristocracy and to eliminate all power and liberty not only for servants but for everyone else who "in a proper sense we call the people."[37] Hume mainly studied feudalism in England after the Norman Conquest. (For him there was no doubt that the military and political aspects of the conquest had a decisive effect.)[38] But he too cannot avoid asking the reasons and consequences of the "great similarity" observable "among all the feudal governments of Europe."[39] The geographical range of feudal Europe remains undetermined for him as well. In fact, his comparison is restricted mainly to England and

France. His analysis of the feudal constitution was an accurate instrument for historical understanding, and was far from those broader generalizations that were being formulated by contemporary Scottish jurists and economists.

John Millar was one of the first men to advance confidently on the new road. For almost forty years, from 1761 to 1801, he taught civil law at the University of Glasgow. His colleagues included Adam Smith and Thomas Reid, and his students included an entire generation of Scottish judges, political figures, and scholars. According to his biographer, Francis Jeffrey, he was an "ardent Whig," and did not scorn "the name of 'republican'."[40] Jeffrey also said that Millar intended to reduce "the history of society to its most simple and universal elements." Moving beyond pragmatic and political explanations, he looked for "the spontaneous and irresistible development of certain obvious principles."[41] How did feudalism appear in this light? He explained it to his students in a long series of lectures. We have the 1771 program; among the topics, he clarifies the origins and nature of feudal property, relates how feudal law was introduced in Europe, speaks of "different kinds of tenure established by the feudal law" and of their mutation over the centuries, and finally reaches the "present state of property in Scotland."[42] Fortunately, Millar took care to publish the essential elements of his thought in his masterpiece, *Observations concerning the Distinction of Ranks in Society,* which came out in 1771.[43] He accepts the results of his predecessors' research (naturally he quotes Robertson and Hume, as well as the French scholars Boulainvilliers and Mably). But in his view, they illustrated special cases of a more general phenomenon whose origins needed to be studied. He saw the roots of feudalism in the unification of the clans that humanity had formed in its early existence. Military requirements, marriages, and mutual hospitality had ended up creating a sort of confederation among these primitive communities. Aristocratic by nature, this government had as its head "a great chief or king."[44] One could find examples in the "government of those kingdoms either on the coast of Africa, or in the countries belonging to Asia, in which a number of distinct tribes or villages are but imperfectly united together."[45] Homeric Greece and primitive Rome had been formed this way. But, Millar also admits, "the most noted examples of that species of government which arises from the first union of different clans occurs in the early history of the modern kingdoms of Europe." The Germanic tribes that had invaded the Roman Empire, "the Gothic nations," had introduced it in Europe.[46] The feudal element in this government was the relationship between the leaders or barons and their adherents or vassals. Later, a very similar bond formed and spread when medieval hierarchies became established. Further development was helped by the absence of cities and of commerce. "A more complete union appears to have been productive of the feudal subordination which has been the subject of so much investigation and controversy."[47] Millar describes this process of feudalization in detail. It had gone at a different pace in each country. But even where political events seemed to indicate a strong break, it was actually only a matter of a stage of development. He also wonders if there had been a feudal system in England before the Norman conquest. Millar favors the hypothesis that there was not. But more important is his presentation of the problem, not in political or legal terms, but as the evolution of social forms. This is what allowed him to look beyond the chronological limits of the Middle Ages and beyond the geographical limits of Europe. "These institutions by which small bodies of men are incorporated in larger societies under a single leader and afterwards linked together in one great community appear so suitable to the circumstances of a rude people, advancing by slow degrees in their ideas of order and policy, that we may expect to find something of the same kind in every extensive kingdom that is formed by the association of many different tribes or families."[48] He was so convinced that feudalism was an obligatory stage in the development of mankind that he saw it born both from the crumbling of a more civilized state and from a nation's first steps toward civilization. The decaying Roman Empire had encountered the Germanic invasions midway, on paths going in opposite directions. "Some authors have thence been led to imagine that the feudal policy of the German nations was copied from those regulations already established in the countries which they subdued. But this only shows that the growth and decay of society have in some respects a resemblance to each other, which, independent of imitation, is naturally productive of similar manners and customs."[49]

After having read these words, it is not surprising that William Richardson, a colleague of Millar's at the University of Glasgow who was directly in touch with the reality of Russia, came to wonder if it was a feudal country. But John Millar did not investigate in this direction. Rather, he looked for examples in the Congo, in Angola, in Benin, in the East Indies, in Pegu, Laos, and Siam. What attracted him especially was the evolution that led Europe out of the feudal world, that is, the formation of a standing army, the development of cities and of commerce. In the conclusion of his book he pauses to discuss, not the nobles, masters, and barons, but those who had worked and suffered for them. The fifth and final chapter of his *Observations* is entitled, "On the Condition of Servants in Different Parts of the World."[50] Here, too, Russia is missing. His ethnographic viewpoint guided him toward Tartars, Africans, and Americans. Historiographical tradition led him to consider the gradual disappearance of Roman slaves and medieval serfs. On the other hand, problems that were closer to home attracted his attention. (One such problem concerned the survival of servants in Scottish coal mines in his own age.)[51] Yet, though he did not discuss the Russian case, the general condemnation of all forms of servitude and slavery with which he ended his work could not but stir others to apply his principles to areas that had remained outside his field of vision.

Millar's *Observations* had only been out a year when, in 1772, the Marquis de Chastellux published *De La Félicité publique, ou considérations sur le sort des hommes dans les differents époques de l'histoire* (On public happiness, or considerations on the lot of men in the different periods of history). It was soon translated into English and published with numerous explanatory notes.[52] Chastellux, too, had attempted to write a general history of humanity. The "Troisième Section" of his work, "wherein is discussed the lot of humanity among the modern nations," begins with a chapter entitled "Du gouvernment féodal" (On feudal government). "Excellent, à mon gré," noted Voltaire, who had provided the first and principal inspiration for it.[53] In these pages Chastellux finally broke the spell that seemed to have concealed feudalism in non-Germanic Northern and Eastern Europe from historians. He was confused; in fact, he muddled the languages and origins of the various nations that had invaded the Roman Empire. But the comparative method, even if it was more intuitive than rational, helped him override these omissions and errors. Having mentioned the Germans, he unexpectedly writes, "Now let us examine what is happening today in the homeland of these same conquerors, I mean, in Russia and in Poland—and it should not be surprising that I compare two such different governments. In the first, the great, oppressors of the people, are oppressed in their turn by a despot; in the second the great succeeded in delivering themselves from the tyranny that they exercise over others; but everywhere I see thanes, boyars, *piastes* or magnates (it doesn't matter what they are called), sole masters, sole possessors of land, sole participants in government, whereas a populace of serfs has difficulty claiming any part of the livelihood that it creates . . ." Everywhere in this Northern and Eastern Europe that seemed to be expanding before the inquisitive eyes of the Marquis de Chastellux, he seemed to see "vestiges of the primitive government of the barbarians," a form of government "brand-new and so extraordinary" that the ancients could never have imagined it. In the Ukraine, "feudal government" still existed "in all its purity and much as it must have been in primitive times." "The czars gave this province to the Cossacks, on the condition that they farm it and that they would be obliged to serve the czars whenever it should be required. No establishment, no legislation except military forms. . . . The hetman stays in a sort of capital, which is an enclosed field where there are some cavalry and infantry, kept always on full pay. The rest work and farm on the condition that they take up arms when there is need."[54]

In Scotland in the 1770s, interest in feudalism as the root of modern political liberty was too strong for such parallels to go unchallenged. When Lord Kames looked at Russia in his 1774 world history, he saw not a feudal system but despotism. He appreciated Catherine II's civilizing effects, the attempt to establish a new code of laws "founded on principles of civil liberty, banishing slavery and torture and expressing the utmost regard for the life, property and liberty of all her subjects, high and low."[55] That is, she tried to "humanize her people and to moderate despotism" by introducing "a code of laws fit for a limited monarchy." The despotism with which she was dealing was like that of the Turks, full of conspiracies and murders. Monarchs and ministers changed, but the populace always remained "abject slaves as formerly." Nor did the more recent social evolution of Russia, the development of economic life, seem to Lord Kames to have succeeded in altering the condition of the peasants. He quotes a passage "from a late Russian writer" (whom unfortunately I am unable to identify) in defense of serfs in his country. "It is a truth founded on experience that commerce polishes manners; but it is also a truth that commerce, by exciting luxury, corrupts manners. With the increase of foreign fashions and foreign commerce in Russia foreign luxury has increased there in proportion, universal dissipation has taken the lead and profligacy of manners has followed. Great landlords squeeze and grind their people to supply the incessant demands of luxury; the miserable peasant, disabled by a load of taxes, is frequently compelled to abandon his habitation and to leave his land uncultivated. And thus agriculture and population diminish daily, than which nothing worse can befall a state."[56]

These ideas had also spread throughout Scotland in the late 1760s and early 1770s, that is, from the time when Catherine herself had weighed the advantages and disadvantages of landed peasants. The famous question of the St. Petersburg economic society had been introduced, for example, in the *Scots Magazine,* the most widely circulated magazine in Edinburgh.[57] This same periodical had followed with great interest the Empress's convocation of deputies to the Kremlin, called to provide Russia with a new code of laws.[58] In November, the journal clearly identified the heart of the problem. "The debates ran pretty high amongst the deputies... on the question whether the good of the state requires that the bondage in which the peasants are subjects be entirely abolished or that it should still subsist under some restrictions. The example of the peasants of England and Holland, and that of the peasants of Poland, Hungary and Denmark are alledged on this occasion, in opposition one to the other. Those of the deputies who have at heart the maintenance of the sacred rights of humanity, are for giving the peasantry an entire liberty, like to that of the rest of the inhabitants: 'The husbandman (say they) being the most usefull of all subjects, what pretence can there be for making his condition worse than that of the others? To render it such is certainly to commit the most cruel injustice.'"[59]

Sympathy for peasants was becoming apparent in Scotland in the 1770s. One of its manifestations was the consideration given to the Highland clans that had lost military and political power in 1745. The losers gradually acquired a halo of primitive equality, warlike liberty, and patriarchal democracy in the minds of the victors. Economic progress, commerce, and cities were not the only possible good. The values of a slowly vanishing world could and should be appreciated and maintained. Adam Ferguson shows sensitivity to this atmosphere in his famous *Essay on the History of Civil Society,* written in 1767.[60]

In Gilbert Stuart, follower of a whole school of interpreters of feudalism, the evocation of the primitive social world that existed before the advent of laws, selfishness, calculation, and inequality takes the form of regret.[61] He criticizes Lord Kames, and especially Robertson and Hume, who in his eyes are too inclined to accept, without the benefit of an inventory, the evolution that had finally overcome "the venerable oak which had expanded his branches so widely and carried its aspiring summit to the skies."[62] Stuart too knew perfectly well that the end of feudalism represented progress, just as he knew that, to use Montesquieu's metaphor, the feudal tree had both reached toward the sky and rooted itself in the servitude of peasants and the despotism of the nobles. Nevertheless, he could not avoid reminding those who seemed to forget that at the beginning "the strength of the nobility must have rested in their influence with their followers," and that then "the people ... could not be in a state of oppression," since "the genius of the feudal system was purely democratical."[63] He compares these origins with the ways of life that slowly arose from the ruins of feudalism. "The rise of commerce" had certainly begun the movement of "the middle and the lowest classes of men" giving "the killing blow" to the age of chivalry. But even in the decline, the very ruins of the "system" seemed to him to have "an interest and importance that bring back to the memory its magnificence and grandeur."[64] The free army was replaced by mercenaries, and taxes were established to support them. The transition period was characterized by a "general corruption" that pervaded the entire society.[65] Stuart ends at this point. Even in his chronological division he opposes William Robertson who begins with that very period in relating his history of modern Europe. Instead, faced with this era, Stuart stops, as he was convinced that the end of the feudal world could not just be considered as the beginning of a better era.

While Stuart was thus viewing the past, a new book was published in 1776. This work, Adam Smith's *The Wealth of Nations,* crystallized for future generations many of the thoughts of the most optimistic Scottish historians. At the root of the "disorderly state of Europe during the prevalence of the feudal government" lay not the rights of nobles but their military and social strength. Privilege derived from the fact that "the sovereign was obliged to content himself with taxing those who were too weak to refuse to pay taxes."[66] Baronial jurisdiction was born from the "authority which the great proprietors necessarily had in such a state of things over their tenants and retainers." "It is a mistake to imagine that those territorial jurisdictions took their origin from the feudal law. Not only the highest jurisdictions, both civil and criminal, but the power of levying troops, of coining money and even that of making bye-laws for the governments of their own people, were all rights possessed allodially by the great proprietors of land several centuries before even the name of the feudal law was known in Europe." The Norman Conquest had only given legal sanction to a situation that was widespread in both France and England. Adam Smith did not have to look far for an illustration of this. Thirty years before the publication of *The Wealth of Nations,* "Mr. Cameron of Lochiel, a gentleman of Lochabar, in Scotland, without any legal warrant whatever ... used ... to exercise the highest criminal jurisdiction over his own people. ... That gentleman, whose rent never exceeded five hundred pounds a year, carried in 1745 eight hundred of his own people into the rebellion with him." In Scotland's recent past, it was possible to observe a reality that had dominated Europe in the previous centuries. It was equally easy to observe "the silent and insensible operation" that always took place in similar societies with the introduction of commerce and the development of cities. It was a process that Smith described in detail.[67]

To what extent was this interpretation of the rise and fall of feudalism valid for other countries? Adam Smith, like all his contemporaries, was open to the ideas brought to him by travelers, by explorers, and by the rapidly expanding knowledge of the world in his era. As regards Russia, he, like many others, stops to consider the peasants and not the structure of the nobility. He says that, for centuries, large landowners everywhere had reduced those who cultivated the land to serfdom. Smith describes this in detail and is severely critical. "This species of slavery still subsists in Russia, Poland, Hungary, Bohemia, Moravia and other parts of Germany. It is only in the western and southwestern provinces of Europe that it has gradually been abolished altogether."[68]

A contemporary of Smith's had tried to associate the feudal nobility of the West with the nobles and landlords of Northern and Eastern Europe. After a five-year sojourn in these areas, John Williams began writing two large volumes of historical recollections and political accounts.[69] His ideas are not very important, but his terminology is interesting. He mentions the "abject slavery" of the great majority of the Russian people along with the "monkish superstition" that reigned in Russia. In his view, these two elements created the fundamental obstacle to progress, and he was convinced they would make Catherine II's good intentions come to naught. He examined to what extent peasant servitude was implicit in the "feudal tenures" of the lords and at what point in Russia and Denmark it became a question of usurping, of "wicked practices" intended to "oppress and tyrannise over the poor farmers," making them "fief slaves." "When the sovereigns of these states invested these feudal lords with power to punish their farmers, and even to deprive them of their lives and properties as they thought proper, which is the case in Poland to this day, there cannot be said to be any civil government existing in such a state, but rather a system of tyranny and oppression more proper for Hottentots than for rational beings."[70] This situation was reflected in the causes and effects of revolutions that occurred in Russia. In Sweden "the people always endeavoured either to support or to regain their ancient rights and privileges"; in Denmark, in all the revolutions but the last, the nobility and clergy had wrested some advantages from the Crown. In Russia, however, the population, kept "in a state of the grossest ignorance and barbarity, as well as in the most abject slavery," had never attempted "to gain anything for themselves, I mean no real advantage," always remaining susceptible in their veneration of their sovereigns, despite the fact they were "tyrannical and oppressive."[71]

The political consequences of the ten-year-old debate were exposed by William Thomson, among others, in 1786 in the pages of the *Political Herald and Review*, a periodical to which Gilbert Stuart and William Richardson had contributed.

Great Britain seemed alone in the world. Tyranny reigned everywhere. Britain alone had managed to maintain those liberties whose roots reached toward the distant past. "Liberty is suitable to the dignity of human nature, and it is the birthright of mankind, but how small a portion of the human race, in fact, enjoys it!" Everywhere there was "the same melancholy prospective of human slavery." There had been a period when "the Persian *timariots* possessed similar privileges to the feudal chiefs of the modern Europe and the Persian kings themselves were subjects to the control of laws." Now the Persians lived in the "most deplorable and degrading slavery." Italy was "enslaved by priests and the emissaries of foreign powers." "Spain with Portugal scarsely recognizes the traces of its ancient parliaments." Liberty was banished in Denmark and Sweden. Almost all the European countries that had known the Romans were "in a state of slavery." There were a few exceptions in some cities in Germany and in Brabant. Only in the British Isles did "the genius of liberty survive."[72] In his article, William Thomson had referred to Russia, saying that she was as yet incapable of achieving liberty. It was a theme that was dear to his heart, and which he had presented in a previous essay in the same journal. "The efforts of the Czarina" he had written, "for the introduction of liberty amid her people have not been wholly in vain." It was always a long and extraordinarily difficult process to transform a "despotic and military throne" and carry out "so mighty a revolution as the rise of the people on the ruins of their powerful and lordly chieftains." The size and internal diversity of the Russian Empire created a further obstacle. Catherine had done everything possible. "Privileges accorded to all who have borne arms . . . rights and immunities granted to the tenants or possessors of the imperial demesnes . . . and, above all, the introduction of the arts of civilization and the light of literature." He concluded, "Already we discern in Russia, as in America, that ardour of pursuit which is the usual result of novelty of impression."[73] To sum up, enlightened absolutism was the only possible route for a country that had not had the ancient roots of liberty.

William Richardson had come to a similar, if more rigorously reasoned, conclusion, expressed in his *Anecdotes of the Russian Empire,* which appeared in 1784. Of all these Scottish professors and writers, he was the only one to have had direct knowledge of Catherine II's empire. As a young man (he was born in 1743) he had accompanied the British ambassador, Lord William Cathcart, to St. Petersburg, acting as secretary to the ambassador and as tutor for his children. Born in southern Perthshire, and being a Scot but not a Highlander, he was closer to the English mentality and literature than some of his compatriots. He was a man of good taste, a poet (one of his collections that is often reprinted bears the delightful title of *Poems, Chiefly Rural*), a literary critic (his Shakespearean commentaries were highly regarded), and a professor of humanities at Glasgow with Adam Smith and John Millar as colleagues. He was always receptive to the political passions of his age and to the historical problems that the Scottish school had raised.[74] In his convictions he was openly a liberal. He found in Pasquale Paoli and in the Corsican revolution an ideal of energy, simplicity, and humanity that could be contrasted with the corruption and cowardice of the English rulers in the period following the Seven Years' War. The poetry he wrote shortly after his arrival in St. Petersburg, as he said himself, came from the heart as he grew increasingly dismayed by the innumerable evidences of despotism that surrounded him in that country. Other and more frequent outlets for his feelings were the letters he wrote from Russia during the four years of his stay. After his return to Scotland in September 1772, he hesitated for about ten years before collecting these letters. In 1783 the work was completed, and the resulting book, published the following year, was naturally dedicated to Lord Cathcart.[75] It is a pleasant and varied miscellany, held together by the delicate thread of Richardson's presence in Russia, and includes the most unexpected topics. He even presents an English version of the story of the abdication of Vittorio Amadeo II, by Adalberto Radicati di Passerano. There are numerous poems, his own and translations from, for example, German literature of the time. As a good citizen of the Age of Enlightenment, Richardson is as interested in meteorological observations as in religious ceremonies, statistics of commerce, or penal systems. Naturally, there is no lack of pages on current events. When Richardson was in St. Petersburg, Russia was at war with Turkey, and technical assistance from England, especially naval aid, was the order of the day. But what attracts our attention in particular are his judgments on Russia, present and past.

Richardson senses what a distance separates Catherine's programs from the actual results obtained. He recognizes the false tones of official Russian propaganda, and he scolds Voltaire for having allowed himself to be corrupted by the flattery that came from St. Petersburg. In these pages irony and sentiment alternate, almost as if to demonstrate his detachment in his role as both judge and participant in Russia's efforts and hopes. His conclusions on the character of the inhabitants—he finds them incapable of control, carried away by passion, rather than being the cheaters and liars they were traditionally considered—prove his sympathy for the people and also offer a veiled comparison with the British character, for Britain always remained in his thoughts. His views on criminal law, on the death penalty, on forced labor, clearly reflect the deepening debate that was developing at the same time all over Europe. He successfully penetrated this field too, presenting the reality of Russia. To limit the spread of crime, was it advisable to establish an omnipresent police force armed with great power, as had been done in France? The English constitution and the liberty it guaranteed would never have allowed such a system, filling large cities with spies. "It is only in arbitrary governments that such great and regular systems of police have been carried into execution, and there is reason to believe that they are supported at great expence, and with unremitting attention, much more from reasons of state than from any regard to the security of the subject or the good order of the community. The end which they have in view does not appear to be so much the punishment or the prevention of crimes as the safety of the prince's person and the maintenance of

his authority" (*Anecdotes*, p. 346). As for forced labor, it too was rapidly transformed into an instrument of degradation and corruption.

Slavery was always the worst of human relationships whether administered by
the state or domestic. According to Richardson, slavery under the state was down-
right incompatible with political freedom; it could be reconciled with the latter
only in the case of an aristocratic regime. He was evidently thinking of Russia
under Catherine II's programs. It had not been difficult for him to ascertain the
truth about slavery in the empire. He dedicated Letter 28 of his *Anecdotes*, entitled "The Slavery of the Russian Peasants," to the topic. In Russia, a noble's
wealth was measured by the number of his serfs rather than the amount of land
he owned. Prince Shcherbatov had 127,000 of them. They were slaves to whom
land was conceded from which they were allowed to cultivate the minimal amount
needed for subsistence. All the rest of the crops went to the landowner. "In fact,
a Russian peasant has no property, every thing he possesses, even the miserable
raiment that shelters him from the cold, may be seized by his master as his own"
(p. 194). Slaves were rented or given over, sometimes in exchange for a dog or a
horse. They were liable for any kind of punishment, although the law excluded
the death penalty. "Yet it happens, sometimes, that a poor slave dies of the
wounds he receives from a passionate and unrelenting superior" (p. 195). Is it
surprising that they were often lazy and sluggish? "I am confident that most of
the defects which appear in their national character are in consequence of the despotism of the Russian government" (p. 197). The fate of servants who depended
on the state rather than on nobles was only slightly better. In general, all social
categories in Russia, aside from the nobles, were in a state approaching slavery.

But what was the fate in Russia of the only class that seemed to escape this
universal despotism? Did it have the rights enjoyed by nobles in other countries?
This was a question that William Richardson, good Scot that he was, expressed in
historical terms, asking if "the feudal system was ever so fully established in Russia
as in the other countries of Europe." This is the topic of his Letter 45, "Concerning the Progress of the Feudal System in Russia" (p. 364). It may be that he was
already writing about this when he was in St. Petersburg between 1768 and 1772.
But the text as it stands now was undoubtedly revised in the following years. Perhaps while still in Russia he had read "the elegant and ingenious" *Account* by John
Millar, published in 1771, and maybe even the 1772 *Essai* by Chastellux, from
which he translates a page directly from the French without awaiting the English
edition. But then he quotes Gilbert Stuart's *View of Society in Europe,* which as
we have seen came out in 1778. Whatever the situation, it is clear that from close
at hand and from afar he continued his dialogue with his Scottish colleagues and
friends, extending their common concern about the nature and value of the feudal
past to Russia.

Richardson's answer is cautiously negative. For nearly a thousand years, Russian
sovereigns "seem to have reigned with unlimited power." Despite the assertions of

those who also searched in Russia's past for the roots of liberty, it was not true that the sovereigns had ever avoided general despotism. As he says, "I have never found, notwithstanding the fond assertions of some patriotic Russians, that in all that period they ever beheld a simple glimpse of freedom." This was a product of the "situation of this country," exposed to invasions and sacking by its neighbors. "Russia has been the thoroughfare, in some measure, by which the Eastern tribes have entered and taken possession of Europe" (p. 364). It was an immense plain without mountains and could only be defended by a standing army commanded directly by the sovereign. "He gave them regular pay, he kept them in readiness to obey his commands, and never dismissed them from his service. . . . Every thing was entrusted to the Velike Knez, known, after the reduction of Casan, by the name of Czar, and of late by the more fashionable name of Emperor" (pp. 365–67). Thus the military nobility did not live on its own land, "separately from one another, surrounded by their dependents and in a state of rural magnificence." Leaving the management of their holdings to their bailiffs, the Russian nobles felt more secure and better accepted at the court in Moscow. Any possibility of conspiracy against the sovereign was curtailed by distance and detachment. "They were removed to a distance from their dependants; their dependants themselves had no other connection with them than to render them obedience, or the fruit of their labour, and were not present to partake of the glory or adopt the resentment of their superiors." As Gilbert Stuart had explained in his *View of Society in Europe,* these were all conditions needed for the success achieved by the feudal lords in the West in the conquest of their own independence and liberty.

Thus the situation in Russia was much more similar to that of the "eastern monarchies" like Persia and Assyria, with their great walled cities and absolute monarchs. The capital tended to completely dominate the population, even in its designation. The king of the Chaldeans became the king of Babylonia, and similarly Russians became Muscovites. Conquest was the principal goal of such monarchies. The great princes of Russia had conquered Kazan and Astrakhan and had advanced toward the Baltic. "These conquests contributed in a variety of different views to confirm his [the Czar's] absolute power at home. He rose, accordingly, to the state of an Oriental Despot." Ideas about legal guarantees or about a constitution were entirely foreign to such governments:

So totally were all notions of real rights and privileges extinguished in the breasts of the nobility, that when the line of Rurik, which had reigned 700 years, was extinct, and when a new Sovereign, or Dynasty of Sovereigns, was to be appointed, the Russians never thought of binding their race of rulers by any such covenant or regulations as would even tend to emancipation. Even of late, when the Empress Anna Ivanovna was exalted to the throne, and was in such critical circumstances as would have induced her to grant any privileges to her subjects, those which were demanded had little respect to the general freedom of the people, or even of the nobility; and, therefore, that she was not compelled to grant them, need not be regretted. Such absolute and undisputed authority has the Sovereign of this empire continually maintained; and so little opposition has he ever encountered from his great lords or chieftains, that I have not learned of his ever having found it expedient, in order to encumber their ambition, to interpose in behalf of their vassals; or countenance among them any pretensions to independence. [Pp. 367-69]

Yet as these and other episodes regarding, for example, the usurper Dimitri or Czar Michael show, a political life among the nobility had existed, just as their mode of behavior in some ways resembled the Western feudal system.

No doubt, in so far as feudal principles are common to all men, in a certain state of society, and may be traced among the Greeks and Romans, no less than among the ancestors of the modern European nations, the Russians also may have exhibited some corresponding appearances. But the chief particulars in their manners, that display any such pretension, arise from the supreme authority of the Emperor over the nobility over their slaves.

The peasantry were obliged to obey their superiors, either in labouring the ground, or in going out to war; but it does not appear, that the terms on which they were allowed to derive subsistence to themselves from tillage were, that they should, on demand, perform military service. If they transgressed against the will of their owner, they might no doubt be driven out of his estates. But the master was unwilling to inflict this kind of punishment; it was like depriving himself of a dog or a horse. The most common punishment would be the seizure of their effects, or corporal suffering.

Quoting from Millar's *Account,* Richardson concluded, "In this we see nothing like the incident of *escheat*" (pp. 370-71).

Even the authorization that lords had to give their serfs for marriages took on a different character in Russian hands. "It is not to be looked for in the power of the master to make the slave espouse whom, or at what time, he appointed. He did something similar for the propagation of his herds and flocks" (pp. 371-72). The entire taxation system was also different. "Considered as having no property but what depended on the good will of their owners, we need not search among them for *wardships, non-entries,* or *aids*" (p. 372). The relationship with vassals differed, too.

Nor does any relation of a feudal nature seem to have subsisted between the Sovereign and his nobility. He was as absolute over them, as they were over the labourers of the ground. If he wanted them to recruit or augment his army, he told the rulers of certain districts the number of men he wanted, and they were bound to supply them. In cases of great emergency, no doubt, they mustered all their vassals, and this force has been termed a militia; it is manifest, however, that it could only be employed for defense, and that other forces were necessary for

the wars waged at a distance, and the extensive conquests achieved by the Czars.
We have nothing, therefore, in the early accounts of his country, corresponding
to the *military service* of the west of Europe. [P. 372]

The judicial traditions and customs that feudalism created elsewhere had never
existed in Russia.

The Russian history, if I mistake not, furnishes few instances of the judicial combat, nor of the manners and customs flowing from such practice or institution.
Neither have I found any thing in the early state of this country that has the
appearance of an assembly of chieftains, met together for the purposes of enacting
laws, administering justice, or of deciding concerning the expediency of peace and
war. The Senate, as it is termed, seems to me to have been originally no other
than a certain number of leading men, nominated by the Sovereign, to assist him
in his deliberations. But what clearly shews that feudal customs were never very
much known in Russia, is the manner in which a man's family succeeded to his
estate. The right of *primogeniture,* till of late, was never much recognized or
regarded. The wife generally succeeded to one-fourth part of a moveable subject,
and one-seventh, or one-eighth, of immoveables. The husband, in like manner,
succeeded to the fortune of his wife; and if she had no children, the remainder
of her effects was divided among her relations. [P. 373]

Nevertheless, Richardson ended by expressing some caution about his conclusions. It was difficult to obtain precise information in Russia. "I tell you what I
was told...I believe I am founded in the account I have given you...yet you
may set them down, if you please, under the head of conjecture" (p. 374). In any
case, the difficulties that Peter the Great had encountered, and that still created
obstacles to Catherine II's plans, also seemed to prove that Russia remained fundamentally "an oriental empire" like Assyria, Chaldea, and Persia had been, where
the emperors commanded great armies "which enabled them not only to make
extensive conquests, but to extend their authority at home." If Peter's and Catherine's will to give Russia "some resemblance to other European states" lapsed
momentarily, their country "will again return, I will not say relapse, into its former oriental condition" (p. 375).
    But if not in Russia, was there feudalism at least in the other lands under the
Empress? Was Chastellux perhaps right to speak of the Ukraine as a perfect example of this political and social system? Here, too, the answer seems negative.

According to this account, no doubt, there is in the Ukraine an appearance of
feudal institutions. But, as was hinted above, the principles, so to say, of feudal-
ity may be found in all nations; among the Romans, in the relation of Patrons and
Clients; among the Greeks, at the siege of Troy; in Mexico, when that country was
subdued by Cortes; in Otaheite, and the South Sea Islands. Nor has the above
quoted author asserted that the particular incidents of the feudal system, and

which gave its peculiar character, are to be met with among the Cossacks. I confess, though the outlines of the system may be traced among them, I doubt much whether they ever had it in its full completion. [P. 377]

By now, the Ukraine had become "in all respects a Russian province," and it did not have "pretensions to independence." The hetman was chosen by the Empress, and his appointment could be revoked ad libitum. Nor was it true that he always stayed with his men, a soldier among soldiers.

He resides in a splendid palace at St. Petersburg, and exhibits all the indolent magnificence and gorgeous luxury of a Magabazus, or Artabazus, or any other Persian satrap in the reigns of Darius or Artaxerxes. I have been informed that the peasants in the Ukraine, who were not, as in Russia, attached to the lands they laboured, the sole property of their masters, and to be bought and sold at their pleasure, but might hire their services on any estate, or to whom they chose, have lately undergone a deplorable change, and have been reduced, by an edict of the present Empress, to the condition of her other Russian subjects. [P. 378]

Thus the debate of feudalism returned to where it began, to the slavery of peasants, not without having exposed, as we have seen, a series of problems of great interest. It was the opening of a long debate. It would be interesting to hear the first echoes of it in Russia. But that would require a reexamination of Russian historiography in the second half of the 18th century. This is a problem of great importance, but here we cannot even scratch its surface.[76] It will suffice to mention two Russian students of the University of Glasgow, I. A. Tretyakov and especially S. E. Desnitsky, the greatest lawyer of Catherine II's time, who brought to the University of Moscow in his own original elaborated form, the thought of Lord Kames, John Millar, Adam Smith, and other Scottish scholars we have discussed.[77] The very term *pravleniye feodalnoye* is used by them.[78] This could form the main thread for further indispensable research. We need only note that, if the *Oxford English Dictionary* is about twenty years behind in its first mention of the English term "feudal system," the dictionary of the Academy of Sciences of the USSR dates the use of a similar term about fifty years too late.

Notes

1. N. Pavlov-Silvansky, *Feodalizm y drevney Rusi* (St. Petersburg, 1907); and N. Kareev, *V kakom smysle mozhno govorit o sushchestvovaniy feodalizma v Rossii? Po povodu teoriy Pavlova-Silvanskogo* (St. Petersburg, 1910); from *Izvestiya Peterburgskogo Politeknicheskogo Instituta Imperatora Petra Velikogo*, vol. 14 (1910).
    2. See Marc Szeftel, "Aspects of Feudalism in Russian History," in *Feudalism in History*, ed. Rushton Coulborn (Princeton, N.J., 1956), pp. 167–82.

3. I. M. Toybin, "Formula Pushkina: 'Feodalizma v nas ne bylo, i tem huzhe,'"
in *Iskusstvo slova*. Sbornik statey k 80-letiyu Dimitriya Dimitrievicha Blagogo, ed.
K. V. Pigarev et al. (Moscow, 1973), pp. 112–21.

4. N. M. Karamzin, *Istoriya gosudarstva rossiyskogo* (St. Petersburg, n.d. [but
1818]), 1:116–17. Referring to the events of 1864, he concluded: "Thus, together
with the supreme princely power, it appears, a system of both feudal landed gentry and independent principalities was established in the new civil society of Scan-
dinavia and in all of Europe where the Germanic people ruled." This was a system
suited for the period when everyone stubbornly defended his own independence
and "obeyed only him who held a sword over his head."

5. M. Pogodin, "Vzglyad na russkuyu istoriyu" (1832), in *Istoriko-kriticheskie
otryvki* (Moscow, 1846), p. 4.

6. Ibid., p. 422.

7. See Andrei Walicki, *Una utopia conservatrice: Storia degli slavofili*, ed.
Vittorio Strada (Turin, 1973).

8. From Toybin's essay, "Formula Pushkina," p. 114.

9. Ibid., p. 115, n. 12.

10. V. V. Pugachev, in *Iskusstvo slova*, ed. Pigarev et al., pp. 101–11.

11. A. S. Pushkin, *Polnoye sobranie sochineniy* (Moscow, 1949), 11:436–37
(there exist several variations on similar thoughts, to which the poet frequently
returns).

12. Ibid., p. 438.

13. Ibid., p. 440. See vol. 12, a note from the same period: "The feudal lords
had duties and rights toward one another."

14. Ibid., 12:203. See ibid., pp. 205–6, for other unusual observations by
Pushkin on this problem.

15. Quoted from William C. Lehmann, *Henry Home, Lord Kames and the
Scottish Enlightenment* (The Hague, 1971), p. xvi. On Home, see Ian Simpson
Ross, *Lord Kames and the Scotland of His Day* (Oxford, 1972).

16. See N. T. Phillipson and Rosalind Mitchison, eds., *Scotland in the Age of
Improvement* (Edinburgh, 1970); and A. J. Youngson, *After the Forty-Five: The
Economic Impact on the Scottish Highlands* (Edinburgh, 1973). These two books
mark a new stage in the study of the Enlightenment in Scotland.

17. Henry Home, Lord Kames, *Essays upon Several Subjects concerning British
Antiquities... Composed Anno 1745* (Edinburgh, 1747).

18. These are the titles of the different essays that divide Kames's work (ibid.).
The introduction was dated in Edinburgh, 10 November 1746. See also the third
edition "with additions and alterations" (Edinburgh, 1768).

19. Henry Home, Lord Kames, *Historical Law-Tracts* (London and Edinburgh,
1758), pp. v ff., "Preface." We note that the term "feudal system," supposed to
have been coined in 1776 by Adam Smith (*Oxford English Dictionary*, s.v. "feudal
system") actually dates from at least twenty years earlier. It became common not
only in books by jurists and historians but also in popular writing. See, e.g., in the
Middlesex Journal, or Chronicle of Liberty, John Wilkes's paper, no. 86 (October
17–19, 1769), the lead article, signed by Sidney and entitled, "How Far the Char-

acter of Majesty Is Sacred," in which we read: "Then the feudal system of government prevailed in Europe, the majority of the people being mere slaves of the grandees and to the sovereign, held their persons and characters in the highest veneration..."

20. John Dalrymple, *An Essay toward a General History of Feudal Propriety in Great Britain* (London, 1757).

21. *Esprit des lois*, bk. 30, chap. 1.

22. Dalrymple, *An Essay*, pp. 1, 7.

23. Ibid., p. 5.

24. Ibid., pp. 1–2.

25. Ibid., p. 2. Voltaire stressed the bellicose character of the Turkish institutions: "Their *zaimats* and their *timariots* are small farms rather than manors. The warrior spirit appears supreme in that establishment.... There is no right for these *zaims* and *timars* other than that of furnishing and leading soldiers for the army, as among our first Franks; no titles, no jurisdiction, no nobility" (*Essai sur les moeurs*, chap. 91 [ed. René Pomeau (Paris, 1963), 1:824–25]). See George Vernadsky, "On Some Parallel Trends in Russian and Turkish History," *Transactions of the Connecticut Academy of Arts and Sciences*, "In Honor of Alexander Petrunkevitch," 36 (July 1945): 25–36, esp. 32–34.

26. Dalrymple, *An Essay*, p. 222.

27. Ibid., p. 311.

28. Ibid., p. 332.

29. William Robertson, *The History of Scotland during the Reign of Queen Mary and of King James VI till His Accession to the Crown of England* (London, 1760). There is an Italian translation from the same period by Pietro Crocchi who was the language tutor for the young John Montstuart, the eldest son of Lord Bute, during their stay in Tuscany: Guglielmo Robertson, *Notizie preliminari alla storia de Scozia avanti all morte di Giacomo V nelle quali si contiene un succinto ragguaglio dell'origine, de' progressi e della decadenza del sistema del governo feudale* (Amsterdam [Siena], 1765).

30. William Robertson, *The History of the Reign of the Emperor Charles V* (London and Edinburgh, 1769), 1:1 ff., "A View of the Progress of Society in Europe from the Subversion of the Roman Empire to the Beginning of the Sixteenth Century." See Giorgio Falco, *La polemica sul medioevo*, new ed., ed. Fulvio Tessitore (Naples, 1974), pp. 154–90.

31. Ibid., p. 13.

32. Ibid., p. 15; "The sources of anarchy were innumerable."

33. Ibid., p. 20.

34. Ibid., p. 21.

35. David Hume, *The History of England from the Invasion of Julius Caesar to the Accession of Henry VII* (London, 1762), 1, 2:397.

36. Ibid., p. 402.

37. Ibid., p. 404.

38. See Giuseppe Giarrizzo, *David Hume, politico e storico* (Turin, 1962), pp. 250 ff.

39. Hume, p. 409. On p. 412 he mentions "feudal kingdoms of Europe."

40. William C. Lehmann, *John Millar of Glasgow, 1735-1801* (Cambridge, 1972), p. 67. On the University of Glasgow, ibid., p. 36. See Ronald L. Meek, "The Scottish Contribution to Marxist Sociology," in *Democracy and the Labour Movement: Essays in Honour of Dona Torr*, ed. John Saville (London, 1954), pp. 84-102.

41. Lehmann, *John Millar*, p. 67.

42. John Millar, *A Course of Lectures on the Private Law of Scotland Given Annually in the University of Glasgow* (Glasgow, 1771), pp. 5 ff.

43. John Millar, *Observations concerning the Distinction of Ranks in Society* (London, 1771).

44. Ibid., p. 156.

45. Ibid., p. 157.

46. Ibid., pp. 161, 164.

47. Ibid., p. 165. Later, he also noted how "the system of feudal tenures" was "regarded as the most distinguishing peculiarity in the policy of modern Europe"; John Millar, *An Historical View of the English Government* (London, 1803), 1:103.

48. Ibid., p. 174.

49. Ibid., p. 178.

50. Ibid., pp. 193-242.

51. See B. F. Duckham, "Serfdom in the Eighteenth Century Scotland," *History* 54 (1969): 178 ff.

52. François-Jean de Chastellux, *An Essay on Public Happiness, Investigating the State of Human Nature under Each of its Particular Appearances through the Several Periods of History to the Present Times*, 2 vols. (London, 1774). The chapter on feudalism is in vol. 2, pp. 1-75.

53. François-Jean de Chastellux, *De La Félicité publique* (Paris, 1822), 2:1. Voltaire's fundamental pages on feudalism are in the *Essai sur les moeurs*, 2:217-48, chap. 96 ("Du gouvernement féodal après Louis XI, au XVe siècle"), chap. 97 ("De la chevalerie"), chap. 98 ("De la noblesse"), chap. 99 ("Des tournois"), chap. 100 ("Des duels"). For him, feudalism was "a very natural and very common effect of reason and of human cupidity," which led the "possessors of land" to try to be "the masters of their homes." He gave an example: "From the end of Muscovy to the mountains of Castile, the great landowners always had the same idea..." (p. 18). But after this fleeting mention of a Russian feudalism, he no longer speaks of it. On Voltaire, and on the discussion on France generally, see J. Q. C. Mackrell, *The Attack on "Feudalism" in Eighteenth-Century France* (London, 1973), which, however, does not even mention Chastellux.

54. François-Jean de Chastellux, *De La Félicité publique*, ed. Marc-Michel Ray (Amsterdam, 1772), pp. 15-16, 22. Note that Chastellux had considered the pages of the Scottish historians: "Let us ask Hume and Robertson..." (p. 13).

55. Henry Home, Lord Kames, *Sketches on the History of Man* (Edinburgh, 1774), 1:253n.

56. Ibid., pp. 401, 421.

57. *Scots Magazine* 29 (January 1767): 45.

58. Ibid., 29 (February 1767): 97; 29 (May 1767): 272; 29 (September 1767): 492.

59. Ibid., 29 (November 1767): 603.

60. Adam Ferguson, *An Essay on the History of Civil Society, 1767*, ed. and with an introduction by Duncan Forbes (Edinburgh, 1966). As the author of the preface says, for Ferguson "civil order, regular government are an undoubted improvement, but not if they become ends in themselves and destroy that vigor and group spirit and loyalty of which the quarrel of parties and classes is a symptom." "Ferguson was a Highlander... and undoubtedly behind the *Essay* lies a deeply felt experience of the contrast between two societies, and the question: what happens to men in the progress of society" (pp. xxxv, xxxix). On feudalism, see ibid., p. 131.

61. Gilbert Stuart, *An Historical Dissertation concerning the Antiquity of the English Constitution* (Edinburgh, 1768).

62. Gilbert Stuart, *Observations concerning the Public Law and the Constitutional History of Scotland with Occasional Remarks concerning English Antiquities* (London, 1779), p. 146. The author considered this work so important that he published it again as an appendix to his *History of Scotland* (London, 1783), vol. 2, *Appendix I* pp. 1–148. See also in Gilbert Stuart's main work, *A View of Society in Europe in its Progress from Rudeness to Refinement, or Inquires concerning the History of Law, Government and Manners* (London, 1778), "Lord Kames, whom I am ashamed to contradict so often" (p. 225), and the statement that Hume and Robertson, in a polemic against the aristocracy, "seem to take a pleasure in painting the abjectness of the people" (p. 318).

63. Stuart, *Observations*, p. 222.

64. Ibid., p. 118.

65. Ibid., p. 141.

66. Adam Smith, *An Inquiry into the Nature and Causes of the Wealth of Nations* (London, 1776), bk. 5, chap. 2, p. 461.

67. Ibid., bk. 3, chap. 4, pp. 497 ff.

68. Ibid., bk. 3, chap. 2, p. 471.

69. John Williams, *The Rise, Progress and Present State of the Northern Governments, viz. the United Provinces, Denmark, Sweden, Russia and Poland, or Observations on the Nature, Constitution, Religion, Laws, Policy, Customs and Commerce of Each Government, the Manners and Dispositions of the People, Their Military Forces by Land and Sea, the Revenues and Resources of Each Power and on the Circumstances and Conjunctures Which Have Contributed to Produce the Various Revolutions Which Have Happened in Them*, 2 vols. (London, 1777).

70. Ibid., 1:259–61. See also, ibid., p. 304, where he calls the property of Russian nobles "fiefs."

71. Ibid., 2:338.

72. *Political Herald and Review* 2 (1786): 396 ff.

73. Ibid. (1785), pp. 31 ff.

74. See Peter Putnam, ed., *Seven Britons in Imperial Russia, 1698–1812*,

(Princeton, N.J., 1952), pp. 125 ff. (where, after a biographical profile, extracts from his *Anecdotes* are published); H. J. Pitcher, "A Scottish View of Catherine's Russia: William Richardson's Anecdotes of the Russian Empire (1784)," *Forum for Modern Language Studies,* University of St. Andrews, 3 (1967): 236–51; and Anthony Cross, ed., *Russia under Western Eyes: 1517–1825* (London, 1971), pp. 208 ff. (he reproduces the letter on the servitude of the Russian peasants, but, like Putnam, omits the one on feudalism).

75. William Richardson, *Anecdotes of the Russian Empire in a Series of Letters Written, a Few Years Ago, from St. Petersburg* (London, 1784). There is a photostatic reprint of the original published by Frank Cass (London, 1968); the following quotations are also from this edition.

76. See S. L. Peshtich, *Russkaya istoriografiya XVIII veka,* 3 vols. (Leningrad, 1961–71). This book deserves the fashionable term "stimulating," also in the sense that, once having read it, one gets a great desire to rewrite it.

77. See Michael P. Alekseev, "Adam Smith and His Russian Admirers of the Eighteenth Century," in William Robert Scott, ed., *Adam Smith as Student and Professor,* Reprints of Economic Classics (New York, 1965), pp. 424–31; M. T. Belyavsky, "Semen Desnitsky i novye dokumenty o ego deyatelnosti," *Vestnik Moskovskogo Universiteta, Istoriya,* no. 4 (1969), pp. 61–74 (with a vast bibliography); and Archibald Braun (Archibald Brown), "S. E. Desnitsky i I. A. Tretyakov v Glazgovskom universitete (1761–1767)," ibid., pp. 75–88 (containing many important new documents about John Millar and Adam Smith, among others).

78. See Peshtich, *Russkaya istoriografiya* (1965), 2:89, where he quotes an example taken from I. A. Tretyakov. A certain number of important texts are collected in *Yuridicheskie proizvedeniya progressivnyh russkikh mysliteley. Vtoraya polovina XVIII veka,* ed. S. A. Pokrovsky (Moscow, 1959). However, one should see the translations, such as that of William Robertson's *History of Charles V,* which was published in Moscow in 1775–78.

Two

A Portrait of
Alexander Radishchev

In a chapter in one of the stages of his *Journey from St. Petersburg to Moscow,* Alexander Radishchev depicts a father taking leave of his children who are on their way to the city. The father is a provincial, bound to the soil and deeply rooted in the daily life of the fields. He raised his children to love work and freedom, and now their destiny as young nobles tears them away from the paternal home and tosses them into the struggles, the ugliness, the vanities and vices of the distant capital. Before them lie, not the wide horizon of the plains, but palaces, barracks, positions as aristocrats, officers, and officials. It is a heartrending farewell; tears spring to the father's eyes. The children weep. It resembles a painting by Greuze, the French painter so much admired by Diderot. As in the artist's pictures, in Radishchev's pages the embellishments of baroque drapery and rococo scrolls cover a hard and severe form that approaches neoclassicism. The tears, the sentimentality, the moralism in those pictorial and literary images, in which reality is accepted as destiny, do not disguise a conception of family, society, and nature that is solidly based on enlightened reason. It is terrible to leave the paternal home and dreadful to be taken and swallowed up by the machinery of the state. But there is no alternative. The natural life is left behind, and civilization serves as its substitute. Family ties are now broken and cannot be reconstructed by means of reason. It is not gratitude but calculation that now unites fathers and sons, not manual labor but science and art that affect the fate of a man who has left primordial simplicity behind. Before him stands a new reality: schools, careers, riches, culture. New virtues and vices lie in the path of those who have abandoned the natural state.

Radishchev had experienced a similar separation in his youth. Born in 1749, by 1755 he had already left for Moscow. Later he frequently returned to this theme of detachment, and his father eventually became the symbol of all that had connected him with the past, of all the bonds that civilization and reason had forced him to break, but that still remained strong within him. His father represented the religious and moral tradition from which he had begun and to which he turned for support. Yet it was a force he always rejected because it contained things that were unacceptable, contrary to reason, to justice, and to the enlightened will, which had become his raison d'être. One never returns to the past, just as one does not return to the natural state. But both had a great attraction for Radishchev, and for Jean-Jacques Rousseau, and for all those who experienced the drama and contrast of nature and civilization with a religious intensity.

Radishchev's relationship with his family is not spoiled by idolization of the aristocracy or by the regret of having left the "house of gentlefolk" too early, or by the pain of not being able to return to that refuge. He has a moral quest; he continually asks what is alive and what is dead in his relationship with his father and the land. In his family's past he sees the roots of the problem that torments him.

The Radishchevs were of Tartar origin. As they recounted from one generation to the next, Alexander's ancestors had fought against Ivan the Terrible, defending Kazan. When conquered, they had converted to Christianity and thus became part of the Russian *pomeshchiki.* For them, orthodoxy, nobility, and the homeland sprang from the same source. In the eyes of Nikolai Athanasevich, Alexander's father, it was sacrilege to muddy that source. When Alexander's first wife died and he lived with his sister-in-law, by whom he had two children, he heard his father say that his was a truly Tartar manner of living and he would certainly not be forgiven for this sin. And how could Nikolai accept, if not as a divine curse, his own economic difficulties and the fate of his son, who was condemned to death, then exiled to Siberia, and eventually a suicide? Nikolai Athanasevich reacted by immersing himself in religion, in monasteries, and in the forests; he built a church on his own land to placate the wrathful deity, and tried to enter a monastery in Saratov. When the son returned from Siberia he found his father more alone than ever and dressed in a traditional caftan, with a long beard, blind, and far from any worldly thoughts. It was a tragic and disturbing image. Yet, in his youth, Nikolai Athanasevich had been anything but poor and idle. He had inherited more than two thousand serfs from his father, a typical noble of Peter the Great's time. Alexander's grandfather had begun his career as a soldier and by fighting and struggling had become an officer, a judge, and a wealthy landowner. Thus in the middle of the century, when Alexander was born, the Radishchevs' future seemed secure. Nikolai Athanasevich administered his vast holdings in Verkhnoe Obliazovo, in the Saratov province, and watched his family of seven sons and four daughters grow up. Alexander, the writer, was the eldest son. But even in this *pomeste,* as among all Russian nobility, greater worries developed as the decades of that century passed. In this family, as we have seen, fortune had come with state employment, with money and land that Peter had granted to his officers and officials. Without this support, how could one maintain an estate based on the labor of serfs, on traditional agriculture, on a primitive technology, without markets for products, without means of communication with the distant and poor cities on the Volga? Like many other Russian nobles of his age and era, Nikolai Athanasevich had only one desire. That was to remain on his own land, to free himself from the

burden of state service, and to try to remove the weight that Peter the Great had
also laid on his family. In 1761, during Peter III's brief reign, the ruler seemed to
have contented the nobles by releasing them from the obligations of service. They
were finally free to dedicate themselves entirely to living peacefully on their own
land. They had dreamed of being released from the cities, from military service,
from burdens, maybe even from wealth. They had had hopes of returning to a
simple and healthy life in their houses with the peristyles, the neoclassical pedi-
ments, the vast yellow-and-white servants' quarters. But behind the facade, the
problems and worries increased. The nobility were free; why not the peasants?
The entire burden of servitude fell on the *muzhiki.* All the advantages of freedom
were enjoyed by the *pomeshchiki.* The more enlightened nobles in St. Petersburg
were beginning to discuss and be concerned about the imbalance. Above all, the
peasants themselves were asking about it with suppressed rage. Why not serve the
czar and work for him instead of being slaves of the nobles who, with their freedom,
had revealed they were of no use to their sovereign, nor to the state, nor to anyone but themselves? The rebellion that had long been simmering on the borders
of the Russian state, on the Caspian and in the Ural areas, found a leader in the
Cossack Emelian Pugachev. In 1773 a great *jacquerie* flared up among much of
the Russian peasantry around the Volga. A true revolution *manquée,* it placed the
throne in serious peril, and for the next two or three generations the nobility bitterly reinforced their position. Between fear and battles, massacres and executions,
the nobility strengthened the tie between *pomeschiki* and the state. The economic
needs, the problems of a difficult agrarian transformation desired or hoped for by
the nobles, the need for new territory, new roads, ships, ports for commercial
development, the need for new techniques and for continually increasing credit,
in themselves created a greater symbiosis between the nobles and the state. Thus,
at the beginning of the 1770s, the war against the Turks and the Pugachev revolt
precipitated an effort at enlightened despotism and active and independent autocracy which were personified in Catherine II.

The shadow of these conflicts and tensions fell on the Radishchevs' Verkhnoe
Obliazovo, too. Nikolai Athanasevich was convinced that strict goodness and unswerving justice would allow the normal system of servitude to function and that
the peasants, if they were well directed, would support him in his role as an enlightened and efficient landlord. In a sense, this is what happened. When the great
wave of the Pugachev revolt passed through his area and all the surrounding nobles'
houses were burned, not to mention the death toll among nobles of all ages, Nikolai
Athanasevich was able to hide with a group of household servants. He was ready
to defend himself with them to the end, and his hiding place was not revealed—
quite exceptional in those days—by any of his thousands of serfs. He had entrusted
two small sons and two daughters to the servants' care. Later it was told how the
peasants had soiled the children's faces so that they would be indistinguishable

from their own, and the rebels could not identify them. Thus the Radishchevs were saved from the *pugachevshchina*. But their attempts at defending themselves from economic difficulties were less successful. Nikolai Athanasevich's will and Christian virtue could capture the respect and perhaps the love of his peasants, but these qualities could not make Verkhnoe Obliazovo a success; debts, land sales, and all kinds of difficulties multiplied. One after another the children left for the city to gain culture and technical knowledge; they were seeking careers and fortunes that only the state could offer.

The eldest, Alexander Nikolaevich, left for Moscow at the age of six. He had learned to read from the Orthodox Psalter and Book of Hours, which had served this educational function for generations. The young Peter, the future emperor, had learned by the same method. But when Alexander reached Moscow in 1755, this tradition too was fading. In that year the first Russian university opened in Moscow. The director was a relative of Radishchev's mother, and thus his early formative years were spent among professors and students, until 1762 when the newly crowned sovereign Catherine II chose her pages. Alexander was selected, and so he moved to St. Petersburg in 1764. For two years he lived in the Winter Palace, mixing in life at court, seeing its most splendid and its most humiliating aspects. The distaste, disgust, and horror he felt from this experience was like a poison in his veins that never left him. But, as he later noted in his *Journey,* even poison can be useful if one has the wisdom necessary to use it.

An unexpected stroke of luck in 1766 gave him the opportunity to acquire an exceptional scientific training. His name was included on a list of twelve young Russians whom Catherine was sending, at her own expense, to Leipzig to learn "Latin, German, and if possible the Slavic languages ... moral philosophy, history, and in particular, natural and universal law and something of Roman law. The study of other sciences is left to each according to his choice." This was preparation for a political and administrative career, a school for high civil servants but, one must admit, liberally and broadly conceived. This program represented a great advance over the training that had been offered previously in Russia. At the time of Boris Godunov, there had been a first attempt at sending students abroad: not one returned. Under Peter the Great, dozens of young nobles had been sent to Holland and Italy. Technical training, medicine, and military and civil arts had dominated Peter's programs. Now Catherine wanted these young people to investigate the very bases of knowledge. She intended to put the young men in direct contact with the natural sciences, with moral philosophy, and with the juridical discussions of the German *Aufklärung.* She was acting like the enlightened sovereign she claimed to be. In her choice, she had not let herself be guided only by a desire to satisfy certain families such as the Orlovs and the Nesvitskys, who had had so much influence in the coup that had brought her to the throne. Nor was she only trying to please aristocrats such as the Trubetskoys. She also included the son of Nikolai Athanasevich Radishchev, the *pomeshchik* from Verkhnoe Obliazovo—for reasons which, incidentally, are not at all clear—and the two Ushakov brothers, who were not linked with the aristocracy either.

As happens with autocrats, even Catherine's best intentions were distorted by the choice of those who were to carry them out. She chose Gerhard Georg Bokum, a Russified German from the Baltic, to supervise the twelve boys. Thus Radishchev and his companions, willy-nilly, took with them to Leipzig a fine example of that mixture of caprice and discipline, of corruption and Spartan life, of dullness and reverence for learning that characterized so many absolute states of the old regime, especially in Germany, but which undoubtedly was found in greater quantities in the St. Petersburg autocracy. It was not the fact of being sent abroad with a particularly despicable supervisor that was new or exceptional, but the fact that the youths, exposed to this system, protested, rebelled, and attempted in every way to free themselves. Theirs was the first student revolt in Russia, and one can understand why it became famous.

However, one must not exaggerate its importance. If it had not been for the presence of Radishchev, who later recalled the episode in an account of one of his companions who died in Leipzig, this protest would have remained as one of the many conflicts between learned people and despots that were common throughout Catherine's reign. More significant are the ideas, the philosophical and moral problems to which the Russian youths were exposed. In this little drama, Bokum is the despot and all enlightened people, in the students' eyes, are on the other side. The shadows deepen as the boys' intellectual curiosity brightens.

Behind the facade of official culture, whose purpose was a practical economic and administrative one, they rapidly searched for and discovered a newer and more vivid culture. Their exposure, even though it was purely academic, to theories of natural law and the rise of human society provided Radishchev and probably others with a juridical grounding which they explored further under the influence of Jean-Jacques Rousseau. For Radishchev, at least, this grounding remained intact. The nature of law, the rise and imposition of laws, and the value of juridical norms always remained cornerstones in his political conceptions. Here and there in the *Journey,* he still recalls the lessons of his teachers, the Leipzig jurists. The absolute power and despotism reigning in his country, both in the relationship between nobles and serfs and in that of the czar and his subjects, appear even more dreadful to him. In his view, the want of laws became one of the most serious and profound ills of his country. He searched persistently for a remedy for this terrible void, this weakness which was at the root of all the cruelty, fear, and insecurity suffered by people who were subject to the whims of those in power everywhere in Russia. The pages in which Radishchev explains and clarifies the origin and value of law may seem pedantic and dry to a reader. Similarly, his notes on the legitimacy of the court that condemned Charles I of England to death may seem strange. It is enough to read his pages dedicated to censorship, which derive chiefly from 18th-century German culture, to fully understand the importance of all he learned in Leipzig, of that sense of law that his teachers impressed on him. There are not many Russian writers open to the value of law. In fact, Radishchev is one of the first, if not the very first, of this small group, and he is certainly one of those most deeply convinced of the value of law. Some elements of the thoughts of his Leipzig professor, K. Hommel, called "the German Beccaria," were clearly passed on to Radishchev.

The period spent in Germany was also fruitful for Radishchev in the field of economics, though less obviously so. August Witzmann, a German professor whom Radischev considered a protector in the conflict with Bokum, opened his eyes to the economic world. Witzmann went beyond the German cameralism to touch on the problems of the poor and backward countries, and treated subjects such as the duties of landowners and the poverty of peasants. On a trip to Italy, Witzmann had read many works on economics, and of them he selected Antonio Genovesi's *Lezioni di commercio* as the most worthy of being translated. When he had completed this considerable task, he wanted to dedicate the edition to his young Russian friends, remembering their common life and battles. He always remained in contact with Radishchev, and one of the few copies of the *Journey* given away by the author was sent to Witzmann, who was then in St. Petersburg. Radishchev's economic ideas matured slowly as he gained direct knowledge of commercial and customs problems of Russia and Siberia. But at the heart of his conclusions are the teachings of Witzmann and, indirectly, the wisdom of the Neapolitan master.

Alongside economics was politics. How could one not be interested in what was happening in the world in 1770 when the Russian fleet, after completing a long voyage through the Baltic, the English Channel, and the Atlantic, was penetrating the Mediterranean Sea and fighting victoriously against the Turks? When Catherine was dangling the image of their freedom before the Greeks to lure them to revolt against the Ottomans? When on the Danube the fates of Crimea and the Black Sea were being settled? Leipzig was on the route from St. Petersburg to Leghorn and Naples, the Russian bases in the Mediterranean. Officials and messengers came and went, bringing the twelve Russian students the news of the world. Was Radishchev even then gaining insight into the other side of such excitement and military glory? It seems so, since he was persuaded to translate into Russian a manifesto that appeared in the Clèves gazette on July 20, 1771. It was written by a Greek from Epirus, Antonio Gicca, who was serving the Russians in Naples and was associated with Mario Pagano and others in Southern Italy who were hoping for a Greek renaissance. He had written to the Russian Empress, strongly urging her not to abandon the Hellenic cause, not to allow those who had rebelled in her name to be massacred, and not to treat the Balkans as a pawn in her military and political game. Gicca expressed these ideas with both sagacity and diplomacy, hoping to convince the Empress rather than shock her. This program that united officers such as the Orlovs, who were inclined toward expansion and adventure, with those who, in Italy as in Russia, attributed a sense of liberation to Russian politics seemed to interest the young Radishchev. In fact, the version of the Gicca manifesto which he began was preserved among his papers and provides evidence of his initial enthusiasm, hope, and perhaps disenchantment.

His most profound experience in Leipzig was a philosophical one. It was not just his contact with the German *Aufklärung* that left significant traces. It was not just Ernst P. Platner's instruction on the relationship between the physical and moral man. It was not only the loss of the value and significance of traditional religions and his acceptance instead of the criticism and ideas of European deism. Above all, Radishchev and his companions discovered the more daring views of the French thinker Helvétius and the Italian Beccaria. It appears that while he was traveling between Russia and the Mediterranean in 1768, Fedor Gregorovich Orlov brought Radishchev *De l'esprit*. On one occasion Orlov discussed metaphysics with Ushakov until one in the morning. The book by Helvétius was read over and over, summarized, and discussed by the Russian students. As Radishchev later said, he and his friends "learned to think" with *De l'esprit*. Soon after that, Professor Hommel gave them Beccaria's *On Crimes and Punishments* in French. Utilitarianism and philosophic radicalism thus became a point of departure for their thought. Self-interest offered a rational explanation for the conflicts between individuals, and explained the origin and nature of society. The essay that Ushakov wrote then, and that Radishchev published twenty years later in memory of his vanished friend, showed traditional Leibnizian and Wolfian philosophy corroded internally by the acid of utilitarianism. It demonstrates the conquest by Enlightenment ideas of a young mind that fights and defends itself, but that in the end is won over, even if not entirely, by the new empirical and utilitarianistic logic of Helvétius and Beccaria. When Grimm, the encyclopedists' friend (whom Pushkin later called "philosophy's traveling salesman"), passed through Leipzig, he was able to ascertain the success of Helvétius's book. He informed the author, who was certainly amazed and surely equally pleased to see how much interest his work had generated among a group of Muscovite students. Helvétius's ideas spread much further in later years. Russian nobles young and old, obscure or famous like ambassador Golicyn, turned to the author, revealed their admiration, and offered to help distribute his books. What was the significance of all this? The French philosopher wondered about this, as did Beccaria in those same years when he was asked to go to St. Petersburg to help Catherine in remaking the laws for her empire. Despite even recent and valuable studies, we cannot help asking the same question ourselves, two centuries later. What caused this unexpected success of philosophical utilitarianism among the Russian nobility? To ascribe it to fashion is too easy. It is a fact that the Orlovs stayed up late at night discussing metaphysics. The Golicyns became followers of Helvétius; Catherine plagiarized Beccaria in her *Nakhaz*. Students struggled with that seductive, lucid thought. We are faced with one of the strangest periods in the long history of the ambiguous relationship between *philosophie* and 18th-century Russia. Helvétius's ideas lent themselves to a double interpretation. He exalted the passions and made them the moving force in society. The Orlovs, the Golicyns, and the young students seemed to read into this affirmation the explanation and justification of the energy that surged within them, of the drive that led Russia to change internally and to expand externally. But would self-interest offer a strong enough embankment—or at least a useful channel—for these passions, directing them, as Helvétius or Beccaria wanted, toward a juster, more rational, freer world? Or would the philosophy of self-interest end by serving as a justification for the tyranny of the nobles, for the despotism of the emperor, or the luxury of the court? They read and re-read *De l'esprit* (and later, when it was published posthumously in 1774 by Golicyn, *De l'homme*). It presented a new and revolutionary thought. But what kind of revolution was it?

As he approached the end of his stay in Leipzig (he returned to Russia in October 1771), Radishchev asked himself this question again and again. All his life he firmly upheld the utilitarian principles that Helvétius and Beccaria had taught him. Yet in the following years he tried to fill these outlines with a moral and political will, with a protest and reform that he felt stirring within his soul beyond the logical tools the *philosophie* had taught him to use. Utilitarianism was the indispensable weapon. But what hand would wield it?

Naturally, the Empress expected to use the students who had returned from Germany in the service of the state, employing them to administer customs, embassies, offices, and courts. Many, including Radishchev, submitted to being employed according to the abilities and knowledge they had acquired. None of them opposed the work on principle. But soon there re-emerged in many of them, including Radishchev, the basic attitude of the Russian nobility, who saw service to the state as a necessity, not a vocation, an obligation, not a duty. Between one of Frederick II's officials and one of Catherine II's *chinovnicks* is all the distance found between the Prussian *Beruf* and the Russian service. The direct contact with culture that the students had sought and found in Leipzig accentuated these distances, this distaste, and made their burden seem even heavier. One of the rivulets that later flowed with the mainstream intelligentsia springs from the encounter between the nobles' old desire for liberty and the budding search for intellectual truth and freedom. Many of these young men became poets, travelers, and writers. None excelled in careers in the state or in court or ministerial politics.

However, a new, intense political will awakened in them, which no one illustrates better than Radishchev. But by now, this consciousness could not find peace without a complete transformation of social relationships in Russia, and could no longer fit productively into the framework of Catherine II's state. Thus Radishchev became at the same time the first member of the intelligentsia and the first Russian revolutionary.

It took twenty years for his experiences to mature. These were the years between 1771, when he returned to Russia, and 1791, when he published his *Journey from St. Petersburg to Moscow*. They were years full of experiences, of withdrawal, of efforts and rejection. With two of his Leipzig companions, to whom he

was growing closer, Alexsei Mikhailovich Kutuzov and Andrei Kirillovich Rubanovsky, he was nominated to the First Department of the Senate, in the very heart of
the judicial control of internal affairs of the country. Here were made nominations
of some of the most important officials and decisions about some of the most
delicate commercial affairs, domestic and foreign. Problems regarding rebellious
serfs and the dreadful punishments that befell them, embezzlement, favoritism,
requests for privileges, the functioning of schools and art academies, irregularities
in court jurisdiction, efforts to make the law respected in the provinces and in the
peripheral bodies of the state—all this and more passed through Radishchev's hands
in his role as a high official of the Senate between 1771 and the spring of 1773. He
tells us the personal significance of this experience in a kind of diary, in an intense
description of his life during a symbolic week of his existence in St. Petersburg.
A sense of duty drives him on in his work. He feels the weight of responsibility in
all he does each day. He is dealing with other people's lives; he feels it too acutely.
Yet the voice of his conscience continually risks being smothered by the daily routine, by the worry, by the futility of each act. He tries to withdraw into himself,
to find refuge in solitude. But he is caught by a sense of emptiness. Reason does
not stand the test. With reason alone, solitude is a poison, pain, ruin. Nor do the
distractions of modern life, conversation, or theater help. The only hope lies in a
different society, in a relationship among people outside that bureaucratic, legal,
official world. He is sustained only by the hope of being with friends, by the desire
to enjoy again the free and natural bond that unites people. This helps him pass,
however painfully, one day after another, to overcome the grayness of his daily life
in the hope of finding again the light and warmth of a spontaneous and natural
world. But why continue tormenting himself thus? Why not follow his friends?
Why stay in the capital? Why not seek a different and more natural life? The diary
follows the ups and downs of his restless and insecure state of mind. At the same
time he treats the external objective reasons for the uncertainty that torments him,
that makes the work to which he is bound seem vain, and that makes him place all
his faith in a separate world of emotions, of truth, far from so much ambition and
suffering.

This *Diary* seems to have been written in 1773. A year later comes an expression
of his torment in political terms. He took advantage of a job translating one of
Mably's main works, *Observations sur l'histoire de la Grèce,* to renew contact
with one of the authors whose juridical and diplomatic works had inspired him in
Leipzig. He compared the ideas of the French publicist with the utilitarianism and
contractualism which had been consolidating in his own mind, not only through
Helvétius and Beccaria but above all through the writings of Rousseau, especially
the *Social Contract.* Mably's ideas greatly attracted Radishchev and his friends. In
Mably's pages, the natural state was presented in the appealing colors of ancient
virtue, of Spartan values, of renunciation of worldly goods, luxury, and power in
the name of goodness and equality. It had been a heroic and just world that had

become more conspicuous as the years and centuries passed and, according to Mably, the shadows of evil, injustice, lust, and corruption had covered humanity. How could one turn back? How could equality be attained again? In later years, after the writing of *Observations,* Mably grew increasingly pessimistic. But in 1764, when he had taken up this work to prepare it for a second edition (which Radishchev used for his translation), the road to regeneration had not seemed completely closed. Archaic aristocratic republics and despotic monarchies were certainly not accessible for "successful revolutions." Yet there still remained monarchies that had not yet "degenerated into despotism," that had not yet broken the springs of virtue and courage in the souls of their subjects. If the sovereign so desired, it was possible to create "a new nation" from these governments. Did Radishchev hope that this could happen in the Russia of Catherine II, just as Mably seemed not to have altogether lost hope of reform in the reign of Louis XV? It is difficult to say. He was certainly attracted by the French philosopher's portrayal of the virtuous Spartan republic, or Lycurgus's constitution that combined "all the advantages of aristocracy, monarchy, and democracy." But these were distant images. The immediate task was to fight against autocracy and despotism, and to remember the rights of citizens and the liberty that everyone had a duty to defend against oppression. With this aim, Radishchev added a note, in rather scholastic terms, but precise and exact, to clarify his opposition to despotism. The fundamental element lay in the expression of his innermost sentiments: "Despotism was repugnant to human nature." A few pages later, he used a note on the Spartan ephors to again stress the value of liberty. It is often said that the note was historical or erudite in nature, but 'its political significance seems evident. Contrary to Mably, he said one should not attribute the creation of the ephors to Lycurgus. As Aristotle and Plutarch had confirmed, this was a later development. It was incompatible with a free and well-balanced constitution in which the limits and relationships between different powers were clearly defined. Thus in Lycurgan Sparta the institution of the ephors was inexplicable and must have arisen with the decay and breakdown of the old constitution, when it had become necessary to have a force from above to regulate and control the state. Montesquieu had already said that the ephors were a "tyrannical magistrature." One had only to open the *Encyclopédie* under "Ephores" to find Aristotle's opinion, which Radishchev claimed as his own. "He compares their government to tyranny, that is, to kingship." Thus Radishchev presents an antidespotic polemic. It is based on his view of ancient Spartan virtue; he does not seem to give up hope of a possible regeneration of a state in which the various powers still preserve their autonomy in a reciprocal balance. His soul aspires toward equality, but he stresses the value and organization of liberty.

At the time when Radishchev was reasoning thus, he had just abandoned his job in the Senate offices. Like many others before and more after him, he must have been attracted by the idea that the great and high magistrature where he had worked would have been able to lay the cornerstone for a Russian regime based on a balance of power, thus opening the way to the dismantling of despotism. (It is a great pity that we cannot read his history of the Senate, which he burned shortly before his death.) Yet, in May 1773, this experience of his seemed definitely over. Perhaps he convinced himself that the barrier was too fragile compared with the enormous weight of imperial autocracy. Was he already overcome by the sense of weakness and despair before the immense problem that he regarded with increasing anxiety: what was the road to liberty in Russia? To understand this turn in Radishchev's life one must remember at least two facts. The years 1773–74 were the Pugachev years. Looking more closely, one must not forget that his resignation was not just an individual gesture. On May 10, 1773, Radishchev set the example. On May 17, Kutuzov followed, and on May 29 Rubanovsky did the same. The group of friends was scattering. Neither the political mirage nor their secret hope had stood the test. By now, even he and Kutuzov, who had always been his closest friend and who was still dear to him, were growing ideologically further and further apart.

Since the atmosphere of officialdom was intolerable, the three friends chose the only other road that was open to them: the army. Kutuzov and Rubanovsky left the capital, while Radishchev became a member of the military court in St. Petersburg. Each day he saw new aspects of the brutality and cruelty of the world around him. He did not even last two years in this position; he resigned in March 1775. He too seemed to have arrived at the long-desired end of so many nobles' careers: the return to the land, marriage (he then married Anna Rubanovskaya, his friend's sister), and raising three sons (he had three and a daughter before 1783, the year in which his wife died). Would he also bury his delusions and his disgust in the country?

That was not his fate. In December 1777 Radishchev was back in St. Petersburg, destined to take on an important position in the Commerce Collegium, something like a ministry of foreign trade. In this turning point in his life, as well, perhaps, as in all his pilgrimages into the labyrinth of the state, the Vorontsov family must have carried great weight. Their property was not far from Radishchev's, and with the accession of Catherine II they had gained a place among the most educated and cultured liberal aristocracy in Russia. After the Pugachev rebellion and the victory over the Turks (both these decisive events occurred in 1774), the times no longer favored adventurous officers of the guards like the Orlovs. Catherine's government was settling around a constellation of aristocrats with immense power and wealth. Potemkin soon became the symbol of such satraps and magnates, full of unbridled energy, competent and violent figures who dominated the mature and final phases of the Empress's reign. Near them in her court, and charged with similar responsibilities, were other aristocrats. Their concern for culture, civilization, and the arts helped limit and transform the immense power in their hands and set some limits to the authority with which they lived and acted. Next to the Naryshkins and Elagins, the Vorontsovs offered the best example of the difficult but fruitful symbiosis between educated men and the higher Russian nobility in the second half of the 18th century. As their power rapidly increased during the short reign of Peter III, they had clung to a political vision that can be summarized as follows: (1) liberty for the nobility; (2) abolition of the secret police; (3) no privileges in commerce. Their culture, which was especially vast and rich, gave a liberal and liberalistic tinge to a program that Catherine II well knew was contradictory to her own desire for absolutism, but which for a long time she tried to neutralize rather than eliminate. Only after many years of uneasy alliance did the Empress consign Alexander Romanovich Vorontsov verbally to the devil. But even in opposition he retained great influence. In 1775, he was the minister under whom Radishchev worked as commercial assessor. A mutual faith and a solid friendship eventually bound the two men together. It was a link impervious to persecution and difficulties (Vorontsov risked his personal and political position by openly declaring solidarity with his friend Radishchev when the latter was condemned to death and then exiled). It was a morally sound bond that overcame the great social gulf that separated the two men (Vorontsov was a great lord, Radishchev a petty noble from the provinces looking for employment in St. Petersburg). They also overcame differences in their ideas and in their political attitudes. (The difficult relationship between the noble opposition represented by a Vorontsov and the liberal and revolutionary slant of a Radishchev is merely a particularly original and significant case of a *concordia discors* that was found all over Europe at the end of the 18th century, right up to the French Revolution and beyond. Mirabeau's family is another example.)

Supported by Vorontsov, and showing exceptional juridical and economic competence along with the even rarer quality of honesty, Radishchev rapidly advanced his career. For about ten years, beginning in 1780, he was the assistant director of the St. Petersburg customs office. In April 1790 he became the director. All the problems of administering the economic affairs of the capital and handling commercial relations between Russia and the Baltic and Atlantic worlds passed through his hands.

In the fifteen-year period between 1775 and 1790, Radishchev dedicated himself with great intensity to writing. Again he returned to the themes of his youth, participating in the current discussion of the value of Peter the Great's reforms and on the rhythm of the process of civilization in Russia. In 1789 he exalted the virtue of "patriotism" and in 1790, in a final moment of enthusiasm, concluded his voyage of discovery, aversion, uncertainty, and rebellion by writing and publishing his *Journey from St. Petersburg to Moscow.*

Radishchev's initial expression, and perhaps his highest, full of his experiences of those years, is the "Ode to Liberty." It was born from the drive and desire of one who knows he is living enclosed in a despotic world. He invokes, almost implores permission to eulogize liberty ("Permit a slave to sing of you"), and in his heart he is convinced of the great power of the goddess to whom he addresses his

verses. Liberty will be able to overcome oppression everywhere, "changing the darkness of slavery into light." Liberty has found the political formula on which to
rest. The social contract and democracy make liberty secure, and men enlightened
by her turn to the conquest of happiness and justice. But the monsters they must
confront are terrible. The church and despotism rise as dreadful forces, cynical
and violent. The struggle dates from the time of Brutus and Tell and from 1649
when the English executed their king. In Cromwell Radishchev sees the great defender of the English revolution.

... you taught generations
how the people could find revenge:
You, following the letter of the law, undid Charles.

The sovereignty of those who fight and of those who work, of those who forge
arms and of those who make the bread was thus being affirmed. Undoubtedly the
heads of state and of the military continued to take advantage of these battles in
order to establish their own domain and their own glory, to fulfill their own ambition. Had not even Cromwell followed a similar path? Yet through this oppression
and evil, men continue in their struggle. By now they see before them "nature's
citadel" rising out of the ruins of perfidy and tyranny. By now the church has
been struck by reform:

The torch of culture Luther raised high
and reconciled the earth with the sky.

Columbus and Galileo expanded the limits of the earth and sky. Newton brought
their work to completion. Over men's houses is the promise of fruitful and secure
work, that transforms even sweat into dew when the shadows of authority are dissipated and lords and suffering vanish. In the West, on the other side of the ocean,
a distant land of liberty had emerged where armies were no longer flocks of men
obliged to fight. There every soldier is a volunteer.

Oh, soldier inflexible
You were and are invincible
—Liberty, Washington are your guides.

The American colonies had won their victory (it is 1783):

You exult while here we suffer.
What you have, we too desire;
Your example has shown the way.

As the Abbé Raynal had written in his pamphlet on the *Révolution d'Amerique*,
published in 1781 and echoed here by Radishchev, "the name of liberty is so
sweet that all those who fight for her are sure of our secret good wishes. Their

cause is that of the entire human race; it becomes ours." How can one avoid being carried away by struggles for liberty even when they take place far from one's own country? "We will avenge ourselves on our oppressors by at least breathing freely our hatred of foreign oppressors. At the sound of breaking chains, it seems to us that our own chains become lighter, and we seem to breathe a purer air when we learn that the universe holds one tyrant the less." Besides, these great revolutions for liberty were the only lesson the despots heard. "They warn them not to count on the people's patience to last forever, and on eternal impunity." This was the conclusion that Abbé Raynal drew from the American Revolution, stressing its value and universal significance. He could write these words because France had been an ally of the rebels, and the relations that linked the free men of France with those across the waters were growing closer. Radishchev's echo shows both the effort and the despair of one who is convinced of the exemplary value of the American Revolution yet who does not for an instant forget the great geographical and political distance that separates those events from Russian lands.

As a result, the sense of victory is mixed with a profound sadness, and the stoic resignation of a man who knows that in human affairs every advance of liberty is followed by a return to servitude. It is a law of nature, the rhythm of life and death, to which everything in the universe must submit. Those populations who were fated to have liberty should not forget that in an instant strength can be changed to weakness and light to darkness. Thus, in his ode the image of death briefly overshadows that of victory, and he asks that one day his ashes be taken to the other side of the ocean.

But he quickly recovers. No, he says, he too must accept the fate by which he was born in Russia. Even his tomb must remain in his country. In passing by the tomb one day, a young man would say:

Born in the power of the yoke
Wearing shackles of gold,
He was the first to prophesy liberty.

Liberty was far away for him and for everyone in Russia. But one day it would arrive, arising from the immense ruins, the fire, the rivers of blood, cruelty, and pain. Before yielding, power and despotism would become more dreadful. But he ends,

Oh, the day, the highest of days!

While waiting, all he can do is to again seek refuge in his thoughts, his memories of the age before he was hurt by painful impressions, thus trying to continue the discussion with his friends which began when they were boys. In 1789 he wrote the *Life of Ushakov* about his companion who died in Leipzig. In some ways it is the first biography of a Russian intellectual, the first attempt to relate how a young man emerges from a vain and corrupt atmosphere and finds the light of wisdom and truth. It tells how he combats evil and indifferent people and how his death seals the defeat of his sick body (the theme of venereal disease appears here and recurs often in the *Journey*). But Ushakov survives in the memory of his friends and in the discovery of a truth that can never be obscured. The "internal flame" that consumed Fedor Vasilevich Ushakov did not burn in vain.

The memory of Ushakov also brought Radishchev back to his central thought, to the despotism that every day he seemed to know more closely. It was a monster with a hundred heads, as he eventually described it in his favorite terms in the *Journey*. He was increasingly convinced that these heads were the magnates, the nobles, the true lords of Russian land and labor. In fact, seen from close by, absolutism appeared like a great boat "that moved according to the winds that were controlled by others." It was an illusion to think that one could act and acquire influence over the sovereign. She too was dominated by uncontrollable, powerful forces. Was it not Helvétius who had said that despotism was not reformable, that either one changed the very bases of the government or one simply passed from one evil to another? "The enlightened man feels that in these governments any change is a new evil, because one can follow no plan; the despotic administration corrupts everything." The French philosopher had continued that by not keeping this fundamental truth in mind, the very founder of Russian autocracy, "the famous Czar Peter," had not "perhaps acted for the happiness of the nation." Just so he had not foreseen that one great man is rarely succeeded by another. "Having changed nothing in the constitution of the empire, the Russians, through the form of their government, could soon fall back into the barbarism from which he had begun to lead them."

In 1782, Radishchev had begun by considering these ideas of Helvétius while reflecting on the inauguration of the monument dedicated by Catherine to Peter the Great. It was inaugurated in that year in the Senate Square. He had written just a few pages published later as a *Letter to a Friend Living in Tobolsk by Necessity of His Work*. It was a short but significant contribution to the discussion on Peter, which had been rekindled and intensified in those years. Just when Catherine's reign was increasingly under the control of the aristocracy, the myth of Peter was becoming more widespread and official. It was a symbol of absolutism which naturally opposed the constitutionalism, conservatism, and liberalism of the nobles. At the same time, Prince Shcherbatov was writing his essay *On the Corruption of Morals in Russia*. It expressed a negative view of the pressure that Peter had imposed on Russian history, and it condemned the Emperor's too rapid steps in drawing Muscovy and the West together. For Prince Shcherbatov, this polemic against Peter was linked to a vision—or, to use other terms, a constitutional and aristocratic utopia—for Russia in the future. His answer is at once conservative and liberal, while Radishchev's response to the same problems is democratic and libertarian. Nearly a century later, Herzen inherited all the efforts of the Russian intelligentsia and nobility in the late 17th and early 18th centuries. In 1859, in exile in London, he published Shcherbatov's essay and Radishchev's *Journey* in one volume, almost as if to indicate the common antidespotic origins of these two works which nevertheless were so different in their social and political conclusions.

In his *Letter to a Friend Living in Tobolsk*, Radishchev combatted both the myth and the official acclaim of Peter the Great without yielding to the criticism coming from those who exalted the aristocracy. His tone is anything but laudatory. He certainly did not outdo himself with vain praise and rhetorical approbation, though he did recognize that Peter "had given the first impulse to great masses who previously had had no motivation," and that he had been "a powerful auto- crat who destroyed the last vestiges of the natural liberty of his country." He would certainly have been more worthy of glory if he had conquered liberty for himself and his country. Here Radishchev seems to argue against Voltaire, who had affirmed that Peter had not dared to "destroy serfdom directly" but had nevertheless prepared its end by the formation of a new army and the creation of a third estate in Russia. This is praise that Peter did not deserve, according to Radishchev. The Emperor was merely a "powerful autocrat" and could not claim a higher function in Russian history. Besides, Radishchev concluded, what other sovereign had ever showed willingness to make the leap from his own power to liberty?

When Radishchev published his *Letter* in 1790, he added a footnote saying that his final mistrustful thought might have been different if he had been able to take into account Louis XVI and the concessions he had been obliged to make to the Assembly and to the Parisians in the year of the fall of the Bastille. Evidently, a new era had begun in which not only the populace but also the sovereign behaved differently from the manner Radishchev had expected in the past.

Before following Radishchev into this new era (of which the *Journey from St. Petersburg to Moscow* is also a part), we must consider in a different dimension the two- or three-year gestation of what was to become his main work. We have seen his prose and poetry against a background of politics under Catherine and the nobility, officials, and aristocrats. However, these works are actually difficult to comprehend if we do not briefly insert them in the close dialogue that developed in the masonic organizations. We must compare the works with the ideas that domi- nated the various trends in the masonic world in Russia at the time. The conflict between Radishchev and despotism is not a duel. Standing with him is the develop- ing intelligentsia and all the intellectual and moral ferment of Russia in the 1770s and 1780s.

We must return to Mably and his view of ancient Greece, which had been Rad- ishchev's point of departure fifteen years earlier. Radishchev was well aware how in the 1770s Mably had reached a kind of desperation, becoming further convinced that a primeval equality, a primitive communism—the only means of assuring hap- piness for man—was irrevocably lost. What was left was the regret for what one no longer had and the knowledge that now nothing remained but to live in an unhappy, distorted society, dominated by the will to power and the greed for wealth. It was a blind alley from which escape seemed impossible. It was a time when the enlightened, those on the threshold of revolution, paused and doubted. It was the origin of so many overflows, retreats, and false starts, in France and all over Europe in the 1770s and 1780s. How could such a state of mind not take on extreme and violent forms in a country like Russia? There was a striking difference between the promises of enlightened men, the great ideas of liberty and equality, and the political, social, and moral reality of the entire country, from Catherine herself to the last *muzhik.* Such contrasts were particularly harsh and painful to those who knew the ideas of Diderot, Rousseau, Mably, and Raynal. Only the call for morality, for internal reform, for a religion of the good and beautiful which remained above the sad daily reality seemed to be able to support and console anyone who felt such conflicts and dilemmas.

Russian freemasonry became the receptacle of this strange development of delusions and hopes, of dejection and conviction. It retained the exterior forms, the rituals and phraseology that came from England, France, and Germany. But around the middle of the 1770s (a significant time for Russia, with the victory over Turkey and with the Pugachev rebellion), it underwent a series of attempts to find the synthesis, the absolute truth that enlightened empiricism seemed incapable of providing, as well as the moral certainty that skepticism appeared to have destroyed. In a troubled and impetuous flood, the mysticism and gnosticism that originated with Boehme, Paracelsus, and Renaissance psychology poured into Russian freemasonry. The result was a confused and grandiose system that seemed to have the merit of again uniting man and the cosmos, dreams and reality, and at least furnishing the imagination with a reply to the enigmas observed by the new intelligentsia. For anyone who is amazed by the Russian freemasons' strange response to the queries of their time, it will suffice to point to contemporary happenings in Paris, where mesmerism was having incredible success. It was answering the same need, to unite in cosmic unity that which modern science seemed to be fragmenting into numerous little islands of light in a sea of darkness. A fascinating recent study by a young American historian, R. Darnton, showed how men who were to hold major roles in the revolution were carried away by the magnetic movement on the eve of the event. Here is the pathology of enlightenment, revealing a moment of arrest, when the entire movement of 18th-century ideas was bottlenecked. We see a similar crisis, with its own contours, in the Russo-German conjunction. Under its influence, a large part of the culture of the University of Moscow was dominated by Schwarz, by the Novikov publishing house, and in the solitary Gatchina palace Paul I, heir to the throne, found in such mysteries the symbols and forms of his own strange personality and capricious domain.

It was not with this aspect of Russian life that Radishchev had a score to settle, for he was convinced that it was a matter of aberrant phenomena which, at the most, would simply confirm the beliefs he had already expressed in his ode to liberty. He felt that each advance was inevitably followed by a step back, and that even the great victory of enlightened men at midcentury was now entering a stage of retrogression, a decay that seemed to be leading back to the Middle Ages, to the age of superstition and irrationality. The mysticism of the sects was merely evidence of the extremely difficult struggle in which he was engaged. Here again he had to swim against the tide, in this case at the cost of appearing to support Catherine, who was increasingly hostile to the Martinist and Rosicrucian lodges. The Empress had a twofold reaction to these sects. She hated them because they were an independent force outside her control, and at the same time she considered them a return to the past, to superstition, to all that Montesquieu, Voltaire, and Diderot had taught her to despise and combat. In 1786 she received a letter from her adviser and confidant, Dr. Zimmerman, in which he seemed to express a sense of repulsion and condemnation toward these increasingly numerous sects. He knew his sentiments were shared by the Empress, just as they could be shared by a liberal and independent man like Radishchev. "Ah, what a sight!" Zimmermann had written from Hannover on February 15, 1786, "to see the world truly mad, to see Germany full of princes, generals, men of letters, and men of all types dancing like men possessed to the tune of each cheat who calls himself a visionary or magician, to see that in this century of humanity, when we no longer roast or burn, it is true, thousands of poor women, in the best houses of Paris and Berlin witches are invited to dine; and then to see the greatest sovereign in the universe laugh publicly at all these follies and set an example for the women of Paris, for the legions of educated men, for the greater part of the German court, for so many princes and perhaps even for some present and future kings!"

Thus, when faced with the rising tide of irrationalism at the end of the century, a faith in certain enlightened principles brought to similar positions the Empress of all the Russias and her discontented, rebellious, restless head customs official from St. Petersburg. In fact, Vernadsky has pointed out that in the capital freemasonry abandoned with greater difficulty and to a lesser extent the plan of alliance between the government and educated men, that is, a collaboration between the powerful and the intellectuals.

Radishchev could not help feeling close to another aspect of mystical life in Russia—not religion, but morality. It was not *gnosis* but *ethos* that moved these men (some, such as Kutuzov, were old friends) to theorize on detachment from all external activity in order to withdraw into themselves and find the happiness the world could not give them, to feel the sense of certainty (as opposed to disillusionment and death) that is reserved for courageous men who are decisive in not lying to themselves or others. Radishchev was continually tempted to adopt this psychology of disenchantment and renunciation. Yet in the period between his ode to liberty and his *Journey,* he had the strength to keep his distance from this attitude. Once again he threw himself into research and discoveries in the external world, into his struggle and polemic against the cruelty and wickedness of political

and social life. Thus he dedicated his two most important and engaging works of
those years, the *Life of Ushakov* and the *Journey from St. Petersburg to Moscow,*
to Alexei Mikhailovich Kutuzov, almost as if to show him that the ways of the
heart drew them closer but that reason could not accept the conclusions Kutuzov
reached.

If we look at the Russian masonic journals of those years, we cannot avoid
being struck by what they all have in common and also by what distinguishes
them from Radishchev's attitude. *Utrennyy svet* ("The Morning Light") of 1777
is totally immersed in the idyll and the pathos of Gessner, Young, Wieland, Moses
Mendelssohn, and Campe. The desire to find different and distant worlds, the need
for a utopia, are expressed on every page. Of all Montesquieu's works, the authors
choose his chapter on the troglodytes. Fénelon returns again with one of Tele-
machus's voyages. The Essenes and Therapeutae make their appearance. From
Bacon, they translate the pages on the ancient myths. *Antiquité dévoilée,* by
Nicolas-Antoine Boulanger, is also discussed. They insist on criticizing themselves
morally, on exposing their own defects, saying, among other things, that nothing
could seem more ridiculous in their eyes than the arrogance, pride, and prejudices
of the nobility. The etchings illustrating this carefully printed journal could not be
more expressive. Socrates's death, a meditation in prison, opens the first issue. An
altar with a serpent of eternity, an acacia, a trowel, a T-square, a map of the world
mounted over a triangle in brilliant light create the masonic seal over these pages;
it is the bric-a-brac of an eclectic world searching continuously for truth.

They themselves state their leanings: "Morality is the first, most important,
and most useful of the sciences." The journal was not an end in itself, but a means
of collecting the money necessary for sustaining philanthropic efforts. Schools for
orphans would arise in St. Petersburg "if God protects our sincere intentions."
They would provide for the support of the poor and old. Having set out on this
path, they tried to establish all kinds of useful institutions. They even founded the
first insurance scheme in Russia. In this and in many other philanthropic manifestations of the 18th century we observe the attempt to replace the state in the indispensable tasks of education and aid. A new capacity for making a contact, creating a bridge between the privileged and less fortunate classes was born. Russian
freemasonry is a contrived school, as are all schools, but like all other schools it
is useful and effective in creating a new consensus.

To understand the significance of the freemasonic movement in Russia, one
need only consider the souls of those who are now active in the lodges, turning
their eyes to the morning light. The hardened men of Peter's era, all involved in
the technicalities of state construction, gave way to their sons who were full of
a new sensitivity, of scruples and uncertainty, and poured all their souls, their
energy, their money into trying to supply what despotism, enlightened or not,
failed to accomplish. It is enough to cite the example of the Tatishchevs: the father
was a scientist, politician, and historian; the son, a Rosicrucian. Nor was there a

lack of effort, at least among some freemasons, to draw closer, from a moral and religious standpoint, to the worst ills of Russian society of their time. If they combatted anger, it was to prevent themselves from exercising over their "serfs or household servants" what they called "instruction or punishment." They reminded themselves that "our servants and peasants are our brothers. All we have that is good and beautiful, all that is useful and that we like, comes from them." Why say they are born to serve? "If they are born to serve, then you, too, are born to serve them." But they did not draw the immediate social conclusions. They were convinced that only an ethical transformation could improve the situation in the villages. "Not the liberation of the serfs; it is impossible to free their souls. . . . One cannot clean with soiled hands, one must wash them first." Thus philanthropy is self-education for the noble classes, who are well aware of the limits and boundaries beyond which they cannot pass.

These sons of the masonic light tend to be gloomy, and they cry easily over the harshness and cruelty of the world surrounding them. A sense of guilt and of a fall weighs on them. Here and there we see judges abandon their duties because the right to punish, and especially the death penalty, are contradictory to their consciences. Some nobles go abroad, not for amusement or curiosity, but because they are irresistibly driven to search the world for a sect containing the authentic masonic truth, where they can find the ritual of salvation and perhaps also the secret of the philosopher's stone. Some officials renounce all, abandon everything in order not to feel oppressed by the weight of daily responsibilities. I. V. Lopukhin (whose memoirs are perhaps the most interesting document of these masonic conversions and aversions) had placed two typical phrases under a portrait of Jean-Jacques Rousseau. They were: "The wildest solitude seems to me preferable to the society of the wicked," and "He is truly free who has no need to use the hands of another to do his will." These men were seeking liberation, but did not find it. They were overpowered by pain, or perhaps only by melancholy from a continual and fruitless search. The "morning light," dawn, soon changed into "evening light," dusk. In fact, the 1782 journal was called *Vechernaya zarya.* Here Kutuzov, Radishchev's friend, published his most significant articles. The editors explain that the title itself is "a beautiful and ethical hieroglyphic." "The noon light of wisdom" has faded now. The incarnation of Christ has not brought man back to his primitive purity: "Human reason is almost entirely obscured, like the light at dusk." The sense of the fall cannot avoid bringing with it the need for a revelation. In their eyes, this seems like a secret that must be unveiled, a riddle for which only a few have the solution. A harsh and mysterious sense of authority insinuates itself and grows into such a concept. Their moral aspiration dissolves into blind submission and solidifies into strict discipline. This is the only way the mystery can be unveiled. We are observing the birth of an authoritarian and hierarchic sect. Their political conceptions are also modified by religious fervor. In *Evening Light* they still seek the vindication of enlightened reform and of a classicist mythology of liberty; Aristides and the heroes of Thermopylae are the true patriots. Conquests are condemned. Laws are above the power of the sovereigns. Fiscal privileges are absurd. Freedom of commerce is necessary. The lords of property must also be the masters of its fruit. They recall that tyrants, called czars, were exiled from Athens. But this enlightened and classical tradition becomes corroded and eventually overturned by a continuous polemic against ideas coming from France, against all those who, by exalting reason, diminish the sense of guilt and the related need for a more profound truth and for liberation. Helvétius became the main target of Schwarz, the young German professor who left his mark on the University of Moscow in the early 1780s. To be utilitarian meant to subject oneself to passion and greed, and to extinguish the light of and interest in research. The external world became incomprehensible. What kind of knowledge could derive from a human reason that is weakened and obscured by sin? As "Eques ab aquila crescente" (as Schwarz was called in masonic jargon) explained it, the intellect *(Verstand)* is always limited and subordinated. Only superior reason *(Vernunft)* can truly satisfy man. Similarly, the political world, rejected at first as wicked and cruel, is further denied as vain and empty of significance. True reality lies elsewhere, in the clear soul of each individual and in the sects of the initiated.

The evolution of the Russian Rosicrucians was long and tormented and drew men such as Novikov closer to the Berlin obscurantists of the time of Johann Christoph von Wöllner. In his own country, it brought Novikov closer to the reactionary group led by the heir to the throne, Paul I, at the Gatchina Palace, while it led Radishchev's friend Kutuzov to stress, in letters written to friends at the time of Radishchev's arrest, how profoundly he differed with the political opinions of those who had been his companions in Leipzig and later.

In 1774, Radishchev had been the guest of the Urania Lodge. He had lived and acted in the same environment in which the sect had grown. He had lectured on topics close to masonic themes to the Society of Friends of the Literary Sciences, a group that had emerged in imitation of and in conjunction with a similar group under Novikov in Moscow. "Who Are the True Children of the Fatherland?" was the title of his speech, which was published in a journal which was also not far from the mystical world, *Beseduyushchii grazhdanin* ("The Conversant Citizen"). But in his very words one could see how he remained faithful to the themes of the Enlightenment, how he clung to utilitarian ideas, to reform, to the struggle against arrogance and injustice.

When they read his *Journey,* at least some of Radishchev's friends could confirm how far he had strayed from them. And with typical sectarian mentality, they tried to explain this by thinking and saying that he belonged to a different mystical organization which they knew had also emerged from the main line of masonic tradition, although it had reached political conclusions that were contrary and opposed to Rosicrucian ideas. They called him one of the Illuminati, that is, a member of Weishaupt's sect, with its democratic and revolutionary tendencies. Thus they were only continuing the Berlin Rosicrucian's condemnation of the Illuminati, accusing them of being "déistes et sociniens." They added that it was necessary to double their vigilance and especially to reinforce their own organization "so as not to be surpassed by nations that are still somewhat barbarous—like the Russians, for example—in the huge empire of which the glorious activity of our brothers has pushed so far with their efforts that there are clubs all the way to the Chinese border." The Rosicrucians were extraordinarily successful in Russia. However, their enemies, the Illuminati, probably only existed in the imagination of their adversaries and persecutors. In his *Journey,* Radishchev too had described the Illuminati as a product of the sleep of reason at the decline of the Enlightenment.

In fact, Radishchev had found his own road. He remained convinced of Helvétius's idea that it is impossible to remedy a population's ills without modifying its laws. It is necessary to stay in the realm of politics, economics, and law, for only thus could one face the evil that made him suffer and mourn. These ills were also intolerable and repugnant to him, yet it was necessary to analyze them to understand how one should really combat them. Ethical distaste alone was insufficient. In a supreme enlightened effort, Radishchev began a voyage to become acquainted with and to describe the political and social reality of his country.

As always, he was assisted in this effort by the thoughts and writings of the 1780s from all over enlightened Europe. As in the past and as was to happen again (at least from Peter's time onward, and for decades into the present), Russia seemed to need a mirror, a reflection from Western countries, in order to be herself. This was particularly true at the time of Catherine II. The root of Russia's ills, that is, the despotism of the state and nobles and the slavery of the peasants, was described repeatedly by travelers and writers. A few years after the Empress's accession to the throne, the French scientist Chappe d'Auteroche had explained in three splendid folio volumes dedicated to Louis XV and the French Academy, "The lords sell their slaves as elsewhere men sell beasts." Using the *knout,* "they have morally given themselves the right to punish [their serfs] with death." There was such a dreadful rapport between masters and slaves that it rendered both sides despicable and cruel. "The Russian nobility, having cruel and wicked slaves perpetually before them, have developed a hardness which is not in their character. Cringing toward the despot, toward their superiors, and toward all whom they think they need, they treat with the greatest severity those over whom they have some rights, or who have not the power to resist." By freeing the nobility from their obligation of service, Peter III had only made the situation worse. Under him, Russia had run the risk of "remaining in its first state of barbarity." Chappe d'Auteroche concluded that one must hope that Catherine II would not limit herself "to granting liberty to the nobility" and that "all her subjects would enjoy the same favor." If this were not to happen, Russia would remain "a feudal government" with innumerable minor tyrants and without any real power in the hands of the state.

It was the Empress herself who answered him in 1770 with a long pamphlet entitled *Antidote*. Between the lines, this *pro domo* oration revealed a powerful and penetrating political intelligence. It directed the debate toward questions of national honor, and to the defense of Russian traditions and characteristics. It accused Chappe d'Auteroche of having made himself the spokesman for French politics, hostile to Russia, but when it came to the heart of the problem, it was not difficult to detect the hand of one who realized what was actually happening. Catherine skipped over peasant slavery but confessed, "There is nothing more difficult than to abolish a thing when the general interest is in contradiction with the particular interest of a great many individuals." How could the nobility be confronted? One certainly could not do so by speaking ill of despotism in the Russian state. Was it not in fact the state that was the prime mover for all progress in Russia? She said that for several hundred years it was "the government that encouraged society as much as it could." Absolutism existed as much in Paris as in St. Petersburg. The Secret Chancellery was equivalent to the Bastille. And had not France also experienced revolt, conspiracies, upheavals, and coups d'état? What was characteristic of Russia, the Empress remarked acutely, was the fact that there revolutions occurred to *strengthen* the government's power, and they broke out when people feared a weakening of government, not despotism. "We have had hard reigns, but we have always suffered weak ones impatiently. Our government, by its constitution, requires vigor; if there is not this, discontent becomes universal and, following that, if things get worse, revolutions follow."

Not more than three years later, in 1773, a new dimension was added to this reasoning on the relationship between power and class in Catherine's empire. Did she think that the peasant revolt, the *pugachevshchina,* derived from the fact that she too had proved too weak and liberal, with her plans for state reform and the improvement of the situation of the serfs? Certainly, as a consequence of the experience, and at the expense of the peasants, there was a reinforcing of autocracy based on a compromise between the state and the nobles. Even foreign travelers' expressions of horror over the despotism, suffering, and oppression in Russia became calmer in tone and were transformed into technical and historical affirmations of the backwardness of the peasants and of the whole country. "The backwardness of the Russian peasants," said William Coxe, a writer well known to Radishchev, in 1784, "in all the mechanical arts, when compared with those of other nations of Europe is visible to the most superficial observer..." Russia was in the state in which Europe had been in the 11th and 12th centuries, "when the unbounded authority of the land holders over their slaves was beginning to be counterbalanced by the introduction of an intermediate order of merchants; when new towns were continually erecting and endowed with increasing immunities, and when the crown began to give freedom to many of its vassals." In Russia, this process encountered a fundamental obstacle. Without removing it, the Russians would not be able to progress toward becoming more civilized. "A general improvement cannot take place while the greatest part continue in absolute vassalage." As is evident, the knots that bound and choked Russia, preventing her development, were widely and lucidly discussed by enlightened men in Europe in the second half of the 18th century.

These problems were the central theme of Radishchev's *Journey*. His contribution was not to offer new technical aspects or practical solutions, for these had not matured. What he did contribute was the spirit with which he looked at the state, at nobles, and at the Russian serfs. Like Chappe d'Auteroche and Coxe, Radishchev is a traveler; but he is in his home territory, among his own people, and bound by many ties to the reality surrounding him. He need not make comparisons with other countries; he feels no need to measure the distance that separates Russia from the rest of the world. Everything either wounds or attracts him, makes him either bleed or smile. His *Journey* is a *via crucis*, but he does not turn his back on it. He must travel that road, among those people and those houses, one stage after another, trying to discover all of Russia's horrors and all its strengths and hidden virtues. At each way station a new emblem of the reality of his country rises before him. A most ordinary journey along Russia's main highway, the one linking the old capital with the new, becomes a voyage of discovery and an extraordinary adventure. It is no longer a world of *isbas* and *kibitki*, but a hidden and secret world which he alone can reveal. It is the moral world of those who live in slavery but are not resigned, of those who are subjects of despots yet dream of rebellion, of those who are privileged but do not accept their privileges, of those who feel small and weak before the immense outstretched Russian plain and under the iron yoke of power, but who find within themselves the strength to lift their heads, to consider themselves free, if necessary at the cost of renouncing wealth, power, and perhaps even life.

Thus Radishchev's *Journey* becomes a Russian version of Diderot's *Jacques le fataliste*. The similarity does not arise from the fact that the literary form of both masterpieces is rooted in a shared admiration for Sterne's sentimental journeys. Nor does the resemblance arise from possible contact or influence between the two books (as we know, *Jacques le fataliste* was published posthumously and had not been printed when Radishchev's work appeared). The connection arises because both works play on the same fundamental opposition: the conflict between despotism and chance, between necessity and liberty. "It was written in heaven" is Jacques the Fatalist's recurring phrase. But in the French novel the richness of life and the continual rebirth of liberty cast destiny aside and celebrate an unbroken triumph over necessity. In Radishchev's *Journey*, despotism is fate. Nothing is written in heaven; everything depends on the whim, the arbitrary authority, the cruelty of those who control the life of peasants and citizens and the destiny of the state. The lack of any laws, the tyranny, make absolute power supreme. Liberty is not a force that springs up irresistibly; it is a rebellion, a revolt, or renunciation and death. The true limit to the power of the nobles is the *pugachevshchina.* The true enemy of despotism is the individual conscience of the newborn intelligentsia. Thus Radishchev's *Journey* is as much an internal voyage as a trip along the Russian roads, a search for a new way of feeling as well as a new reality. In *Jacques le fataliste,* as in Spinoza, liberty and necessity coincide at their limits. In the itinerary of this Russian *philosophe,* morality and reality *must* coincide: it is his task to make them do so. He knows how difficult this is, how much pain and effort it costs, how difficult is the road he wants to travel, but to give it up would be worse than death.

This *Journey* toward a free and just world is also a voyage back through the author's past experiences. He reviews the hopes that he and his generation had nurtured for an enlightened sovereign, for a government capable of taking charge of Russia's transformation. He does not close his eyes to the political affirmation Catherine had made in her *Antidote,* that the government was more advanced than the society. He dreams once more of a collaboration between the intellectual who is capable of telling the truth and the sovereign capable of listening to it. But he cannot stop at this. He is driven by the reality that he sees around him, and he proceeds toward a political vision based on equality and liberty. The strength of this book lies in the fact that he does not hide the hesitations, the doubts that accompanied its preparation. This was the only way he could show us how difficult it is to be a rebel, a free man in a country where there are no limits to the powers of those who govern and where the pliability of those who obey is infinite. The tone of these pages, sometimes pathetic, sometimes bittersweet (Sterne and Raynal serve as models), veils but scarcely hides a kind of unlimited desperation, a pain without resignation.

Radishchev published this book in his own house using a printing press he had acquired by taking advantage of one of the Empress's concessions which allowed the legal existence of such domestic enterprises. Naturally, as Radishchev explained in one of his digressions in the *Journey,* she reserved the right to censor the manuscripts to be printed. Radishchev's work was a precursor of the 19th-century and modern *samizdat.* The first eyes to glance over the book were the censor's. He was clearly distracted and was evidently unaccustomed to being presented with dangerous or rebellious writings. As a result, the words that close the original edition, "with permission of the government," are true. Six hundred copies of the *Journey* were published legally in May 1790, to be distributed to friends and sold in the capital. The book commanded collectors' prices at once, for it had aroused no small amount of curiosity and interest.

Among the first readers was Catherine II herself. Alarmed, she declared to a courtier that "it was worse than Pugachev." She ordered an inquiry, had the bookseller who distributed the work arrested, and on June 30 the author was imprisoned.

The Empress continued her careful reading, took notes, and was eager to let the accused man know, through the channels of the investigation, with what care she was examining the text. It was a strange dialogue that took place across the Neva between the Winter Palace and the Fortress of SS. Peter and Paul, between the luxury of court and the dark and humid little cell where Radishchev was confined. The Empress was too indignant and too disgusted to maintain the detached and skillful tone that she had used when discussing Chappe d'Auteroche's book. The Voltairian charms vanished. Without being shocked, but showing remorseful reproof, she recognizes that the author is not faithful to Orthodox dogma; he is a deist, and often argues against religion and superstition. From under Catherine's veneer of enlightenment emerges her political realism, her will to get to the heart of the matter, to understand the actual reality. The appeal to the heart that she finds in every page of Radishchev's book seems to her mistaken. "The author says, 'Ask your heart, it is good; do what it says.' He does not tell us to follow our reason. Such a proposition cannot be correct." Catherine's reason above all served the state and power. Why, the Empress wondered, was Radishchev so opposed to conquest, the army, the defense of the country? How could he arrive at such defeatism and talk about that "assassination called war"? "What did he and his friends want? To be left without defense and taken prisoner by the Turks and the Tartars, or be conquered by the Swedes?" And why be so sentimental about the free republic of Novgorod, beaten and conquered by Ivan III? Radishchev forgot to mention that the czar was punishing the city for having become allied with Russia's enemy, Poland, and thus the city deserved to be considered a felon and traitor. How poorly the author presented the sentiments of one who held great and immense political responsibilities! How clearly he showed his distance from the throne! The desire for power, the pleasure in commanding that he saw in sovereigns were, at least for her, unknown sentiments. "I do not know how great is the desire for power among other leaders; in me it is not great." As for the nobility, Catherine notes with composure Radishchev's various accusations against the class, and she makes no effort to defend it except when it comes to the highest aristocracy, the magnates and the dignitaries of the court. She smiles at the author's hopes, the illusions he has of possibly inducing the *pomeshchiki* to hasten the liberation of their serfs: "He is trying to persuade landowners to free their peasants, but no one will listen to him." To her horror, she has to admit that the political game in Russia is no longer limited to nobles and sovereigns, to autocrats, conservatives, and reformers. She must admit that people such as Radishchev exist, ready to support the peasant revolt and to say that the end of the regime of serfdom could come soon, without awaiting a concerted liberation by the government and landowners.

But now, the energetic and enlightened sovereign, the stateswoman, is overcome by the inquisitor, searching not for reality but for the intentions and the thoughts of her adversaries, the secret intrigues and plots of her enemies. It is here that the

Empress errs and becomes reactionary out of blindness, and not just out of hatred and fear. Where Radishchev had written, "One must not expect liberty from the council of landowners but from the very weight of slavery," she notes, "Thus he rests his hopes on a peasant revolt." Radishchev is fixed, nailed, to only one of the parts of his vision of Russia (though it is undoubtedly a true and important one), whereas besides the *pugachevshchina* there are so many other hopes of rebellion and political and moral transformation. Catherine goes even further astray when she tries to understand the origins of Radishchev's discontent. After all, it was she who sent him to Leipzig, who allowed him to develop his career, entrusting him with one of the most sensitive and important services in the economic administration of the state. From whence did his disdain and anger over state careers, the court, and government arise? Why did Radishchev insist on painting everything in "yellow and black"? The sovereign repeatedly comes back to this problem. "It is a sure wager that the author wrote this book because he did not have *entrée* to the palace. Perhaps he once had it and lost it, and since he is now excluded, he is bitter and thus ungrateful, and is now struggling with his pen to re-enter." As she progresses in her reading she feels she is gaining greater understanding of the author's mentality. "He must have been born with unbounded ambition, prepared for the highest positions, but because he did not succeed, his gall and impatience turned on everything, and gave rise to this philosophizing." She was reducing the drama of men like Radishchev, and others of the Enlightenment (for example, Beccaria), to a hackneyed tale of frustrated ambition. These men tried to collaborate with absolutism, to accomplish through political efficiency what they knew they could not achieve alone. But they suffered or resigned or rebelled before the limits, the failures, the falsity of this compromise, even though it was often fruitful. Was it ambition or greed that had driven Voltaire, d'Alembert, Diderot to collaborate with Catherine a decade earlier? Was it ambition that persuaded Turgot to become minister for Louis XVI? By now all these *philosophes,* whom Catherine had once admired and praised, were dead. A generation had passed. The Empress was no longer able to judge the Russian *philosophe* in the spirit in which she had regarded his French predecessors. The possibility of a true collaboration between educated men and absolutism was gone. It had not only ceased in Radishchev's heart (he was now studying the ancient republics, modern liberty, and the right of the oppressed to revolt) but also in the heart of the Empress. All she could see in the prisoner locked in the Fortress of SS. Peter and Paul was a man moved by spite because he had not achieved a high position in the Winter Palace.

In her notes, the Empress attributed her own change not to logic and to the limits of her power but to the change in the times, to the new situation developing in France in recent months. Give or take a day, it was the first anniversary of the fall of the Bastille when Catherine read Radishchev's book. The Empress was not just frightened but terrified by the revolution. How could she avoid recognizing the French "poison" and "madness" in Radishchev's attempt to "overcome all respect for authority, to stir up popular indignation against his superiors and against the government?" When Radishchev attacked the court, Catherine noted, "One must assume that he is thinking of the evil example of present-day France." The specter of Paris in 1789 hangs over Catherine's comments. And just because of this, she ends by attributing to Radishchev intentions and ideas that he did not have. It is true that in the last phase of his long manuscript he had added two allusions to the French Revolution; a few words in praise of Mirabeau (who, Catherine noted, "deserves to be hung not just once but many times"); and, significantly, in defense of freedom of the press, which in his opinion was not sufficiently respected even in Paris under the Constituent Assembly. In no other part of the *Journey* is there even an echo of the French Revolution for the simple reason that the book, composed over a ten-year period, was nearly finished in 1789. As we have seen, it originated not from an external impulse but from a long and tormented process of reconsideration and revolt before the reality of Russia. When Radishchev thought of revolutions he still returned to England, to Cromwell and Charles I. (Catherine noted, "These pages are written with criminal intent, and are entirely revolutionary. One must ask the author what is the significance of the ode [to liberty [and who wrote it.") Radishchev had the opportunity to meditate on the French Revolution after the publication of his book and after his sentencing, when he was in Siberia. It is characteristic of him that he did not accept and was even explicitly critical of Robespierre and his terrorism. Despite Catherine's suspicions, Radishchev was not a propagandist for other people's ideas, but a man feeling and living in great depth his own libertarian experience.

Eventually, the Empress and the investigators became convinced that there were no revelations to be obtained from Radishchev other than the ideas he had offered publicly in his work. Despite the advice of his friend and protector Vorontsov, and despite the insistence of his jailers, Radishchev would not express regret for having written the *Journey*. He did not disown it, and he insisted on defending the truth. The works of Sterne and Raynal, which had provided the framework and ornamentation for his book, became the weapons with which he tried to protect himself by claiming that he had a burning literary ambition and perhaps even the desire to create a scandal. He appealed to Catherine's magnanimity and mercy and tried to turn to his advantage the obvious fact that no revolution would begin because of a book printed in an edition of six hundred copies, in an affected literary style, among a generally illiterate population. He did not hide his despair at being separated from his children and having to abandon them to their fate. Reading his deposition is like perusing another mislaid manuscript found along one of the stages of his *Journey*. The book and the character match, even in the reader's uncertainty of where emotion ends and irony begins—when, for example, Radishchev speaks of the exemplary character of Catherine's reign and of the madness that drove him to write such a distasteful book as the *Journey*. Here are penitence and despair, but also a basic refusal to discuss the true issues with the Empress, who, with her notes, had requested such a discussion insistently and in detail.

In reality, Radishchev had closed himself off more and more, almost as if going back over his whole life, to his childhood, to the world of his father. In prison, he even began to paint an icon of himself, seeing himself in the features and recognizing himself in the thoughts of an ancient monk, Filaret, condemned for having spoken the truth. He even wrote a biography of Filaret and wanted to have an image of the saint with him, bearing the inscription, "Blessed are those who are persecuted for the sake of the truth."

On July 26, 1790, Radishchev was sentenced to death. On August 8, the Senate confirmed the sentence, adding that the guilty man should be sent in chains to Nerchinsk, almost on the Chinese border, and be beheaded there. The sentence was commuted by the Empress to ten years of forced labor, to be spent in the distant land of Siberia. Radishchev was taken far from St. Petersburg, first in chains, then unfettered, as a political prisoner, a journey that lasted for sixteen months. Vorontsov continued to watch over him. At the time of Radishchev's condemnation, this high aristocrat had abstained from participating in the government committees as a sign of protest. This courageous gesture contributed greatly to mitigating Radishchev's fate, and sealed their long friendship. The letters that Radishchev wrote him from Siberia are proof of the mutual esteem that united the two men. "You are the man who made me love life," Radishchev was to tell him later.

At Ilimsk in Siberia, where Radishchev was eventually exiled, a complete cycle of his existence had ended. He felt he was beginning another life. He formed a new family. He participated fully in the poor and desolate world in which he was obliged to live, bringing his improvised medical cures to the local inhabitants, taking an interest in the economic problems of the area, trying to determine the advantages and disadvantages of Siberian and Russian trade with China. Yet he never forgot distant Europe, at the height of its phase of revolution and war at the end of the 18th century. One thread continued to tie him to the European world: he received books that were precious and rare when they arrived in Siberia. Scientific journals, works by Condorcet which he requested, the French translation of Filangieri, and other pamphlets and volumes represented for Radishchev, at the edge of Europe, the distant echo of the great storm that was shaking the civilized world.

He soon withdrew this glance toward the outside world and returned, as always, to his own existence. He viewed the simple and basic life of those who passed their days near him. His interest in the rural world became sharper. He turned his observations to the peasant community, the *obshchina,* and became one of the first persons to see it as an answer, arising spontaneously from the Russian soil, to the need for equality that was then developing in the West. The problem of the similar needs arising from the lower classes in Russia, and their relationship to the great machinery of the Russian state, confronted him with renewed intensity. There were also practical problems that in the solitude of exile continued to present themselves without ever being completely reconciled with the moral, religious, and philosophical questions that filled his mind. His long treatise, *On Man, His Mortality and Immortality,* was written during the Siberian exile and published posthumously in 1809. In it he returns to culture that he had explored and acquired earlier, often of German origin, including Mendelssohn and especially Herder. It is an obviously sincere attempt to reconstruct a coherent and harmonious universe compatible with his strong ethical needs. Yet it is also an eclectic effort to synthesize a morality and religion for the educated. To put it another way, this work is a Russian or even a Siberian version of the attempts of Robespierre and others after him to find a new religious answer to the many questions that multiplied once the old religion had been overcome.

Catherine's death and the accession of Paul I to the throne opened the way for Radishchev's return to European Russia in 1797, though he was not allowed to re-establish contact with the world of the capital. His return was saddened by the death of his second wife, the sister of his first, and he was increasingly insecure in the precarious atmosphere of the whole country in those years.

Only with the accession of Alexander I to the throne did a brief, new, and tumultuous era in Radishchev's life begin. In the dawn of the new century, the drama of his life seemed to be beginning again. His hopes for a new enlightened sovereign, the attempt to find a constitutional road to liberty, the contrast between the desire for reform and the aspirations of the nobles, aristocrats, and *pomeshchiki* all seemed to reimmerse Radishchev in the machinery of political responsibility and burdens of state. While the first part of his life had ended with a death sentence, he himself brought an end to the second part on September 11, 1802 by committing suicide, an act still shrouded in darkness and mystery. Although it was rich in thoughts and hopes, the second life of the author of the *Journey* was ended.

Annotated Bibliography

A photostatic reproduction of the original edition of Radishchev's *Journey,* which appeared in St. Petersburg in 1790, was published in 1935 by Academia (Moscow and Leningrad). It was accompanied by an indispensable volume of notes and comments edited by Ya. L. Barksov. The Institute of Literature of the Academy of Sciences of the USSR (Moscow and Leningrad: Pushkinsky dom) published Radishchev's complete works, *Polnoye sobranie sochineniy,* edited by I. K. Luppol, G. A. Gukovsky, V. A. Desnitsky, N. K. Piksanov, D. C. Babkin, and B. B. Kafengaus, in three volumes between 1938 and 1952.

Basic Works in Russian

Alekseev, M. P., ed. *Radishchev: Stati i materialy* [Radishchev: Articles and materials]. Leningrad: Leningrad University, Institute of Philology, 1950.
Marks the renewal of studies on 18th-century Russia after the war. Here, G. P. Makogonenko, Yu. Lotman, and P. N. Berkov present the first results of wide research which continued in the next twenty years.

Babkin, D. S. *Protsess A. N. Radishcheva* [The trial of A. N. Radishchev]. Moscow and Leningrad: Institute of Literature of the Academy of Sciences of the USSR (Pushkinsky dom), 1925.
The greatest documentary contribution published on Radishchev after the war.

Babkin, D. S. *A. N. Radishchev, Literaturno-obshchestvennaya deyatelnost* [A. N. Radishchev, literary and social activities]. Moscow and Leningrad: Nauka, 1966.
Useful, erudite clarification.

Karyakin, Yu. F., and E. G. Plinak. *Zapretnaya mysl obretaet svobodu* [Forbidden thought conquers liberty]. Moscow: Nauka, 1966. A dedicated attempt to reconsider all the current themes in the Soviet interpretation of Radishchev.

Lotman, Iu. M. "Radishchev i Mabli" [Radishchev and Mably]. *XVIII vek* [The 18th century], no. 3 (1958), pp. 276 ff.
An incisive investigation by one of Russia's best contemporary critics. A requisite starting point for a deeper understanding of the relationship between Radishchev and the Enlightenment in Western Europe.

Luppol, I. K. "Tragediya russkogo materializma XVIII v.: Filosofskiye vzglyady A. N. Radishcheva" [The tragedy of Russian materialism in the 18th century: philosophical conceptions of A. N. Radishchev]. In *Istoriko-filosofskiye styudy* [Studies in the history of philosophy]. Moscow and Leningrad: Gos. Soc. Ekon. Izd., 1935.
Shortly after having published this essay, Luppol was eliminated during the Stalin purges. The tragedy of materialism, of the ideas and hopes of the Russian intelligentsia which began with Radishchev's condemnation and suicide between the 18th and 19th centuries, found its echo in the 1930s.

Makogonenko, G. P. *Radishchev i ego vremya* [Radishchev and his era]. Moscow: Gos. Izd. Khud. Lit., 1956.
The most important recent monograph, with many new elements and no small amount of exaggeration deriving from current Soviet "patriotism" and above all from a desire to include Radishchev in the pantheon of the eternal Revolution.

Orlov, A. S., ed. *A. N. Radishchev: Materialy i isseldovaniya* [A. N. Radishchev: materials and researches]. Moscow and Leningrad: Academia Nauk SSSR, 1936.
An excellent miscellany. I. M. Trotsky enhances our knowledge of Radishchev in the early part of Alexander I's reign, G. Gukovsky examines the author's style, V. P. Semennikov contributes valuable elements about the atmosphere in which the *Journey* was conceived, and P. G. Lyubomirov offers a superb essay on the ancestors and family of the author.

Semennikov, V. P. *Radishchev: Ocherki i isseldovaniya* [Radishchev: essays and researches]. Moscow and St. Petersburg: Gos. Izdatelstvo, 1923.

This work considers some of the fundamental themes in critical terms: the "Ode to Liberty," the relationship with the French Revolution, Radishchev's activities at the beginning of Alexander I's reign, his relationship to Pushkin, etc.

Shtorm, Georgy. *Potaennyy Radishchev: Vtoraya zhizn "Puteshestviya iz Peterburga v Moskvu"* [The hidden Radishchev: the second life of the *Journey from St. Petersburg to Moscow*]. Moscow: Sovietsky Pisatel, 1965.

An unusual and adventurous attempt to make the circle of those who read and were influenced by Radishchev's work between the end of the 18th and the beginning of the 19th century less restricted.

Startsev, A. *Universitetskie gody Radishcheva* [Radishchev's university years]. Moscow: Sovietsky Pisatel, 1956.

Startsev, A. *Radishchev v gody "Puteshestviya"* [Radishchev during the *Journey* years]. Moscow: Sovietsky Pisatel, 1960.

Interesting for the new material presented but restricted by the "patriotic" and "revolutionary" interpretation.

Significant Works Not in Russian

Confino, Michael. *Domaines et seigneurs en Russie vers la fin du XVIIIe siècle: Etude de structures agraires et de mentalités économiques.* Paris: Institut des Etudes Slaves, 1963.

Confino, Michael. *Systèmes agraires et progrès agricole: Assolement triennal en Russie aux XVIIIe-XIXe siècles.* Paris and The Hague: Mouton, 1969.

These two works by Michael Confino constitute the most important investigation into economic life in the Russian countryside in the 18th century.

Dukes, Paul. *Catherine the Great and the Russian Nobility.* Cambridge: Cambridge University Press, 1967.

An accurate clarification of the discussion both in and outside Russia on autocracy and its relationship with the nobility in the second half of the 18th century.

Hexelschneider, Erhart, ed. *A. N. Radishchev und Deutschland: Beiträge zur russischen Literatur des augehenden 18. Jarhunderts.* Berlin: Akademie-Verlag, 1969.

La Franc-Maçonnerie en Russie: Bibliographie préparée par Paul Bourychkine, completée et mise au point par Tatiana Bakounine. Paris and The Hague: Mouton, 1967.

Indispensable bibliographical guide for a study of the masonic movement in Russia.

La Révolte de Pougatchev, presentée par Pierre Pascal. Paris: Juillard, 1971.

The most recent and lucid study of the *pugachevshchina.*

Lang, David Marshall. *The First Russian Radical: Alexander Radishchev, 1749–1802.* London: Allen & Unwin, 1959.

McConnell, Allen. *A Russian Philosophe: Alexander Radishchev, 1749–1802.* The Hague: Martinus Nijhoff, 1964.

The best non-Russian book on Radishchev.

Raeff, Marc. *Imperial Russia, 1682–1825: The Coming of Age of Modern Russia.* New York: Knopf, 1971.

A quick summary and the work of one of the finest experts on Russia in the old regime.

Raeff, Marc. *Origins of the Russian Intelligentsia: The Eighteenth-Century Nobility.* New York: Harcourt, Brace & World, 1966.

Rogger, Hans. *National Consciousness in Eighteenth-Century Russia.* Cambridge, Mass.: Harvard University Press, 1960.

Thaler, Roderick Page, ed. *A. N. Radishchev: Journey from St. Petersburg to Moscow.* Translated by Leo Wiener. Cambridge, Mass.: Harvard University Press, 1958.

Three Destutt de Tracy and the Liberal Revolutions

When in 1817 the publisher J. F. Desoer presented Destutt de Tracy's *Commentaire sur l'Esprit des lois* to French readers, he expressed the conviction that he was rendering "a real service to liberals of all countries."[1] In fact, the clear and original political and economic ideas of the French ideologist created a distinct echo, which resounded throughout the whole period of the liberal revolutions, from the Spain of 1820 to the Russia of 1825. The *Commentaire,* along with his writings on *Idéologie,* must be placed beside the widely read and influential works of Benjamin Constant, of Bentham, of the French theorists, and of the English radicals without being confused with them. A clear stream of distinct ideas runs through the age of Riego and of Pestel.

Like all liberal thought, Destutt de Tracy's ideas arose from reflections on the consequences of the Enlightenment and of the revolution during the transition from the 18th to the 19th century. What makes his views original is the cosmopolitanism of his vision, his lively interest even in countries lying beyond and outside revolutionary and Napoleonic Europe, especially the United States and Russia. At the same time he maintains his 18th-century legacy with particular freshness.

His bond with America stemmed from his youth when, like so many promising sons of the French nobility, he took an active part in the English colonies' war for independence. More significant is the fact that after the age of Robespierre, the Directory, and Napoleon, he returned to the problems of America. He had reached his philosophical conclusions on the Enlightenment, on Condillac, on what he called "ideology" while he was in prison in the days preceding 9 *thermidor,* when his life hung in the balance. He waited until 1806, about twelve years later, to formulate his political conclusions and again referred back to the 18th-century masters, discussing and arguing with them in light of the extraordinary events of the age of revolution. It was not just practical problems—the desire to evade censorship—that led him to introduce his ideas to a man like Thomas Jefferson and to try to publish his commentary on *L'Esprit des lois* in America. Destutt de Tracy was evidently convinced that his work could be as useful—and even indispensable— on one side of the Atlantic as on the other.[2]

59

Distance and censorship delayed matters, but they did not obscure the initial response to his writings. "It is the most valuable political work of the present age," Jefferson stated on September 16, 1810. Jefferson obtained as faithful a translation as possible and succeeded in having it published in 1811 in the guise of a work by a French emigré in America.[3] When a copy was brought to Destutt de Tracy by General Lafayette, the author thanked Jefferson, saying that his highest aspiration had been to gain "the approbation of the most virtuous and most truly enlightened statesman over the destiny of a great people." Nothing could have pleased de Tracy more than to see his works approved and then disseminated by such a man. "It is the destiny of truths to go around the world, once they are known." He added that he had almost finished the "preliminary discourse" of his "treatise on the will" and "the whole first part, which deals with political economy."[4] A month later he sent Jefferson the manuscript of this work, hoping once again to see it published in English and in America; for America was not only a free country but also seemed particularly well suited to accept his economic ideas, now that it had welcomed and spread his political views. Once again, Jefferson said he was convinced that he was dealing with the best existing essay on the subject: "It may be considered as a review of the principles of the Economists, of Smith, and of Say, or rather an elementary book on the same subject.... He has in my opinion corrected fundamental errors in all of them, and by simplifying principles has brought the subject within a narrow compass."[5] Later, Jefferson again expressed his conviction that it was an excellent book. "Its principles are so profound, so logically demonstrated and so briefly expressed, that it must become the elementary book of the world for the science of political economy, as the other [the *Commentaire*] will be that of government."[6]

But by now world events were hampering the publication and distribution of Destutt de Tracy's work. When Jefferson wrote those words, the war between America and England had already begun and the Napoleonic empire had entered its final crisis. After the great era of the Chathams and the Turgots, the world seemed to have fallen back into the immorality of the age "of the cabinets of the age of Machiavel." It was a world of bandits which, Jefferson said, "sickens my soul unto death."[7] It was only later, in 1816, that he could write to General Lafayette that at least the result of the fierce struggle could be considered positively. "The loss of the battle of Waterloo was the salvation of France. Had Bonaparte obtained the victory, his talents, his egoism and destitution of all moral principle would have rivetted a military despotism on your necks."[8] In 1817, in the subdued atmosphere at the culmination of the postwar crisis that every country experienced after Napoleon's fall, the English translation of Destutt de Tracy's *Traité d'économie politique* appeared, and the French edition was published in Paris the following year. In 1819 the original version of the *Commentaire* was published in Liège. Both works, begun during the empire, thus came to be at the center of current discussions and polemics, and in the midst of the world "of lying and blindness" in which the author was obliged to live, his works prepared the way for the liberal revolutions of the 1820s.[9] As de Tracy said, these two works formed his testament, a testament that would increasingly arouse the interest of constitutionalists, of liberals, and of Carbonari.[10]

Once again, Destutt de Tracy was convinced that America would lead the way to recovery: "I await the avenger from America."[11] Once again, as in his youth, the spark would come from the New World. This time it was the Spanish colonies, now in open revolt against their mother country. With renewed enthusiasm de Tracy wrote to Jefferson, trying to persuade him and his countrymen to help the South American rebels. "It is on you, dear sir, that all my affections, my hopes, and my esteem are focused. It is enough to say to you with what impatience I wait for you to help our South American brothers living in Buenos Aires, because their conduct seems to me admirable and their principles excellent."[12] Destutt de Tracy's daughter-in-law, a descendant of Newton, describes with what enthusiasm the old ideologist, now almost completely blind, considered the new countries that were just emerging in the historical scene, and how in his view they appeared potentially even more interesting from the political and economic standpoint. "He wanted to be able to run to the aid of the less advanced countries, to offer them advice, to help them understand that by giving a more precise meaning to words one would see more reasonable ideas being born.... De Tracy carried on a correspondence with Rivadavia, and passed on his ideas to him. He wanted to visit Buenos Aires, Mexico, Chile, Peru, all of the America he loved so much ..."[13]

Concern for the "less advanced countries" is constant in Destutt de Tracy's works, and both in the *Commentaire* and in the *Traité d'économie politique* it is polarized especially between North America and Russia. Certainly his personal experience and intellectual knowledge of the two countries were very different. He was not as familiar with and as close to Russia as he was to the United States, but his interest was not less because of this, for Russia was an example and an experimental area for economic and political problems faced by advancing civilization. At the beginning of the 18th century, had Russia not tried to escape from a situation that Montesquieu called despotism and which in reality, according to de Tracy, was the position of all monarchies "surrounded by ignorance and barbarism"? "If the monarch, like Peter the Great, is desirous of changing so abominable and precarious a state of society, or if he is placed among a people already somewhat civilized, and consequently disposed to advance in refinement, then he ought to devise a rational system."[14] An overall view and a coherent political system were the first requirements for any change. De Tracy had always vigorously defended this enlightened conviction without ever giving in to the temptation offered by the defenders of traditions and of spontaneous and organic developments. Already in 1790 he had explained to Burke that it was for this very reason that Burke's whole approach to the revolution was radically wrong. "Burke has not grasped the spirit of our revolution ... I think that the long-standing habit of considering what governments really are has prevented him from calculating what they could be."[15] It was not a matter of "reforming, that is, consolidating and repairing an oppressive and corrupt government, whose tendency was to divide all the classes of citizens and all the parts of the empire among themselves, to set one against the other and dominate them all." Rather, it was a question of creating a new state based on "the love of equality and of union, that precious sentiment that Montesquieu himself, that illustrious apologist for the government under which he lived, did not hesitate to honor with the name of true virtue, and from which he derived the principle of republican government."[16]

These ideas and programs did not deal only with constitutional forms and the structure of states and governments; they were meant above all to tackle economic problems. Everything depended on the ability to restrain useless and unproductive expense, which in Destutt de Tracy's 18th-century viewpoint was luxury. "When a nation first takes its place in civilized society, in order for the success of its efforts to be complete, the progress of its industry and culture should be greater than that of its luxury."[17] Three examples demonstrated this point. Eighteenth-century Prussia had furnished proof of what a monarchy opposed to luxury could do. The United States had managed to "double their agriculture, industry, commerce, wealth, and population, . . . in less than twenty-five years," while systematically continuing to produce more than they consumed.[18] Russia, with her luxuries, her splendor, her spending for prestige, risked providing the opposite example, rendering "true prosperity and true civilization difficult and imperfect," though in so many other ways they had seemed promised to this country as well as to the others.[19] Like America, Russia had the great advantage of being a nation at least parts of which could still be colonized. A sure means of prevention and a very effective remedy for peasant poverty everywhere was, in fact, "the proximity of unsettled but fertile lands."

But the very attitude of these two countries toward this favorable element in their situation showed the difference between them. "Their different ways of responding to this fortunate circumstance show the difference between the two governments, or more precisely between these two nations, one of which is incapable of self-government and will be for a long time yet."[20] Evidently it was not sufficient to offer free land and provide some tools and livestock, as was done in Russia (while in America the land was sold "very reasonably").[21] It was necessary to remove the obstacles that kept people from profiting from such offers. The monopoly in the grain trade, which existed in Poland, for example, could only be deleterious. "In Poland, where a small number of men own not only all the land but all the people who cultivate it, when these proprietors gather all the wheat that their serfs have been able to produce in order to sell it abroad and buy in exchange luxury items which they consume, everyone is made more miserable. It would be better if these magnates could find no market for their grain. They would perhaps try to nourish men with it, and endeavor to teach them, little by little, to make at least some of the things that they desire." In Russia the monopolistic spirit had reached the point of prohibiting the production of certain goods in order to protect foreign traders. "No doubt, in this case, it would be better not to have any relations with the outside world."[22]

Only by overcoming such obstacles could Russia too have benefited from the great advantages of being a nation with a growing civilization. De Tracy was convinced that "ease is general, among the new and industrious nations."[23] He also knew the reason for this privilege, "especially if the race of men which forms the new society comes from an industrious and enlightened nation and if it has relations with other civilized countries; because then it does not need to invent and discover, which is always a very slow process, but merely to profit from what is known, and to put what is known into practice, and to put into practice what one knows, which is easy."[24]

Static and retrograde civilizations only produced poverty. "Such is the sad state of the old nations."[25] But if this seemed to be the fate of old monarchic and feudal Europe, how could one believe that in the same period the United States and Russia could benefit in their own way from the possibilities open to them? De Tracy did not have illusions about either country. "The state of full prosperity is necessarily transitory." It was no use complaining about this fact or attributing the blame "to those vague words, degeneration, corruption, the old age of nations,... all metaphorical expressions which have been strangely abused."[26] In the final analysis, everything depended on the ratio between population and means of subsistence. If "in the actual state of our old societies"—that is, in Europe—the population increased, even slowly, it was all to the credit of intellectual progress. "It is because the arts and sciences, and notably social science, are constantly being cultivated there, more or less well, and their progress adds from time to time some small facilities to the means of livelihood, and opens some new markets to commerce and industry." Otherwise the population tended to stabilize or even decrease Russia's case was particularly significant from this standpoint as well. "I don't pretend to either eulogize or satirize this nation, which I do not know." The situation there seemed paradoxical. Russia certainly could not boast of greater luminaries and greater technical progress than other European nations. Yet it was a fact that her population was increasing at a faster rate than in other countries. Only the existence of large amounts of free land could explain such a development. Then why did the population not increase as rapidly as in the United States? "It is because her social organization and her industry are far from being as perfect." One need simply consider Poland and imagine that the great landlords were abolished and that the land had become "the property of those who cultivate it" to see the peasants "promptly become industrious and multiply rapidly."[27] Spain in the past fifty years served as an example of what one could obtain by freeing "industry from some of its shackles" and by brightening "the lights a little."[28] By refusing to believe in the myths of an inexplicable decay and flowering of nations, Destutt de Tracy seemed to indicate, even for countries that did not enjoy the privileged situation of the United States, a compelling need for a vigorous program of reform based on the search for a new equilibrium between equality and economic initiative, between population growth and intellectual and technical development.

But who should put such a program into effect? What political means could be used for such a transformation? Destutt de Tracy, convinced that Montesquieu "understood political economy very poorly," wrote his whole *Commentaire* to argue with him over political ideas and institutions. He thus intended to free liberalism from the traditionalistic, historicist element that had accompanied its birth and its development in the transition between two centuries, but which, in his view, would only make it less vigorous and less active in the struggle against the privileges, inequality, luxury, and poverty that smothered the old European nations. Thus, despite all the dangers, he had always been on the side of revolution. He had refused to emigrate and had faced persecution fighting, but not complaining, and as soon as he was able to, he had again tried to clear the road of republican France of all the obstacles that still blocked it. He had not given way on religion (he was very attached to a synthesis he had written of Dupuis's *Origine de tous les cultes*) much less on philosophy or ideology, placing all his works under the label of a renewed Condillacian logic. He had become a close friend of Cabanis and had done everything in his power, both during the writer's life and after his death, to make his works and ideas known.[29] When, in 1807, Madame de Staël sent him her *Corinne,* Destutt de Tracy responded with an exquisite letter which is a courteous and complete denial of all romantic liberalism. "You love enthusiasm, madame; I confess that I dread it."

The hero of the novel, the Englishman Oswald, seemed to de Tracy "a Chinaman devoted to ancestor worship" and, like many Englishmen, looked more toward the past than the future. As for the "delicious Italian girl," Corinne, "she is of her country, she falls in love at first sight, she loves what is shadowy and vague, without dreaming that obscurity is the refuge of all imperfections." (Destutt de Tracy's mother was a "devout Italian" and, apparently, "very remarkable for her spirit and character.")[30] "You may believe, madame," he continues, "that I was not able to follow you into the tombs, and still less to raise myself as often as you to the heavens, because my soul, though it is neither hard nor cold, is all the same a bit terrestrial, and holds to the surface of the soil because it needs a firm foundation which it finds only there." He felt a need to defend the revolution even to Madame de Staël. Why, already in 1791, represent France "as a monster"? "It is at least premature, it seems to me, but this subject leads me far afield."[31]

The core of Destutt de Tracy's political thought is in the polemic against monarchy, be it legitimate like the French monarchy or constitutional like the English one. Both were an expression of the static and unjust society that he felt was weighing on old Europe. It was not that he wanted to return to ancient forms of democracy, to the republics of the past. Either they had never really existed (even in Greece the power of the cities lay in their embryonic federalism, not in democracy) or they were always destined to have aristocratic or oligarchic forms and had been incapable of creating a representative government. One could look at Berne or Venice, where the monopoly of culture and power had fallen into the hands of a limited aristocracy, "precipitating the people into disorder, crapulence, and vice."[32] Nor could primitive populations serve as an example, as many over-indulgent writers, including Montesquieu, had believed. As for Spartan virtues, he said, "I confess naively that I don't admire Sparta any more than Trappism.... Men need clothing, not hair shirts."[33] Montesquieu's great mistake had been to confuse ancient and medieval republican tradition with the modern idea of popular sovereignty. For him, a republic meant both democracy and aristocracy. "When he speaks of republican government, one no longer knows which of the two he means."[34] The American and French revolutions had severed the tie that, in the 18th century, had linked the idea of democracy with past republican experiences. Now only two forms existed. They were the only one which could answer the needs of the world that had emerged out of the "fifty prodigious years" from 1748 to Napoleon:[35] (1) the "federal government . . . , appropriate to new countries, to virgin lands that feudal privilege has not soiled," and (2) the "representative government" suitable for Europe, which "this deleterious regime, after so many centuries, has beaten more or less to servile sterility."[36]

But would it really not have been possible to renew Europe by creating a federation of its states? Destutt does not exclude the possibility, saying that it was considerably more difficult to pass from "the original state of man to the Achaean league, than [from] the actual state of Europe [to] the confederation of all its parts."[37] But meanwhile, the only possible government that would be active and would reform the old nations was a representative one. It was the only kind capable of realizing the democratic and liberal ideal for a large nation. According to Montesquieu, monarchy had been nothing but "aristocracy under a single head." Pure monarchy was a "government of barbarians." Only representative government would have made "democracy for a long time and a great space" possible. Such a government, unknown in the past, had taken on different forms in the last decades: "representative government under a single head, as in the constitution of the United States of America" or "the constitution made for France in 1791."[38] Destutt proposed another variation. He suggested that the executive power not be entrusted to an elected president or to a hereditary monarch but to "a council composed of a small number of persons elected for a time and renewed successively."[39] He also felt there was a need to introduce a sort of constitutional court, a "conservative body" with wider jurisdiction than that of the American model.[40]

The possibilities for a modern state were as follows: (1) the constitution of the United States of America; (2) Louis XVI's constitution or, as his readers must have thought when the *Commentaire* reached Europe after the fall of Napoleon, the constitution of Cadiz of 1812 which took up the essential elements of the French constitution of 1791; or, finally, (3) the constitution of year III with the Directory. The constitutions omitted from the list are as significant as the ones mentioned. Nothing was accepted of the Napoleonic constitutional forms (the "conservative body" that de Tracy envisaged would have had the merit, if it had existed in 1799, of helping to avoid the coup d'état of 18 *brumaire*). On the other hand, despite some formal concessions, the entire *Commentaire* was basically directed against constitutional monarchies that arose from the restoration, and against the Bourbon monarchy of the *Charte*. In his eyes both were evidently too similar to the aristocracies presided over by a king which he had criticized in the *ancien régime* and in Montesquieu. Thus he rejected the English constitution. His proposals for a directory and a "conservative body" were a clear effort to eliminate any monarchical remains in representative governments which arose from the revolutionary events between the 18th and 19th centuries.

Thus we can understand what Jefferson meant when he read the *Commentaire* for the first time: Destutt de Tracy had confuted Montesquieu and substituted a true principle for a false one, "and the true principle is that of republicanism."[41] The republic was the basis of the French ideologist's thought. Nevertheless, Jefferson was not willing to accept the idea of the executive power being entrusted to a body of people who were elected and then periodically replaced. Destutt de Tracy had touched a fundamental point for the president of the United States. "When our present government was first established, we had many doubts on this question, and many leanings towards a supreme executive council." In 1784 a council of states had been formed with thirteen members, one for each state, to govern during the congressional recesses. This body soon proved completely unable to function. France's experience ten years later convinced Jefferson and the Americans that a single executive head of state was indispensable. To follow Destutt de Tracy's suggestion would have meant substituting a council of ministers for the individual executive power and bringing to the head of the state all the differences and rivalry that are inevitable in all governments. Nor would a collective body have created, as de Tracy had hoped, a greater obstacle to the designs and ambition of a potential usurper. For this function, the constitutional court, the conservative body which he had rightly recommended in his *Commentaire,* would have been more to the purpose. But Jefferson insisted that the strongest support of public liberty lay in the federal character of the American republic: "The true barriers of our liberty in this country are our State governments." In France, liberty had been lost without even being defended, "without a struggle," "because the party of *un et indivisible* had prevailed." "No provincial organizations existed to which the people might rally under authority of the laws, the seats of the directory were virtually vacant and a small force sufficed to turn the legislature out of their chamber and to salute its leader chief of the nation." The federal government was undoubtedly exposed to the danger of the secession of one or more states, but not to the hazard of a coup d'état and usurpation.[42]

Jefferson's complete and natural defense of the American constitution struck something fundamental in Destutt de Tracy's thoughts; the French ideologist doubted whether the old countries of Europe were actually capable of adopting authentic federalism. The past—and not just the *ancien régime,* but even the revolution itself—seemed to present too many obstacles to such a radical measure. With his division of peoples into new and old, Destutt de Tracy was actually trying to overcome an inherent contradiction in his ideas. His thoughts were divided between the ideal of a representative regime and that of a true democracy in which the rights and desires, not only of individuals but also of different territories and groups making up the community, were respected. But, as he well knew, to realize this second hypothesis, a socially balanced society was needed. It must not be seriously threatened either from far or near, it must be prosperous without luxury, it must be expanding rapidly without seeking colonies outside its boundaries. Under these conditions the federal government could resolve the problems of democracy "in the easiest and surest manner." But who could guarantee that, even in America, executive power entrusted to a single person would not end up creating a serious danger? The facts mentioned to him by Jefferson seemed not only to show that "the predominating voice of a president" had been very useful in the crisis after 1784, but "you show me more than that, that it is almost necessary." The power of the president had become predominant. But as for France, how could one assume that the people would wait calmly for ten months, as they had in America in 1784, "for the national will to manifest itself legally," remaining quite composed during such a long interregnum? How could one find in France a president who, like Jefferson, could write to him that he could not even understand how a rational being "could propose happiness to himself from the exercise of power over others"? And above all, how could a federal government similar to the American one be adopted in a country like France, surrounded by powerful enemy governments? "If our France had been divided in a certain number of states that are truly separated, truly independent from one another, and united only by a weak federal bond, we would never have been able to sustain the terrible struggle from which we have emerged victorious only by the effect of the most energetic central power that has ever existed; lacking that, our country would have been subjugated or torn asunder; that is what all those who have lived in this time of crisis and calamity would tell you." If one were not to despair of the possibility of a free government even in old Europe, one had to find some "clever schemes" capable of "supplying the advantages of federation." "I like well the federal system, sir, I sense in it truly all the advantages, thus I hope to distance myself very little from your way of thinking, but you force me to believe that liberty is even a bit more difficult to conserve than I had imagined."[43]

The only thing that consoled de Tracy in the difficult years following this exchange of ideas between Monticello and Paris was to see how, after so many disasters and so much disillusionment, his ideas began to be revived all over Europe after 1817. They first reappeared in Italy. He wrote to Jefferson on April 11,

1818, "I want to brag to you, sir, that my first three volumes [on *l'Idéologie*] were very well translated into Italian in Milan and that the fourth volume [the one containing the *Traité d'économie politique*] is going to follow them."[44] The thick volumes, ten in all, entitled *Elementi di ideologia* appeared in rapid succession between 1817 and 1819.[45] They were a veritable bastion of the ideas of Locke, Condillac, and French ideology, patiently erected by Giuseppe Compagnoni against the innumerable enemies of the Enlightenment who had arisen in the preceding ten years, including traditionalists, metaphysicists, Kantians, and romantics. Compagnoni defended the fortress with skill, trying to avoid attacks from the constituted authorities and from the dominant church by using as a screen long passages on the existence of God or on the immortality of the soul, taken from the works of Antonio Genovesi and of Father Vincenzo Bini; invoking the authority of Father Soave ("if Father Soave were still with us...") and calling on all of modern science from Bacon to Hobbes, from Bonnet to Lavoisier; and persistently recalling the Italian tradition of the Enlightenment personified by Verri and Beccaria.[46] After all these preliminaries, the "valentuomo" whose works Compagnoni had decided to translate was proclaimed "the first man to give a marvelous clarity to subjects which are abstruse and very subtle." In this he was similar to Lavoisier, "in that on one hand both contain new discoveries, and on the other both purify the old elements they had."[47] Of special importance was the return of the idea of a philosophical grammar, which Compagnoni was proposing in a vast and detailed preface to the second part of *Principi d'ideologia*. When he reached the fourth part, the *Traité de la volonté* (that is, *Traité d'économie politique*), he had to redouble his defensive devices (he even managed to speak well of the Holy Alliance), but at the same time he emphasized the contractual and egalitarian elements in Destutt de Tracy and the tradition of political thought that de Tracy headed, defending Rousseau and Beccaria, referring back to Romagnosi, "one of the most profound Italian publicists of our time," and seeking vindication for his *Elementi di diritto costituzionale,* which Compagnoni himself had published in 1797. He said he was certain that the new generation would shoulder the burden of transforming and regenerating a society which seemed to have stopped advancing and to have been stifled: "It is particularly to the young that we address our discussion, because with these studies they have come to a happier era than ours, and now they are rightly entrusted with the fate of all national glory."[48] At the end of the ten volumes, Compagnoni even presents a sort of catechism so that readers may learn his and Destutt de Tracy's essential ideas.[49] As can be seen, Destutt de Tracy could not have found a better intermediary in Italy. It was probably gratitude that led de Tracy to give Compagnoni an unpublished text to be included in the last volume of *Principi d'ideologia*. The text, *Dell'amore*, thus first appeared in Italian (it only came out many decades later, posthumously, in French) and closed the great work on a subtle and penetrating psychological note.[50]

The reaction in Italy to the *Principi d'ideologia* disillusioned Compagnoni. He well knew that he was going against the current, but he had not expected such cautious silence: "Few newspapers that I know have spoken of my work, and my notes could have merited some mention. The 'Biblioteca Italiana' is the one that did refer to it, and perhaps one day this work will be discussed more freely than it has been until now. That will come when reason removes the slanderous sophisms that some meticulous and unenlightened minds tried to spread."[51] But there were some signs of interest in Destutt de Tracy's philosophical ideas. Three collections of his works appeared in the *Collezione dei classici metafisici* published by Defendente Sacchi in Pavia: *Principi logici e memoria inedita sulla metafisica di Kant* in 1822, *Memoria sulla facoltà di pensare* in 1824, and *Memorie scelte di ideologia* in 1826, all translated by Giuseppe Sacchi. In presenting the second of these works, the editor of the series noted how the French philosopher continued to exercise a kind of hidden influence that was not even admitted by those who had felt it most. *Principi d'ideologia* was "an almost inexhaustible source from which many people in France and Italy drew, copying the ideas without even thinking to cite them . . ."[52]

Something better can be said about Destutt de Tracy's political ideas. They spread all over Italy in the years leading up to the movements of 1820–21 and came to light during the uprisings, especially in Naples. But after the defeat of the liberal revolutions the ideas faded into the shadows; they were condemned to obscurity during the restoration because of their boldness and incisiveness. In 1824 Defendente Sacchi noted the close link uniting the French ideologist's philosophy with his politics. He clearly expressed the sense of amazement that affected even the Italians when faced with the force of de Tracy's conclusions: "It was he who took in the philosophy of experience when it was just a hesitant child; he encouraged it, nurtured it, and when it became dominant, brought it to the field of ideology, of the science of languages, and what is more amazing, to the field of politics." "The Nestor of living philosophers," moving from Montesquieu and from Condillac, "in corrupt times, recalled the era of Socrates by his example and domestic virtues."[53]

Giuseppe Sacchi, the translator of this *Memoria,* recalled how the author had held the Italians "in special affection."[54] Our brief excursions in search of traces left by de Tracy in the peninsula must begin in the transition zone between France and Italy, still involved in the memories and problems of the revolutionary and Napoleonic ages. Henri Beyle (Stendhal), the great novelist who boasted of being "Milanese," will naturally be our guide. In Milan between November 1817 and June 1818, Beyle worked feverishly on his *Vie de Napoléon,* leaving the manuscript with his friend Brezzi when he left the capital of Lombardy. Passing through Paris on his way to England at the beginning of August he delivered a copy of his *Histoire de la peinture en Italie* to Destutt de Tracy. The old ideologist went to see Beyle at his hotel on his return, on September 4, and the two men had a long discussion. "Two days later, Beyle received in his turn a copy of the *Commentaire*." When Stendhal left for Milan in October, Destutt de Tracy gave him a letter for Defendente Sacchi. In recording this encounter and exchange of books, Stendhal declared himself to be a "disciple" of Destutt de Tracy and again recognized not only how great his admiration was for the ideologist, but also the considerable debt he owed de Tracy in his interpretation of Napoleon and, in general, in the fields of political and economic ideas.[55] "For me," he noted in the manuscript of the *Vie de Napoléon,* "the last state of the science of government, and consequently my political credo, is the *Commentaire sur l'Esprit des lois de Montesquieu,* printed by Desoer in Liège in 1817."[56] From Destutt de Tracy he had taken the explanation of 18 *brumaire;* the events had been possible because the constitution of year III had not foreseen a conservative senate. Stendhal had also derived from de Tracy the basis of his criticism of the government structure established by Napoleon. While he accepted the fundamental ideas of his master, Stendhal nevertheless modified them under the influence of the liberal theories prevalent in the age of the *Charte.* According to him, Napoleon should have established "five directors renewed annually by one-fifth and nominated by a conservatory Senate, two chambers elected by the people, the first among the people paying one thousand francs in taxes; the second among the people who pay ten thousand, and renewed annually by one-fifth."[57] Destutt de Tracy had spoken of only one chamber and had not accepted the principle of an election based on the census. More personal and typically Stendhalian is his forcing of Destutt de Tracy's concept of political liberty. Stendhal actually uses his master's ideas in his apologia for Napoleon. The ruler had certainly suppressed all political liberty. But had Destutt de Tracy not explained that liberty should be measured exclusively according to the degree of intensity with which it was desired, according to the force and energy of the will expended to obtain it? "Thus, to be free, it is necessary to want it." Under Napoleon, the French were still monarchic and had not had the strength to be free. Rather, the true fault of the Empire—and in this Stendhal was in full agreement with Destutt de Tracy—lay in the indifference and disdain that Napoleon had shown for "les lumières," knowledge and education. "His greatest crime" against the French "is this: he could have advanced their education."[58] With regard to Napoleon's foreign policy and his wars and conquests, Stendhal relies on Destutt de Tracy and what he had asserted about the positive function of the expansion carried out by the French Revolution in Europe, on the necessity and usefulness of spreading the new ideas and political and constitutional forms everywhere. According to Stendhal, Napoleon had been wrong in never being decisive and consistent enough in such policies, in having accepted the compromise with the Pope at Tolentino and with Austria at Campoformio, with Prussia and again with Austria in the following years. "He abandoned the old Jacobin principle of seeking allies against kings in the hearts of their subjects. As a new king, he already husbanded, in the hearts of the people, respect for the throne."[59] It was what Destutt de Tracy had maintained. He had written, "It is this that makes a representative government so formidable to all the others: because, in their quarrels with it, the interests of their own subjects are against them.... If the French had truly profited from this great advantage, by not deviating from their principles, after setting themselves the natural limits that they could desire, they would have immediately been surrounded by states constituted like theirs..."[60] Thus, according to Stendhal, both in internal affairs and abroad Napoleon had proved incapable of overcoming the limits of his monarchic upbringing. The views expressed in the *Commentaire* on the *ancien régime*, on its aristocratic and religious character, its fundamental identification with despotism, the fallaciousness of all the justifications that Montesquieu had tried to offer, its radical opposition to a free and republican system, all profoundly affected the portrait that Stendhal painted of Napoleon. Apart from any intention to give an apologia, or personal admiration or idolatry, Destutt de Tracy's political categories provided a solid framework for this *Vie de Napoléon*.

These were all the personal ideas of Henri Beyle. But to fully understand them we must compare them with what was being said all around him, even in Italy, about the ideas of his political mentor. There are indications and scattered traces, and further investigation would no doubt reveal more, but even in their fragmentary state they are significant. Among the Piedmontese, Santorre di Santarosa became acquainted with the *Commentaire* during his exile, but when he obtained a copy of it he read it "making notes at each step" as he wrote to Victor Cousin on June 19, 1822.[61] In Tuscany, during the revolutionary years, one of Destutt de Tracy's most interesting pamphlets was published. It concerned penal reform, which is hardly astonishing in the land where Peter Leopold's very modern penal law was created in 1786.[62] In the era of the restoration, Destutt de Tracy was approached by the cream of Tuscan youth. Among them were Gino Capponi and the Marquis Giuseppe Pucci. Capponi, writing to Foscolo, described Pucci as "my very dear friend..., a true and good gentleman, and Italian."[63] Destutt de Tracy met him at the beginning of 1820 and found that his ideas and spirits were similar to his own. He wrote to Melchiorre Delfico, who had introduced him to Pucci, "I took the greatest pleasure in chatting with him, and I must boast that from the first word we were in complete agreement on all points."[64] Giuseppe Pucci, a great traveler (he also went to Russia and took an interest in Alexander I's military colonies),[65] was one of those who shared the high hopes and enthusiasm which Riego's revolution in Spain had aroused in Capponi in the early months of 1820. As for Capponi himself, he always remembered the conversations he had with Destutt de Tracy, colored by memories of the American Revolution, Franklin, and above all, the blind hatred that Napoleon had felt toward intellectuals in general and the ideologists in particular. Capponi later related:

It is well known how Napoleon, having just fled from the Russian snows, placed the blame on ideology; he meant those ideas that came under the heading of liberal. Yet from the beginning, it was those ideas that had cleared the seat for him to sit upon and opened the way to it; nor were they any great impediment to him during the course of his domination; nor did he fall because of them. But they reigned after him and he hated them as a despot hates his successor, a laughable and impotent hatred. Old de Tracy told me how on the day of that famous address to the Senate, following the custom, the senators encircled the Emperor. He passed before the patriarch of ideology without saying a word but scowling at him. Then, after exchanging a few words with two or three men near him, he suddenly turned back and said straight to the ideologist's face, "L'idéologie a tout gâté [Ideology has spoiled everything]," and continued on his way. The great can become so small.[66]

What Destutt de Tracy was to Capponi and Pucci in Florence, he was to Melchiorre Delfico in Naples. Delfico sent de Tracy his work on Roman jurisprudence and history in September 1816. When de Tracy received it, he recognized ideas that coincided with his own. He also saw an effort parallel to his own to pursue boldly, in the new century, the 18th-century Enlightenment's attempt to give life to a new and real science of politics and economics. In a letter written on September 23, 1816, he reminded Delfico that Napoleon, the enemy of enlightened men, had abolished moral and political science from the Institut français.[67] On February 20 of the following year, he told Delfico of his treatise on will, that is, the *Traité d'économie politique*. In August 1817, with great caution and without openly admitting his authorship, he spoke to Delfico about the *Commentaire*, sending him a copy of the anonymous edition published in Liège. In February 1820, he was finally able to give Delfico a copy of his work bearing his own name. The precautions arose from de Tracy's great fears about his situation in France, "poor France," which certainly deserved "the interest that you take in her, because she sustains the cause of all nations." But freedom of the press was continually threatened: "It is only too true that it could be lost at any moment, with all the other freedoms."[68]

Through Delfico, Destutt de Tracy came into contact with Neapolitan scientists such as the doctor Luigi Chiaverini, who seemed to him to "embody the oath of Hippocrates and of my illustrious friend Cabanis," bringing "philosophy into medicine, and what is more, medicine into philosophy."[69] Chiaverini's *Fondamenti della medicina generale o comparativa,* published in 1816,[70] was based on the ideas of Destutt de Tracy and Cabanis, and contained a *Piano de antropologia,* a complete plan of anthropological research, which would certainly have interested the French ideologist.[71] Chiaverini had written his *Piano* in France, where he had gone "to visit hospitals, museums, and schools of natural history in Paris." He illustrated his conclusions in his "academic prolusions," which Delfico attended and which were published under the title, *Dell' oggetto della medicina comparativa, de' suoi rapporti con altre scienze e della sua influenza sull'economia civile* (On the purpose of comparative medicine, on its relationship with other sciences, and on its influence on civil economy).[72] Here again, the mark of the French ideologists was noticeable.

During the eight months of constitutional government in Naples between 1820 and 1821, Cabanis and Destutt de Tracy, ideology and politics, reappeared together in the form of some lively journalistic and editorial works. On October 2, 1820, issue number 1 of *L'imparziale: Foglio politico* announced the work by Cabanis, "Rapporti del fisico e del morale dell'uomo . . . colla giunta della vita dell'autore e di una tavola analitica del conte Destutt de Tracy" (The relationship between the physical and the moral in man . . . with a life of the author and an analytical table by the Count Destutt de Tracy). It was referred to as "a product of the most sublime French mind of the last century" and a work which "according to Ginguené, is most useful for the philosopher, the moralist, the legislator, the doctor." It was so useful that the Neapolitan publishers, Marotta and Vanspandoch, had decided "to facilitate everyone's acquisition of such a famous work . . . [by publishing] an economical edition." This was actually the second Italian edition of this book, which had already been published in Naples in 1807.[73] But the two volumes published in 1820 were different, as they were based on the third French edition and accompanied by a preface by Destutt de Tracy. The *Giornale costituzionale delle Due Sicilie,* which had advertised this work on January 16, 1821, had already mentioned, in a footnote in the issue of November 23, 1820, another expected return: *Mezzi di fondare la morale d'un popolo. Operetta del Signor conte Destutt de Tracy, tradotta in italiano da G. M.* (Means of founding the morals of a population: a work by the count Destutt de Tracy translated into Italian by G. M.), which, as we saw, had been published in 1799.[74] And finally, unannounced by any of the papers, comes *Il comentario sopra lo Spirito delle leggi di Montesquieu, opera del conte Destutt de Tracy, membro dell'Istituto di Francia e della Società filosofica ecc., seguita dalle Osservazioni di Condorcet sopra il ventesimo nono libro dello Spirito delle leggi. Prima versione italiana.* It was published without any indication of place and only the date, 1820, and had neither notes nor a preface.

A perusal of newspapers, magazines, and pamphlets of the times shows us that, though Destutt de Tracy's influence was present in Naples, it was less visible and active than the more widely diffused and discussed ideas of Bentham and Benjamin Constant. On August 16, 1820, the *Giornale costituzionale delle Due Sicilie* announced the publication of *Trattati di legislazione civile e penale di Bentham* (Treatises on civil and penal legislation by Bentham), translated into the Italian by D. Michele Azzariti: "After their unfortunate reception they are becoming available again. These *Treatises* are famous proscribed works, until recently banned from the land of Gaetano Filangieri, and after being exiled they have come back to us."[75]

As for Benjamin Constant, the same newspaper said, on September 6, 1820, that "the literary center at Largo del Gesú is accepting subscriptions for *Corso di politica costituzionale del signor Beniamino Constant, tradotto dal Sig. Oliver Poli,*"

promising "two issues per week." Still in 1820 the *Biblioteca costituzionale* began
its series with a "Progetto di costituzione di Benjamin Constant, prima versione
italiana corredata di note relative alla costituzione spagnola" (plan for a constitution by Benjamin Constant, first Italian version accompanied by notes relating to
the Spanish constitution). Elsewhere, the works and ideas of the French liberal
were often reproduced and discussed. An important part of the debate about and
defense of the Spanish constitution was carried out using Constant's ideas as a basis
of argument.[76] In *L'imparziale* he came to be called "Beniamino Costante."[77]
Despite the frequent return to the traditions of 18th-century political thought
from Pagano to Filangieri, from Galanti to Delfico, despite the return to the problems of the revolutionary and Napoleonic eras imposed by the presence of the
Carboneria, by the attempt to apply the Cadiz constitution, and by the very need
to prepare for a Spanish- or Russian-style partisan war, attention was increasingly
turned to the French constitutional debates, toward the more refined and more
doctrinaire liberalism of Benjamin Constant, toward the problems of a constitutional monarchy in the age of restoration. Despite the interest aroused by Destutt
de Tracy's ideas, which tended to be more republican, more egalitarian, more
broadly cosmopolitan, and thus more abstract, the ideologist was nevertheless
destined to leave a less noticeable mark in Naples than in other parts of Italy.

One could probably say something similar about constitutional Spain between
1820 and 1823. There too the resurrection of ideas of the enlightened tradition,
the search for the passions and ideas of the revolutionary and Napoleonic ages
(consider the secret societies and the Cadiz constitution) were accompanied by
the birth. and development of a new liberalism and a different radicalism which in
Spain can also be symbolized by the names of Benjamin Constant and Jeremy
Bentham.[78] But in Spain there was also space, if somewhat restricted, for the ideas
of Destutt de Tracy. This was related by Ramon Salas, a "Spanish citizen and doctor of Salamanca," who presented his successful translation of the *Comentario
sobre el Espiritu de las leyes de Montesquieu,* which was printed in Valencia in
1821 and 1822, in Bordeaux in 1821, in Madrid and Toulouse in 1822. He said
that the political and economic works of Destutt de Tracy "are somewhat weakened by his passion for ideology," fending off the accusation of being "excessively
metaphysical." But one must never forget that he had actually "studied politics in
two great schools, France during her great revolution (which is not yet finished) and
the United States of America which today is the classic land of liberty." Destutt
de Tracy's ideas reached Spain with the assurance of having been opposed by
Napoleon, who had called "all men with liberal ideas ideologists," and with a
guarantee from Jefferson, the great American. Ramon Salas thus hoped that
Destutt de Tracy's work would receive a worthy welcome in a Spain that was
fully engaged in conserving its own "carta sagrada" and in "popularizing liberal
ideas."[79] At the same time, while translating Bentham's *Tratados de legislación
civil y penal,* he explained how the English author had carried out a revolution

"in the science of laws." It was a revolution that Montesquieu had only begun, proving himself to be more a historian than a critical philosopher of existing laws. "Montesquieu taught what laws were rather than what they ought to be." Beccaria, who "gave us the greatest book that I know on legislation," could be considered the true forerunner of the ideas that were finding their most complete expression in the writings of Bentham.[80] English radicalism and French ideology seemed to find a point of contact and union in the will to rebuild the political and legal institutions in Spain; they maintained a clear view of what ought to exist rationally in the future, not of what had been transmitted in the past. The same urge drove others in those years to introduce the Spanish public to the works of Destutt de Tracy. Already in 1817 Manuel Maria Gutierrez had published the *Principios de economia politicia,*[81] Destutt had been both amazed and pleased. Writing to Jefferson, he said the work had been done "with all permission" and the translator had even been proposed "for a chair in political economy created for him at Malaga."[82]

In 1821, "the priest Don Juan Justo Garcia, professor emeritus of mathematics at the University of Salamanca, representative of the province of Estremadura to the *Cortes* for the years 1820 and 1821," wrote an abbreviated version of the first three volumes of the *Ideologia.*[83] "This valuable work, though it stops short of all that could be desired, is in my opinion sufficient so that the young can acquire truthful and solid ideas in that science stimulating them to the study of the others." He was defending Destutt de Tracy against accusations of materialism. Was this not the usual polemical method, he asked, used to condemn Galileo and which, during the absolute and inquisitorial regime before the revolution, had led to the prohibition of the works of Bonnet and of Condillac, "and would have proscribed those of Destutt-Tracy on the pretext that they induce materialism, if it had lasted one more year?"[84]

There was a tension between reason and tradition, between "what ought to be" and "what is." We find this dichotomy at the center of the ideas of Francisco Martinez Marina. He was one of the most dedicated and accurate historians of the old Spanish liberty and also, after the Napoleonic invasion, one of the first to request the convocation of the *Cortes* from which the Cadiz constitution arose.[85] The works and ideas of Destutt de Tracy interested him greatly, especially when he began writing, in the years of constitutional liberty between 1820 and 1823, his *Princípios naturales de la moral, de la política y de la legislación,* which was destined to remain unpublished for a long time.[86] In this work he quoted Bentham extensively, fought once more against all absolutist principles, and—without actually saying so—based his struggle on Destutt de Tracy's ideas. Reading his work, we occasionally find complete passages that are nothing but translations from the *Commentaire,* particularly, and this is characteristic, when he engages in controversy over the monarchy and explains how the passage from barbaric to modern and civilized governments took place. Thus, in chapter 15, "Sobre la mejor forma de gobierno" (On the best form of government), we read: "Absolute monarchy is with one small difference equally as intolerable as democracy, because it almost always is identified with despotism and with tyranny. The one is a government of savages and the other a government of barbarians. Both are almost impossible for any length of time: the one and the other are like the infancy of society, and each is necessary and natural in any nation beginning to take shape."[87] Familiar words to us: "pure democracy, despite the elegies produced for it by pedantry and lack of reflection, is an insupportable state of affairs. Pure monarchy is nearly as intolerable: the one is a government of savages, the other a government of barbarians, each is very nearly impossible for long. They are merely, one and the other, the childhood of society, and almost the necessary state of any beginning nation."[88]

Martinez Marina continued translating, summarizing, and exposing the thoughts of an author he never named, but who certainly must have impressed him. Yet his conclusions remain eclectic: "In a century so enlightened, in which reason and experience have shown us the goods and evils of all the governments of the world, we can finally observe with a certain kind of security and profit from the errors and foolishness of our past."[89] He, too, turns toward the haven of a constitutional monarchy that respects the liberty and privileges of individuals and groups. Like so many others inside and outside Spain, he had been attracted by Destutt de Tracy's cool and incisive examination of monarchies and aristocracies. Yet he could not manage to follow the French ideologist on this difficult path and was content with a compromise between traditional and modern liberty.

In Germany and in Poland, too, the twenties marked a time when Destutt de Tracy's political writings were translated and discussed. Between 1820 and 1822 a German version of the *Commentaire* was published in Heidelberg, edited by C. E. Morstadt, a well-known jurist.[90] In Poland at about the same time, as the historian Szymon Askenazy assures us, this work had become "the oracle not only for our constitutionalist deputies, but also for members of the secret societies."[91]

In that same period, undoubtedly a greater effect of Destutt de Tracy's ideas was felt in Russia, less as a philosopher than as a political theorist. His name recurs often in the Decembrists' depositions and memoirs as one of the sources of their ideas on liberty, even though in Russia too he is mentioned less frequently than the classical figures of the previous century, from Montesquieu to Beccaria and Filangieri, and than other contemporary writers such as Benjamin Constant and Bentham. Mikhail Pavlovich Bestuzhev-Riumin said that in the Northern Society, after having refused to accept Pestel's *Russkaya pravda,* at the outbreak of the revolution Nikita Muravev, N. Turgenev, and he had planned to entrust to a ten-man committee the framing of a constitution which would then have been sent for approval to Benjamin Constant, Destutt de Tracy, Bentham, and Guizot.[92] While it is evident that in the Northern Society Destutt de Tracy was only one of the representatives of European liberalism, though one of the most important, in the Southern Society his influence was undoubtedly greater. Nikolai Alexandrovich

Kryukov admitted knowing, among "works concerning changes in government," *L'Esprit des lois,* the *Commentaire* by Destutt de Tracy, and works by Filangieri and Beccaria. In another instance he mentions a reading list that was even longer, including "Beccaria, De Tracy, Helvétius, Bentham, Condillac, Say, d'Holbach, Vattel, A. Smith, Machiavelli and others."[93] There is a list from M. D. Lappa, a young man who had been introduced to liberal ideas and initiated into secret societies by his Italian master Mariano Gigli, a former Carbonaro at St. Petersburg. Lappa's most recent reading before his arrest had been Montesquieu and the *Commentaire sur l'Esprit des lois.*[94] Nikolai Petrovich Repin spoke of "Montesquieu, Filangieri, Destutt de Tracy, Adam Smith and Say."[95]

We must conclude that Destutt de Tracy's influence spread widely throughout Russia among the members of the secret societies, more so than in the same period in Italy, and perhaps in Spain, if such things are at all measurable. His impact in Russia seems to stem from only one book, the *Commentaire,* and is therefore more concentrated in one field. In the West his influence is broader and at the same time less intense as it covers his ideas on logic, grammar, and psychology. The intensity of the Russian reaction is typical of masonic and clandestine life and of the enormity of the tasks that the Decembrists faced. In their hands, a military and constitutional upheaval was turning into a social revolution that would have to abolish peasant servitude, face great national problems including that of Poland, and change the very character of the ruling class. And it is precisely this development of political and social problems that explains not only the dedication with which the young officials mentioned above read the *Commentaire,* but also the interest shown in it by the greatest economist of the Northern Society, Nikolai Ivanovich Turgenev. Above all, it explains what we might call a true conversion which the *Commentaire* wrought in the soul and mind of Pavel Ivanovich Pestel, the head of the Southern Society and the most brilliant and innovative of the Decembrists.

Nikolai Turgenev read the *Commentaire* between April 9 and 12, 1821. He was not convinced by the division between forms of government which Destutt de Tracy had proposed in opposition to that of Montesquieu. In this area he remained attached to Helvétius's distinctions (or rather those of Abbé Lefebvre-La Roche, who had published his criticism of Montesquieu under Helvétius's name): "The bad and the good, or those who exist and those who are still to come."[96] On the other hand, Turgenev was very attracted by Destutt de Tracy's economic ideas. "He considers work as the only element of value and the only source of wealth; he considers land as an instrument on an equal level with machines." Smith, too, had viewed work as "the sole measure of the value of things." Recalling Lemontey's words, Turgenev says, "Production is nothing but a transformation: when an object is transformed, it acquires greater value. Here in de Tracy, there are some excellent things." Drawing a parallel with Rousseau, Turgenev noted the formulae with which this approach to work was expressed in the book he was reading: "The laborer does more good for humanity, even without intending to, than the idle philanthropist could ever do with all his zeal."

Entering into more technical discussions, de Tracy said one could undoubtedly measure the wealth of a country by its exports and imports provided that "this wealth is well distributed," a concept Turgenev had always maintained in his writings on Russian commerce. Quoting the passage on the monopoly over land and the labor force which existed in Poland, he agreed fully with de Tracy on the bad effects this had in that country, adding that the author nevertheless "did not know what was happening in Russia." Rather than have foreign trade based on such foundations, it would have been better if landowners had not had their own grain to sell abroad. "I always believed the same thing about Russian commerce. Thus serfdom makes all calculations erroneous and truth itself false. Slavery is a lie." However, he did not accept Destutt's monetary ideas. Money, even assignats, even paper money, was a sign of wealth. Money was not wealth itself, but a sign of it.

In the pamphlet published as an appendix to the *Commentaire*—called *Quels sont les moyens de fonder la morale d'un peuple?*—Turgenev was especially struck by the author's defense of divorce from a moral point of view, while he noted the phrases with which de Tracy had expressed his conviction that it was necessary to act not by force but by creating conditions in which men would naturally tend to become "reasonable and virtuous." He was also struck by de Tracy's affirmation that punishments for crimes were certain and inevitable. In the middle of these notes, Turgenev mentions what he happened to hear about the movements of the Russian troops. It was April 1821. Were these movements for show or for an expedition against the liberal revolutions in Italy and Spain? Thus the words of the *Commentaire* took on an air of painful reality.[97]

Pestel read the *Commentaire* in the spring of 1820, probably in the edition bearing the author's name, published, as we have observed, in July 1819. He was then in St. Petersburg, and it was a critical time in the development of his ideas.[98] He was debating with himself and with his friends in the conspiracy about the problem of passing from a monarchical-constitutional conception to a republican one. Destutt de Tracy's book was decisive in crystallizing his new political ideas and in establishing a new direction for all his activity. As he declared six years later to the committee of inquiry:

From the monarchical-constitutional conception, I was brought to a republican one by the following facts and thoughts: ... the work of Destutt de Tracy, in French, had a great influence on me. He shows that all administrations where the head of government is a single individual, especially if such a position is hereditary, will inevitably end in despotism. ... All the newspapers and books on politics applauded so strongly the development of prosperity in the United States of America, attributing it to their political system, which seemed to me to be clear proof of the superiority of the republican form of government. ... I recalled the glorious times of Greece when it was composed of republics, and its pitiful situa-

tion after that. I compared the great glory of Rome in the days of the republic
with its pathetic fate under the government of the emperors. The history of Great
Novgorod also strengthened my republican ideas.—I saw that in France and in
England the constitutions are nothing but masks that do not prevent the English
ministers and the French king from doing as they please, and from this standpoint
I preferred autocracy to such a constitution because in an autocratic government,
I thought, absolute power is visible to all, while in constitutional monarchies such
power exists, but it acts more slowly and therefore is incapable of rapidly correcting evil. As for the two chambers, they only exist as a mask. It seemed to me that
the principal trend in this century is toward the struggle between the popular
masses [*mezhdu massami narodnymi, la masse des nations,* as he had written in
French in 1820] and aristocracy of all kinds, whether founded on wealth or on
hereditary rights.[99]

The rapid overlapping and mingling of the various arguments that led Pastel to a
republican conception explains, better than any orderly exposition, the catalytic
effect that Destutt de Tracy's ideas had on him. Onto the memories of the classical
and medieval background is grafted a new analysis, no longer Montesquieuian but
rather opposed to the *Esprit des lois,* of political power and of its relationship to
social class. A new vision is born, as vigorously antidespotic as it is anti-aristocratic,
both liberal and egalitarian.

   The process by which Pestel arrived at this maturation of ideas is very difficult
to follow in detail. The dating of his various sketches and fragments, which later
came together in *Russkaya pravda* (Russian law), is often uncertain and conjectural.
An echo of the discussions he had then with the other members of the secret society
has reached us through his depositions and those of his friends. Naturally, these
documents are dubious and hard to interpret. Nor can we forget that the general
situation in Europe, just at the critical period in the maturation of Pestel's ideas,
was changing rapidly. The revolutions that had broken out in Spain, Naples, and
Piedmont were constitutional, not republican. Many Decembrists, in fact, the vast
majority, thought that for Russia too, this was the road to follow. But the liberal
revolutions in the West were fairly rapidly overcome. The republican road suggested
by Pestel represented a countercurrent, animated mainly by the hope for a committed renewal of persistence and courage among Russians, the only remaining
European "Carbonari" in 1823, 1824, and 1825. This will to continue when all
was quiet around them demonstrated the energy and drive of Pestel and his friends.
Their effort found its expression and its symbol in the desire to make Russia a
republic.

   At the beginning of 1820, Pestel had committed to paper a sketch of a general
political plan. His vigorous criticism of all privilege, his condemnation of all social
disparity created by modern economics, his battle against all aristocracy whether
of wealth or birth, and his overt anticlericalism are reminiscent of the 18th-century
egalitarian tradition of Sismondi (Pestel read his *Nouveaux Principes* at the begin-

ning of 1820), and of the atmosphere created in England and in Europe by the
crisis of 1817 (which he did not fail to remember). He did not call for "agrarian
law," nor for "an imaginary leveling," but for "merely the abolition of all privilege
and all caste." He was convinced that "the government must concern itself with
the national wealth and, in my opinion, take a more active role than the greater
part of modern economists would wish. But this role should consist in industrial
legislation and not in the industrial distribution of the nation." Thus the state,
using methods of liberty, should be the protagonist in the struggle against all aristocracy. "All good government" should openly struggle against it, making sure to
prevent the new forces of money and industry from taking advantage of the situation to surreptitiously impose their own rule. "It appears in general that in the
actual struggle between the titled aristocracy and the masses, while each is trying
to knock down the other's pretensions, the aristocracy of wealth raises its egois-
tical head and, supported on piles of gold, accompanied by the horrible misery of
the poorer classes, prepares for the world new encumbrances and new disasters."

Pestel knows the mechanism by which the rich, the *nouveaux riches,* dominate
the poor and the workers. "The poor man lives only by his work, the rich only by
his possessions, his capital. The poor cannot suspend his income for, having no
capital other than his work, lacking that he would die of hunger. The rich man can
suspend his, live for some time on his capital, and in that way force the poor man
to meet any conditions he wishes to impose on him. . . . It is this difference, by
which one can wait and the other cannot, which is the cause of all the evil." Thus
the state should intervene with legislation for public assistance which would put
the poor "beyond the caprice of the rich." "I know that all the aristocracies imag-
inable, those of title and those of wealth, are going to rise up against these principles, but has the genius of evil ever permitted good, and has it not constantly declared ever crueler and more opinionated war as the stakes became higher? The
government that wishes to enter into such a noble course must pay no attention
to their cries of invective. The love and benedictions of a whole people fully compensate for the impotent hatred of a few reprobate egoists."

But to what government could one entrust such an enormous task? One can
understand why Pestel, when reconsidering such a plan in prison in 1826, said
that at least absolutism would have been decisive and quick enough in the struggle
against such social ills, against evil itself, in the form in which modern man faced
it. Enlightened despotism might appear much more suited to such a battle than
the constitutionalism in France and England. And in fact, in this work in French,
one read: "The sovereign should place himself at the head of the spirit of the century, march before it and direct it in its course. . . ." Parliaments, with their desire
to vote every year on the budget, for example, only retarded the sovereign power's
impulse for reform. "It is not by placing the bodies of the state in constant opposition to one another that one arrives at the great goal of public health, but by
giving each one precise and unvarying attributions," preventing everyone from
spending their lives "in trying to prevent one another from getting anywhere."[100]

When Pestel read what Destutt de Tracy had written, he found both a confirmation of what he thought and an invitation to abandon his hopes for a beneficent and provident absolute government. The French ideologist was also convinced that "all these systems of checks and balances are nothing but vain affectations, or a real civil war." But he hastened to add that one should not go to the opposite extreme and entrust executive power to the hands of one individual because of of this. "The only reason that has been given in favor of the contrary opinion, is that they say one man is better able to take action than many assembled men. This is false." One had only to go from theories to concrete facts to realize that the absolutism of kings was a fable. Those who really governed were the ministers. The executive power was always actually divided or controlled by assemblies and constituent bodies. "The legislative body and the cabinet, those are really the government. The king is merely a parasite, a superfluous cog in the movement of the machinery, which serves only to augment its friction and its expense." He concluded, reaffirming that he was certain that "the majority of a less numerous council produces the same unity of action as a single chief and, as for speed, it is found there as often if not more so."[101] This was true whether "this single chief" was hereditary or elected. Thus Pestel found in Destutt de Tracy's work a reasoned confirmation of his ideas on governments. A new vision of a republican world opened to him; it was independent of whether the head of state was elected or hereditary, now that it was linked to a different conception of the whole state structure.

What Pestel read must have interested him even more since the question of a monarchy or a republic, of a sovereign or a president had formed the main discussion of one of the most important meetings of the Union of Welfare. It was held at the house of F. M. Glinka on a date that is difficult to ascertain precisely, but certainly in early 1820, perhaps in January. Pestel had the responsibility for the report. Everyone seemed to agree on the excellence of the system in the United States of America. But there were serious and persistent doubts about the possibility of transplanting that system to Russia. While N. Turgenev seemed to support a "président, sans phrases," others, affected by what was happening in the West, felt they should stop with a constitutional monarchy. It seems certain that for Pestel and for the other members of the society, the discussion took place before they became acquainted with Destutt de Tracy's ideas. Only the *Commentaire* could provide the method for advancing beyond the clash between more traditional forms of constitutional monarchies and republican ones.

Already in the plan for a constitution that Pestel had written down once he had returned to Tulchino, the seat of his command in the region of Podolsk, there seems to be a search for a new road. Unfortunately this text was lost and we only know of it through the words of Nikita Muravev in his deposition.[102] The head of state was still the emperor. An assembly of a thousand members would exercise legislative power. They would be elected, and half of them would be replaced each year. The moderating power *(umeritelnaya vlast)* "was in the hands of the

Senate, whose members were selected by the emperor from among candidates proposed to him by the assembly. The senators were appointed for life and could not accept any other position without giving up their title. There could only be governor generals in the provinces or attorney generals in the ministries." The Senate would own land which could provide the less prosperous senators with appropriate compensation for their services. Behind these plans, with their auto-chthonous and Russian flavor, we nevertheless easily recognize the ideas of Destutt de Tracy on the functions he would have liked to give to the "corps conservateur": "This body would be composed of men who would remain there all their lives, who would no longer be able to hold any other position in society, and who would have no interest other than maintaining the peace and tranquilly enjoying an honorable existence."[103] Pestel moved immediately from constitutional to social problems. "All the nobles' peasants would be liberated and would receive as social property *[obshchestvennoye vladeniye]* half the land of the landowners, still pay-ing the same rent they did henceforth in money."

One only need read *Russkaya pravda* to find the ultimate document expressing Pestel's ideas; in his view it presented the foundation and guarantee of the political future of the government that would evolve from the revolution. This work con-firms how much more thoroughly he had investigated ideas from both constitu-tional and social aspects. V. I. Semevsky's study has shown how, regarding the organization of the state, Pestel had worked on the basis of Destutt de Tracy's ideas, accepting the essential elements and at the same time trying to fit them into the reality of his country.[104] The French philosopher was particularly admired in Pestel's circle. We know this from the deposition of Mikhail Fedorovich Orlov, a contemporary of Pestel and, at first, a fellow conspirator. Orlov was the general to whom Paris surrendered in 1814, and was one of the most brilliant men of the generation of the Decembrists. When he was at Tulchin in 1823 he noted

a great change in the theories and spirit of the officers. For example, Destutt de Tracy's book, *Commentaire sur l'Esprit des lois,* offered them the highest degree of wisdom; to them, the English constitution seemed extraordinarily burdensome for the population and organized for the aristocracy alone; the French *Charte* in their eyes was nothing but a useless piece of paper for the citizens; American fed-eralism, the events in Spain, the Napoleonic revolution played a large role in all their discussions. One could say that these men denied the force of circumstances and the gradual concession of rights and were guided only by an intellectual theory that did not recognize any fine distinctions in the customs and habits of populations.[105]

A similar energetic spirit and a desire to develop fully the ideology from France are also evident in *Russkaya pravda* and make this text one of the most important examples of Destutt de Tracy's influence on the Europe of the liberal revolutions. The impact of de Tracy's works is also confirmed by Alexander Poggio, the Italian Decembrist, when he describes his meeting with Pestel in 1824 and his initiation into the Southern Society. Pestel, starting as far back as biblical times,

slowly and in detail went through all the changes in governments and through all the conceptions that peoples had had about forms of rule. He mentioned the age of liberty in Greece and Rome, saying how little it was then understood, as it lacked the principle of representation. He quickly passed over the barbaric centuries of the middle ages which had buried liberty and culture. He paused briefly at the French revolution without failing to stress how it had not achieved its goal and how its foundations and its results were not solid, and finally he came to Russia. . . . He spoke of the monarchy, how it contradicted the principle of representation, how the strength of the monarchy brought the principle to ruin, how essentially different one was from the other, how under such a government it was impossible to establish a strong system of balance of power, how both the conflict between these powers and the hereditary aspect of the throne passing to the eldest son opposed the goals of any well-organized government: how could one expect that the firstborn sons would possess the qualities necessary for governing? He spoke of the hereditary monarchy without hiding all the ruinous consequences that it produced by arousing civil discord, and he finally led me to his proposed republic based on popular representation. He asked my opinion on all this. I told him my convictions; I verified that he had taken this from Destutt de Tracy, and very ably transformed de Tracy's *Commentaire sur l'Esprit des lois* into a mathematically constructed system; and I expressed agreement with it all, finding that our predecessors in the task of transforming the state had been apprentices, that their science was still immature, while now it had finally achieved positive and immutable principles.[106]

Scientific pride, certainty in political analyses and conclusions—Destutt de Tracy had given these to Pestel and his followers.

In *Russkaya pravda* there is no longer any trace of the emperor. But the president of the republic has also ceased being the head of state. In their place is a *Derzhavnaya duma,* a council of state composed of five members in office for five years. Each year one of them resigns his position. The member who is in his last year presides. Each province *(guberniya)* proposes the candidates, and the national assembly makes the final choice from those. The council of state exercises supreme executive power, presides over decisions over wars and treaties, but does not declare war and does not conclude peace agreements. All the ministries and, in general, all the administration are under its authority. As for the national assembly *(Narodnaya vecha),* "it consists of representatives of the nation chosen by the population for five years. Each year one-fifth must resign, and they are replaced through new elections. The deputies can be reelected. The Assembly decides on its own internal organization. The president, chosen from those in their last year, serves for one year. The Assembly constitutes a whole and is not divided into chambers. It exercises all legislative power. It declares war and makes peace treaties."

It nominates a temporary body for the periods of its vacations. It cannot be dissolved by anyone. As for the conservative power, it is called the supreme council *(Verkhovyy sobor)* and is composed of 120 members called boyars, who are nominated for life and cannot have any executive or legislative function. They are nominated by the assembly from a list of candidates proposed by the provinces. The supreme council "does not judge the content of what is proposed to it, but only considers the form so that everything may be carried out according to the law." Laws are valid after this confirmation. The ministries and the administrative districts *(oblast)* are controlled by people nominated by the supreme council (attorney generals and governor generals). The council also appoints military commanders in the country and commands the army when it goes beyond state borders, relinquishing this power on the return of the army. It proclaims martial law in the provinces.[107]

By remembering the constitution of the United States of America and of the French Directory, and by transforming words taken from the past in Russia, we can recognize the heart of Destutt de Tracy's ideas. Among the points that Pestel did not accept from his master's teaching was the question of the appointment of those who should exercise executive power. As we have seen, Pestel thought they should be nominated by the national assembly. Destutt de Tracy had a different opinion: "It is not for the legislative body to nominate them or to judge them. Because they must depend on it, in the sense that their actions should follow its will, but they should not depend passively, since they should execute its will only when it is legitimate."[108] Thus he had thought to leave the selection of the executive power to the conservatory power, "whether by receiving from the electoral body a list of candidates to choose from, or on the contrary by sending them a list of those from whom they can choose."[109] This was too complicated and too similar to a system of opposing powers, which Destutt de Tracy had taught Pestel to criticize in monarchies, to persuade Pestel to accept it. Similarly, he had tried to simplify the attributes of the conservative power, while still maintaining the essential rights of control and appointment of the high offices. Besides choosing the highest judges, the conservatory power, according to the French ideologist, had to "pronounce on the unconstitutionality and therefore the nullity of the actions of the legislative and executive bodies."[110]

As for the legislative power, in his first constitutional plan, which we know from Muravev's summary, Pestel seems to explicitly accept the idea that the national assembly should be elected by universal suffrage. Everyone would vote, but only to choose the electors, who in turn would designate the deputies. Destutt de Tracy wrote, "They tell me that this renders each citizen's influence on the drafting of the laws quite indirect; I admit that. But I ask you to take into account that I am speaking here of a populous nation, spread over a vast territory, and which has not yet adopted a federal system, but that of indivisibility."[111] This was exactly the hypothesis which was Pestel's starting point when he thought of

Russia. As for specific details regarding the composition of the national assembly, Destutt de Tracy had either kept silent or had been satisfied with very general principles. It was up to Pestel to fill in with his plans, while still keeping intact the principles of his master.

While following the French liberal and ideologist, Pestel had never been able to set aside, much less forget, the reality of the Russia in which he lived. Nor could he forget that a few years earlier he had been forced to say, as he was made to repeat later in his depositions, that absolutism and the lack of complex controls and knowledgeable opposition could at least bring hope for a more rapid and stronger struggle against political and social ills. Afterward he had lost all illusions that absolute and efficient power could be incarnated in a Russian emperor. With the passing years, the leader was increasingly enmeshed in conservative and reactionary politics, both inside and outside Russia. But it was not because of this that Pestel no longer felt a need for an unhindered power capable of facing the struggle to transform Russia. In fact, absolutism reappeared in a new and different form, in the guise of the provisional government, a revolutionary dictatorship which, according to Pestel's declared intention, could precede and prepare for the installation of the well advised and delicate institutional structure that Destutt de Tracy had taught him to admire and appreciate. An important part of *Russkaya pravda* is dedicated to the description of this provisional government, the indispensable instrument of a revolution that wants to overcome autocracy and establish the entire society of the country on a new basis. "Two things are indispensable in Russia: the first is a complete transformation of the order and structure of the state; the second is the promulgation of a new code that conserves all that is useful and destroys all that is harmful." For this reason it was necessary to have a plan, which he treats in *Russkaya pravda,* and a provisional supreme government. The country was vast and varied; it was essential that the rhythm of introduction of reform be gradual, a pace which only the temporary dictatorship would have accepted; the risk of opposition and disorder was too great. All the events of the last decade in Europe had demonstrated what dangers lay in a revolution that was not controlled by a strong and clear will. Otherwise, how could one introduce the principles of a representative government for which no precedents existed in Russia?[112]

A Bonapartist temptation arose from Pestel's strong personality, but above all from the circumstances in which he had to act. Those who were close to him in the months preceding his arrest describe his character as frequently imperious. They describe the double temptation, felt by each of his followers, to either love him or hate him, to either idolize him or condemn him utterly. Despite everything, right to the end Pestel continued to cling to the idea that the provisional government should be only a temporary instrument for achieving a legal and constitutional regime. He never denied his French master, who had incidentally explained in a hypothetical and doubtful page (no less significant just because of this), that perhaps it was a good idea to entrust to one man the task of legislating in the name of a whole nation.[113] "With a single legislator, it is probable that legislation would be wider and more apt than with a legislative assembly, and it is certain that it would be more comprehensive and consistent."[114] He certainly did not hide from the possible objections to this proposal. "Moreover, I do not pretend to be obstinately attached to an extraordinary opinion that might seem paradoxical."[115]

What had been a paradox for Destutt de Tracy became crystallized in the idea of a revolutionary government in Pestel. Only Pestel would have been capable of making Russia into a republic, one and indivisible (and the same French ideologist had taught him to subordinate the elements of federalism to a republic capable of defending itself in the midst of powerful neighbors). Only the provisional government would have been able to conduct foreign affairs as Pestel treated them, trying to solve the Polish problem and make Russia's weight felt in the Balkans (and here, too, what Destutt de Tracy had said about conquests and liberations by revolutionary governments supported Pestel's political will). Above all, only a revolutionary government would have been able to realize the liberation of the serfs and the transformation of the whole Russian economy, the most crucial and innovative point in the plan exposed in *Russkaya pravda*. In the end, Destutt de Tracy's pupil was convinced that only the sword could cut the Gordian knot of Russia's problems.

Notes

1. *Commentaire sur l'Esprit des lois de Montesquieu, suivi d'Observations inédites de Condorcet sur le vingt-neuvième livre du même ouvrage* (Liège: J.-F. Desoer, 1817), p. v. The phrase is repeated in the 1819 edition published in Paris by Delaunay, p. v. See Pierre-Henri Imbert, *Destutt de Tracy, critique de Montesquieu, ou de la liberté en matière politique* (Paris: A. G. Nizet, 1974).

2. Gilbert Chinard, *Jefferson et les idéologues, d'après sa correspondance inédite avec Destutt de Tracy, Cabanis, J.-B. Say et Auguste Comte* (Baltimore: Johns Hopkins Press; Paris: Presses Universitaires de France, 1925).

3. Ibid., pp. 59 ff.

4. Ibid., pp. 87, 89 (letter from Paris dated 21 October 1811).

5. Ibid., pp. 105–6 (letter dated 22 January 1813).

6. Ibid., p. 150 (letter dated 17 May 1816).

7. Ibid., p. 112 (letter dated 4 April 1818).

8. Ibid., pp. 150–51 (letter dated 17 May 1816).

9. Ibid., p. 157 (letter dated 10 January 1816).

10. Ibid., p. 165 (letter dated 4 February 1816).

11. Ibid., p. 179 (letter dated 11 April 1818).

12. Ibid.

13. Mme. de Tracy, *Essais divers. Lettres et pensées* (Paris: Plon, 1852), p. 393. On the influence of Destutt de Tracy's ideas in Argentina, see Hernan Rodriguez,

"John Locke en el Rio de la Plata," in *Anuario del Instituto de investigaciones históricas,* Universidad nacional del Litoral, Rosario, 3, no. 3 (1958): 41 ff.; and Ricardo Piccirilli, *Rivadavia y su tiempo,* 3 vols. (Buenos Aires: Penser, 1960), which contains numerous important letters between Destutt de Tracy and Rivadavia.

14. *Commentaire sur l'Esprit des lois de Montesquieu par M. le Comte Destutt de Tracy . . . suivi d'Observations inédites de Condorcet . . . et d'un mémoire sur cette question: Quels sont les moyens de fonder la morale d'un peuple?. . .* (Paris: Théodore Desoer, July 1819), p. 51. The quotations are translated from this edition, edited by the author. After the American version and the two French versions printed in Liège in 1817 and in Paris in 1819, Destutt de Tracy finally decided to give up his anonymity. The differences in these three editions are worth noting, but they are not essential, as they generally seem to be dictated by questions of style or prudence.

15. *M. de Tracy à M. Burke* (Paris: Imprimerie nationale, 1790), p. 2.

16. *Commentaire,* p. 96.

17. Ibid., p. 9.

18. Ibid., p. 89.

19. Ibid., p. 97.

20. Ibid., p. 275.

21. Ibid., p. 291.

22. Ibid., pp. 359–60.

23. *Traité d'économie politique, par le comte Destutt de Tracy, pair de France* (Paris: Bouquet & Levi, 1823), p. 179.

24. Ibid., p. 184.

25. Ibid., p. 186.

26. Ibid., p. 187.

27. Ibid., pp. 191–92.

28. Ibid., p. 183.

29. See George Boas, *French Philosophies of the Romantic Period* (Baltimore: Johns Hopkins Press, 1925); and Sergio Moravia, *Il tramonto dell'illuminismo. Filosofia e politica nella società francese, 1770–1810* (Bari: Laterza, 1968).

30. Mme. de Tracy, *Essais divers,* 1:306.

31. "Lettre de M. de Tracy à M.me. de Staël pour la remercier de l'envoi de *Corinne,*" in *Société des amis des livres, Annuaire* (Paris, 1881), pp. 91 ff. Her reply to these measured words cannot help sounding conceited and apologetic: "It seems to me that a spirit as superior as yours, at present already detached from all that is material by the very nature of its quest, must one day take pleasure in religious ideas; they complete all that is sensitive, and, without this hope, I am seized by such an invincible terror of life and of death that it staggers my imagination." Destutt de Tracy, who for thirty years lived alone and isolated and almost completely blind, having fallen "into a great sadness," had as his only consolation "to have Voltaire read and reread to him. . . . He knew it by heart, and called him the hero of human reason" (François-Auguste-Alexis Mignet, *Notices et portraits historiques et littéraires,* 3 vols. [Paris: Charpentier, 1854], 1:373).

32. *Commentaire,* p. 40.

33. Ibid., pp. 29–30.

34. Ibid., p. 63.

35. Ibid., p. vii (the emphasis is Destutt de Tracy's).

36. *Commentaire* (Paris: Delaunay, 1819), p. vii. (It may be that these words are not Destutt de Tracy's, but rather those of the publisher; nevertheless, they seem to summarize his thoughts well.) On the relationship between Destutt de Tracy and the republican movement in France (e.g., Joseph Rey), see A. Galante Garrone, *Filippo Buonarroti e i rivoluzionari dell Ottocento (1828–1838)*, new enl. ed. (Turin: Einaudi, 1972), pp. 77 ff.

37. *Commentaire* (Paris: Théodore Desoer, July 1819), p. 130.

38. Ibid., p. 22, pp. 65–66.

39. Ibid., p. 199.

40. Ibid., pp. 205 ff.

41. Chinard, *Jefferson et les idéologues*, pp. 54–55 (letter dated 12 August 1810). For a comparison of Jefferson's republicanism with that of Destutt de Tracy, see Adrienne Koch, *The Philosophy of Thomas Jefferson* (New York: Columbia University Press, 1943). I used the reprinted edition (Chicago: Quadrangle Books, 1964), pp. 152 ff.

42. Chinard, *Jefferson et les idéologues*, pp. 75 ff. (letter dated 26 January 1811).

43. Ibid., pp. 89 ff. (letter dated 21 October 1811).

44. Ibid., p. 180 (letter dated 11 April 1818).

45. *Elementi d'ideologia del conte Destutt de Tracy, pari di Francia, membro dell'Istituto di quel regno e della Società filosofica di Filadelfia, per la prima volta pubblicati in italiano, con prefazione e note del cav. Compagnoni* (n.p.: A. F. Stella, 1817), pt. 1, *Ideologia propriamente detta*, 2 vols.; pt. 2, *Grammatica generale*, 2 vols.; pt. 3, *Logica*, 3 vols. Part 4, *Trattato della volontà* (3 vols.), was also published in Milan, by Gianbattista Sanzogno, in 1819.

46. F. S. Salfi's important article, "Du génie des Italiens et de l'état actual de leur littérature," published in *Revue encyclopédique* (1819), 1:521, mentions the notes that Compagnoni had included in his version of de Tracy and observes that they were sometimes theological, "but all who know the mind of M. Compagnoni will blame, not him, but his circumstances."

47. *Elementi d'ideologia*, pt. 1, 1:xx.

48. Ibid., pt. 2, 3:xi.

49. *Saggio di un trattato di morale in forma de catechismo pubblicato in seguito degli Elementi d'ideologia del Sig. Conte Destutt de Tracy. del cav. Compagnoni* (Milan: Gianbattista Sanzogno, 1819).

50. *Elementi d'ideologia*, pt. 4, 3:63 ff. See Chinard, *Jefferson et les idéologues*, pp. 189 ff.; and Yves Du Parc, "Destutt de Tracy, Stendhal et *De l'amour*," *Stendhal Club* 2, no. 8 (15 July 1960): 335 ff.

51. *Vita letteraria del cavaliere Giuseppe Compagnoni, scritta da lui medesimo* (Milan: Fortunato Stella, 1834), p. 40. For repercussions of Destutt de Tracy's philosophy, see Silvio Pellico's letter to his brother Luigi in Milan, dated 1 April 1817: "We see how Condillac and recently Destutt-Tracy have anatomized, so to speak, down to the most hidden fibril, and without pedantry, the theory of Locke"

(Silvio Pellico, "Lettere milanesi [1815-21]," ed. Mario Scotti, in *Giornale storico della letteratura italiana*, suppl. 23 [1963], p. 107).

52. *Memorie sulla facoltà di pensare di Destutt conte di Tracy* (Pavia: Pietro Bizzoni, 1824), p. 10. See Eugenio Garin, *Storia della filosofia italiana* (Turin: Einaudi, 1966), vol. 3, index.

53. *Memorie sulla facoltà di pensare*, ibid., p. 17.

54. Ibid., p. 20.

55. Jules C. Alciatore, "Stendhal et Destutt de Tracy: La vie de Napoléon et le *Commentaire sur l'Esprit des lois*," *Modern Philology* 67, no. 2 (November 1949): 98 ff. See H.-F. Imbert, *Les Métamorphoses de la liberté ou Stendhal devant la Restauration et le Risorgimento* (Paris: J. Corti, 1967), pp. 240 ff.

56. Alciatore, "Stendhal et Destutt de Tracy," ibid., p. 99, n. 8.

57. Ibid., p. 100.

58. Ibid., p. 101.

59. Ibid., p. 103.

60. *Commentaire*, pp. 135–36.

61. Santorre di Santa Rosa, *Lettere dall'esilio (1821–1825)*, ed. Antonino Olmo (Rome: Istituto per la storia del risorgimento italiano, 1969), p. 217.

62. *Quali sono i mezzi di fondare la morale di un popolo? Del cittadino D. T. ***. Traduzione dal francese* (Florence, year vii of the French Republic [1799]).

63. *Lettere di Gino Capponi e di altri a lui*, collected and published by Allessandro Carraresi, 2 vols. (Florence: Le Monnier, 1884), 1:48 (letter from Paris dated 5 January 1820).

64. *Opere complete di Melchiorre Delfico*, ed. Giacinto Pannella and Luigi Savorini (Teramo: Giovanni Fabbri, 1904), 4:239 (letter dated 25 February 1820). The originals of these letters, which are poorly published in this edition, can be found in the State Archives of Teramo, Carte Delfico, III/75.

65. On Russia, see Robert Lyall, *An Account of the Organization, Administration and Present State of Military Colonies in Russia* (London, 1824). Gino Capponi refers to it in *Lettere*, 1:180 (letter dated 6 February 1824, in which the word "Rossi" should probably read "Russo").

66. *Scritti editi e inediti di Gino Capponi*, ed. Marco Tabarrini (Florence: Barbera, 1877), 2:477. On other contacts between Gino Capponi and Destutt de Tracy, see *Lettere*, 1:192 (letter of 24 January 1825 from Guglielmo Libri, who terms himself "enamored" of the French philosopher); p. 193 (Capponi's reply to Libri, dated 9 March 1825: "I had a letter from Tracy who was pleased with you. It is important to me that you regard him as a great and excellent man because he is both"); p. 207.

67. *Opere complete di Melchiorre Delfico*, 4:232.

68. Ibid., p. 239 (letter dated 25 February 1820).

69. Ibid., p. 234 (letter to Luigi Chiaverini dated 20 February 1817).

70. Luigi Chiaverini, *Fondamenti della medicina generale o comparativa* (Naples: Tip. Chianese, 1816).

71. A part of this work, including the *Piano d'antropologia*, was reproduced by the *Giornale enciclopedico di Napoli* 9, no. 4 (October–December 1817): 113 ff. On this aspect of ideology, see Sergio Moravia, *La scienza dell'uomo nel*

Settecento (Bari: Laterza, 1970), which actually broadly covers the early 19th century but does not mention Italian reactions to such anthropological efforts.

72. Luigi Chiaverini, *Dell'oggetto della medecina comparativa, de'suoi rapporti con altre scienze e della sua influenza sull'economia civile* (Naples: Tip. Chianese, 1818).

73. Pierre J. G. Cabanis, *Dei rapporti del fisico e del morale,* 2 vols. (Naples: D. Sangiacomo, 1807).

74. I was unable to find a copy of this work, nor could I identify the translator.

75. They were printed by Angelo Trani in 1818.

76. See, for example, the complete collection of the *Annali del patriottismo, giornale politico e letterario* and of *L'amico della costituzione* which, on 4 October 1820, reprinted Benjamin Constant's "Ragionamento di un elettore con sé stesso."

77. *L'imparziale* (1 December 1820).

78. On all the Spanish liberal and revolutionary ferment of the twenties, there is little in the book by Luis Sanchez Agesta, *Historia del constitucionalismo español* (Madrid: Instituto de estudios politicos, 1964); and in the fuller monograph by Miguel Artola Gallego, *La España de Ferdinando VII,* Historia de España dirigida por Ramón Menéndez Pidal, vol. 26 (Madrid: Espasa-Calpe, 1969). More useful is the work by José Luis Comellas Garcia-Llera, *El trienio constitucional* (Madrid: Rialp, 1963). The book by Iris M. Zavala, *Masones, comuneros y carbonarios* (Madrid: Siglo XXI de España Editores, 1971), is rich in facts and points of departure. See also the fundamental work of Alberto Gil Novales, *Las Sociedades patrioticas (1820–1823),* 2 vols. (Madrid: Editorial Tecnos, 1972).

79. The edition used was *Comentario sobre el Espiritu de las leyes de Montesquieu, por Destutt de Tracy . . . Traducido del frances al español, por el doctor Don Ramon Salas* (Burdeos: Lawalle, 1821).

80. *Tratados de legislación civil y penal, obra extractada de los manoscritos del Señor Jeremias Bentham por Esteban Dumont . . . , traducida al castellano con comentarios, por Ramon Salas, ciudadno español y doctor de Salamanca,* 5 vols. (Madrid: Firmin Villapando, 1821), vol. 1, translator's prologue, pp. vi ff.

81. *Principios de economia politica* (Madrid: La imprenta de Cano, 1817). They were published again in Madrid by the Libreria de Rosa in 1824.

82. Chinard, *Jefferson et les idéologues,* p. 180 (letter dated 11 April 1818). In 1821 the chair had become "de constitución, economia pública y comercio." In the subsequent decades M. M. Gutierrez continued to write numerous books on political economy which I have been unable to consult.

83. *Elementos de verdadera lógica. Compendio ó sea extracto de los Elementos de ideología del senador Destutt-Tracy . . .* (Madrid: Mateo Repullés, 1821).

84. Ibid., pp. vii, x.

85. All is narrated in the introduction to his *Théorie des cortes ou histoire des grandes assemblées nationales des royaumes de Castille et de Léon* (the title itself reveals the tension and the desire to make the "théorie" and the "histoire" coincide), in the French version by P. F. L. Fleury (Paris: Baudoin, 1822), 1:lxxi ff.

86. F. Martinez Marina, *Princípios naturales de la moral, de la política y de la legislación, con un estudio preliminar de D. Adolfo Posada* (Madrid: Academia de Ciencias morales y políticas, 1933).

87. Ibid., p. 384.

88. *Commentaire*, pp. 66–67.

89. Martinez Marina, *Princípios naturales*, p. 388.

90. A. L. C. Destutt de Tracy, *Charakterzeichnung der Politik aller Statten der Erde. Kritischer Commentar über Montesquieu's Geist der Gesetze . . . übersetzt und glossirt vom Professor Dr. C. E. Morstadt* (Heidelberg: K. Groos, 1820–21). The book was dedicated by its presenter "to the most noble cosmopolitan, his greatest teacher in the field of moral philosophy, Count Destutt de Tracy, the most famous investigator of political science, and to Professor Ritter J. B. Say, the Copernicus of political economy, his undying friend, with admiration and thanks." In the introduction and in the copious notes in these two volumes, C. E. Morstadt demonstrates not only great enthusiasm for 18th-century tradition represented by the author of the *Commentaire* (it is no wonder he selects the motto *Sapere aude*) but also a profound knowledge of all European political literature during the transition from enlightenment to liberalism.

91. Szymon Askenazy, *Lukasiński*, 2 vols. (Warsaw: Lazarski, 1929), p. 128.

92. *Vosstanie dekabristov. Materialy* [The Decembrist insurrection. Materials] (Moscow: Glavnoye arkhivnoye upravlenie), 9 (1950): 77.

93. Ibid., 9 (1954): 353, 372. A series of notes on these authors, including Destutt de Tracy, is conserved among his papers in the Central Historical Archive in Moscow. See *Zapiski, stati, pisma dekabrista I. D. Yakushkina* [Memoirs, articles, and letters of the Decembrist I. D. Yakushkin], ed. S. Ya. Shtraykh (Moscow: Akademiya Nauk SSSR, 1951), p. 590.

94. V. I. Semevsky, *Politicheskiya i obshchevstennyya idei dekabristov* [The political and social ideas of the Decembrists] (St. Petersburg, 1909), p. 222. See De Tracy, *Memoria sulla facolta di pensare*, p. 12 (preface): "Coloro che da Leibnitz fino a Gigli si occuparono di formare un linguaggio universale, mentre diedero da vèdere di avere un alto intelletto, non fecero che accrescere di nuove chimere la storia della filosofia, delle quali anche di troppo ne ridonda [Those from Leibniz to Gigli who were concerned with the formation of a universal language showed their great intellectual power yet did nothing but increase the number of chimeras in the history of philosophy, which were already too abundant]." Instead he is remembered with praise in Giuseppe Sacci's presentation *Memorie scelte di ideologia di Destutt conte di Tracy* (Pavia: Pietro Bizzoni, 1826), p. 80. On M. Gigli, see F. Venturi, *Il moto decabrista e i fratelli Poggio* (Turin: Einaudi, 1956), p. 42n., where one must mention in addition the article *Lingua filosofico-universale pei dotti, preceduta dall'analisi del linguaggio, opera de Mariano Gigli, già pubblico professore di varie facoltà* (Milan: Società tipografica de' Classici italiani, 1818), and the recollection of his linguistic ideas in the above-mentioned article by F. S. Salfi on Italian culture in 1819 (see n. 46 above), p. 462.

95. *Vosstanie dekabristov*, 2 (1926): 361.

96. See Richard Koebner, "The Authenticity of the Letters on the *Esprit des lois* Attributed to Helvétius," in *Bulletin of the Institute of Historical Research of the University of London* (1951), pp. 19 ff.

97. *Arkhiv bratev Turgenevych* [Archive of the Turgenev brothers] (St. Petersburg: Rossiyskaya Akademiya Nauk, 1913), 3:261–63. A careful examination of the evolution of the political and social ideas of N. I. Turgenev is contained in

V. V. Pugachev, *Evolyutsiya obshchestvenno-politicheskikh vzglyadov Pushkina* [The evolution of the social and political ideas of Pushkin] (Gorkii: Gos. Universitet im. N. I. Lobachevskogo, 1967). See also the recent publication of unknown texts by N. I. Turgenev, ed. E. B. Beshenkovsky, M. Ya. Bilinkis, and V. V. Pugachev, in *Osvoboditelnoye dvizhenie v Rossiy* [The liberation movement in Russia], issue 1 (1971), pp. 105 ff., issue 2 (1971), pp. 108 ff.

98. See Eufrosina Dvoichenko-Markov, "Jefferson and the Russian Decembrists," *American Slavic and East European Review* 9 (1950): 162 ff.; and especially S. S. Landa, "O nekotorych osobennostyakh formirovaniya revolyutsionnoy ideologii v Rossiy. 1816-1821 (Iz politicheskoy deyatelnosti P. A. Vyazemskogo, N. I. i S. I. Turgenevych, M. F. Orlova)" [On certain characteristics in the formation of revolutionary ideology in Russia, 1816-1821 (On the political activity of P. A. Vyazemsky, N. I. and S. I. Turgenev, M. F. Orlov)], in *Pushkin i ego vremya* [Pushkin and his times] (Leningrad: Gos. Ermitzah, 1962), pp. 136 ff.; Boris Evgenevich Syroechkovsky, "Perekhod Pestelya ot monarkhicheskoy kontsepcii k respublikanskoy" [Pestel's passage from monarchic to republican conceptions], in V. E. Syroechkovsky, *Iz istoriy dvizheniya dekabristov* [History of the Decembrist movement], ed. N. M. Druzhinin, I. V. Porokh, L. A. Sokolsky, and V. A. Federov (Moscow: Izd. Moskovskogo Universiteta, 1969), p. 127 ff.; and V. V. Pugachev, "O spetsifike dekabritskoy revolyutsionnosti (Nekotorye spornye voprosy)" [On the revolutionary character of Decembrist activities (Some controversial problems)], in *Osvoboditelnoye dvizhenie v Rossiy* [The liberation movement in Russia], issue 2 (1971), pp. 11 ff. See also the interesting articles of B. V. Vilenskiy, "P. I. Pestel o gosudarstae" [P. I. Pestel on government], and V. A. Kalyagin, "Pervyy Konstitucionnyy proekt P. I. Pestelyv" [The first constitutional project of P. I. Pestel], in *Voprosy istoriy gosudarstva i prava* [Problems of history of government and law] (Seratov, 1977), 1:3 ff. On the formation of Pestel's political and economic ideas, see E. M. Kosachevskaya,*M. A. Balugyansky i peterburgsky universitet pervoy chetverti XIX veka* [M. A. Balugyansky and the University of St. Petersburg in the first quarter of the 19th century] (Leningrad: LGU, 1971), pp. 181 ff.

99. *Vosstanie dekabristov,* 4 (1925): 91.

100. *"Russkaya Pravda" P. I. Pestelya i sochineniya ey predshestvuyushchie, pod red. M. V. Nechkinoy* [*Russian Law* by P. I. Pestel and the works preceding it, edited by M. V. Nechkina], in *Vosstanie dekabristov,* 7 (1958): 289 ff. The date of this work is also uncertain. I believe that V. E. Syroechkovsky is probably right in attributing it to the beginning of 1820 rather than M. V. Nechkina, who dates it at the end of 1820 or early 1821. V. V. Pugachev believes it is from early 1820.

101. *Commentaire,* pp. 185 ff.

102. *Vosstanie dekabristov,* 1 (1925): 302.

103. *Commentaire,* pp. 205-6.

104. Semevsky, *Politicheskiya i obshchevstvenniya idei dekabristov,* pp. 545 ff. and index.

105. M. F. Orlov, *Kapitulaciya Parizha. Politicheskie sochineniya. Pisma* [The

capitulation of Paris. Political works. Letters], ed. S. Ja. Borovoy and M. I. Gillel-
son (Moscow: Akademya Nauk SSSR, 1963), p. 85.
106. *Vosstanie dekabristov,* 9 (1954): 75.
107. Ibid., 7 (1958): 214–15.
108. *Commentaire,* p. 202.
109. Ibid., pp. 203–4.
110. Ibid., p. 204.
111. Ibid., p. 179.
112. *Vosstanie dekabristov,* 7 (1958): 118.
113. *Commentaire,* p. 196.
114. Ibid., p. 183.
115. Ibid., p. 184.

Four   The Army and Freedom:
              Alexander Poggio and the
              Decembrists of the Southern
              Society

Alexander Poggio departed from St. Petersburg dismayed by the situation he was leaving. The progress made in the last months of 1823 seemed to him insufficient. The differences of opinion between the Northern and Southern societies ran deep. Organizational ties were weak, and he had not seen in the capital evidence of the desire for rapid action that he knew was strong in the south, especially in the group headed by Matvei Muravev-Apostol. Those who met Poggio shortly after his departure described him as "very dissatisfied with the Northern Society leaders, especially with Nikita Muravev."[1] He shared the views of Muravev-Apostol, who was also about to leave St. Petersburg to return to the south. Both were convinced that in order to proceed it was necessary to replace Nikita Muravev. They also felt that within the heart of the society they must secretly and autonomously organize the group destined to suppress the entire ruling family.

This chapter is taken from *Il moto decabrista e i fratelli Poggio* [The Decembrist movement and the Poggio brothers], published in Turin in 1956. Other publications up to 1959 are listed in *Dvizhenie Dekabristov. Bibliografiya. 1928-1959* [The Decembrist movement: bibliography], ed. M. V. Nechkina (Moscow, 1960). Works written in the last fifteen years include: S. N. Chernov, *U istakov russkogo osvoboditelnovo dvizheniya* [The origins of the Russian liberation movement] (Saratov, 1960); S. B. Okun, *Dekabrist M. S. Lunin* [The Decembrist M. S. Lunin] (Leningrad, 1962); V. A. Fedorov, *Soldatskoye dvizhenie v gody dekabristov* [The soldiers' movement in the Decembrist years] (Moscow, 1963); Hans Lemberg, *Die nationale Gedankenwelt der Dekabristen* (Cologne and Graz, 1963); V. V. Pugachev, *Evolyutsiya obshchesvenno-politicheskikh vzglyadov Pushkina* (Gorkii, 1967); B. E. Syroechkovsky, *Iz istoriy dvizheniya dekabristov* [From the history of the Decembrist movement] (Moscow, 1969); *Literaturnoe nasledie dekabristov* [The literary legacy of the Decembrists], ed. V. G. Bazanov (Leningrad, 1975); O. V. Orlik, *Dekabristy i evropeyskoe osvoboditelnovo dvizheniya* [The Decembrists and the European liberation movement] (Moscow, 1975); S. S. Landa, *Duch revolyutsionikh preobrazovaniy* [The spirit of revolutionary transformations] (Moscow, 1975).

Every year in Kiev during the last two weeks of January a large fair was held, known traditionally as the *Kontrakty*. Merchants and nobles from the surrounding area converged on the city for the occasion. The Southern Society had for some time taken advantage of this event to gather its followers in order to discuss the fundamental problems of the day. Poggio, Matvei Muravev-Apostol, and Obolensky were headed there in January 1824, bringing news from the north. Poggio had with him a copy of the plan for a constitution which Nikita Muravev had revised and rewritten for a third time and which showed the full extent of the ideological disagreement between St. Petersburg and Kiev. Other participants in that year's *Kontrakty* were Davydov, Yushnevsky, Volkonsky, Bestuzhev-Riumin, and Sergei Muravev-Apostol, Matvei's brother—that is, all the leaders from the south except Pestel. The latter had decided to leave for St. Petersburg to observe the situation with his own eyes and to try to reach the agreement that his envoys and partisans had failed to achieve. He shared his southern companions' passion for action; it was he who had given them those Jacobin ideas that contrasted with Nikita Muravev's liberalism and constitutionalism. But he strongly maintained that nothing would be possible without coordination between the two groups, and perhaps he even feared Muravev-Apostol's activism. Did Muravev-Apostol's contacts with the capital perhaps signify an attempt to override Pestel's authority and to try to reach a decision without taking into account his broader view of the movement? Did the disagreement with St. Petersburg not create the risk of repercussions in the south, of impeding the unity of direction that he felt was indispensable and which he was determined to maintain in his own hands? Pestel was convinced that there was little point in listening to the recriminations that were bound to be heard that year in the *Kontrakty*. For the moment, his place was in the capital, where he arrived in March 1824.[2]

The Kiev meeting did not bring about any new results. Poggio related what he knew.[3] Sergei Muravev-Apostol proved particularly impatient: "We cannot expect anything from the Northern Society," he said. "We must act on our own. We have sufficient strength and numbers to do so."[4] Others pinned their hopes on the Kronshtadt group of naval officers. This group had maintained contact with Ryleev and seemed to him to be the starting point for the insurrection. "Kronshtadt will be our Isle of Leon," Ryleev said, alluding to the first center of the Spanish revolt of 1820. In the heated atmosphere, plans for an attempt to assassinate the emperor flourished, and there was much talk of exterminating the whole royal family. But even the participants in this meeting saw that only Pestel could achieve a positive goal and obtain what everyone desired, "the union and common action of the North and South."[5]

The Kiev gathering permitted Alexander Poggio to grasp the political and organizational configuration of the southern group he was to join and in which he would participate. At the center of the group was Pestel, whose headquarters were in the little village of Tulchin in the Podolsk region, about two hundred kilometers south-west of Kiev in the southern part of the Bug valley. The little town of Tulchin in itself summarized the history of that region.

Annexed to Russia during the second division of Poland, in 1793, it belonged to the Pototski princes.... Their luxurious mansion stood in the center of the village. It was built in 1782 by the French architect Lacroix. It was surrounded by a large park.... At a distance, at the edge of this palatial residence lived the inhabitants of Tulchin, Jews and lesser Polish nobles. Overlooking the village stood a large Catholic church constructed in 1817 and later transformed into an Orthodox church in the thirties. The ruins of a Dominican monastery could still be seen. A fair held twice a year brought together the nobles, peasants, and merchants from the surrounding countryside.[6]

This was the center of Pestel's activities. There the members of the Southern Society often gathered, meeting in the evening in the Pototskis' palace. Their meetings were not exclusively dedicated to politics and conspiracy. The atmosphere of friendship and interest in literature is gracefully evoked in the verses which Baryatinsky addressed to Pestel in 1824:

Quatre lunes déjà–j'y pense avec effroi,
Prime sodalium! me séparent de toi.
Sans doute, il te souvient des tranquilles soirées
Où par l'épanchement nos âmes resserrées,
Trouvaient dans l'amitié tant de charmes nouveaux.
Alors, te reposant de tes nombreux travaux,
Ou las d'avoir sondé quelque grande penseé,
Ma muse sous ta main fut souvent caressée.
De deux Natchez pour toi j'ai tracé les revers
Prends pitié de leurs maux et surtout de mes vers.[7]

[Already four months–I think it with dread, prime sodalium! separate me from you. No doubt you remember the tranquil evenings when through their outpourings our constricted souls found in friendship so many new charms. Then, resting from your many travels, or weary, having sounded some great thought, your hand caressed my muse. I traced the sufferings of two Natchez for you. Take pity on their ills and especially on my verse.]

At Tulchin, Pestel commanded the Viatka infantry regiment, which had been entrusted to him in 1821 and which he had managed to transform from one of the worst units in the Russian army to one of the best.

The second center of the Southern Society was located in Vasilkov, a small town in the Kiev region about twenty kilometers from the city. There Muravev-Apostol and Mikhail Bestuzhev-Riumin were garrisoned. They were the most ardent and decisive members, wishing to imitate the example of Riego and Quiroga at any cost, certain that in Russia, as in Spain, even a small revolt would be enough to bring about a flood of general declarations.

In Kamenka, located about two hundred kilometers southeast of Kiev in the Dnieper valley, was the third secret nucleus. V. L. Davydov, with whom Poggio had been in contact since the previous year, was one of the principal members of this group. At its head was Prince Sergei Grigorev Volkonsky, general of the 19th infantry division and thus Alexander Poggio's superior officer. Born in 1788, Volkonsky was older than the average official in the secret societies. All the tendencies, the strengths and the weaknesses, of the Decembrist movement seemed to meet in him. An active freemason, he had taken one step after another toward the military conspiracy. Cultured and generous, born and raised in the highest and most brilliant ruling class of the empire, Volkonsky embodied the hopes and aspirations that the more enlightened Russian nobles had dreamed of realizing under Catherine II and then under Alexander I, and which had been constantly frustrated by the burdensome reality of absolutism, by the expansionist foreign policy, and by the social configuration of Russia. He was among the few who now, through the conspiracy and declarations, were trying to resolve all these accumulated problems. Confident and persevering, he nevertheless recognized the terrible difficulties of their chosen road more readily than the young men around him. His doubts and hesitations were many in those years. Thus he saw the obstacles and contradictions that were hidden from Pestel's view by his iron will to succeed; from the most ardent activists, such as Muravev-Apostol and Bestuzhev, by enthusiasm; and from the more doctrinaire figures, such as Nikita Muravev, by confidence in the intrinsic ability of the best ideas to win out.[8]

Besides Davydov and Volkonsky, the Kamenka group included such secondary but characteristic figures as twenty-four-year-old Vladimir Nikolaevich Likharev, Count Polignac, a French immigrant who like many others had come to join the Russian Army. He was preparing to return to his country around that time, and was charged by his friends with the task of seeking links with French liberals.[9] Others included Andrei Vasilevich Yantaltsev, and, finally, Joseph Poggio, who had become an active member of the group in April 1824.

Alexander's brother had resigned from the army in 1818. Far from the military life, he had not been attracted by the first awakening and development of the secret societies. Nevertheless his thoughts and state of mind had followed a path similar to that of his brother. Later, when arrested and asked to explain the origin of his attitude of political opposition, he had given the following reasons: "It came from reading *Le constitutionnel* and reflecting on the fact that the United States of America was in an excellent position compared with its situation before the war with Great Britain. . . . It sufficed on the other hand to compare Spain's dreadful condition with that of France and England."[10]

These were sufficient arguments to convince even him of the advantages of liberty. Thus it had not been difficult for Davydov to persuade Joseph Poggio, when he was in southern Russia, to join the Society. Moreover, the presence of his brother was probably another factor that drove him to take this step. From that time onward, their companions often referred to the two young men of Ital-

ian origin as "the Poggio brothers," alluding to the fact that they were both engaged in the same struggle.

Looking closely at the little nucleus in Kamenka, it is interesting to note that
here too the bonds between members of the secret societies were not solely military and political. Behind the formal organization of the Society was not only a
military hierarchy, which bore some weight, but also a society of the nobility,
with lands not far from the garrison, with intertwining family ties between one
clan and another, and with the parties and receptions that constituted so much of
the life of these *pomeshchiki* and that now served as a pretext and opportunity
for meeting and talking about politics and the hoped-for action.

Davydov was the half-brother of the hero of the patriotic war, Nikolai Nikolaevich Raevsky, the "glory of our days . . . cool leader in the hazards of war . . . in calm
times, wise," as Zhukovsky says in the famous poem written to recount his exploits.
In 1824 the daughter of N. N. Raevsky, Mariya Nikolaevna, married General Volkonsky, the head of the Kamenka group, and in Siberia they were close to Alexander Poggio. The wives of Likharev and of Joseph Poggio were sisters. A son of
Likharev later married a Muravev daughter. And when Joseph Poggio married a
second time he chose a relative of Davydov. The godfather of their son Lev became
the "glory of our days," Nikolai Nikolaevich Raevsky. We could continue to inter-
weave the threads of relationships in that world of nobles gravitating around Kiev
at the time and which "an old inhabitant of the city" recalled many years later in
his memoirs: "That was a happy and glorious epoch for the Russian element in the
oldest capital of Russia and in the whole region of Kiev. The Raevskys were among
the wealthiest noble landlords of the region. They lived in luxury, as did their
wealthy relatives..." There follows a long list of *pomeshchiki* of those lands,
which includes the Poggio family.[11]

To get an idea of what this worldly atmosphere was like, we can read accounts
by Pelagya Rostsiszewska, an educated woman who left an interesting diary about
this period and this society. Here, for example, is how Sergei Muravev-Apostol and
Mikhail Bestuzhev-Riumin appeared to her:

The former had been educated in Paris, where he had stayed for seven years.
He seems to be an outstanding man, intelligent, full of French spirit and gaiety,
of pleasing appearance. His friend is younger, a finished product of the currently
fashionable Romanticism. He is always enthusiastic, speaks in aphorisms, and
quotes endlessly, all inflamed by the spirit of the genius of Byron. He speaks of
himself as a volcanic soul; he says that he is amazed to find *salons* like those of
civilized Europe here, that his main enemy is moderation, that there is nothing
more poetic than the seven deadly sins, etc.[12]

This is the atmosphere in which the Poggio brothers also lived. Their mother too
lived in the Dnieper valley, in Yanovka's house in the district of Chigirin, about two
hundred kilometers below Kiev. She remained there for a long time, at least until
1842 when her two sons had been in Siberia for many years. The land that their

father, Victor Poggio, had acquired now created an additional bond that united the two men. One a military man, the other a retired widower with four sons, they both found themselves in the Kamenka group.

This seemed to be a time when this provincial, familiar noble world would re-absorb Alexander Poggio, tearing him away from the ideas that he had formed in St. Petersburg. We have only a few hints from the trial documents, but they suffice to show us this moment of reflection and doubt in the course of his life. "The elder Poggio brother then began to waver in his faith in the Society and thus drew away from it."[13] One cannot exclude the possibility that the domestic affairs of his brother had some influence on his own attitude. Apparently Joseph shared Alexander's more extreme ideas. Shortly before, at Kamenka, he had had a conversation with Bestuzhev-Riumin, and the discussion had led again to the necessity of freeing themselves from the emperor.[14] A plan for this was already prepared, he told Bestuzhev-Riumin, and he added that a group of men had already been recruited to carry it out. Alexander, present during the conversation, pointed out that a "schism" existed in the very heart of the Southern Society over this matter; some believed that it was necessary to suppress the whole ruling family, and others, such as Bestuzhev-Riumin himself, foresaw rather a direct attempt on the person of Alexander I, with the promise of sending the other members of the family into exile.[15] Joseph Poggio brought up the example of France, which seemed decisive to him. If one wanted to avoid the danger of a future restoration one had to re-member that "Louis XVIII, returning to his country, had again taken the throne."[16] And with some hesitation, he declared himself ready to participate in the assassina-tion attempt. Joseph Poggio, nevertheless, did not go beyond these extremist in-tentions. At that time his private life absorbed all his energies. His love for Mariya Andreevna Borozdina, violently opposed by her family, began to sow the first seeds of that romantic tragedy that made up a large part of his existence. The senator lieutenant-general Andrei Mikhailovich Borozdin had refused this daughter to Poggio. The marriage took place anyway, but the differences and fights were only beginning. Joseph withdrew from all conspiratorial activities.[17] Alexander was momentarily discouraged too. It was Prince Volkonsky who tore Alexander away from the Kamenka atmosphere and put him directly in contact with the driving force of the Southern Society. It was he who "advised Alexander Poggio to become acquainted with Pestel during maneuvers. At the same time he asked Pestel to encourage Alexander to take heart and to strengthen his convictions, which he was able to do: Poggio, in fact, ... after having revealed his feelings to Pestel, ended up a more enthusiastic liberal."[18]

Pestel was the true center of the southern organization. We do not know its exact structure, as all the statutes on which it was based were either lost or de-stroyed. However we do know that it was more complex than its northern coun-terpart and that it maintained stronger and more lasting traces of the different masonic and hierarchical grades used in stratifying the members of the first secret societies.[19] It was thus meant to satisfy more effectively the need for secrecy and to provide action from an accepted and disciplined military command, from top to bottom. Three fundamental categories (boyars, brothers, and friends) are reminiscent of the Union of Salvation. Probably a fourth category existed composed of persons who were "not initiated but in whom there was hope." An oath was required of those who became members of the Society. In it they promised to maintain secrecy, to show total dedication to the common goal, to display zeal in recruiting new members, and to threaten with punishment "without pity those who violated the secret." A *directoire occulte* was at the head of the entire southern organization and was composed at first of Pestel and Yuzhnevsky; later Sergei Muravev-Apostol was added.

Pestel had reached St. Petersburg at the beginning of March. He remained in the capital for a month and a half and then spent two more months on his lands, returning to Tulchin in July. In September he met Alexander Poggio. He wanted to "test his knowledge, his capability and decisiveness." The meeting, which was extended over several days, took the form of a true "tour d'horizon" concerning all the problems of the secret societies.

Like all those whom Pestel met, Poggio was impressed by Pestel's culture, his political strength, and the arrogance of the man described by another Decembrist who was present as "one of the most outstanding men of his times" and a "gifted man."[20]

Pestel was a great admirer of Napoleon, and like his hero he was the object, both to his contemporaries and to later men, of "undying hate and overpowering love." An American scholar, A. E. Adams, stresses the profound contradiction in Pestel's mind between "the authoritarian dogmas of the eighteenth century" and his planned "liberal reforms." The need for "order, efficiency and authority" was as strong in him as the desire for liberation.[21] This evaluation is valuable even if it seems that it could be applied to all Decembrist thought, in which the legacy of enlightened absolutism and the seeds of liberalism and revolution constitute ever-present elements in a synthesis that varies with different phases of development and various personalities. Are the federalist elements contained in Nikita Muravev's constitution not also an attempt to find a way out of the dilemma of combining a powerful state with a guarantee of liberty? What distinguishes Pestel is the very fact that he brought these differences to their climax, trying to resolve them without turning to half measures or compromises.

"Authority" does not exist for him in its traditional monarchical form. Rather, Pestel sees it incarnated in the Committee of Public Safety, or in Napoleon, whom he divests of his counterrevolutionary disguise, thus following the evolution of that Napoleonic myth which throughout Europe accompanied the struggle against the restoration of monarchies. Pestel is a republican, and he stresses this point with particular vigor in his discussions with the northern group. For him the republic has become a principle, and he wants to eliminate not just the czar, but the entire ruling family.

He sees "liberty" more as a problem of transforming Russian society than as just a problem of checks and balances and guarantees. Not only in Russia but everywhere in Europe "it seemed to him [these are his words] that the main tendency of the present century consisted of the struggle between the mass of the population and aristocracies of all kinds, based as much on wealth as on hereditary rights."[22] In Russia, the basic problem was achieving a true liberation of the serfs. Only the transfer of half the land to the peasant communities would have made a definitive break in the reign of serfdom. Other Decembrists intended to abolish slavery by following the example set by the Prussians and Austrians or by the application of ideas of a free economy. Alexander Poggio was not mistaken when he saw the main feature of Pestel's originality in his program for the peasants. "Many were our plans and thoughts about the liberation of the serfs, and everyone wanted the personal liberty of the peasants with the payment of a compensation in money to the landlords, but the idea of freeing the peasants and entrusting them with land was Pestel's alone."[23] The very form of this transformation of all the agrarian relationships in Russia proposed by Pestel was impressively original. He was trying to find an answer to all the Sismondian criticism of liberalism, attempting to give economic impetus to the Russian countryside without damaging peasant interests, introducing a modern concept of property and at the same time maintaining the traditional collectivist elements of the Russian villages. The debate between "authority" and "liberty" taking place in his mind thus led him toward solutions which later arise in the visions of Chernyshevsky and of the populists.

For him, this republican and reformed regime hinged upon a "provisional government" capable of handling Russia for at least ten years, carrying out the social transformations, creating an initial basis for a future representative government, and laying the foundations for the institutions of a "popular government."

This solution naturally stems from Jacobinism but bears clear and explicit traces of the events of the thirty years that had passed since Robespierre's life had ended on the guillotine. The "provisional government" must be both the ideal continuation of the Committee of Public Safety and a political organ capable, by its very nature, of correcting from the start the historical errors committed by the Committee. The liberals' criticisms of the French Revolution had not been in vain. A dictatorship is conceived both as a revolutionary instrument and as a means of avoiding the ills and disorder of revolution. "The terrible events that occurred in France during the revolution," Pestel says, "induced me to seek means to avoid them, and this led me to the idea of a provisional government."[24]

In Pestel's conception, next to the provisional government and acting as a spur and as an incentive would be a party. But it too appeared in a form very different from the Club of the Jacobins. Secret societies would not disappear with the installation of the provisional government. They would continue to exist with their own disciplined clandestine organization and their own hierarchy. The military sect, the *carboneria*, had definitely taken the place of a party in a time of restoration, of reaction, far removed from the revolutionary expansion of the end of the 18th century.

These organs of power desired by Pestel were modeled on the French constitution of the year III, and perhaps on the Napoleonic consular structures, rather than on the 1793 constitution, to which, as far as I know, neither Pestel nor any of the other Decembrists referred. The influence of Destutt de Tracy's ideas in this area is decisive and seems to have guided a large part of Pestel's elaboration on the constitution.

On the other hand what is lacking is the basic drive found in Jacobinism: the armed insurrection, the constant pressure of the "revolutionary days," and the popular threat. Pestel foresaw a "military revolution," a *pronunciamento,* at the beginning, followed by the work of transforming and reforming from above, through the provisional government.

It was this that the northern liberals disliked. It made Pestel's political passion appear to arise from personal ambition or dictatorial desires. *Quis custodiet custodes?* The eternal question that spontaneously arises with any revolution from above arose in the minds of almost all those who listened to Pestel defend his political vision. Evidently the freedom of the press and of religion which he promised were not enough. Would the authority of the Society have been sufficient to guide and control this provisional government?

Pestel tried to overcome this moot point with his life's major work, a document that he wrote and rewrote over a period of ten years—*Russkaya pravda.* This document was not intended as a book of propaganda, nor as a plan for the Society, but as something more ambitious. It was to be a fundamental plan of the future provisional government, the solemn responsibility that it would assume before the entire Russian population—what one could call the plan of the political and social structure that was to arise from the ruins of the czarist autocracy. This man who not only admired the clear thought of Destutt de Tracy but was also an attentive reader of Machiavelli, who often impressed his contemporaries, including Ryleev and Poggio, with the element of cynicism that he inserted into his evalution of the liberal, humanitarian, and well-intentioned concerns of his companions, in the final analysis was placing all his faith and hope in an ideological document, in a political theory.

One way or another, all the Decembrists felt the paradox inherent in their desire to give a liberal regime to Russia. Pestel resolved the paradox by an act of faith in ideas, in the will to remain faithful and adhere to a political ideal. By doing this he revealed the deepest roots of the movement. The spirit of sacrifice and dedication expressed, on a moral plane, the impetus that made it active. Pestel had known better than others how to carry this enthusiasm to an intellectual level: with *Russkaya pravda* he established one of the first and most revealing departure points for the "intelligentsia" that was arising.

Russkaya pravda was discussed in St. Petersburg during Pestel's stay in 1824. It had also been discussed the year before. The economic plan was criticized by Nikolai Turgenev. There were few people who allowed themselves to be convinced by the most innovative and personal economic ideas contained in this document. Nikita Muravev objected to the electoral system (which was not based on the census) envisioned by Pestel and to the agrarian reform he proposed. The idea of the provisional government with "unlimited powers" aroused widespread distaste.[25]

It was the ideological value of *Russkaya pravda* that risked deepening the political dissension between north and south. Nevertheless, Pestel also knew how to maneuver, and perhaps how to impose his own will, and steps were taken toward the acceptance of the formula he insisted upon with special vigor, that is, the republic. Alexander Poggio later said, "Although he encountered much resistance, nevertheless, eventually beating his fist on the table he had said to them: 'Then it will be a republic.'"[26] He even added that "he had persuaded the members of the Northern Society to accept his whole constitution without exception. Nikita Muravev would burn the one he had written."[27] This last affirmation, even if Pestel himself related it, was certainly too optimistic. In reality, the differences of opinion between north and south continued to exist and were never entirely resolved.

Moreover, indissolubly linked to *Russkaya pravda* was Pestel's conception of the "military revolution," of the elimination of the ruling family and the installation of the provisional government. Nikita Muravev opposed this plan with a different view of the *pronunciamento* and of its political consequences. He was counting on propaganda and on the support of public opinion. He proposed to: "(1) spread among all the classes in the population a great number of copies of his constitution...(2) arouse a revolt among the troops and make it public. (3) With each military success in each region and province occupied by the troops, proceed to gather the electors, choose local administrators, judges, and form regional chambers, and in case of great success, the national assembly. (4) If the imperial family then did not accept the constitution, he then proposed, as an extreme measure, to banish it and establish a republican regime."[28]

Faced with this plan, Pestel could not help returning in his own mind to all the arguments he had long since marshalled against constitutional monarchy. In St. Petersburg, Nikita Muravev proposed following the example of Naples, Piedmont, and especially Spain. But it was through his criticism of those very examples that Pestel had decided on a republic. What had occurred in Western Europe had not happened in vain for him. Following the same reasoning that had led him to the idea of the provisional government to avoid the ills and errors of the French Revolution, he now insisted on the initial elimination of the monarchical problem in order to try to avoid following the pattern of recent defeats. "Events in Naples, in Spain, and in Portugal, exerted a profound influence on me. They provided incontrovertible proof of the instability of constitutional monarchies and gave sufficient reason for not believing in the sincere acceptance of the constitution on the part of the monarchs."[29]

On the organizational level, the consequences of these different conceptions were clearly evident. Nikita Muravev's plan used the Society as an instrument for organizing the *pronunciamento,* to spread propaganda, and not, as Pestel desired, as a weapon to carry out both the military revolt and, later, Russia's long transformation. Only in this way would the Society have been able to strike the country's center without losing time and energy in the provinces, without worrying about the election of judges and of local administrators before having established the provisional government.

Given these different views, it is not surprising that no firm agreement was reached in St. Petersburg in the spring of 1824. Concerning organization, there was only a vague promise to amalgamate the Northern and Southern societies after a period of two years, and an "agreement to decide together where, when and what to do at the time of the insurrection" and a "promise of reciprocal assistance if either center had to take action."[30]

Had the choice of the critical moment been left to the Northern Society? It is likely that Nikita Muravev interpreted the agreement in this way, as he had been worried for some time about the activism of the southern group. But it is equally evident that many members of the Southern Society did not feel restricted in this aspect by what had been stipulated in St. Petersburg. Plans for an assassination attempt on the emperor, for the coup de main, for the takeover of vital centers continued to blossom one after another. It became increasingly evident that there was a desire to wait no longer, to enter the field as soon as possible. Yet Pestel continued to hold to his conviction about the absolute necessity for coordinated action with the northern group, and controlled more vigorously his own impatience and that of his companions.

All these ideological, political, organizational, and military problems are reflected in the conversations that took place between Pestel and Alexander Poggio in September 1824. We can get an impression of this dialogue from the depositions that both men wrote later. Of course, this source is often distorted or unfaithful because of Poggio's concern with appearing shocked or showing regret to the investigating authorities. Yet this echo of their words still has a clear and lively tone that brings the personal ties and ideas of the two men to life.

Pestel maintained it was necessary to begin with the rudiments of politics. Starting as far back as Nimrod,

Slowly and in detail, he went through all the transformations of governments and through all the conceptions that populations had had about forms of rule. He mentioned the era of liberty in Greece and Rome, saying how little it was understood, as it lacked the principle of representation, he quickly passed over the barbaric centuries of the Middle Ages which had buried liberty and culture, he paused briefly at the French Revolution without failing to stress how it had not achieved its goal and how its foundations and its results were not solid, and finally he came to Russia.

He remarked how Russia's present state structures were incompatible with a representative regime. "They contradict each other and are by their nature incapable of harmonizing, so that it would be impossible to establish a strong system of balance of powers." Hereditary monarchies impeded the establishment of good governments, but an elected monarchy would also have "disastrous consequences."

He finally led me to his republic based on the principle of popular representation. He asked my opinion on all this. I told him my convictions and affirmed, "You have taken this from Destutt de Tracy and have very ably transformed de Tracy's *Commentaire sur l'Esprit des Lois de Montesquieu* into a mathematically constructed system." I added that I agreed with him in all this.

Our predecessors were only apprentices in the task of transforming the state; their science was still young. Now finally we are adopting positive and immutable principles in this science.

Thus ended the test of my political knowledge and of my attitude toward the introduction of this system of government into Russia.[31]

Regarding Russia's social problems, Pestel read him the articles from *Russkaya pravda* dealing with the subdivision of land and the liberation of the peasants, and about "the creation of districts under collective property, all things that concerned him more than anything else, as he himself admitted."[32] Pestel thus exposed the nucleus of his social ideas and his plans for agrarian reform to Poggio.

On another day, the two men discussed the initial act of the revolt, the tyrannicide. Once again Pestel reveals his desire to avoid all the ills and dangers that had accompanied the revolutions in Europe in the preceding decades. Preventing the risk of restoration is now translated into the desire to carefully count the members of the imperial family to be eliminated at the start. "Let us make a list of the victims," said Pestel, and he began counting them on his fingers. There were thirteen, and he added that "Bestuzhev-Riumin had already prepared twelve men committed to this goal."[33] Although Poggio declared to the Investigating Commission that the plan had seemed "terrible" to him, he went on thinking that once begun, it was no longer possible to stop the successive elimination of the side branches of the imperial family and their descendents. Despite this official repentance, his own words show us how even then he continued to view the assassination plan with particular delight. The tone of "horror" which he used in prison to describe his dialogue with Pestel reveals a certain unconscious complacence.

They then spoke of the composition of the future government. Pestel told Poggio, "You know that a provisional government will have to be established. Who do you think could take part in it?" He had already exposed his plan for a *senat conservateur* and a national assembly that would support and complete the provisional government.[34] Poggio's reply was obvious. He well knew of "Pestel's superiority over all others" and, he added, of the ambition in Pestel's heart. So he gave the name of his questioner, calling him the founder of the republic. But the response was, "I do not want to be accused of personal ambition, and besides my surname is not Russian, so I am not suitable." Poggio noted then that the accusations of ambition were not unknown to Pestel and that he could have followed the model of "Washington's glory" and, like him, return to being a private citizen after having established the basis for the new government: "I expect it will not last more than a year or two." "Oh, no," replied Pestel, "not less than ten years; the mere division of land will take a long time." Poggio protested that such a long period of power would frighten many people. "What could be done? One could create a distraction using some foreign policy goal, such as a declaration of war on the Turks and restoration of an eastern republic in favor of the Greeks, thus demonstrating politically their best intentions toward other European populations." This idea of Pestel's was too reminiscent of the classic example of the Roman republic for Poggio to fully accept it. He, too, desired the liberation of the Greeks, but he did not want the internal problems of Russia to be forgotten as a result.

They discussed the future capital of the republic and the future ministers. Pestel advised Poggio to join with Davydov and follow his orders when the action began. "I myself will go to St. Petersburg and will take Bariatinsky with me." The coldness shown him by the people in the capital, and especially by Nikita Muravev, continued to worry him. In the south, too, all was not well. His relationship with the Muravev-Apostols was not satisfactory. "I myself will go to St. Petersburg to see with my own eyes.... Perhaps the czarevich Constantine Pavlovich will have been warned. If the imperial court moves to Moscow, then all the action will take place there." Finally, Poggio asked Pestel what he intended to do when "the work of the Society was finished." "You would never guess," replied Pestel, "but I will go away to the Pechersky monastery in Kiev. I will become a hermit, and why? Because then I will become a believer." Poggio answered that Pestel should never withdraw but should "always continue to be the watchful sentry for the cause he founded."[35]

In one of these conversations, Pestel had spoken to Poggio about another problem of central importance, that of the contacts that the Southern Society had established with the Polish secret societies. He even showed Poggio a document sent by Bestuzhev-Riumin: *Rapport au directoire secret sur les conférences secrètes avec la Société polonaise.*[36] Poggio was thus brought up to date about the negotiations that had taken place in the spring of 1824.

The development of the Polish secret societies had paralleled and sometimes converged with that of the Russian groups. Their common bond with the Western European sects, the phraseology and atmosphere of both the masons and the Carbonari that had penetrated the Polish and Russian societies, the parallel reaction to Alexander I's policies, seem to explain their similarities and their common rate of development. In Poland, too, the first nuclei had formed around 1817, based on the conspiracies and the military sects that had spread through the Napoleonic empire, or on the German *Tugendbund.* In Warsaw in 1817 the Association of Friends, also called *Panta Koina,* had formed. In 1819 the Central Organization was formed. Like the Russian society, it had a legitimate side (cultural associations, etc.) and a clandestine side (Association of Free Poles, which in May 1820 became the Great Orient of Warsaw). In Wilno, starting in October 1817 the Philomatic Society had begun to spread. It was known particularly for its intellectual activities, but, beginning in 1819, it also contained a clandestine element. The Philarets and later (in 1822) the Philadelphi are affiliations or transformations of it. The organization that was politically most important was undergoing a parallel development. In 1819 it bore the name of National Masonry, and soon it absorbed the most active and most military elements who were more disillusioned with Russian policies. Under the direction of Łukasiński it was modeled on the French movements of the Union and the Amis de la Vérité.

In the autumn of 1820, with impetus from the groups formed in the Posnan region (the most openly revolutionary groups, generally called the Reapers), the National Masonry carried out a more or less fictitious dissolution. The same thing occurred in Russia at that time; it was simply a way of creating a more political, more decisive secret society by moving away from weak, uncertain, or weary elements. Thus the Patriotic Society developed under the direction of Łukasiński in collaboration with the Reapers. It spread through all the historical centers of Poland, especially in the Polish-Ukrainian land along the Dnieper, and gathered a few hundred followers. One of its centers, or rather one of its meeting places, was the fair, the Kiev *Kontrakty* which, as we have seen, served an analogous function for the Southern Society.

The Patriotic Society was accompanied by another parallel group, with which it had nearly entirely amalgamated when the Russians and Poles made direct contact. This group was called the Templars, or Knights of the Temple, and had gathered in January 1821 in Kiev and derived or claimed to derive from Scottish masonry.

Although the rhythm of development of the Polish groups was parallel to that in Russia, their content was often different. The Carbonaro and masonic formulae often hid another reality. The participation and initial prevalence of student elements, inspired by the German Burschenschaften, was one new aspect. The prevalence of the national problem over institutional and ideological problems became a characteristic of the Polish groups. The main goal of the Patriotic Society was the resurrection of the Polish state in its historic boundaries. Thus, among the Polish groups we do not find broad political discussions like those of the Russian societies. There is no debate similar to the one we observed between members who wanted to adopt and adapt the American constitution and those who believed in the necessity of a provisional government to accomplish a profound political and social transformation. Among the Poles, we find a more restricted and precise aim, and we observe their strong faith or hope of obtaining support from European powers (from England and Sweden). Poland's historical tradition was much stronger than Russia's myths and romantic recollections of the medieval free communes of Pskov and Novgorod. The group's political moderation had strong roots in the social and national character of those who were members of the Patriotic Society. As in Russia, they too were nobles, but often they were of different nationality than their peasants in the Russian and Ukraine regions.

As long as the Poles could sustain their hopes in the constitutional and pro-Polish policies of Alexander I and his brother Constantine, they felt it was not advisable to draw closer in their relationship with the Russian secret societies. It was only the disillusionment of the recent years that made them view collaboration with those who were planning the overthrow of czarist absolutism as useful.[37] From the Polish standpoint, the Decembrists had taken a step backward. They had begun by reacting with a mixture of envy and national resentment to Alexander I's concession of a constitution for Poland and his promise, even if in uncertain and vague terms, of future restitution of the eastern lands that had previously been part of the "Polish republic." Some men had moved toward the opposition and toward the secret societies, driven by the czar's policy, which they considered an offense to the national dignity of Russia. Then the revolt deepened; the mounting desire to fight imperial absolutism at any cost led them to welcome the idea of uniting their efforts with those of the Polish secret societies.

The negotiations which extended throughout 1824 and 1825 were inevitably influenced both by the diverse origins and political nature of the two movements and by the diffidence that had kept them separate and distinct until then. The problem of the republic, stressed so much by the Southern Society, eventually had to be set aside and shelved. The Poles admitted that the United States could be an appropriate model for Russia. But for Poland, they evidently preferred a constitutional monarchy. The question of boundaries was also a heated one. But it is interesting to note that, in this realm, an agreement seems to have been reached, based on Russian concessions. A map was drawn; Wilno, Minsk, and Lvov would be Polish while Vitebsk, Mogilev, Zhitomir, and Kamenec would be Russian.[38] Nevertheless, Pestel clearly intended to solve this problem by coolly calculating the value of what he could obtain in exchange for the concessions made. The important element for him and for others dealing with the Poles was to gain their help in the effort to initially eliminate the forces that would have opposed the Russian *pronunciamento*. These included the Grand Duke Constantine, who must be detained in Warsaw and possibly eliminated, and the Lithuanian Corps, commanded by Constantine, which was assigned to Russian territory and could become a dangerous instrument of repression. In case of war, they hoped for an alliance and thought the Poles would be able to help them make contacts with the secret societies in Western Europe as they were reputed to be linked with the Prussian, Hungarian, Italian, and English societies.[39]

Despite these immediate political needs, the institutional problem persisted. The reticence in the documents still conserved in the archives does not allow us to follow precisely the fascinating interweaving of nationalistic and ideological motives in the Russian-Polish relations. However, we can affirm that, despite all the concessions, Pestel maintained a clear and precise idea of the ultimate goals he wanted to achieve. These included: setting fixed borders, not according to history but according to "convenience" for both countries, perhaps using popular will to override the legacy of tradition, that is, a concession of independence for Poland on the part of the Russians and not "separation by Russia's will"; a strict alliance between the two countries in both peace and war; and finally,

Since relations between countries develop through their governments, and since the strength and significance of these relations depend basically on the structure of the governments, to be certain that the very structure of the Polish government will be Russia's guarantee, the following three fundamental conditions, without which Russia will not give Poland independence, must be met: (A) The supreme power in Poland must be constituted in the same way as it is in Russia, on the basis of chapter 6 of *Russkaya pravda* (that is, it must have a similar republic, provisional government, and assembly). (B) The selection and nomination of all political and administrative officials and persons must follow the exact criteria used in Russia, based on chapters 4 and 9 in *Russkaya pravda.* (C) All aristocracy, whether based on wealth, on land, or on privilege as with traditional nobility, must be broken down entirely and forever. Thus the Polish population will form only one class, on the basis of chapter 4 of *Russkaya pravda.* It is only on the basis of these conditions and guarantees that the restoration of the Polish government will take place.[40]

Such were the ideas that Poggio heard Pestel expound on the Polish problem. And with this ended the rapid "course in politics" which he had heard. Like all those who heard the voice of the head of the Southern Society, Poggio had been impressed by the vastness of these plans and by the consistent logic of their architect. But was he truly convinced? Poggio denied that he was when he wrote his confession in prison and depicted Pestel's energy in dark yet grandiose tones. Even as he repudiated Pestel's words, he said that they had made a deep impression on him. They had reawakened his enthusiasm and his desire for action. Though he could not be entirely convinced of the possibility of realizing the plans, they had an irresistible effect on him. After the defeat, and having calmed down, he said that Pestel's ideas "satisfied the soul, but not reason."[41] Yet he certainly accepted the tasks he was given willingly.

In the autumn he was in Orel to establish the foundations for a new secret group and to ascertain the mood of the troops quartered there. Pestel had heard through Bestuzhev that a squadron of Kirasirsky's regiment, a part of the first corps, had shown signs of insubordination.[42] Poggio had hoped to contact the officers of this squadron; and, on the other hand, he knew the members of one of the most important families, the Golicyns, whose lands were situated near where this revolt had taken place. Many years earlier in St. Petersburg, he had had a conversation with Prince Pavel Alexandrovich Golicyn, who was close to the Union of Welfare. Although he had not wanted to become a member of the Society, he had "promised to spread the ideas on liberty and representative government across the lands where he lived (in the governorship of Orel and Tambov)."[43] In the capital, Poggio had also become friendly with Prince Valerian Mikhailovich Golicyn, "whose mind was no less tempestuous than his own" and who, if we are to believe Poggio's deposition, agreed about the necessity of tyrannicide.[44] In other words, Poggio could hope for support from that family. But his mission was unsuccessful. Pestel declared that "Poggio returned without having seen Golicyn and without having accomplished anything."[45]

It could be that there was a political difference. "When he was at P. Golicyn's in 1824, Poggio did not find him favorably inclined towards the Society, and particularly towards the idea of a republican government."[46] Even Valerian Mikhailovich, who would pay for his liberal ideas with a long deportation in the following years, was a member of the Northern Society, and—contrary to what Poggio had thought when they had met in St. Petersburg—he did not share the southerner's strong ideas on republicanism. What perhaps at one time could have been the "sixth secret group" or "oriental group," next to those of St. Petersburg, Moscow, Tulchin, Kamenka, and Vasilkov, remained an unfulfilled dream.[47]

Poggio recounted this failed mission at the meeting held during the Kiev *Kontrakty* in January of the following year, 1825.[48] On his return from St. Petersburg, Pestel related the dissension (not without diminishing it considerably) that his constitutional ideas, his initiatives toward the Poles, and his social conceptions continued to arouse in the Northern Society. Nevertheless, he said that a basis for understanding had been found.[49] But not even this seemed to solve the fundamental problems. The atmosphere was agitated. As Poggio said, "The agreement, the unity that had existed before, was missing."[50] A new year was beginning; it was the last year of life and liberty for these men, and already the difficulties of getting a result from the conspiracy weighed on them. The secret society was prolonging its life without being able to take action, which increased the risk of its discovery. Impatience grew, plans multiplied, and everyone was intent on finding a way out of the uncertainty in which they found themselves at any cost. The last fruit of the European cycle of revolutions in 1820–25 was reaching maturity when already the situation inside and outside Russia no longer allowed a fight with any probability of victory.

The last great organizational success of the Southern Society developed at the end of August when they made contact with the Society of United Slavs. The liaison became even closer the next year. Not far from their center in Vasilkov, Muravev-Apostol and Bestuzhev-Riumin had found a particularly promising group of young officers who had formed a secret society two years previously. Here democratic ideas, Polish and Panslavic ideologies, and the revolutionary spirit had fused into a strong desire for propaganda and action.[51] The Society of United Slavs demonstrated the fertility of the land where the Russian secret societies were working. At the same time this group reintroduced the Southern Society to all the problems it thought it had solved. With its vivid aspirations and its youthful extremism, the United Slavs seemed to openly expose all the contradictions in the "military revolution" desired by Pestel. From the organizational standpoint, the Slavs were dominated and absorbed by the Southern Society, but the discussions that led them to this position again brought to light all the difficulties in the plans proposed by the conspirators and contributed toward making the crisis in the whole Society more acute, driving it even closer to immediate action at any cost.[52]

The Polish problem, now "diplomatized" by Pestel's negotiations, took on a broader and more general form. The United Slavs declared that their plan included the formation of a federation of all Slavic populations from the Adriatic to the Arctic Ocean, from the Black Sea to the White Sea. New military and commercial ports would be constructed for the defense of the federation and for the development of maximum trade for Slavic populations. In the center, "at the center of the earth," a common capital would enthrone the "goddess of civilization." "In the Slavic ports commerce and naval power will flourish, as, in the city in the midst of these lands, will justice for all."[53] The resurrection of Poland was thus becoming a factor and perhaps the secret trigger for this great Pan-Slavic utopia. Bestuzhev-Riumin managed to persuade them that one had to begin with action in Russia: "The transformation of Russia," he said, "will certainly open the road to liberty and well-being for all Slavic populations. . . . Once liberated from tyranny, Russia will openly contribute to the attainment of the goal of the Union of Slavs: it will free Poland, Bohemia, Moravia, and other Slavic lands, and will establish free governments and will unite them all in a federal union."[54]

The organizational problem also seemed more difficult to solve, at least at first. The United Slavs still maintained numerous traces of their masonic and Carbonaro origins, from which the whole Decembrist movement had arisen, with rituals, oaths, formulae, and terminology that still naively reflected a state of mind that Pestel's "machiavellianism" had long since undermined and removed. It was only with difficulty that the small but tightly knit group of Slavs submitted to the scheme of the southern secret groups which by now were more centralized and hierarchical.

The discussions that accompanied the difficult process of assimilation revealed that the basic differences lay in the diversity of their prospective policies. The United Slavs began to criticize the "military revolution," not so much because they considered it inappropriate and inadequate, but because they felt it to be unjust. In their youthful democratic fervor they were repulsed by the idea of using soldiers simply as instruments, as a maneuverable mass that the officers would manipulate without even explaining the goals and ideas of the *pronunciamento* and of the revolt. The memorialist who gave us a vivid picture of these discussions has probably rigidified the contenders' positions and attributed to them ideas that seem more clear and precise than they actually were. Nevertheless, even after so many years, the recollection of these differences emerges in his writings with the power of deeply felt problems. Contrary to earlier beliefs, the author of these memoirs is probably Petr Borisov, the actual founder of the United Slavs.[55] He relates how he had proposed a plan for propaganda for the troops. "I was convinced that sincerity and frankness would have had more effect on a Russian soldier than all the cleverness of machiavellianism. Muravev had a different view. To him it seemed not only useless but also dangerous to reveal anything to the troops that had to do with the aims of the Society. The troops were in no position to understand the advantages of the revolution. For them a republican government, class equality, and the election of officials would have been like the sphinx's riddle."[56]

At the most, they could and should have acted on the soldiers' spirit, using religious rituals perhaps taken from the Old Testament where it mentions the election of kings and liberty. But this attitude was also criticized as machiavellianism by Borisov. As a Voltairian and an enemy of all positive religion, he could not give in to the use of any instrument in which he did not believe.

The problem of propaganda among the soldiers thus remained open and continued to be discussed in the whole Southern Society toward the end of its existence, as the time of action gradually drew nearer. It was only the most immediate and urgent aspect of a broader problem. Did one have the right to use arms to impose a revolution that presupposed the passivity of the whole Russian population? According to the memorialist, the United Slavs were convinced that: "(1) No uprising can succeed without the agreement and cooperation of the entire nation; therefore first of all it was necessary to prepare the population for its society's new form of government and then present it, (2) a population cannot be free without becoming moral, enlightened, and industrious. Although military revolutions achieve their goal more rapidly, they are not the cradle but the coffin of liberty, in whose name they are carried out."[57]

It is not surprising then that the Slavs, faced with Pestel's central idea of a dictatorship that would last at least ten years, had a typical libertarian reaction. Petr Borisov then asked: "Who would elect the members of the provisional government? Would only the military take part in it? With what right, and with whose consensus and agreement would it govern Russia for ten years? Where would its strength lie, and what elements would there be to guarantee that a member of our government, elected by the army and supported by bayonets, would not usurp absolute power?"

In replying, Bestuzhev-Riumin too was carried away by the logic that had made tyrannicide the center of his ideology. "How can you ask this?" he answered, his eyes blazing. "We, who somehow will kill our legitimate sovereign, we would tolerate a usurper? Never! Never!" "This is true," said Borisov, feigning cold-bloodedness and with a smile of doubt, "but Julius Caesar was killed in the middle of Rome, falling under his own greatness and his glory, yet a boy of eighteen, the feeble Octavius, triumphed over the killers and the excited patriots."[58] This reminder of the classical era, even recalling Trajan, obviously could not solve such a deep contradiction. Only the spirit of sacrifice and the will to fight at any cost could silence or drive away these doubts. As Bestuzhev-Riumin said, for the conquest of liberty neither sects, statutes, nor constitutions are needed. Only enthusiasm is necessary. "Enthusiasm transforms a dwarf into a giant. It destroys all and creates new things."[59]

Thus it was enthusiasm and not just the respect that the young Slavic officers had for these nobles with their great names, who appeared so powerful with their wealth, their military rank, and their links with the world of culture, that served to fuse the Society of United Slavs with the Southern Society. On September 13, 1825, Bestuzhev-Riumin gave a final speech on the future successes, on the fortune of sacrificing oneself for the good of one's own countrymen, and after this, everyone immediately wanted to swear the required oath.

In a burst of enthusiasm, everyone swore to come forth at the first signal, arms in hand, at the given place, using all possible means to bring along their subordinates, to act with dedication and a spirit of sacrifice. Bestuzhev-Riumin, removing the holy image he wore, kissed it fervently and called providence to witness. With great passion he pronounced the oath to die for liberty, and he passed the holy image to the Slavs next to him. One cannot imagine this solemn, moving, and at the same time strange scene. With their imaginations stirred and with heated and indomitable passion, they expressed themselves in ceaseless exclamations. Pure, sincere, solemn, and terrible oaths were mixed with the shouts of "Long live the constitution! Long live the republic! Down with class distinction! Let the nobility die along with imperial dignity!"[60]

The *cohorte perdue*, the section destined to eliminate Alexander I, was to be recruited from among the Slavs. The extremist fervor of the young officers was channeled toward the assassination attempt which would then give the signal for the uprising and would cut the Gordian knot of the disputes between constitutional-monarchists and jacobin-republicans. The plan of action was taking shape. Pestel and Sergei Muravev planned to use Muravev's battalion to capture the emperor in May 1826 during maneuvers. They would do so just at the moment when the third and fourth army corps were to meet.[61]

In the final months of 1825, Trubetskoy, the head of the Northern Society, was warned that the Southern Society was absolutely set on starting action the following year. Two military camps would be established, one in Kiev under Pestel's command and one in Moscow under Bestuzhev.[62] But how could they gain control of these centers? The coup de main on the headquarters at Kiev was to be carried out by Focht and Maibord, two men very close to Pestel. Pestel had proposed this plan in the presence of Lorer and Alexander Poggio the year before, after the summer maneuvers in 1824. The same problem that was being discussed at that very moment at Vasilkov with the young Slav officers was raised again by Focht, who pointed out to Pestel that it was not easy to make soldiers march against their superiors in headquarters. Pestel responded, "You must know how to lead soldiers. You have all the necessary gifts for doing so."[63]

Faith in the officers' capacity to command and to take initiative, and faith in their military abilities, tended to mask the political problem contained in all these

uncertainties and doubts. Moreover, it was thought that the task would be facili-
tated when the guards of the Kiev command were entrusted to the Viatka regiment, which was that of Pestel and of the men charged with carrying out the coup.
The soldiers in this corps could be prepared for the task awaiting them by adapting
military discipline to the political aims they wanted to achieve. Pestel said that he
"intended to make the troops understand that the farther the czar was from them,
the more benevolent were their superiors, whereas the nearer they were to the czar,
the harsher and more detached were their superiors." Still in the presence of Lorer
and Alexander Poggio, he planned to divide the troops into two categories and to
try to appeal to the sympathies of the first group. He was certain that the second
group would follow the example of the first and support their fellow soldiers, who
would have been better informed and better treated.[64]

To broaden and solidify the base of support for the revolt, at one point there
was a plan to make use of the endemic discontent that existed in the military colonies created by Alexander I on the model of the Austrian colonies along the
Turkish border. But while they were a marginal phenomenon in the Hapsburg empire, the Russian emperor intended to make them one of the fundamental institutions of his state, reforming the existing recruitment system, allowing a reduction
in military spending, and thus diminishing the fiscal burden on Russia. The colonies
constituted the most hated of Alexander I's "reforms." They were detested by the
nobility who were afraid of losing control of their servants and thus also over the
primary material for the czarist army. They were also hated by the enlightened
and cultured nobility, who saw the military colonies as an instrument of tyranny
and almost as an attempt to replace the guard of the nobility with a praetorian
guard. They were viewed with dismay by the victims, who were obliged to cultivate the land and live with their families in a strict barracks atmosphere (plowing
in uniform, obeying the sound of a trumpet for waking, for mess, and for taps in
the evening). Finally, they were considered a curse by the peasants from the districts where the military colonies were installed, as they were sent away from the
land they tilled.[65]

The revolts had begun promptly. One of the first and biggest was the one in
the Chuguev district, not far from Kharkov and Taganrog. The uprising had taken
place in the summer of 1819 and is described by Poggio in his depositions as one
of the current themes of discussion among the young officers in St. Petersburg
and as one of the reasons that led him to participate in the clandestine groups.[66]
About a thousand tenant farmers had been arrested; about a hundred had been
whipped, and four hundred deported. Economically the colonies soon had proved
to be counterproductive. Far from relieving the state budget, they aggravated it.
Yet in 1825 about 750,000 people lived in these colonies and they were not suppressed until the time of Alexander II's reforms.

The Decembrists often thought that the colonies might have served, if not as a
starting point, at least as a possible avenue of retreat. The conspirators thought
they might find refuge and support in the colonies if the *pronunciamento* failed.

Thus it is natural that Pestel welcomed with interest and hope the contact with the southern colonies offered by General A. K. Boshnyak. After he had contacted Likharev and Davydov, Boshnyak offered his services to the Society and brought news that General Ivan Osipovich Vitt, head of the military colonies in the Kherson and Ekaterinoslval regions, also had rebellious sentiments. If he did not contact the conspirators directly it was only out of prudence. Nevertheless, he guaranteed his support and that of the colonies under his command. Meanwhile, he offered to reveal the names of some spies.[67] Pestel, Likharev, and Davydov soon became mistrustful of these offers. In fact it was a provocation. Boshnyak had been ordered by Vitt to take advantage of the fact that he knew Davydov's family, "a nest of enemies of the government," to "penetrate the shadows that concealed the evil-doers."[68] In August 1825 he made his report, and only an illness and the obvious diffidence of the Kamenka group prevented him from proceeding with his work.[69] He died in an ambush during the repression of the Polish rebellion in 1831, and his end was attributed to his "denunciation of the 1825 conspiracy."[70]

The hope of being able to count on the military colonies was developing into an additional reason for fearing that the Society would soon be liquidated if it did not act in the shortest possible time. As Pestel said, "After the contact with Boshnyak, we are in continual danger."[71]

Thus, Sergei Muravev-Apostol kept repeating that they must pursue these plans with increased vigor. Why continue, as Pestel did, to use any means to find an agreement with St. Petersburg to link the action of north and south? Even if they were small, they must begin with the forces that were ready and not postpone action any more. Why wait until 1826 and not take advantage of the summer of 1825? Muravev-Apostol said that nothing was being done in the capital and little or nothing was happening in the south. One could count on only one thing—decision. The problems arising from the rapport with the troops only delayed action. "The masses are nothing, they will only be what the individuals who are everything wish them to be,"[72] he said one day to Poggio. His men would certainly follow him. The Chernygov regiment was a unit that was firmly in his hands. "The soldiers adored him," remarked Alexander Muravev-Apostol.[73] "He had succeeded in attracting not only officers but also a large majority of the soldiers, especially in the battalion he commanded. He had shown great benevolence and helped the men in their needs."[74] The idea of mutiny and a military revolution reappeared in its original and spontaneous form after the long political elaborations of the secret societies.

As we have seen, Alexander Poggio was present at the discussions held in Kiev in January 1825. The agitated atmosphere surrounding him and the general situation of the whole Society in that period had a profound effect on his spirits. The crisis that Pestel had helped him overcome in September of the preceding year began to recur. When the eager desire to participate in an extreme and definite action no longer seemed to have a real outlet, Poggio seemed to withdraw into himself and lose faith in his own strength. As Sergei Muravev-Apostol wrote to his brother Matvei in April 1825, "You have known Poggio for some time and therefore I have nothing to add about him. Only I find he distrusts his own strength greatly, which slows the general movement of things when it should be his duty to lead others."[75] More and more tormented by doubts, he gave in to the temptation of following his brother's example. He resigned from the army and gave up his uniform. While maintaining a close relationship with the Society, his return in extremis to private life made it more difficult or even impossible for him to participate actively in the approaching events.

He asked to retire on December 30, 1824. Pestel did not approve of this step and made this clear to him when they met in Kiev in January of the following year. Poggio answered that he would always remain faithful to the Society—"If you need me, you can always send word"—but he planned to go away, to spend a few months in the Caucasus. Before leaving Kiev, he saw Matvei Muravev-Apostel, who asked Poggio to investigate whether there were any clandestine centers forming in Georgia and to contact them. In fact, Volkonsky had heard rumors of their existence. Poggio left in May. But despite a stay of almost two months, he could find no trace of a clandestine organization. The personality of General Ermolov, who was in command of the troops in the Caucasus, attracted the attention of everyone who was thinking about reform and changes; the officers were faithful to him to an "unbelievable degree," but this did not signify they were ready, nor could Poggio confirm that there was a real movement afoot.[76] In September, he returned. The head of his secret group, Davydov, believed that they should not take action if St. Petersburg did not give the signal. They must wait. The atmosphere grew heavier and led to personal disputes in the heart of several groups. In October, Poggio decided to abandon all, "to go to Berlin and beyond, leaving my mother, my family, and my country. I wanted to go far on my voyage, God knows to what destination."[77]

The news that reached him in mid-December was a great blow to him. On December 13, Pestel had been arrested. A detailed report to the emperor on the secret societies was provided by Maiborod, who had often attended the most confidential meetings held in Tulchin. The report made the government decide to strike the most active and dangerous section of the entire clandestine movement. Pestel, who naturally was unaware of the denunciation, continued to hope for several days after his arrest that he had been taken blindly and that the government would not know how to carry out further repression. The southern secret groups held the same illusion for some time.

But the pace of events accelerated. Alexander I had died on November 19. The uncertain period of the interregnum had already lasted a month under the new emperor Constantine. He had renounced the throne yet he inexplicably delayed completing the necessary acts so that his brother Nicholas could legitimately succeed him. In St. Petersburg on December 14, upon hearing the announcement of the new oath that the army had to give Nicholas I, the Northern Society had put all its forces into attempting to lead the garrison to mutiny and trying to bring an important and strong nucleus of troops into the Senate square. The *pronunciamento* kept the destiny of Russia in suspense for a long and decisive day. Then the logic of the "military revolution," so much discussed and theorized upon in previous years, immobilized the conspirators, making it impossible for them to pass from a military demonstration to a coup de main against the Winter Palace and against the person of the new emperor. All the conflicts revealed during the long evolution of the Russian Carboneria, between the responsibility of officers and of soldiers, between the call for force and the faith in persuasion, between the exclusive duties of the army and its function of providing an incentive to influence large state bodies from the Senate to the autocracy, between the desire to impose or to ask for a constitution—all these differences reappeared at the moment of the revolt. They appeared during the period of waiting, of faith, and of indecision which signaled the fate of the *pronunciamento* of December 14 and led to the scattering of the troops and the arrest of all those who from near or far had had anything to do with the secret societies in the capital.

The first confused news of what had happened in St. Petersburg reached the south at the same time as the orders to arrest those who had been closest to Pestel. Soon the arguments of those who favored an immediate uprising in order to support the Northern Society and avoid a passive fall into government hands prevailed over the proposals of those who still believed it was possible to "wait until the storm passed." One figure who in those difficult days showed great passion in trying to find a way out of the overwhelming difficulties was Alexander Poggio.

Poggio was at Kamenka. On December 21 he was dining at Davydov's house. Likharev was also present, and there they heard the news of the arrests of Pestel, Yushnevsky, Kryukov, and the search through Baryatinsky's papers, though he was absent. Shortly after, Colonel Yantalchev arrived. He had seen General Volkonsky. The Society had been discovered. He was sending out advice to burn any compromising papers. Volkonsky had already seen Pestel under arrest. Pestel had told him to look after the fate of his *Russkaya pravda* and had urged him not to lose heart. But there was no news from the third southern secret group. What had happened to Sergei Muravev-Apostol? It was decided that Poggio should seek information, and he agreed to go. But upon returning to his home, he reacted against the atmosphere of deep pessimism and fatalistic waiting that had pervaded the meeting with his friends. He had to do something. He would go to Muravev-Apostol when he knew more about the intentions of those who were still free.

On December 22, Poggio wrote a long letter to General Volkonsky. He said that ruin was approaching for everyone, that soon the Society would truly be uncovered, that everyone expected to lose his life, now without hope of clemency, as evidenced by the persecutions already taking place. He reminded Volkonsky that at other times he had heard him say: everyone must do his duty toward his companions; "It is for you to reassemble us and mark for each one of us the duty we must fulfill toward our friends: do yours, and I shall do mine." On a separate page he proposed the only plan that seemed logical and possible to him. They must immediately execute a plan that Pestel had prepared in 1824 and had discussed with him, advising him to take action with Davydov and Volkonsky. The plan was to "join the regiments of the 9th infantry division [Volkonsky's] and the Viatka regiment [commanded by Pestel], attacking Tulchin and seizing the headquarters [of the second division], freeing Pestel and the other prisoners." He added, either in the letter or probably sending the message through Yantalchev, that as soon as he had received a positive answer he would set off to meet Sergei Muravev-Apostol and make arrangements with him. If Muravev-Apostol was in a position to raise the third corps at the same time "there was still some hope that things would move in a favorable direction." Yantalchev himself proposed to support the planned action with an artillery detachment under his command.[78] Yantalchev was convinced that Volkonsky would not do anything, but he agreed to be the bearer of Poggio's letter and to advocate the plans. In any case, they all were responsible not to leave Sergei Muravev-Apostol alone and to support him whenever he decided to mobilize the troops.

The messenger reached Volkonsky in his country home in Boltyshka where the general had gone to join his wife who was about to give birth to their first child.[79] The general immediately gave a negative reply and burned Poggio's letter. He proposed meeting Poggio in person to explain the reasons for his refusal. How could he arouse the 9th division in which there were only two members of the secret society other than himself—that is, Poggio, who had retired, and Captain Focht? He added that moreover he knew for certain that Maiborod's denunciation had endangered the whole nucleus of the Southern Society.[80] He evidently no longer saw a way out.

On the night of December 22, Alexander Poggio stayed up waiting for the reply at Yantalchev's house. The next morning he returned to Davydov's house where he found his brother and Likharev. He read them a copy of his letter to Volkonsky. Joseph approved. Davydov was convinced that it would bring no results. "Alone, Volkonsky is insignificant. To be able to do this he would have to be pushed by someone. If Pestel were here, things would be different." Alexander Poggio replied that perhaps despair would give him courage. After all, Volkonsky did not lack support. His father-in-law, Raevsky, had often promised to save him. But by now he was too compromised to be able to hope for any protection or intercession. In any case they must wait for Volkonsky to decide in order to give Sergei Muravev-Apostol a clear answer.

Then for the last time they discussed the alternative plan that for years had gone against the desire for a southern uprising. The action must begin in St. Petersburg, not in the south, Pestel had always maintained. Not knowing what had already occurred in the capital, they drew up plans for possible action there. If Volkonsky refused, nothing remained but to leave. Alexander Poggio offered his services for the tyrannicide. "I proposed my own two hands and said that on the very day of my arrival they would have heard that the emperor had ceased to live." Muravev-Apostol could have gone with him. Davydov objected that two hands were too few.

Poggio answered that many others could certainly be found in the Society. Besides Muravev-Apostol there were Obolensky, Golicyn, Mitkov. The tyrannicide would be followed by political upheaval. They spoke of Admiral Mordvinov and of others as possible members of the future government. As for the Guards, they could be kept under control by General Mikhail Feodorovich Orlov, who had been one of the most important figures in the first phase of the movement and in the Union of Welfare. He had grown more distant and detached from his friends though they continued to regard him highly and admire him for his preparedness and intelligence. Davydov expressed support for this proposal.[81]

While these plans were being discussed at Kamenka, the situation in the Vasilkov secret group was becoming critical. The warrant for Sergei Muravev-Apostol's arrest, heard about on December 25, along with the more detailed news about events in St. Petersburg made him decide to revolt. Finally, in the most adverse circumstances, he put into action the designs that had been proclaimed so many times.

Arrested on December 29 along with his brother Matvei, Muravev-Apostol was freed by a group of Slav officers. Then, putting himself at the head of a few companies of the Chernygov regiment, the next day he marched on the town of Vasilkov, which he occupied with the intention of making it the center of an uprising that would then lead all the other groups of southern conspirators. Bestuzhev-Riumin and many others joined him. Once again, the conflict between a rapid and rash action (the Slavs suggested marching on Kiev) and the concept of a *pronunciamento* that should spread like a drop of oil, with the gradual adhesion of other troops (this was Sergei Muravev-Apostol's vision), caused the revolt to take a defensive position and close in on itself, halting its development. There were efforts to make the soldiers realize what they were doing, both through the promise to free the peasants and through true religious-political preaching carried out using an "orthodox catechism" composed by Muravev-Apostol. These efforts provide further evidence of the breadth of ideas and the spirit of sacrifice that moved the heads of the southern rebellion. But they did not manage to overcome the conflict between the need for immediate action and the necessarily long task of propagandizing. The words of the *Orthodox Catechism* "read by a parish priest in the square in Vasilkov" remained a symbol, expressing a "military revolution" that tended to go beyond itself to become a revolution of the entire Russian population, but naturally they never had any practical effect. On the night of December 31, Muravev-Apostol's troops reached Motovilovka, another small center, and succeeded in carrying part of the garrison stationed there. On New Year's Day none of the soldiers wanted to march and the movement stopped, losing precious time. On January 2, they moved on Belaya Tserkov, but the garrison there, with its strong sectarian links, had been withdrawn. Then the peregrinations of the revolutionary column from village to village began, at first with the hope of opening a route toward Zhitomir or Kiev, to join the Slavs or perhaps the Polish secret society; then the column was just trying to escape the hunt of the government troops and avoid the circle that was drawing closer around them. On the night of January 3, they encountered a detachment of hussars and artillery carrying out reconnaissance. The thousand men commanded by Muravev-Apostol had no chance of victory in the battle. Seriously wounded from the first, the commander courageously tried to reorganize his troops. The behavior of many of his officers was heroic. But the enemy cavalry and cannons soon dispersed the little nucleus. The southern insurrection too had been crushed.[82]

A few days later, Poggio heard the news that Volkonsky had refused to take the leadership of the movement and Sergei Muravev-Apostol was already engaged. When he heard more details on Muravev-Apostol's movements, it was already too late to reach him. Perhaps there was still a possibility of following the plan "to go to the military colonies, and find a base for action there." On December 29, Iantalcev had spoken to him about the discontent there. But Poggio persisted with the idea of tyrannicide. Those who he believed had escaped the repression (Matvei Muravev-Apostol, Tizengauzen, and Bestuzhev) should concentrate on St. Petersburg, organizing the assassination attempt, perhaps planning it for the coronation day of the new emperor.

The news of the uprising in St. Petersburg on December 14 reached Poggio after a long delay and made the latest plans pointless. The increasingly frequent arrests around him were exasperating and convinced Poggio even further that he must devote himself to carrying out the "fatal promise." This is what he told his brother, Joseph, on December 29 after witnessing Likharev's (Joseph's brother-in-law) arrest, the tears of his pregnant wife, the despair of his mother and sisters. This suffering must be vindicated, and he foresaw "an era of cruel state vengeance was approaching with despair for all."[83]

Soon for Poggio, too, the desperate search for an escape ended in prison. A warrant for his arrest had already been signed on December 27. On January 3, 1826, he was arrested on his estate at Yanovka. General Nagel was in charge of securing him and delivering him to the hands of the emperor. As soon as Poggio was seated in the sleigh, ready to begin the long journey, he gave the General "his word of honor not to escape," assuring him that he well understood the meaning of behaving in accordance with the demands of duty. And, of course, he scrupulously kept his word.[84]

Poggio arrived in St. Petersburg on January 11 and the next day was imprisoned in the Fortress of SS. Peter and Paul in casement number 7. He was next to the members of the Northern and Southern societies, whose numbers were increasing there. Joseph, arrested at Yanovka on January 14, after his warrant was issued on the 7th, joined his brother in the fortress on January 21. For six months the Poggio brothers too lived in the atmosphere of the trial that involved nearly five hundred people and marked the end for an entire "elite."

The harshness of prison, the inquisitorial methods used by the investigating judges, the despair and the enthusiasm of those who were caught up in the machinery of the trial that was created and personally manipulated by Nicholas I to dishearten, eliminate, neutralize, or destroy men and ideas have repeatedly been described to us in the Decembrists' memoirs, and they still come to life, despite the bureaucratic jargon, in the enormous volume of documents from the investigating commission. Torture was not used, although it was threatened against those who were most responsible for the revolt or who resisted most strongly. Numerous other means of pressure were used, from isolation in chains and deprivation of food to persuasive words from the emperor, judges, and priests, in order to undermine the secret societies down to the last member and to arouse despair among those who had participated in the conspiracy. Fear and threats alternated in this long process of elimination of the liberal elements seated in the very hearts of the Russian ruling class.

The individual drama of the men who were arrested and condemned, the repercussions that prison and interrogation had on their spirit, the multiform tragedy of the men involved in the investigation must not make us forget that it was a political trial. The Decembrists' sacrifice gave them an aura of legend and martyrdom which also carried great political influence in the further development of the "intelligentsia." But this must not hide the fact that above all the year 1826 marked the end of an era, the violent closing of an entire age in Russia's history. After their action was brought to a violent halt in that year, the Decembrists became a myth. Nicholas I not only managed to overcome the dynastic and military crisis that had marked his accession to the throne; he also stifled the ideological ferment that had accompanied Catherine II's attempts at enlightened despotism, Alexander I's reforms and patriotism, and the territorial expansion and wars at the end of the late 18th and early 19th centuries. The methods used in presenting and conducting the trial revealed not only the petty realism of Nicholas's mind, and the great servility and blind fear of those who surrounded him, but they also were a mirror of the whole transformation of the Russian ruling class which had already matured in Alexander I's final years and was now completed under the blow of the Decembrists' attempted insurrection.

The judges, and above all the emperor, tried to use the trial to demonstrate that sects and liberal and republican ideas constituted foreign elements in Russian life. They wanted to show that such elements could and should be strictly eliminated because they represented nothing but a monstrous and abnormal excrescence. Throughout the investigation and the sentencing, there was an effort to render impassable the gulf that existed between the enlightened "elite" and the great traditionalistic or ignorant masses. As we have seen, the Decembrists discussed at great length what means would allow them to influence the soldiers, to make contact with the constituted state bodies, and to truly enter the life of the nation. They had been well aware how arduous this task was. Now everything was being done to sever their actions and ideas from the traditions and aspirations of the populace and the ruling class. They were presented to Europe and Russia not only as criminals and rash men, but even as madmen guided only by their overwrought imaginations, "monstrous caricatures," as Poggio said.[85]

Yet, it was not easy to carry out this operation. First of all there was an element that linked the Decembrists' attempts with a well-established Russian "tradition." For the last century, each change of sovereign had been accompanied by some trouble in the nobility and in the army. In 1730, Anna had had to deal with a first attempt at a "constitution." Catherine II had acceded through a military revolt and the killing of Peter III. The death of Paul I, father of Alexander and Nicholas, was still fresh in everyone's mind. The people remembered the conspiracy as well as the fact that those responsible had never been punished. The Guards, the same Guards who had been one of the fundamental nuclei for the Decembrists, had had some crucial declaration to make every time the question of proclaiming the emperor of all the Russias arose. There was a temptation to include the December 14 action in this "tradition." One of the judges in the trial, Pavel Vasilevich Kutuzov, had been a main figure in the conspiracy that eliminated Paul I. Bestuzhev did not fail to remind him of this during his interrogation. But now a great distance separated the past movements of the Guards from the liberal revolution dreamed of by the Decembrists. Going over the past events many years later, Alexander Poggio was still struck by this contrast: *"Là, une révolution de sérail,* there, a revolt of filthy courtesans, a conspiracy dictated by personal interests; and here an integral revolt of the whole society."[86]

Times had changed. Both on the part of the revolutionaries and on the part of the emperor, there evidently was a desire not to recall those specters, not to retrace those steps. This was tyrannicide, a military revolution but not a palace conspiracy. Rejecting the conspiratorial tradition, the Decembrists had hoped to demonstrate their desire for liberalism and modernity. They had stopped every time their revolutionary plans seemed to lead them on paths that had already been trodden. The element of uncertainty, of hesitation, and of chance that was connected with the very idea of the *pronunciamento* was probably aggravated by this aversion. Again, with their sacrifice, they demonstrated that they wanted to open a new road. This concept is best expressed by M. S. Lunin: "The secret society could not approve or desire palace revolutions since such enterprises, even when they are carried out by those who have a right to the throne, do not bring any advantage, and they are irreconcilable with the principles that the secret society had declared, and in which all its strength lay. The Society intended to affirm the rule of law and permanently remove the need to adopt means that are contrary to justice and reason."[87]

Alexander Poggio was equally resolute in his *Memoirs.* After recalling the assassination of Paul I, he concluded: "The killers were compensated but theirs was an easy and miserable success. No, they were not an example for us. They were true assassins, glorified assassins. We instead ... I shall say what we were. I have looked for models for ourselves in the past and I did not find any."[88]

As for the emperor, was he not the champion of legitimism in Europe? Was he not tied to that revived concept of monarchy that had developed through the struggles against Napoleon and in the organization of Europe during the restoration? He too wanted to sever his connections with the past and present himself, not as the head of the Guard, but as the legitimate sovereign of Russia. The long interregnum after the death of Alexander I had severely tested this plan, but he remained faithful to it. Although in the trial the judges concentrated all their attention on the plans for the extermination of the ruling family, on everything that concerned the sovereign's person, they did not manage to present the Decembrists as pure and simple military conspirators. There was almost a secret competition between the liberal revolutionaries and the czar, between the supremacy of constitutional law and the legitimism of the monarchy, both now spiritually far away from the age of palace uprisings. The revolutionaries were defeated. Nicholas triumphed, opening a century of legitimate successions to the Russian throne and closing the era of the revolts of the Guard.[89]

It was more difficult, however, to break the bonds with all the ferment of enlightened and liberal ideas from which the Decembrist movement had arisen. This would have meant denying the historic fruits of the works of Catherine II and Alexander I. Nicholas I used petty yet efficacious means to do so. Again and again he said in his proclamations and declarations that the Decembrists had wanted to act against Alexander I, not against himself, and he laid as much responsibility for the development of the sects on his predecessor as possible. He made it clear that his heredity had been painful but that he would know how to exercise his absolute power without the weakness observed in the past. Thus he denied any responsibility and in doing so he linked the Decembrist movement even more to a man and a world that had now vanished. With equal vigor or equal stubbornness, he publicly denied all links between the Decembrist movement and what had developed in other countries in Europe. "One cannot compare this insurrection with those that arose in Spain and Piedmont.... Thank God we have not reached this stage and we never will..." Privately, Nicholas was not as certain on this point as he wanted to appear to the diplomatic corps, to whom these words were addressed. He well knew what the political content of the Decembrist movement was.[90]

The men in the secret societies were neither simple military conspirators nor innocuous dreamers imagining a liberal Russia. They had linked action and thought as well as they could and as the situation permitted. They had wanted to solve Russia's basic problems. Thus Nicholas I was obliged to consciously and carefully hide their truest and most effective ideas. The trial became a systematic operation to conceal the fundamental results that the Russian "elite" had achieved through a long development that began in the era of Catherine II.

Not a single word was said about the Decembrists' desire to solve the problem of peasant servitude. Many Decembrists were struck by this denial of historic justice that they were obliged to suffer. "The commission was silent about the liberation of the peasants, which should have restored civil rights to so many millions of our compatriots," noted Lunin.[91] Poggio, too, joined in this protest in an era, when after 1861, it seemed to him the injustice committed in 1826 should have been rectified.

Why were we not accused of this aim of ours [the liberation of the peasants] as a crime, and why did the judges and great and lesser figures prefer to remain silent about this problem? . . . Tearing away such a glorious page from our documents, removing Pestel's only legitimate glory—is this not treacherous falsification, is it not obvious expropriation of mind and heart? We had many plans and ideas for the liberation of the serfs, and everyone wanted the personal liberty of the peasants with payment of compensation in money to the lords, but the idea of freeing the peasants and giving them land was Pestel's alone.[92]

Lunin noted the obvious reason for the silence: "In mentioning these problems, the commission would have aroused the public sympathy that they were trying to suppress."[93]

Similarly, nothing was published about another of the Decembrists' characteristic moral concerns, that is, their constant desire to improve the soldier's position, to fight the militaristic spirit, to give discipline a form that was far from the crudeness and violence existing in the Russian army then; in other words, to profoundly reform the army, too.[94] These nobles and owners of peasant-serfs wanted to liberate them. And when wearing uniforms, they refused to subject themselves to the military discipline imposed by tradition. In this matter too, their plans and visions of the future were carefully hidden from public view, thus breaking one of the strong bonds that had united these young officers to the humanitarian and philanthropic spirit of the century that had trained them.

What can be said about the constitutional plans? The hints that leaked out from the trial were few and vague. The whole debate between the supporters of the American model and those who believed in the French Revolution was obscured. Pestel's *Russkaya pravda* was discovered during the investigation, in the place where it had been hidden, but "it was discovered with the purpose of truly hiding it from the people, by sending it to oblivion in the archives."[95] Lunin, the author of this observation, consoled himself saying that his constitutionalism and that of his companions represented for Russia what the will of the nobles who obtained the Magna Carta had represented for England.[96] But his romantic vision only revealed the hopes of a man deported to Siberia. In reality, in no point more than in this question of constitutionalism do we see the break between the world of the Decembrists and that of Russia in the second half of the century. Not one constitution promulgated by the movements from 1820-25 in all Europe, including Spain, Naples, and Piedmont, succeeded in establishing roots and bearing fruit. But in Russia, Nicholas I even managed to prevent the birth of a constitutional tradition.[97]

How did the autocrat succeed in crushing not only the military revolt but the whole movement that had prepared and justified it? The Decembrists asked themselves this when they faced the judges in the secret investigating commission. They thought of their own errors, of what they might have done, of the immensity of the task they had undertaken. They sometimes even tried to continue their work from prison, trying to persuade Nicholas I and the judges of the need for reform. For many, the secret societies and the military revolt itself had only been a means of applying pressure to persuade the ruling powers, to make them recognize their tasks, to force the whole ruling class to feel and do what they felt and were trying to do. Some of them hoped to find adversaries and not enemies among the judges and in the emperor. Others, a greater number, felt the full tragedy of their position. They had managed to lead only a small fraction of the army, and they realized how this group only constituted a very limited part of the ruling class. Confronting the men of the old generation they even found those in whom they had hoped and who they had thought could be given power, including even Mordvinov and Speransky. They sensed how fear was now petrifying all those, among the young, whom they had considered at least as sympathizers. Rostovecev had gone straight to the emperor to express his fears and legalistic scruples on the day before the insurrection. Liprandi became one of the main figures in Nicholas I's police force. Orlov escaped his sentence thanks to a policy of calculated forgetfulness that the emperor used for certain members of the sects when it seemed useful to exercise indulgence in order to isolate the force of the true conspirators from the world of those who had gravitated toward the Northern and Southern societies. Nicholas could use various pressures and means, striking a heavy blow against the most combative core and thus eliminating the political forefront, knowing that this way he would finally place a tombstone on the era of Alexander I. "The *history* of Russia will begin when the romance is finished," said Metternich at the time of the death of the emperor.[98] These words contained the cruel political sense of the Decembrists' trial.[99]

Alexander Poggio also tried to understand the reasons behind the events that were crushing and eliminating him from Russian civilian life. On the morning of July 10, 1826, he was taken from his cell and brought to the judges. He again saw his friends from whom he had been isolated for so many months. Like them, his spirit was in suspense, waiting for the sentence soon to be heard. The High Court of Justice was seated before them. None of the Decembrists had had much to do with these judges who had practically restricted themselves to accepting and validating the conclusions of the secret investigating commission. It was actually the commission, along with the czar, that was responsible for the sentence. Poggio's thoughts naturally returned to this body at the moment of the final decision. The commission represented the Russia that had triumphed over the Decembrists.

The president of the commission had been the minister of war, Count Tatishchev. Poggio wrote in his *Memoirs:* "If a man who was entirely an outsider to the trial was to be chosen for this task, then the selection could not have been better. Always silent, apparently deep in thought about his ministerial affairs, he looked at us with an air of indifference...."[100]

Another Decembrist, A. E. Rozen, recalled how this minister of war impressed his importance on his prisoners: "You, sirs, have read everything, Destutt de Tracy, Benjamin Constant and Bentham and look where that got you, and I, in all my life have read nothing but the Holy Scriptures and look what I have gained," he concluded, indicating a series of shining decorations on his chest.[101]

Next to Tatishchev in the investigating commission was Alexander Ivanovich Chernyshev, "the moving force and, one could say, the only moving force in the whole trial," as Poggio wrote. "There was no form of cleverness, or deceit, or refined baseness, covered by a mask of feigned understanding, that was not ceaselessly employed by that man, who never rested." Next to these members, a member of the royal family, Nicholas I's brother, Mikhail Pavlovich, represented the dynastic element in the drama. "Aside from his truly chivalrous sorties against Pestel, Kyukhelbeker, and especially against myself, one could not help being amazed at seeing him so enmeshed in something that so closely concerned himself and his family. The basic problem was dynastic, and he, as incredible as it may seem, was, as the French say, *juge et partie.*"

Diebitsch, on the other hand, was so full of military spirit that his activity in the investigation, which was limited anyway, seemed to Poggio like an uncontrolled attack, "not toward the center where the fortress lay, but at its flanks, scattered all over Russia." The true representative of the bureaucratic spirit was Benkendorf, later the head of the Third Section created by Nicholas I. And the more characteristic and traditional superstition present in the person of Alexander Nikolaevich Golicyn, "an almost ecclesiastical man," who had fallen from favor in the past and was now brought forth for the occasion "to make him forget his past sins through the sins of his present zeal."[102]

Poggio might have added two personalities to his list, both particularly characteristic of the historic period in which he was living. One of Nicholas I's most active and important counselors regarding the organization of the investigation of the court that was to condemn the Decembrists, and of the propaganda that accompanied the change of regime, was Speransky, the main representative of Alexander I's reformism. It was he who gave a bureaucratic if not legal form to the investigation; it was he who provided the czar with the administrative instruments for penal action and even corrected or drew up the manifestos that Nicholas I was to publish.[103] Next to Speransky, even if in a very different position, one must not forget that Admiral Mordvinov took part in the trial. He was one of the most enlightened, balanced, and cultured members of the group of men who had surrounded Alexander I. Mordvinov had spent the years preceding 1825 in contact with Ryleev, Kyukhelbeker, and in general, with the young liberal intelligentsia of St. Petersburg. A follower of Adam Smith for all that concerned economics, and of Bentham for matters of state administration, he represented something very rare in Russian society: a tenacious and patient will for reform.[104]

As we have said, Speransky and Mordvinov had been designated *in pectore* by the Northern Society, as leading figures in the state structure that the *pronunciamento* would have established. They were certainly not unaware of the existence of the sects although they did not join. They represented the generation of older men in Russia, sons and followers of enlightened despotism of the old regime or of the Napoleonic era, men that all the European sectarian movements of the age of restoration found along the way and variously tried to use or involve in their action. They used them occasionally as a screen, relying on their technical and administrative capacities or simply taking advantage of the spirit of tolerance and legality that moved these men for their own goals. In Piedmont, we might think of Prospero Balbo. Everywhere a contrast existed between the mentality of these men and that of the Carbonari, of the liberals of the new generation (a contrast that again aroused all the difficulties and obstacles in the transformation of enlightened despotism into a constitutional regime), making the political alliance with the sects difficult or even impossible. This contrast contributed toward delaying the success or consolidation of the *pronunciamentos* of 1820 and 1821. It was the fate of Russia under Nicholas I to see the men of the era of enlightened despotism seated on the judge's bench, now active collaborators not only in repression but also in the elimination of the matured liberal and revolutionary fruits of their own ideas and their reforming activities.

Speransky was led to assume this function just because of the czar's suspicions about him. Nicholas I knew of his political links with the Decembrists even if they were not strictly organizational. By forcing him to recant the new sovereign wanted to confirm the break with the hopes and aspirations of the first years of his predecessor's reign. The secret tears shed by Speransky over the documents that he zealously prepared for the czar are a symbol of this break. Mordvinov, instead, became part of the court as a member of those state bodies (the senate, the synod, etc.) which so many Decembrists had planned to counterpose against autocracy, making them the prime instruments and main foundations of a constitutional evolution in Russia. Now Mordvinov too was led to become an instrument of the restored autocracy, He was more successful than Speransky in maintaining the internal coherence of his position: he alone pronounced himself against the death penalty for the Decembrists, thus reaffirming, at least personally, that ideal continuity of 18th-century reform spirit that Nicholas intended to eliminate from the Russian political scene.[105]

Alexander Poggio mentions neither Speransky nor Mordvinov in his *Memoirs*. All his attention is focused on the more immediate instruments of repression. The drama taking place on a high level in the private rooms of the new court was not accessible to him, just as for many years it remained hidden from the eyes of observers and historians. Yet he could not fail to recognize, even in the people making up the secret commission, the same problems that stirred the souls of Speransky and Mordvinov. Even the inquisitors were sons of the enlightened era and of the struggle against Napoleon in the name of liberty.

Why [he wondered] were these judges, born in Catherine II's time and brought up under Alexander, not imbued with the spirit of tolerance of these two reigns? Why could they so suddenly, so quickly deny all the past and dive headlong into the abyss of death sentences and persecutions? Why did they decide so quickly and without considering how to overcome the limits that clearly divide a benevolent philanthropic government from a cruel one lacking in humanity? Where and when in their long lives had they ever seen the use of these gallows and this forced labor in such great abundance? What could have driven them to such a complete break with our system of government? Let us assume that the ideas revealed by the investigation threatened their own interests, that the goal of limiting the monarch's power would have deprived them of necessary support, that the introduction of the representative system and of the electoral system in general in all branches of administration would have weakened their position as well as that of all the dominant bureaucracy, that the planned abolition of peasant servitude would have affected their way of life. Let us assume that the latter would concern them more closely than any of the other factors. But were we the only ones who held these views? And all these problems that had come to the surface, did they not necessarily require a long sane discussion, in cold blood, rather than a decision in one stroke of the pen to kill not only the men but also the very spirit that had motivated them? They killed, and then? Power in Alexander's time was at least dormant; but under Nicholas it became oppressive, reaching the height of harsh and immovable absolutism like a fatal yoke on all thinking people in Russia ... A lack of talent, of energy, of ability appeared everywhere and Nicholas, with his power, became the object of reproach, of criticism, the cause of all the causes.

No, Nicholas was not the only one to blame for all that had been lost. The guilty were precisely those judges before whom I stood [on the morning of July 10, 1826] ... They were men of their era in Russia, who had grown and matured under the influence of the limited, unilateral, state military spirit of the times. The mark of that both glorious and miserable era was on them.

All their personalities manifested all the contradictions, all the extremes of social characters that had formed. But most unilateral, exclusive, and superficial of all was the military preparation. It existed under conditions of uninterrupted and bold courage, of second-rate ambition, of coarse behavior before inferiors and a profound servility before superiors, mixed with great magnanimity before a foreign enemy. Their life was spent in military campaigns, they had marched against the Circassians, the Turks, and above all against the French. In between, especially in Alexander's last years, they had studied military rules and had memorized the regulations. This was the only measure of the merit of officers of the times. Tirelessly they read the orders of the day, saw to the line up and maneuvers; but in their estimation, the greatest thing of all, shining above everything else, was military presence and bearing...[106]

The military spirit that had stirred hearts in the preceding years and decades had become crystallized at the end of Alexander's reign in that military mania that characterized the era of Nicholas I. We can add that the condemned Decembrists represented the moral forces and sentiments that had accompanied the wars against Napoleon. The judges that sent them to the gallows or to Siberia were the incarnation of blind obedience, of formal discipline, of hierarchy that the wars had rooted more deeply in the ruling class.

The attempt by the secret societies to turn the army from an instrument of absolutist domination, as it was at the time of Bonaparte, to an instrument of liberal revolt failed. In their judges, the Decembrists could see the incarnation of oppressive militarism, which they had vainly tried to counter with the idea of a "military revolution." Nor were they the only ones in Europe to undergo this experience. In fact, they were the last in a long chain of failed attempts and unsuccessful military uprisings that moved from Spain to Russia through France, Portugal, and Italy.

But in Russia the defeat had been so harsh and the recovery period was so long in coming that many (including Poggio) believed that Russia was too different from other countries, and that the attempt had fallen on terrain that was entirely unsuited for acceptance and development of this kind of revolution. After thirty years of isolation in Siberia, Alexander Poggio returned with both an exalted and pessimistic vision of his country and its history. As the years passed, he felt he was searching more and more through Russia's past and present for justifications for the moments of discouragement from which, as we have seen, he was not exempt even when he was surrounded by men like Pestel, Bestuzhev, Muravev-Apostol, or Volkonsky. He now seemed to find a terrible confirmation in the long silence that accompanied their condemnation, their deaths, or their deportation. "Who were our predecessors," he asked, "and who are our followers? No one! We were the initiators and everything ended for all the centuries."[107]

A great weight seemed to immobilize all Russian history. Any attempt to transform the country was in vain. Peter the Great had also tried. Yet not even he had understood "the Russian man," "seeing in him only a two-footed creature made in order to realize his own goals."[108] Pure, absolute power had become the only law of Peter and of the state he founded. Even in his own family life he had not managed to create continuity. Yet a man like him "who shows a certain inclination, like Saturn, to devour his own children" ought to have seen the dynastic problem with very different eyes. In reality, his personality did not fit the Russian mentality. "Peter became intolerable to his country. . . . He was different from his land in everything: he expressed movement and she expressed calm."[109] Peter was inspired, "a new prophet and follower of Christ," as he demonstrated by preferring manual labor to science, by abolishing the patriarchate and making himself head of the church, by the very grandeur of his tasks. But not even Peter the Great succeeded in removing the central obstacle to Russia's historical development.

Pugachev, the peasant rebel, had also tried. The whole drama of Russia's past was reflected in him. Pugachev was both a citizen and a bandit. In the "Russian Spartacus" one could see a man capable of fighting for his own rights, affirming a principle of liberty and at the same time incapable of bringing the revolt to the level of a revolution similar to the one that shook the countries of Western Europe. Slavery, the habit of serving, had impeded thousands of peasants from following him. His revolt had done nothing but induce the nobles to bow their heads before absolutism.

Russians seemed incapable of creating a revolution to obtain something new. All their revolts were caused by a desire to defend the past, customs, and traditions at any cost. As long as this supreme good was not touched, Russians would

not move. They had taken action only in order to prevent modification or transformation brought about by a higher power. The *raskolniki* and peasant revolts
proved this; the former in the field of religion, and the latter in the social arena,
and both enmeshed in the history of the 17th and 18th centuries. "Name me an
insurrection, and if not an insurrection at least an event that can be termed as any
sort of political aspiration."[110]

This was the great secret of the sphinx that tormented Poggio while he was in
prison: What was the secret strength of Russian absolutism? "Why did thousands
of people blindly obey one person without complaining?"[111] How did the people,
instead of sympathizing with those like the Decembrists who tried to organize
themselves and to rebel, repudiate them and in a sense collaborate in their execution?[112] According to Poggio, the only possible answer lay in the profound conservatism of the peasant masses, on which the servility of the whole Russian society
was based. Any attempts at reform were destined to fail before this obstacle.
"Strange to say, I do not know a better conservative, who has more good faith,
and, naturally, is more limited than the Russian *muzhik*."[113] This conservatism
is manifested as pride or firmness and is always "a force, and a force that will not
be beaten."[114] The peasant, and with him all of Russian society, defends itself
this way, with unshakable decision and its tradition of servitude. For example,
what application did the enlightened idea of Bentham, that "laws make men,"
ever have in Russia? This idea became an instrument in the hands of the autocracy
and absolute power of the czars. Foreign policy, too, can only be explained by
keeping in mind this immobility. If Catherine and Alexander were able to intervene in Europe, shaken by the French revolution, it was just because the new
principles could not be solidly established in Russian soil. As Poggio said, "Russia
alone is not concerned."[115] "Russia, completely removed from the movements
that were developing in Europe, was distant, immobile, and unshakable. Only this
state of Russian minds could explain the strange politics of Alexander I in the last
years of his reign," that is, Russian intervention in support of the Holy Alliance.[116]

Not even the secret societies could be advanced as an argument in favor of the
revolutionary ferment that had penetrated the czar's empire. No, not even the
conspiracies found suitable terrain. "A Russian revolutionary does not exist in
the nature of things, and if occasionally one appears, he perishes immediately,
just as the monsters perished in Sparta."[117]

The court seated before Poggio and his companions on July 10, 1826, had been
mistaken in viewing the Decembrists as authentic revolutionaries and in consequently treating them as such. A tradition of a real and true struggle against power did
not exist in Russia.

These were the thoughts that stirred in Poggio's mind from the day the cell door
was shut on him. He, too, had been taken in by the logic of the trial. Nicholas I's
plan to eliminate the liberal forces even reached Alexander Poggio's conscience as

well as that of a large number of Decembrists enclosed in the Fortress of Saints Peter and Paul and then separated from the world for decades.

Poggio himself has described his experiences as a prisoner. He tells us how the lack of all contact, of all activity, led some to desperation, to suicide, and others to isolation, and led all to a loss of the balance between thought and action, an effect brought on by prison existence. "Prison, which limits a man to an inactivity that makes him like an object, not only does not dim his mental capacity but almost seems to stimulate it. Thought is normally fed by action; this is the valve without which the mechanism of our brain cannot function properly."[118]

Poggio saved himself from this imbalance and from this very failure of his own action. He did so by never concluding from his pessimism about Russian reality that there was a need to adapt to it and thus become a conservative, too. His experience in prison taught him what he needed: "I found myself alone and had to develop all my forces, both intellectual and moral, against the enemy that had triumphed. Here there was no battle or struggle, no, the sword that had fallen had no strength. What was needed was a cuirass, some armor that would blunt and break all the blows that fell on it. I'll find a cuirass, I told myself, and I did."[119]

He maintained his liberal opinions all his life. They were an asset that nothing could make him give up, not even the conviction that Russia was incapable of assimilating the substance of his ideas. "Our beliefs did not weaken but were reinforced, and we remained faithful to ourselves and to the Russia that had so violently torn us from her heart and had so calmly forgotten us."[120]

With the trial ended, the reading of the sentence vividly pointed out all the elements on which Poggio's reflections were based: bureaucracy, servility, militarism, and at the same time ingenuousness and fresh good will which spilled out from the Decembrists' hearts without finding an outlet in the reality of Russia.

A blond young man who I will call the *expéditeur* was very eager to do his duty. He recited at the right time and to perfection the lesson given to him. He read aloud with conviction. His voice was firm and he showed great art in knowing how to express the commas and periods when it was a matter of separating a minor crime from a serious one. And how many crimes were accumulated, and how heavily they weighed on each of the accused!... The *expéditeur* rapidly read the general sentence. When speaking of the sentence of death by beheading, he exhibited all his dramatic talents. He paused intentionally on this picture, there where the heads were separated from the body, and thought he could impress us deeply with this pause. After a full minute, he again raised his tone and finished the incomplete sentence: "But the czar, in his clemency, etc., has commuted the death penalty to a sentence of life at hard labor." Pronouncing these words, he skillfully turned toward us on his right leg and took his leave. Zhuravlev picked up the documents and passed them to the minister, who jumped up from his chair. This vivacious little man raised his little right hand, indicating the exit. A military man came toward us, murmured something softly, and made us turn to the right, leading us down the stairs. Before us and on the sides of the stairs the observers were silent. From the public the unmistakable head of Mellin emerged (a man for all ceremonies, banquets, receptions and friend of all the officers in the Guards). In a loud voice he told one of his jokes, a dragonade (as he called them, as he had served in the Nizhni Novgorod dragoon regiment, which had been covered with glory in the Caucasus). His joke must have been very amusing as it was followed by general laughter. What a trait of Russian character![121]

Notes

1. *Vosstanie dekabristov, materialy* [The Decembrist insurrection, materials] (Moscow, 1925–), 3 (1927): 113.

2. Ibid., 4 (1927): 210.

3. Ibid., 4 (1927): 241, 11 (1954): 54.

4. Ibid., 4 (1927): 345, 401.

5. Ibid., 10 (1953): 165.

6. V. Bazilevich, "Dekabrist O. P. Yushnevsky. Sproba biografiy" [The Decembrist O. P. Yushnevsky: biographical essay], in *Ukrainska akademiya nauk. Zbirnik istorichno-filologichnogo viddilu. N. 37 b. Dekabristi na Ukraini. Tom II* [Academy of Sciences of the Ukraine: miscellany of the historical-philological section. N. 37 b. The Decembrists in the Ukraine, vol. 2] (Kiev, 1930), p. 45.

7. *Quelques heures de loisir à Toulchin* (Moscow, 1824), p. 38, quoted in M. V. Nechkina, *Dvizhenie dekabristov* [The Decembrist movement] (Moscow, 1955), 2:466.

8. See S. G. Volkonsky, *Zapiski* [Memoirs], 2d ed. (St. Petersburg, 1902); and *Arkhiv Dekabrista S. G. Volkonskogo, pod red. kn. S. M. Volkonskogo i B. L. Modzalevskogo* [The archive of the Decembrist S. G. Volkonsky, edited by Prince S. M. Volkonsky and B. L. Modzalevsky] (St. Petersburg, 1918), vol. 1 (the only one published, which treats the years 1803–16).

9. In order not to be too surprised to find even a Polignac involved in these conspiracies, let us read what "General de Brack, commandant l'école de Cavalerie de Saumur" says about him in 1811: "Colonel count Héraclius de Polignac served in Russia a long time.... In 1793 a cradle, carried by the ebb of the revolutionary flood, was stranded on the sands of the north. The infant it contained was received maternally by Russia, which nourished and raised him.... The first language he lisped was that of the Slavs. Barely had that infant grown up when, at the age of twenty-five, he became, on the field of battle, colonel of the Russian Imperial Guard." He then returns to France. "What should not be the future of a Polignac under the restoration? But he did not know how to insult the great man who had fallen. Before statues of Napoleon the soldier bared his head.... He was outcast.... And it was only in 1829 that he was finally given a regiment, although his old comrades in Russia were all lieutenants and generals." Héraclius de Polignac was wounded at Borodino. When he returned to France he still maintained an interest in things Russian and became the translator of the *Essai sur la guerre de partisans, par le général Denis Davidoff* (Paris, 1841); the above quotations are from its in-

troduction. It also has a translator's introduction in which Polignac stresses the importance of partisan war for France.

10. V. I. Semevsky, "Josif Victorovich Podzhio," in *Gallereya shlisselburgskikh uznikov. Pod red. N. F. Annenskago, V. Ya. Bogucharskago, V. I. Semeskago i P. F. Jakubovicha* [Gallery of prisoners of Shlisselburg, edited by N. F. Annensky, V. Ya. Bogucharsky, V. I. Semevsky, and P. F. Yakubovich] (St. Petersburg, 1907), pp. 17 ff.; and *Vosstanie dekabristov,* 12 (1969): 183.

11. S. Sulima, "Zametski starago kievlyanina" [Notes of an old Kievite], in *Kievskaya starina* [Kievite antiquities], 1882, no. 12, p. 623, quoted in *Arkhiv Raevskikh. Izdanie P. M. Raeskogo. Redakciya i primechaniya B. L. Modzalevskago* [Archive of the Raevskys, edited by P. M. Raevsky, edited and with notes, B. L. Modzalevsky] (St. Petersburg, 1908), 1:246, n. 1. This *Arkhiv* is a vast collection of letters and documents that very effectively depict the society from which—through contrast and derivation—the southern Decembrist movement arose. Rich in information on the "great house of Kamenka" and on its inhabitants, and illuminating about this group of nobles, is the *Arkhiv dekabrista S. G. Volkonskogo,* 1:xviii ff. Poggio's descendants continued to live in the Ukraine. Some of them were present at a celebration of the centenary of the Decembrist movement held in Kiev in the fall of 1925. See V. B-ch., "Jubiley dekabristiv u Kievi" [Jubilee of the Decembrists in Kiev], in *Ukrainska akademiya nauk. Zbirnik istorichno-filologichnogo viddilu. N. 37. Dekabristi na Ukraini. Tom I* [Academy of Sciences of the Ukraine. Miscellany of the historical-philological section. N. 37. The Decembrists in the Ukraine, vol. 1] (Kiev, 1926), p. 199.

12. Volodymyr Porsky, "The Decembrist Milieu in the Diary of Pelagya Rostsiszewska," *Annals of the Ukrainian Academy of Arts and Sciences in the U.S.* 1 (1951): 29, n. 1.

13. *Vosstanie dekabristov,* 4 (1927): 19, 68; see also *Vosstanie dekabristov,* 11 (1954): 54.

14. Ibid., 9 (1950): 101.

15. Ibid., p. 110.

16. Ibid., p. 90.

17. During the investigation, M. P. Bestuzhev-Riumin said, "After that time the Society no longer numbered Joseph Poggio among the conspirators" ("Pizmo M. P. Bestuzheva-Riumina k A. I. Chernyshevu" [Letter from M. P. Bestuzhev-Riumin to A. I. Chernyshev], in *Pamyati dekabristov. Sbornik materialov* [In memory of the Decembrists: a collection of documents], fasc. 2 [Leningrad, 1926], p. 90).

18. *Vosstanie dekabristov,* 4 (1927): 19, 68.

19. On Pestel's relationship with freemasonry, see N. Druzhinin, "Masonskie znaki P. I. Pestelya" [P. I. Pestel's masonic badges], in *Muzey revolyutsy SSSR* [Museum of the revolution of the USSR], fasc. 2 (Moscow, 1929). On the whole question of Russian freemasonry, see Tatiana Bakounine, *Repertoire biographique des francs-maçons russes: Dix-huitième et dix-neuvième siècles* (Paris, 1967), with detailed bibliography.

20. *Zapiski dekabrista N. I. Lorera* [Memoirs of the Decembrist N. I. Lorer] (Moscow, 1931), p. 74.

21. Arthur E. Adams, "The Character of Pestel's Thought," *American Slavic and East European Review* (April 1953).

22. *Vosstanie dekabristov*, 4 (1927): 91.

23. Poggio, *Zapiski*, p. 53.

24. *Vosstanie dekabristov*, 4 (1927): 90.

25. Ibid., 4 (1927): 163, 1 (1925): 324.

26. Ibid., 4 (1927): 145, 9 (1950): 70.

27. Ibid., 4 (1927): 146.

28. Ibid., 1 (1925): 325.

29. Ibid., 4 (1927): 91.

30. Ibid., p. 163.

31. Ibid., 11 (1954): 75.

32. Ibid., p. 49.

33. Ibid., p. 76.

34. Ibid., p. 65.

35. Ibid., pp. 76–78.

36. Ibid., p. 65.

37. Apparently, General Kniaziewicz, who had been living in Dresden for nine years and who was in contact with Lafayette, always advised a prudent and diffident policy toward the Russian societies (M. Handelsman, *Les Idées françaises et la mentalité politique en Pologne au XIXe siècle* [Paris, 1928], p. 81).

38. See the excellent map published in *Vosstanie dekabristov*, vol. 7 (1958), facing p. 130.

39. Ibid., 9 (1950): 54. On pp. 69–71 is the planned agreement with the Poles, reconstructed in prison by Mikhail Bestuzhev-Riumin and written by him in French, "because I must confess to my shame that I am more used to this language than to Russian," as he himself said.

40. *Russkaya pravda*, in *Vosstanie dekabristov*, 7 (1958): 123–24. On the whole Polish question in this period, see Georges Vernadsky, *La Charte constitutionnelle de l'Empire russe de l'an 1820* (Paris, 1933). On the Polish secret societies, the fundamental works are still those by Szymon Askenazy, *Rosya-Polsky. 1815–1830* (Lwow, 1907), and *Łukasiński*, 2 vols. (Warsaw, 1908). A useful overall view can be found in Handelsman, chap. 3, pp. 63 ff.; M. V. Nechkina, *Obshchestvo soedinënnykh slavian* [The Society of United Slavs] (Moscow and Leningrad, 1927); I. Bekker, "Dekabristy i polsky vopros" [The Decembrists and the Polish problem], in *Vosprosy istorii* [Problems in history], 1948, no. 3; G. Luciani, "La Société des slaves unis," thesis (Paris, 1949) (see *Revue historique* [October–December 1949], pp. 308 ff.); Leon Baumgarten, *Dekabryści a Polska* [The Decembrists and Poland] (Warsaw, 1952); and L. A. Medvedskaya, "Yuzhnoe obshchestvo dekabristov i Polskoe patrioticheskoe obshchestvoi" [The Southern Society of the Decembrists and the Polish Patriotic Society], in *Ocherki iz istorii dvizheniya dekabristov. Sbornik statey* [Essays on the history of the Decembrist movement. Collected articles], ed. N. M. Druzhinin and B. E. Syroechkovsky (Moscow, 1954), pp. 276 ff.; and Orlik, p. 184, with large bibliography (see p. 94, above).

41. *Vosstanie dekabristov*, 11 (1954): 51.

42. The movement had taken place in February 1823 and was one of the numerous signs of discontent over the harshness of discipline and of the military service

that we find in that period. Eighteen soldiers were exiled to Siberia after those acts of insubordination (ibid., intro., p. 20).

43. Ibid., 8 (1925): 67.
44. Ibid., 11 (1954): 40, 71.
45. Ibid., 4 (1927): 157, 11 (1954): 78.
46. Ibid., 8 (1925): 67.
47. Ibid., 4 (1927): 142.
48. Ibid., 11 (1954): 51.
49. Nechkina, ed., *Dvizhenie dekabristov*, 2:40 ff.
50. *Vosstanie dekabristov*, 11 (1954): 78.
51. It is interesting to note how the first nucleus of this group, that is, the Friends of Nature who proclaimed themselves to be followers "of the rules of the Pythagorean sect," had taken their ideas from a Russian translation in six volumes, which appeared between 1804 and 1810, of *Voyages de Pythagore en Egypte, dans la Chaldée, dans l'Inde...*, published in 1799 and written by Sylvain Maréchal. See Yu. G. Oksman, "Iz istorii agitatsionno-propagandistskoy literatury dvadcatych godov XIX veka" [From the history of the literature of agitation and propaganda in the twenties of the 19th century], in Druzhinin and Syroechkovsky, eds., pp. 474 ff. (see n. 40 above).
52. Nechkina, *Obshchestvo soedinënnykh slavian.*
53. *Vosstanie dekabristov*, 5 (1926): 17.
54. *Zapiski i pisma dekabrista I. I. Gorbachevskogo* [Memoirs and letters of the Decembrist I. I. Gorbachevsky], ed. B. E. Syroechkovsky (Moscow, 1925), p. 53 (hereafter *Zapiski i pisma*).
55. The identification was proposed, with good evidence, by Nechkina in *Dvizhenie dekabristov*, 2:135 ff.
56. *Zapiski i pisma*, p. 83.
57. Ibid., p. 58.
58. Ibid., pp. 73–74.
59. Ibid., p. 71.
60. Ibid., pp. 80–81.
61. *Vosstanie dekabristov*, 4 (1927): 213.
62. Ibid., p. 151.
63. Ibid.
64. Ibid., 11 (1954): 47–51. On the question of the participation of troops in the Decembrist movement, see Sergei Gessen, *Soldaty i matrosy v vosstaniy dekabristov* [Soldiers and sailors in the Decembrist insurrection] (Moscow, 1930).
65. The major revolt, which occurred in 1831, has been studied in great detail by P. P. Evstafev, *Vosstanie novgorodskikh voennykh poselyan* [The insurrection of the military colonies of Novgorod] (Moscow, 1934), which also describes the creation and the first developments of these colonies. A useful overall view is: R. E. Pipes, "The Russian Military Colonies, 1810–1831," *Journal of Modern History*, no. 3 (1950), pp. 205 ff. Further details from: V. A. Fëdorov, "Borba krestyan Rossii protiv voennykh poseleny (1810–1818)" [The struggle of the Russian peasants against the military colonies (1810–1818)], in *Voprosy istoriy,*

1952, no. 11. The opinions of the Sardinian residents of St. Petersburg fully reflect the concern and disgust aroused by the military colonies. G. de Maistre had given his government detailed information, adding predictions of catastrophes ("it will result in the final destruction of the civil order" [September 17, 1816]) and the strange idea that "military colonies modified according to location will be perhaps the only means of making something of Sardinia" (October 29, 1816). His successor, Count Brusasco, in his dispatch of February 8/ January 27, 1821, lists the advantages of the military colonies but concludes: "All these advantages are little enough compared with the fatal consequences it could have for Russia to establish, in the greater part of the empire, a military population entirely free of civil jurisdiction and having no other laws, no other tribunals, than those of the military. How, in fact, is the nation to protect herself from the oppression and devastations of this immense population in which the government has invested all the force of the state? And how will the government manage to repress the uprisings of these colonies, which could become even more dangerous than the Strelitz were?" (February 8, 1821, A.S.T., Ministry letters, Russia, Group 4). An echo of the interesting discussions that the military colonies aroused in three travelers in Russia around 1822, Marquis Pucci, Count Salazar, and the Englishman Robert Lyall, can be found in the unusual pamphlet by Lyall, *An Account of the Organisation, Administration, and Present State of the Military Colonies in Russia* (London, 1824). A French translation of this work was published in Paris the following year.

66. *Vosstanie dekabristov,* 11 (1954): 38. See V. A. Fëdorov, "Vosstanie voennykh poselyan v Chuguev v 1819 g." [The insurrection of the military colonies at Chuguev in 1819], in *Istoricheskiy zapiski* [Historical memoirs], 1955, no. 52, pp. 305 ff. About two thousand people were arrested; 363 persons were brought before the military tribunal which condemned 273 to death (later commuted to beating), and ninety to flogging. The execution of these sentences lasted the whole of August 1819. This was followed by deportation to other military colonies. Among others, twenty-nine women were flogged and deported. This is only the fate of the soldier-peasants and their families; officers who had in any way sympathized with or supported the insurgents were also sentenced.

67. *Vosstanie dekabristov,* 4 (1927): 84.

68. Ibid., 8 (1925): 42.

69. On the provocation and on the spy network that extended around the Southern Society in the final period of its existence, see I. Trotsky, "Likvidatsya Tulchinskoy upravy yuzhnogo obshchstva" [The liquidation of the Tulchin secret group of the Southern Society], in *Byloe* [The past], 1925, no. 5, pp. 47 ff.

70. *Vosstanie dekabristov,* 8 (1925): 286.

71. Ibid., 4 (1927): 170.

72. Ibid., 11 (1954): 79.

73. "Mon Journal ou mémoires d'Alexandre Mouravieff," in Theodor Schiemann, *Die Ermordung Pauls und die Thronbesteigung Nikolaus* I (Berlin, 1902), p. 167.

74. *Vosstanie dekabristov,* 4 (1927): 402.

75. S. Ya. Gessen, "Iz proshlogo. Neopublikovannye pisma Sergeia Muraveva-

Apostola" [From the past. Unpublished letters of S. Muravev-Apostol] in *Krasnaya niva* [The red field] 1927, p. 19, n. 6, in *Vospominanya i rasskazy deyateley taynykh obshchestv 1820-kh godov* [Memoirs and stories of the members of the secret societies in the twenties], ed. Yu. G. Oksman and S. N. Chernov (Moscow, 1931).

76. See A. Fadeev, "Dekabristy v otdelnom kavkazskom korpuse" [Decembrists in the autonomous Caucasus corps] in *Voprosy istoriy*, no. 1; and Nechkina, ed., *Dvizhenie dekabristov*, 2:110 ff. (see n. 7 above).

77. *Vosstanie dekabristov*, 11 (1954): 41, 49, 50, 59.

78. Ibid., p. 59, and 10 (1953): 138, 140–41, 149, 210.

79. Volkonsky, in *Zapiski*, 1:466 (see n. 8 above), described the destruction of compromising papers, carried out by himself and his wife, as soon as Pestel was arrested.

80. *Vosstanie dekabristov*, 10 (1953): 152.

81. Ibid., p. 60.

82. Vol. 6 of *Vosstanie dekabristov* (1929) is devoted to the revolt of the "Chernygov" regiment.

83. *Vosstanie dekabristov*, 11 (1954): 62.

84. B. Pushkin, "Arest dekabristov" [The arrest of the Decembrists], in *Dekabristy i ikh vremiya* [The Decembrists and their times] (Moscow, 1932), 2:381, 401.

85. Poggio, *Zapiski*, p. 56 (see n. 23 above).

86. Ibid., p. 26.

87. "Razbor doneseniya, predstavlennogo Rossiyskomu Imperatoru Taynoy Komissiey v 1826 godu" [Examination of the report presented to the Russian emperor by the secret commission in 1826], in *Dekabrist M. S. Lunin. Sochineniya i pisma* [The Decembrist M. S. Lunin. Works and letters], ed. S. Ya. Straikh (St. Petersburg, 1923), p. 71. This examination was written in English, in close collaboration with Nikita Muravev when both men were exiled to Urik, not far from Irkutsk.

88. Poggio, *Zapiski*, p. 62.

89. See the penetrating article by E. Tarle, "Voennaya revolyutsiya na Zapade Evropy i dekabristy" [The military revolution in Western Europe and the Decembrists], *Katorga i ssylka* [Forced labor and deportation], 1925, no. 8, (pt. 2), special issue, *100-letie vosstaniya dekabristov* [The centenary of the Decembrist insurrection], pp. 113 ff., which rightly concludes: "It was the events of December that showed how far advanced was the Europeanization of Russia," and it stresses the unity of all the movements of those years, from the "Guadalquivir to the Neva."

90. N. K. Shilder, *Imperator Nikolai I. Ego zhizn i carstvovanie* [Emperor Nicholas I. His life and reign] (St. Petersburg, 1903), 1:635.

91. "Razbor," in Straikh, ed., p. 75.

92. Poggio, *Zapiski*, pp. 52–53.

93. "Razbor," in Straikh, ed., p. 75.

94. See E. A. Prokofiev, *Borba dekabristov za peredovoye russkoye voennoye isstustvo* [The Decembrists' struggle for a progressive Russian military art] (Moscow, 1953).

95. "Razbor," in Straikh, ed., p. 73.

96. Ibid., p. 61.

97. The documents that give proof of Nicholas I's clear desire that nothing should be published about the Decembrists' ideas on reform have been published in Nechkina, *Dvizhenie dekabristov*, 1:429.

98. The true results obtained by Nicholas I's judicial policy are documented, for example, by a letter written by Genz to Metternich on July 28, 1826. After having read the report of the investigating commission, he said, "I have never seen a more horrible document. Compared to these Russian conspirators, our German revolutionaries seem to me like innocent children.... The stigma which this report has placed upon the forehead of the entire Russian nation cannot be washed away in a hundred years..." (*Briefe von und an Friedrich von Genz, herausgegeben von Friedrich Carl Wittichen* [Munich and Berlin, 1910-]), 3, pt. 2:274.

99. *Lettres du prince de Metternich à la comtesse de Lieven, publiées par Jean Hanoteau* (Paris, 1909), p. 333.

100. Poggio, *Zapiski*, p. 25.

101. A. E. Rozen, *Zapiski dekabrista* [Memoirs of a Decembrist] (St. Petersburg, 1907), p. 85.

102. Poggio, *Zapiski*, pp. 25–26.

103. N. V. Golicyn, "Speransky v Verchovnom ugolovnom sude nad dekabristami" [Speransky in the supreme criminal court that judged the Decembrists], *Russkii istorichesky zhurnal* [Russian historical journal], 1917, nos. 1–2, pp. 61 ff.; P. E. Schegolev, "Imperator Nikolai I i M. M. Speransky v Verchovnom sude nad dekabristami" [Emperor Nicholas I and M. M. Speransky in the supreme criminal court that sentenced the Decembrists], in *Dekabristy* [The Decembrists] (Leningrad, 1926), pp. 277 ff. See G. Sacke, "M. M. Speranskijs politische Ideologie und reformatorische Tätigkeit," in *Jahrbücher für Geschichte Osteuropas*, no. 4 (1939), pp. 331 ff.; and M. Raeff's excellent book, *Michael Speransky, Statesman of Imperial Russia* (The Hague, 1957).

104. V. S. Ikonnikov, *Graf N. S. Mordvinov. Istoricheskaya monografiya* [Count N. S. Mordvinov. Historical monograph] (St. Petersburg, 1873).

105. The documents about this were published in *Arkhiv grafov Mordvinovykh. Predislovie i primechaniya V. A. Bilbasova* [Archive of the Counts Mordvinov, introduction and notes by V. A. Bilbasov] (St. Petersburg, 1903), vol. 7.

106. Poggio, *Zapiski*, pp. 27–29.

107. Ibid., p. 75.

108. Ibid., p. 35.

109. Ibid., p. 41.

110. Ibid., p. 77.

111. Ibid., p. 52.

112. Ibid.

113. Ibid., p. 81.

114. Ibid., p. 82.

115. Ibid., p. 78.

116. Ibid., p. 79.

117. Ibid., p. 74.
118. Ibid., p. 48.
119. Ibid., p. 58.
120. Ibid., p. 51.
121. Ibid., pp. 55–57.

Five   Russians, French, and Italians
              in Nice, Genoa, and Turin after
              the Revolution of 1848

"Here I am once again in Nice..." Alexander Herzen had been there more than
two years earlier on his way to Rome at the end of 1847, when the revolution was
beginning to break in Italy. As his disillusionment with events in Paris had deepened, Herwegh had encouraged him to consider returning to Nice.[1] Now he found
there a refuge in defeat after having participated in France's latest efforts toward
democracy and in the demonstration organized against the expedition destined to
crush the Roman republic. In France everything seemed finished to him.

When I had crossed the bridge on the Var, and a Piedmontese carabinier asked for
my passport to write in it—I breathed freely. I am ashamed, I blush for France and
for myself, but I swear that the same feelings seized my soul when I crossed the
Russian border. At last, I left behind me this land of moral torture, of feverish
irritation, of indignation, of anger... The carabinier handed back my passport:
Inspected by reg. carab. at Ponte Varole June 23, 1850. Thus I quitted France on
the terrible anniversary of the 23d of June. I looked at my watch. It was four-
thirty in the afternoon. Two years ago, at that hour, an immense and fatal struggle
was still brewing; I watched, leaning against the corner of a house in torrents of
rain, as they finished an enormous barricade near the Place Maubert.—My heart
beat strongly, and I thought, *"To be or not to be."* "Not to be" decided the outcome. The revolution was defeated. Authority had won out óver liberty, the question which had troubled Europe since 1789 was answered in the negative. The
shame of the taking of the Bastille was washed away in the square itself by the
cannonade of the Faubourg St. Antoine.... But that was enough.... Before my
window lies the Mediterranean, I am on the blessed coast of Italy. I enter the port
peacefully, and I trace on the threshold of my house the ancient pentagram to
separate it from any feelings of agitation and of human madness.[2]

This chapter is taken from *Esuli russi in Piemonte dopo il '48* (Turin, 1959).
The quotations from Herzen's writings are from the now completed edition of
his works, in thirty volumes, published by the Academy of Sciences of the USSR,
and some new bibliographical information has been added.

He felt he was experiencing a rebirth in Nice after "the convulsive, absorbing, irritating, and sick existence" in Paris. "Presently in Nice. Never in my life have I felt such climatological well-being as here; even the heat makes no difference. We have huge rooms, we undress instead of dressing, we bathe in the water and in the sweet, balmy evening air—and to hell with the fierce beauty of Switzerland, those monuments of a geological reign of terror. For no amount of money would I go further north, but I would willingly go as far south as the Basilicate if you wish— for that matter, Piedmont is very livable; I find many changes, much more governmental benignity than in '47 and more resources. All in all, I am quite happy to have left Paris—the general cancer of Europe—and to have made this choice and none other."[3]

Thus Nice ought to have been his refuge, a place set apart from suffering and struggles. What bond could he feel with the conflicts that were taking place in the little city of the Kingdom of Sardinia? Yet in Nice Herzen suffered particularly violent blows, both in his personal life and in politics. In Nice he was stunned by the tragic loss of his son and his mother at sea. There he watched his wife draw away from him and later return only to die in his arms. Yet he continued to live there not only with a moral commitment but also as an active and brilliant participant in the struggle of ideas of his era.[4]

The epigraph in the first of his *Letters from France and from Italy* from Nice, dated July 10, 1850, asked: "Are you a republic, you Gallic flock?" He was turning to Alfieri, asking him for a confirmation of his desire to preserve the individual above and against all ideology, against all states, against religion. He was also remembering Alfieri when he recalled briefly the bitterness of the *Misogallo*. Alfieri, who was regarded as the genius loci of the little world where he had sought refuge, would have helped him overcome the trouble of a failed revolution.[5] And perhaps Herzen thought briefly of becoming a citizen of the Kingdom of Sardinia.[6]

A year later, on June 1, 1851, Herzen boasted: "I have kept my word. I spent an entire year in my hermitage without having written any ethical-political letters, without having read any published by our friends, and attempting to forget those which had previously fallen into my hands."[7] In reality, the political life had touched him and involved him from the very beginning of his sojourn in Nice.

In May 1850, shortly before leaving for the south, Herzen met Mazzini, whom he had seen in Geneva and Lausanne the previous year. "He was secretly in Paris," Herzen related in his memoirs. "He was staying in an aristocratic house and he sent one of his followers to see me. He told me about the plan for an international committee in London and asked if I intended to participate as a Russian. I changed the subject." Shortly after, on July 22, 1850, the manifesto of the Central European Committee appeared, launching the international body that Mazzini had mentioned to him in Paris. But Mazzini had not given up hope of seeing Herzen's name next to his and those of Ledru-Rollin, the Pole Albert Darasz, and the German Arnold Ruge, all of whom had signed the document. At the beginning of

September, Felice Orsini visited Herzen; Mazzini had charged Orsini with the task of making Herzen "a new proposal." Again the reply was negative.[8] From the time of their very first meetings in Switzerland, Herzen had developed strong doubts and objections to Mazzini's politics, although the doubts were mixed with a deep admiration and personal liking for the man. From Paris he had written to his Prussian friend Johan Jacobi: "I tremble for Mazzini, it seems to me that one more step and he will be, not ahead, as he always has been, but behind. He thinks that things are still eternally the same as in the time of the Bandiera brothers. Noble individuality, poor [an illegible word] but not progressive."[9]

Viewed from Nice, Mazzini's new creation, the Central European Committee, seemed to Herzen to be "without any profound thoughts," "without unity and even unnecessary." As for its form, it simply seemed "wrong." "The aspect of the *movement* that the Committee represented, that is, the reestablishment of oppressed nationalities, was not strong enough in 1851 [*sic,* for 1850] to give life to an *open* organization. The existence of such a committee only showed the tolerance of English legislation."

As for the *secret* societies, Herzen had no faith in them either then or later. Thus, in his eyes, the Committee risked becoming a characteristic product of the "formalism" of "revolutionary bureaucracy": "Even the most serious persons are very easily attracted by formalism, and manage to convince themselves that they are doing something when they meet periodically in assemblies and accumulate piles of paper, protocols, convocations, votes, resolutions, print manifestos, *professions de foi,* etc. Revolutionary bureaucracy breaks things down into words, just as our chancellery bureaucracy does."[10]

For these reasons. Herzen refused to give the support that Orsini had requested. In a long and affectionate letter, he explained his state of mind and his ideas to Mazzini. Once again, as he had in Switzerland, Herzen scolded Mazzini for wanting to use his great and noble personality to shelter a mistaken and failing policy, for seeking to pursue and perpetuate the errors of the democracy of 1848. "It is the continuation of the old liberalism and not the beginning of the new liberty; these are epilogues, not prologues. ... Where is our progress since the Montagne of '92? These men are the Bourbons of the revolution, they have learned nothing." He could not accept the political compromises that had been necessary to unite men of different ideas and intentions in one organization. Nor could he accept the religious facade that he felt would be useful to hide their ideological differences. ("Deism belongs only to the rationalists; it is the constitutional regime in theology, it is a religion surrounded by atheistic institutions.") Thus he intended to remain alone and independent, keeping aloof from people whom he considered "incomplete revolutionaries." "From the age of thirteen to the age of thirty-eight, I served only one idea, I had only one flag: war against all authority, against all slavery in the name of the absolute independence of the individual. I will continue this little partisan war, like a real Cossack, "auf eigene Faust"—as the Germans say—

attached to the great revolutionary army, but without enlisting myself on the rolls—until it is completely reorganized, that is, revolutionized."[11]

Mazzini's reply has not survived. It was burned by Herzen himself at the time of Louis Napoleon's coup d'état in December 1851, when Herzen feared a search of his house. But he summarizes it for us in his memoirs: "He answered with some friendly words. Without touching the heart of the matter, he spoke of the need to unite all forces into a single action, he regretted the disagreement, etc."[12]

In his letter of September 13, Herzen explained to Mazzini the "partisan war" that he intended to wage alone, from his retreat in Nice. He had already prepared a long article on Russia, destined for publication in a German journal, which soon also appeared in a French periodical. *Du développement des idées révolutionnaires en Russie* came out as a series, from January to May 1851, in the *Deutsche Monatschrift*. In May of the same year another edition came out marked Paris, but it had actually been printed at the Imprimerie Canis Frères in Nice.[13]

It was a complete history of Russia, painted in broad strokes, leading dramatically to its culminating point, the oppression of Nicholas I and the intelligentsia's stifled rebellion against that mighty tyranny. It answered precisely the questions that all Europe was asking at that time. Where had Russia come from and where was it headed? What was the relationship between its internal development and its foreign policy? What could Europe expect from the ferment that had been and was being expressed through the Decembrists, through the slavophilic tendencies, and now through the voices of the Russian emigrants? Herzen answered, and his brilliant reply was full of profound intuitions and laden with prophecies on the future of Russian political movements in the decades to follow. This work was one of the most Romantic pieces to come from Herzen's pen. It was also the work in which the intricacies of Russian society and politics were most accurately described.

> In general, Europe has an exaggerated notion of the spiritual power of the Russian emperors. This error has its source, not in Russian history, but in the chronicles of the Bas-Empire . . .
> The question of the emancipation of the serfs is not understood in Europe. They think as a rule that it is only a matter of individual liberty, which is of no importance under the despotism of St. Petersburg. Whereas it means freeing the peasants with the land. . . . The great accusation that literature makes against Russian life, this complete and ardent negation of our own faults, this confession which has a horror of our past, this bitter irony which makes the present blush, is our hope, our health, the progressive element of the Russian nature . . .

The state, the peasants, and the intellectuals were the three essential elements in the drama described by Herzen, which ended with a chapter entitled "On the Rural Commune in Russia." This was the first detailed and accurate description of a Russian village and of the hopes the socialists had for it.

Herzen made his work known and distributed it even in Piedmont. On June 13, 1851, he wrote to his wife with instructions to have a copy of *Du développement* sent to Lorenzo Valerio in Turin, to the editors of *L'opinione,* and to the editors of *Il progresso.* He had sent other copies to be distributed by Ivan Golovin, who was in Turin at the time. But the package was returned and the surprised Herzen insisted that his work should be sent "to the editors of some opposition periodicals" in both Turin and Genoa.[14]

Upon opening the August 1 and August 2 issues of *Il progresso* in 1851, Herzen was able to read, not without interest, a long and fine review of his work. It seems that he never identified its author, but if we read the articles by Cesare Correnti devoted to Russia published in the same paper a few months earlier (November 23, 27, and 30, 1850) it is not difficult to guess that the review came from the same passionate pen.[15] Herzen's book seemed to achieve and confirm the reviewer's hopes, satisfying his desire to know the Muscovite empire from the inside, restating all the problems that Russia brought to his mind and heart. "We, the populations of the West, too often feel the nightmare of Russia. We are accustomed to regarding the empire of the czars as the predestined sacrificer of Latin-Germanic civilization. Russia exerts the fascination of terror upon us." Greek orthodoxy, Panslavism, autocracy—these were great ideas that were a moving force for the Russian state and population. But "were these terrors based on truth? Or would approaching the specter make it assume less gigantic and frightening proportions?" Iskander, "the Russian emigré to whom we owe the book we are examining," was right in saying that Russia was unfamiliar to Europe. Herzen was right to scold the Western populations for living "in a continuous state of alarm over an enemy they do not know." "We are practically ignorant of the internal history of Russia." For a long time Peter, Catherine, and her relationship with Voltaire were all that were known about the country. "Yet in the sinister light of the flames from the Kremlin, Europe began to see Russia, and it regarded the new population with a broad and serious attitude." Then the view of Russia was again obscured. But there was no lack of useful works to acquaint westerners with the moral life of the nation. Adam de Gurowski's book had been "quite fashionable with us because it was printed in Italy."[16] It had "unveiled to the Western world the great force of Panslavism, glorifying it." With his "fine work" *La Russie et les Russes,* published in 1846, N. Turgenev had presented many elements of the social and intellectual ferment in his country. One could now form a strong conviction that it was the development of revolutionary ideas that was the main obstacle to religious and Panslavistic enthusiasm. And now we were provided with an instrument for truly understanding this development. "For the study of the development of the various elements that constitute the liberal opposition in Russia, Monsieur Iskander's book is a clear and knowledgeable guide." In it he traced the route that the Decembrists, the Slavophiles, and the pro-Westerners had opened. It was an intellectual history that led directly to the problem of the Russian revolution.

A natural revolutionary call-up exists in the condition of the Russian peasant, or serf, a condition which is just comparable to the slavery of the Africans. There is a true social revolution is brooding; and the day when the Russian peasant will have found his Spartacus, Russia will present us with the spectacle of a complete internal transformation. The emancipation of slavery by now is in the plans of all the liberal parties in Russia, from the moderate Turgenev, who lovingly studied the state of the peasants, to the socialist Bakunin, who is now paying for the noble audacity of his thoughts and the energy of his character in an Austrian fortress.

Thus, by now the battle had begun. In the very heart of Slavic ideology was "an opposing force that tended to paralyze it," a seed of democracy that was dissolving it. It is one of Russia's illusions that the West is falling, decaying. "The force of democracy is becoming powerful in the West; and rather than corroding and putrefying, it is reviving and purifying. Russian pressure is anticipating and accelerating the democratic constitution of the West." Russia itself seems to feel it, and seems to hesitate and draw back from the decisive battle.

But Russia, autocratic Russia, the holy Russia of the "popes," of the imperial synods, the fanatic Russia that in 1812 set fire to Moscow and shattered the fascination of Napoleonic fatalism, today is waiting, marking time, doubting. It has something like a profound instinct that cannot combat Western ideas except through the method used to conquer Napoleon. It withdraws, entrenches itself in its deserts, delays the advance of the triumphant spirit with Scythian devastation, and awaits the moment of tiredness and confusion and the winter storms. Gurowsky in his threatening loquacity has revealed the secret of official Russia, the secret of its weakness. It is waiting for European civilization to topple by itself, and is not thinking so much of conquering as of inheriting Europe. For autocracy ever to prevail, it would be necessary for civilization and liberty to lead to suicide.

A few weeks later, taking up his pen to write *Le Peuple Russe et le Socialisme. Lettre à Monsieur J. Michelet,* dated September 22, 1851, Herzen does not fail to express his admiration for an efficacious formula against czarism which he had read in this review in *Il progresso* ("It was thus admirably put by a contributor to the journal *Il Progresso* in an article published on 1 August 1851"). And it does not seem mistaken to extend this view to the entire article which had so successfully found a connection between the ideas of the Lombard liberal and those of the Russian revolutionary.

In order to develop and complete the thoughts that he had expressed in *Du développement des idées révolutionnaires,* Herzen soon wrote and published, as a short study, the letter to Michelet mentioned above. This pamphlet too was printed in Nice at the Imprimerie Canis Frères at the end of 1851, and should have been distributed bearing the date of the next year and stamped Paris, "A. Franck Librairie étrangère. Rue Richelieu 67." But this edition was ill-fated. As Herzen related when he published a second edition in London, "This letter, printed in

Nice in 1851, was never circulated outside Piedmont and Switzerland. Almost the entire edition was seized by the customs in Marseille, who forgot to send it back, disregarding any claims."[17]

The pamphlet arose from Herzen's reading of a work that Michelet was writing at that time, which was being published as a series in *L'Evénement* (from August 28 to September 15) and then came out as a pamphlet which was also widely distributed in Italy.[18] This rhapsodic account of the *Légende de Kosciuszko* was entitled "Pologne et Russie." All the prejudices and idolatries of European democrats on Poland and Russia are reflected there as in a burning-glass. And while he was feverishly writing the pages on Poland, Michelet met Herzen. It was on June 17, 1851, when Herzen was traveling in France. The meeting was all the more important for Michelet because he intended to follow his Polish legend with a Russian one, and he was gathering books and notes in order to write his *Martyrs de la Russie* on Pestel, Ryleev, and the Decembrists. It is difficult not to recognize a clear echo of Herzen's words and thoughts when we read that Pestel

was a man of genius, practical, not in the least utopian. He did not make an imaginary Russia for himself. He took her as she was, communistic, and he left her so. He supposed that by strengthening the commune, by freeing it, by making it apply its principle (the land is for those who work it), one had the primitive element, the original molecule of the republic, that in ascending to the *arrondissement* (the commune of communes), to the province, finally to the city, one could more easily move from the Russian element to republican government than to Tartar czarism or German imperialism.

But these great problems of Russia's future and the figures of the free men of the country he was describing seemed to make the background against which they stood appear even more dismal and bleak. Michelet's article, "Le Tzar comme pape et comme dieu," contained a particularly violent condemnation of the regime and of the character and history of Russia. At the end of October, almost as if to excuse himself and torn between a profound hatred for Russia and the equally intense sympathy that he felt for a few of his Russian friends, Michelet asked Herzen, who was back in Nice, to send him news and articles on the revolutionary movement in Russia and on Bakunin. When he had received a few pages by Herzen on Bakunin, he thought of publishing them in *National,* but the Napoleonic coup d'état on December 2 put an end to his studies and his plans.[19] Nevertheless, on November 27 he had managed just in time to publish a note on Herzen's book *Du développement des idées révolutionnaires en Russie:* "An admirable pamphlet has appeared recently. The author, a Russian born, but gifted on the other side with the more generous blood of the Rhine, writes in our language with a heroic vigor.... I have read him ten times with stupefaction.... Alas! it is a condemnation, not only of Russia, but of France and Europe.... As long as Europe has such men, however, things are not yet desperate."

On September 24, 1851, *L'Avenir de Nice* reported Michelet's view, adding, "The French literary movement in Nice, as restrained as it is, produced from time to time some works of merit," such as *Du développement des idées révolutionnaires,* "which has had the honor, not only of arousing some uneasiness among the Muscovite despots, but that, much more precious, of kindling a lively interest among French thinkers. We cite the words of the great historian with the more pleasure because we believe we are able to promise our readers a new work that Monsieur Iscander plans to publish in Nice, and which will worthily follow his first."

For Herzen, whose *Lettre à Monsieur J. Michelet* was presented this way, a reply to the French historian seemed called for. "Speech becomes a duty for us when a man, resting on a great and legitimate authority, has just told us that 'he affirms, he swears, that he will prove that Russia does not exist, that the Russians are not men, that they lack any moral sense.'" The political regime in Russia was disgraceful, but the future "of the Russia of the people, the hidden Russia," was full of hope.

The real problem lay in the possibility that the West would have to carry out the revolution imposed by the times, which was about to misfire in those very years and days. Scorn for Russia would certainly not help this revolution. "To me there is something tragic in this senile distraction with which the old world confounds all its notions concerning its antagonist. In this mass of contradictory opinions we see so much fixed knowledge, such a sad flightiness, such tenacious prejudices, that in spite of ourselves we find no other point of comparison in history than the decay of Rome."

As for Poland, Europe did not recognize that the underlying tendencies were not directed toward a struggle among Slavic populations but toward their future federation. Above all, Michelet had only seen the negative side of Russian "communism." Yet it was in Russia's peasant collective communities that the seed and the possibility of socialist development lay. "The commune has saved the man of the people from Mongol barbarism and from civilized czarism, from lords with European polish and from the German bureaucracy; the communal organism has resisted, however deeply affected by, the encroachments of power, it has fortunately preserved itself until the development of socialism in Europe. For Russia, that is a providential fact...."[20]

It appears that no review of Herzen's second pamphlet was printed in Piedmont. But we know that it was distributed, and it was quoted a few years later, along with the book *Du développement des idées révolutionnaires,* in an article by Ausonio Franchi entitled "Il comune in Russia," which appeared in *Ragione* on December 16, 1854. In fact, the works that Herzen had published in Nice were clearly the main source, if not the only source, used by the author, and the ideas expressed in the article are Herzenian. "In Russia, the principle that informs and governs the organization of the commune is a sort of socialism which was broken down and perverted by the tyrannical despotism of the czar and the nobles. Nevertheless, it contains precious elements for regeneration and with luck it will bring about a more rapid and secure social reorganization among the uncultured peoples than among the so-called civilized ones."

Franchi also quoted Custine and Haxthausen about this, but these were the very authors that Herzen discussed in the pages devoted to the "Commune rurale en Russie." "Information about them," *La ragione* added, "was later both confirmed and corrected by a Russian writer who, in exile, nobly represents the youthful democracy of his race, and from him we have especially acquired the following information about the rural communes in Russia..."[21]

Herzen ended 1851 with a despairing letter from Nice to Proudhon on December 24. But this year had actually marked a major step in Herzen's work, and the contents of the latter, following a natural progression or driven by revolutionary propaganda, had also reached Genoa and Turin.

In Nice, a small colony of Russian emigrés had formed around Herzen. Some had been led to mix in local politics, and this too had affected Herzen's life. The Italian emigration between Genoa, Nice, and Turin, on the other hand, had become an integral part of his everyday life, both at the time of his family tragedy and during the crystallization of his new ideas and hopes. At this time, Herzen and his little group of Russian emigrés had achieved the position and significance of a political group, small in numbers but rich in debates and intuition, closely associated with the Italian and, especially after December 2, 1851, with the French groups.[22] Despite all his difficulties, Herzen tried to reinforce and expand this little circle of Russian immigrants. On August 9, 1951, he wrote to Alexander Alexandrovich Chumikov, a Russian intellectual then en route to Paris, describing the moral and political situation of Europe in that difficult time. He told him about France, Germany, and Russia, and concluded: "Emigration is very useful now, but suitable Russians are very few....Wait until the end of May 1852 and join us. (The Russians who want to remain in Europe never take any precautions, and they lose all their belongings—a generous act but one showing immaturity.) If victory comes to our side, we will work together. Until then, work, speak, and send me material."[23]

Thus, Herzen had faith not only in the importance but also in the possibilities of the development of the little nucleus of emigrés. "The Russian emigration is only a seed, but a seed often contains a great future. The Russian emigration will increase, because its opportunity is obvious, because it represents, not hatred or despair, but love of the Russian people and faith in their future."[24]

Anyone who opened the Nice edition of *Du développement* could read these words, along with a description of Russian emigration which was dropped in later editions: "For ten years we have seen Russians settle in France, not only to be out of their country or to rest, but also to protest vigorously against the despotism of St. Petersburg, to work toward the common liberation. Far from becoming foreigners, they make themselves the free organs of the young Russia, her interpreters."

Conditions in Russia at that time were difficult, and the concessions that those who remained had to make were sad, but Russians were no longer inclined toward suffering and passive endurance. The emigrés would lead the way. "Thus, at this time emigration is the most significant act of opposition that a Russian can perform." Some years had already passed since two young Russian nobles, Bakunin and Golovin, had been among the very first to disobey orders to return to their country. It was to Bakunin that the book was dedicated, and it contained this portrait of him: "Bakunin, profound thinker, ardent propagandist, was one of the hardiest socialists, well before the revolution of February 24th. An officer of Russian artillery, he quitted the cannons to study philosophy, and some years later he abandoned abstract philosophy for concrete philosophy—socialism . . ." He had been the first to protest against the German professors' escape into the abstract; he had been the first to revolt "against this inhuman and heartless abstention which wished to participate in none of the suffering and hardships of modern man, by shutting itself up in an apathetic submission to a fatal necessity invented by themselves. Bakunin did not see any other way to resolve the antinomy between thought and fact than struggle: he became a revolutionary."

In Switzerland and Paris, and later, with the revolution in Germany and Bohemia, his words and actions were heard everywhere. Now he was in prison after the failure of the Dresden uprising: "They claim that he is going to be delivered to Russia. . . . That he goes thus into the snows of Siberia to press the hand of those glorious old men, exiled in 1826, that he goes, followed by our prayers, into that great Russian cemetery where so many martyrs of our cause are resting. Bakunin, succumbing at the same time as the German revolution and going to Siberia for Germany, perhaps on the eve of war with Russia, will serve as a sign and a proof of the sympathy that exists between the peoples of the West and the revolutionary minority in Russia."

Only a few months after these words were written, news reached Nice that Bakunin had died in the Schlüsselburg fortress. It was not true, but evidently Herzen and the emigrés who had gathered around him believed the rumor. On October 31, *L'Avenir de Nice* published a long obituary notice about Bakunin, said to be written by "another Russian patriot, a noble and great heart." It contained the words quoted above, and went on: "Alas, Bakunin will not even have had the supreme consolation of mingling his bones with those of the heroes of the 14th of December. But his thought will remain united to theirs, and when the impending day of European liberation comes, Bakunin will take his place alongside the glorious elders of 1826 on the altar which the people raise in their heart to those who live and die for them."

In Nice, in addition to knowing the little group of Russian emigrés, Herzen soon became acquainted with Frenchmen who began to seek refuge there; fleeing persecution, these men preceded the sizable stream of French emigrés who poured into the city after the coup of December 2. In 1850, one typical French refugee was

Jacques Mathieu, a lawyer born in La Garde Freinet (Var) who had democratic and socialist ideas. One of the chapters in *My Past and Thoughts* is devoted to him.

Herzen describes in ironic tones Mathieu's vain attempts at revolution, seeing in him an example of the traditional revolutionary, the professional democrat and conspirator. In those years in particular, such men aroused the resentment of a defeated man and the bitter criticism of a man who, unlike most, could see the moral and political roots of the failure he experienced.[25] The irony of Herzen's prose was so powerful that Jacques Mathieu was virtually erased from the historical record. Even the most recent Soviet editor, punctilious though he generally is, had no explanation to add about who this French emigré was. But Mathieu improves on closer examination. He provides a characteristic example of the socialist, Proudhonian, and rebellious ferment that filtered from France into the Kingdom of Sardinia after 1848. "A young member of the Paris bar . . . wounded on the barricades of February 24, he had returned to his family in La Garde Freinet and, once cured, committed himself with all the ardor of his age to republican propaganda. Sentenced for a political offense, he preferred exile to prison and sought refuge in Nice."[26]

In Nice Mathieu published a little book called, *La Révolution française du février 1848. Détails inédits sur la formation du gouvernement provisoire dans les bureaux du "National," sur la proclamation de ce gouvernement à la Chambre des Députés, et sur celle de la république à l'Hôtel de Ville.* It was printed in 1850 by the same publisher who printed *Du développement.* The author's name was followed by the titles "ex-Procureur de la République, à Draguignan, et ex-Maire révoqúe de la Garde Freinet (Var)."[27] The following year the book was translated into Italian and published in Genoa under the title *Dettagli inediti sui principali avvenimenti della rivoluzine francese del febbraio 1848 per J. Mathieu, ex procuratore della Repubblica. Prima versione dal Francese per G. M.* The writer of the introduction praised "the sincerity of the story" and the interest of the facts described. "Oh, magnanimous hearts, let this offering of mine arouse your indignation against the French republic that assassinated its legitimate Roman sister." One also had to remember "the protests of the minority and of many generous hearts and the deception of the public. For the Italians and the French, let God make the star of disabuse shine in all its clarity." Nor, he concluded, should one give in to despair. Why believe in the prophets of doom, in those who foresaw reactions and tragedies? "The servants of despotism, like owls in a graveyard, predicted the arrival of Russians in Paris, and their views have already been scattered by the winds for three years."

In fact, Jacques Mathieu could still arouse hope and enthusiasm with his vivid account of the events of those years in Paris. Even the most tragic events were explained as errors, as failures on the part of the democrats; he implied or even explicitly added that these could be corrected in the future. "The unfortunate events of May and June 1848" according to him were "due to the fact that the Assembly had shown its opposition to social reforms, had displayed its impatience and a republican lack of discipline."[28] "The demonstration of 1849, because of its peaceful character, was the cruelest of all the errors which the democracy made!... Was it not a true folly to present oneself unarmed, bare-chested before such a bloodthirsty enemy?"[29]

But Jacques Mathieu reserved his true thoughts for a book published in 1852, again at the Imprimerie Canis Frères, entitled *Le Vol et la tyrannie consacrés par la législation française*. Directly beneath the title were a peremptory appeal, "Plus de lois," and some phrases from Proudhon: "Laws! We know what they are and what they are worth. Spider webs for the rich and powerful, chains that no dagger could break for the small and poor, fishing nets in the hands of government." The entire book was inspired by Proudhon's anarchy. It consisted of a systematic examination of the civil code; the procedural codes; the codes of commerce, fishing, forestry, and hunting; the rules of administration, taxation, the army, and the press; electoral laws, etc. As one can see, it was a complete treatise on legislation, or, to be more precise, antilegislation. In fact, Mathieu's book was a rhapsody that contained nevertheless a remarkable nucleus of ideas that were characteristic and symptomatic of the post-1848 years.

The law was his hatred, his enemy. He wanted to shake off the legislative past of France. His great adversaries were absolutist and Jacobin traditions, the legalistic and hierarchical spirit. "National sovereignty has entirely disappeared under the floods of this lying and hypocritical legality.... The legal chain is wrapped with so much art around society.... We are fashioned by this degrading yoke to such an extent, the poison of legalism has so ravaged us, that instead of recognizing legislation as the cause of our oppression and ruin, we see in it the fruits of a model civilization."[30]

Yet one had only to look at life in French society to realize what degradation the laws and the state had led to. The pettiest and meanest exclusiveness prevailed in relationships between Frenchmen and other populations. All provisions concerning foreigners in France were oppressive, not just those emanating from reactionary governments. "The people too were proscribers in February 1848, when, acceding to the perfidious suggestions of the reactionaries, they repulsed at the borders the workers of Belgium, Savoy, etc., toward whom even the monarchy had been hospitable."[31] For political emigrés the situation was even worse, especially when it involved persons coming from countries that expected their subjects to return. "The Russians and the Neapolitans"[32] lost their original citizenship when they resisted the injunctions of their sovereigns. And what France done to help them? Politically, the situation was even worse. One had only to consider the "assassination of the Roman republic."[33] Internally, the law for the French citizens did nothing but consecrate and create injustice. The family situation, the position of women, the insecurity of all who were neither rich nor powerful, described at length by Mathieu, were clear proof of this fact. The situation of the proletariat was the most shocking example.

Until then, what had been done about this situation? Very little, even by the democratic parties.

Revolutions have been constantly the fruit of instinct, of the vague need for novelty and undetermined improvements. Science has counted for nothing in them: it is this that explains their sterility; an idea, though it be essentially useful, can triumph only under the condition that it is grounded on faith and that the entire society takes an interest in its fate. Now, the socialist or revolutionary program has never satisfied these two conditions. For example, all revolutionaries in general have proclaimed the right to education, which alone is capable of creating unshakable convictions; but once this homage has been rendered to principle, they avoid its application and generations continue to wallow in ignorance. Equality has always been their war horse, which has not prevented them from excluding women, that is, a third of the members of society, from political and social life. . . . They rebelled against oppression, only to become oppressors.[34]

To prevent this from occurring in the future, it was necessary to rebuild the entire structure from the bottom up, starting with the commune which would be the basic element in the new social framework of France. "The omnipotence of the commune should succeed the omnipotence of the state."[35] This was the only way to break down bureaucracy and eradicate despotism altogether. The communes would be autonomous in all that concerned education, justice, and administration. There, if anywhere, it would be possible to achieve equality, or at least "the right to live by working."[36] Cooperatives would facilitate the realization of this program, and Mathieu recalled how one had been created during the 1848 revolution in his town, at La Garde Freinet.[37] But he had since begun to appreciate another model. Herzen had introduced him to the peasant communities in Russia, the *obshchina,* and the Russian author's description in his book *Du développement des idées révolutionnaires en Russie* had clearly impressed Mathieu. In fact, he quotes extensively from Herzen's pamphlet,[38] concluding, "It is due to a constitution analogous to communal proprietorship that Russia does not know a proletariat." The condition of the Russian peasants, even if they were serfs, did not seem worse than that of French workers who were free only to die of hunger and were slaves of capital, and who, when they tried to escape exploitation, were "tracked down, like a wild beast, under the pretext of coalition."[39] Certainly the potential in Russia was not identical to that existing in Western Europe. "Unlike Russia, France does not have immense steppes to distribute to her inhabitants, but she does have 80 billion in land, 30 billion in products, merchandise, furnishings . . . the national and communal assets are worth at least 10 billion, and the private and public wealth is thus in the neighborhood of 162 billion, not counting the colonial wealth. . . ."[40]

If all this national wealth had been distributed in the municipalities, the principles that Herzen had taught Mathieu could have been applied in France: "It is the commune that owns the land, and its inhabitants have the use of it."[41]

But for this to happen, it was necessary above all to abolish all laws, according to what Mathieu repeated in concluding his book. Traditional democratic theory derived from Rousseau had led to oppression and hypocrisy. The idea of a direct government by the people, upheld by Ledru-Rollin, Girardin, Considérat, and Rittinghausen, was utopian.[42] Such a government would have also brought about domination by landlords, by the wealthy, by the only people able to look after public affairs. "The people properly speaking, that is, the laborers, the peasants, the shopkeepers, the tradesmen, in a word, the workers, would have been excluded. Would it be possible for them, in fact, to abandon their business, the work by which they earn their bread ... to make laws?"[43] The government of Athens, based on slaves, would have arisen again, only to then fall into the hands of those who did not work. "The laws would no longer be the work of a few hundred reactionaries, but the work of all the reactionaries of France. That would be all that the people would gain from that innovation."[44] There was no alternative but to base oneself on the integral government of the "communes," abrogating at once all existing laws, allowing men and women to find support through the natural principles of equality. "One could mend and remend the law, change its source and its effects, it would not be any less disastrous and incompatible with democratic principle."[45]

In Mathieu, Proudhon's ideas, with Herzen's influence, produced a vision that on one hand was a precursor of Bakunin's anarchism and on the other hand reflected the radicalism of the small bitter rebellion of the French *petits ouvriers*.

After having read Mathieu's book, it is not surprising to learn that the Piedmontese authorities had been worried for some time about his activities. After about a year's stay in Nice, he was expelled at the end of May 1851, to return later. Immediately after the December 2 coup d'état, he asked Herzen for support (also financial) and made a vain attempt to reach the Var insurgents. For this he was again expelled by the Piedmontese authorities. He had been interned in San Remo but was there only a short time before again managing to return to Nice. The French consul was dismayed and discouraged by this. "I went immediately to the Intendant General," who repeated his assurances that exiles would be kept under surveillance. But as for Mathieu, "this refugee had gone to Turin to complain, and as there were no charges against him other than those which were made against the refugees in general, he was allowed to return to Nice, on the condition that he submit to whatever measures of surveillance the Intendant General deemed necessary."[46]

Moreover, as the Judge Advocate General of Nice wrote on October 25, 1852 to the Minister of Justice, even when Mathieu was far from Nice "it was easy for him to find ways to publish his booklets ... as he maintained many close ties in this city." It was a reading of *Le Vol et la tyrannie* that convinced this high magistrate of the need to intervene. "With a virulent style, he combats the laws and institutions" of France, "using this opportunity to present certain absurd and ridiculous doctrines derived from the socialist school to which the author of this booklet seems to belong." On October 18, he was "interned in Turin by ministerial order." There he was notified that he had been expelled. On October 29, he tried in vain to obtain at least a deferment, pointing out that Napoleon III's French government "will not go to war over a ten-day reprieve." But a Turinese official wrote on his letter, "The undersigned regrets not to be able to approve this request."[47] So he moved to Geneva, where Herzen sent him greetings through Carl Vogt at the beginning of April 1853.[48] He sent for "his Luisa" from Nice and ardently hoped to begin life again in Switzerland. But on an unknown date not long before 1854, he was already dead.[49]

Mathieu's fate had been harsher than that of many other French exiles who had found refuge in Nice. They, too, had to undergo the succession of internments, forced residence, expulsions, and intermittent aid. Despite French diplomatic pressures on the Turin government to expel everyone, for a few years they nevertheless managed to continue to live in the territory of the Kingdom of Sardinia, though in a precarious and difficult situation. There were several hundred French exiles, mainly workers from Provence, who eventually became assimilated into the life of Nice. But there were other intellectuals and writers besides Mathieu, whose experiences we have described.[50] Probably the most interesting figure among them was Henri Dameth, who also established contacts with the Russian and Italian exiles gathered in Nice.[51]

Henri Dameth, born in 1812, became a Fourierist and defended his master's doctrines against those of Proudhon. After the 1848 revolution he began publishing short essays on socialist doctrines (for example, a pamphlet called *Solidarité. Propagation et réalisation populaires de la science sociale. Le crédo socialiste,* which came out in Paris in 1849). He attributed a significant role to the "commune," conceived as "a little world," an "integral organization" in which "all the essential functions of social life take place" (p. 14). The commune was to become the realization of Fourierist phalanstery, its incarnation in the real world. "Maître de conférences d'histoire au Collège Louis-le-Grand, professor à l'Institut Polytechnique de Paris," editor of *National,* Dameth, like Herzen, was a victim of the June 13, 1849 demonstration organized by the "Montagne" to fight against the French expedition that was intended to crush the Roman republic. In prison, he watched his situation worsen, and it did not improve even when he was finally freed.[52] Thus he had hastened to accept the offer, made to him in the winter of 1850–51, of a position in Nice on the newspaper financed by Carlone and Avigdor. The paper was to be called *L'Avenir de Nice,* and it became the organ of the left-wing opposition to the Turin government, expressing various degrees of municipalism, sympathy for the French Republic, and anticlerical radicalism. Dameth had accepted the position on condition that he would also be given the post of professor of political economy at the Nice School of Commerce. Only with two salaries would he be able to support himself; only by spreading his ideas both in a newspaper and from the rostrum could his voice be heard. He obtained all that he requested and settled in Nice. Thus he was not a true exile, but his ideas and his political activity made him an adversary of the French government and of his consular representative, Leon Pillet. "*L'Avenir de Nice* is an opposition newspaper that is very advanced in the demagogic sense," said Pillet. "Even though it is published in a monarchy, it openly preaches... the republican form of government.... it threatens despots and reactionaries of all nations incessantly with the rising of the people."[53] In fact, from its first issue (published on August 19, 1850) *L'Avenir de Nice* was openly anticlerical; it often quoted the republican Genoese newspapers and the Parisian *Démocratie pacifique,* printed long extracts from Brofferio's *Storia del Piemonte,* advertised the "Memorie e documenti intorno al governo della Repubblica Romana" by Felice Orsini, and printed articles by F. Pyat. It became a voice of the movement for a democratic and socialist revival in France. Even if its methods were eclectic, it knew how to fight the campaign of left-wing opposition against both Turin and Paris. It expressed particularly vigorous opposition to Louis Napoleon, demanding that he submit to the will of the assembly; it objected to his usurpation and stressed the European importance of the events in Paris in the long months that preceded the coup d'état of December 2, 1851. As for Piedmont, *L'Avenir de Nice* openly and tenaciously upheld the need to "defend and develop" the Statuto, the constitution given by Charles Albert in 1848. In the constitution, the newspaper saw the symbol of the country's hope and a strong starting point (March 3, 1851). "We shall not make a systematic opposition to the Sardinian government"–on condition, naturally, that that government strengthen the struggle against the church, that it create a broad policy of economic improvements and cease to persecute the free press. To Dameth the social situation in Piedmont seemed particularly suited for the development of such a policy. Economic liberalism–without fearing intimidation of the proletariat–this was the economic plan of *L'Avenir de Nice.*

On April 21, 1851, Dameth wrote: "Open wide the doors of the country, don't listen to miserable fears, don't do petty politics when you have the sentiments, the convictions, of the great.... Do you fear the hobgoblin of the millions of industrial proletarians behind whom the protectionists of France and Belgium hide in order to conceal their egoism? Get to the bottom of things and you will see that your reservations have no more value than the false doctrines of your enemies...."

The course in political economics that Dameth taught at Nice was inaugurated at the end of January 1851 in the presence of the authorities, including the superintendent general. Its main purpose was to present modern economic doctrines, to discuss in detail the socialist doctrines of Fourier, Considérant, Louis Blanc, Cabet, and Proudhon, not specifically approving any of them but showing the full importance of social problems and making the ruling class truly aware of the task that awaited it in the world that was emerging from the 1848 revolution.[54]

It was during this course that difficulties began to arise. The course was cancelled temporarily, but when it began again it became an object of suspicion and criticism. "It was not long before his doctrines began to worry the government, the Council of Surveillance of the School of Commerce was equally concerned, and M. Dameth was asked to tender his resignation, which he did."[55] He was able to start again, but the initial impetus was lost and the meaning of his course was no longer so clear and explicit.

Then for Dameth, as for Mathieu, came expulsion from the Kingdom of Sardinia at the end of May 1851. At the same time L'Avenir de Nice was banned in France.[56] Dameth made some political maneuvers; he contacted the French consul and requested and obtained permission to go to Turin to defend his work to the ministers, "and especially to M. Cavour." Eventually he was able to return to Nice. He took up his work again for a little over a year without substantially modifying his political attitude, though by now his situation was becoming increasingly difficult, especially because of the separatist trend that was gaining strength among the backers of his paper, a trend that eventually replaced problems of liberty and political economy with a national problem. A reading of L'Avenir de Nice from the end of 1851 and early 1852 shows how Dameth nevertheless managed to continue to focus on social problems and ideas, devoting long discussions especially to Proudhon's doctrines, reproducing in August 1852 long passages and entire chapters of his works. Politically, Dameth's immediate conclusions were by now clearly constitutional. For example, on October 19, 1851, he wrote, "The instruments of political progress are universal suffrage, a parliamentary regime, the separation of powers, the constitution." Other means would be found in the future, and these could be modified over the years and decades to follow. "But to destroy them before new tools are sprung from their loins, as it were, and are spontaneously substituted for them would be madness." Therefore, he not only supported any effort by Piedmont to maintain liberty, but he also observed with satisfaction, on September 18, 1852, that "neither freedom of the press nor the separation of church and state received any check in Piedmont following the December 2d usurpation."

But it was this very comparison between France and the Kingdom of Sardinia that led to another expulsion. Pressure from the French embassy in Turin (and from the consulate in Nice) became more insistent and vigorous. On December 23, 1851, the minister was able to assure the consul. "I have received from the Sardinian government formal assurance that all the refugees will be the object of rigorous surveillance."[57] And a few months later, on October 5, 1852, he was able to announce that "the Piedmontese government has just ordered Signor Dameth's expulsion from states of the Sardinian monarchy."[58]

On October 9, 1852, Dameth was in Turin, where in a long letter he explained what he had done in Nice, and how, collaborating on L'Avenir de Nice, "I made a purely separatist and ultra-radical journal into a defender of the constitutional institutions of Piedmont."[59] Meanwhile, in Nice, his newspaper protested violently and declared plainly that it no longer wanted to state its views, since the possibility of expressing itself openly had been denied. Its tone was becoming more bitter, marked by increasing diffidence toward the Turin government. This alienation of those who still supported the ideals of 1848, of those who were still fighting against Louis Napoleon's France, rendered the national aspect of political life in Nice more and more bitter. On October 26 *L'Avenir de Nice* published Dameth's farewell letter.

Like Mathieu, Dameth went to Geneva. In fact, he later returned to Piedmont, and at one point was asked to become the director of the School of Commerce in Nice where he had given his course in political economy a few years earlier. The French Embassy became involved in the affair and in 1854 again managed to take the position from him.[60] In Turin, in September of that year, he published *Etude sur la méthode en économie politique,* in which, among other things, he took up his often repeated argument with the socialists and with Proudhon. "If the *socialization* of capital (if I may use the word) is voluntary" (joint-stock company, etc.), it could be regarded positively, but it would hardly change the fate of the workers. Instead, "the forced association of capital" was communism, and this ideal, that had "skirted all of history without ever being able to take its place there, except as an exception..." had always demonstrated its inferiority when compared with the principle of private property.[61] The pamphlet was "presented at the competition for the Chair in political economy at the Academy of Geneva." There he finally became a professor in 1855.[62] He continued to be a prolific writer, though not a very original one. In 1869, in Paris, he published a book entitled *Le Mouvement socialiste et l'économie politique.* Here he again reviewed all the themes of his career as a journalist, not forgetting "Russian and Polish socialism" and the importance he attributed to the "Slavic commune": "It comprises in his eyes, all the elements of social renovation in the communist sense that he pursues."

But we must return to Nice and Piedmont. In the spring of 1851 the government of Turin resolved to abolish Nice's status as a free port, which was considered an unjust and damaging privilege inherited from the past. In the context of general customs reforms and broad financial transformation, Nice too should integrate into the state that had resulted from the trials of 1848 and 1849. In May, the protests of the people of Nice became loud and violent and developed into unrest in the streets. The leaders of this local reaction included Jules Avigdor, an influential figure in commerce and in the city council, and A. Carlone, a banker. Supporting them, naturally, was *L'Avenir de Nice,* which carried out a spirited campaign in defense of the free port and generally in support of the county's interests. The French consul, examining the two sides of the dispute, could foresee in his dispatch of May 18, 1851 that the last word would go to the Piedmontese authorities. But he did not deny that the situation was rather worrying. "Whatever interest the working class of Nice can take in the cause of the free port, in view of the number and dispositions of the garrison, no action appears to me to have any chance of success."[63] In Turin, the semiofficial newspapers, such as the

Gazzetta piemontese and the *Risorgimento,* vigorously defended the general economic principles that had dictated the government's policies and indignantly denounced the attempted defense of the "ancient privileges of the province." The
opposition newspapers drew attention to the extremely difficult position that
would confront the economy of Nice; they stressed how ill-equipped the county
was to face the new customs regime, as it lacked an adequate road network, good
communication, and trade that would link it effectively with other Sardinian states.
While arguing with the municipalistic and Francophile extremism of *L'Avenir de
Nice,* they tried to understand and justify the agitation that was increasingly per-
vading the Mediterranean city. The Genovese newspapers, under Mazzini's influence, were calmer and more moderate in their defense of the Nice disturbances,
partly for nationalistic reasons and partly because they reflected the opinion of
the working class of the port, which was not in favor of competition from Nice.
They could not be insensitive, said *Il povero* on June 1, toward "a population
crying out for bread, a population rising up against the suffering that threatens
it..." But, as for the free port, "they still recognized an anachronism...incom-
patible even with the civilization of the previous century, that in one State there
should be a diversity of contributing countries, those who benefit and those who
suffer, those who are taxed and those who are not." They fought openly against
the government policy, which they considered "harmful, inopportune, and even
reckless," but basically they approved its main purpose.

Finally, after the May 19 and 20 demonstrations, the superintendent general,
Alessandro Radicati di Marmorito, began repressive action.[64] Jules Avigdor was
arrested, a request for the expulsion of two Frenchmen was sent to Turin, and
other measures were prepared against the little foreign world in Nice. "It is unfortunately too true," wrote the consul on May 20, "that among the leaders the
number of French refugees is rather large, and by refugees I don't mean only
political refugees, I mean a crowd of bad workers or small shopkeepers who were
forced by the state of their affairs to leave France."[65] On May 28, Dameth and
Mathieu received orders to leave the Sardinian states immediately. A few days
later, on June 4, *L'Avenir de Nice* announced: "M. Hertzen Iscander, author of
the *Développement des idées révolutionnaires en Russie,* has just been expelled
from our city, where he lived quietly with his family."[66]

Herzen relates this episode in *My Past and Thoughts.* His tone is not without
irony, for the event was even more peculiar for him as he was preparing at that
very time to leave Nice for Switzerland.[67]

It seems that my expulsion was caused by the zeal of two or three faithful
Russian subjects who had come to Nice. Among them I am pleased to name
Minister of Justice Panin. He could not tolerate the fact that someone who had
brought upon himself the most high wrath of Nikolai Pavlovich not only could
live peacefully but could even reside in the same city that Nikolai Pavlovich was
visiting, and that this man should write little articles knowing that His Majesty
the Emperor did not tolerate it. They say that on going to Turin, he asked Min-

ister d'Azeglio, an old friend, to expel me. Nevertheless, in his heart d'Azeglio guessed that in the dungeons of the Kruticky monastery where I had been imprisoned in Moscow, I had learned Italian by reading *La disfida di Barletta,* a novel that was "neither classical nor archaic," though boring, and he took no action . . .

Though this may be what happened, the responsibility had fallen on the superintendent general of Nice, who, when the disturbances mentioned above occurred, ordered the expulsion. Herzen's family was convinced that "Alexander had been expelled for the books he had printed here," as his mother wrote on May 31– June 1, 1851.[68] Herzen went to the highest administrative authority in Nice, the superintendent general himself; he became convinced that the action against him had originated with that very official. "I wrote about my conversation to the famous opposition deputy, Lorenzo Valerio, and then left for Paris."

We do not know whether the two men, Herzen and Valerio, had known each other previously. Nor do we know if Herzen, when he wrote his letter from Nice, had in mind the Italo-Slavic Society that Valerio had tried to create two years earlier. It is known, however, that the two men developed a high regard for each other and later remained in contact. Following a request by Michelangelo Pinto, Herzen sent Valerio the first German edition of his memoirs.[69] In a letter dated September 1861, Herzen recalled how "in 1850 and 1851" Valerio had been a "good and ardent man."[70] In 1863 he consulted with Valerio about the plan (which was never realized) to move the press and editorial office of his *Campana* to Florence.[71] The following year, when V. N. Kashperov, a musician, composer, and friend of Ogarev and Herzen, met Valerio, he wrote on February 14, 1864 from Lake Como, "Is it true that Bakunin is in Turin? Valerio is asking. A propos, could Valerio have a few copies of 'La Cloche'? He wants them very much. If yes, address them to: Como, Lorenzo Valerio."[72] Herzen was very glad of this news and was quick to send Valerio the French edition of his *Kolokol.*[73]

There was never any lack of gratitude in the tenacious bond that linked Herzen to Valerio. In fact, when he received Herzen's letter from Nice with the news of the French and Russian exiles' expulsion, which was also urged by Ivan Golovin, Valerio did not delay in vigorously intervening in the Parliament of the Kingdom of Sardinia. On June 11, the Turin newspapers reported the speech Valerio had given the day before on Nice and on the consequences of the movements that had developed there.

The *Gazzetta del popolo* was more effective than other papers in describing the atmosphere of that session and that debate. "When Valerio took the floor, there was profound silence." For him, and for others in the left-wing opposition, the Nice question was not a matter of "historical rights." "There are no other rights than those that come from the Constitution." It was a political and economic question. He wondered "if it is just to remove from Nice that which forms its life without first putting the city in a situation equal to the rest of the State. First provide the district of Nice with a good road system and then perhaps the Niçois

themselves will ask for the abolition of the free port." For the moment, he proposed to maintain the status quo, "but restricted to the city alone," and also to
preserve differential rights "until a good road system is completed." In other words,
Valerio was suggesting a compromise that convinced only a few members of Parliament, and which was evidently dictated more by his knowledge of the gravity of
the political problem than by economic needs. This was terrain in which Valerio
could boast of having taken a strong position based on a clear evaluation of the
situation. The "ill humor and fatigue" running high in Nice could not be attributed
to the agitators and instigators. It had been the government, with its shortsighted-
ness, that had created the mood. The discontent had not existed two years earlier.
"At that time, I myself saw that the city was enthusiastic about our cause, which
was also its own." Then the government had done everything possible to discour-
age the forces that sympathized with Italy's democratic movement. The most
reactionary magistrates, dismissed from other regions, had been sent, of all places,
to Nice. The "constitutional and Italian" newspaper *Popolare nizzardo* had been
obstructed in every way, "even to the point of the transfer of a postal employee,
because he wrote for the paper." By supporting the clergy, the government had
played into the hands of the separatists, even "preaching that France is more
Catholic than we are." By supporting the reactionary party, the government had
taken the solid ground from under its own feet, and now complained that that
party had undertaken the defense of local privileges, of autonomy, and perhaps
of separation. The expulsions had simply been the final sensational example of
these ruinous contradictions. In the official account of the session, we read:[74]

You are expelling from Nice Mr. Mathieu of Draguignan, who wrote an article
in "L'Avenir de Nice." But the strange thing is, you see, that in this article, in
which he compared the policies of the French and Piedmontese governments,
he bestowed all his praise on Piedmont and all the blame on the French, and yet
you banish him from Nice. You banish from Nice Mr. Dameth, the distinguished
French economist and author. . . . And still that is not enough. At the same time
two famous Russian exiles are banished from Nice. One is Mr. Herzen, a renowned
statesman who not long ago published in one of Germany's main newspapers a
scholarly work with which no one found any fault, on the movement of revolutionary ideas in Russia. Mr. Herzen published the same work in French in Nice
and established its public sale and deposit in France . . . ; in it, with the talent of a
historian and the viewpoint of a citizen, he briefly surveyed the past events of
the Slavic Empire. Well, Mr. Herzen, who had been living quietly in Nice for a
year, who there had spent 100,000 lire a year, who has a mother, a wife, and
children, had the day before obtained a passport to leave the city voluntarily
to look after his own affairs. But the day before his departure, the superintendent
gave him orders to leave within twenty-four hours. Why? Why such a useless and
beastly act? When questioned, the superintendent answered, "Because you are a
republican." But the distinguished exile rightly responded, "Have I made republican propaganda in Piedmont?" And the superintendent was silent because Mr.

Herzen respected Piedmont's hospitality and had never even shown an inclination to spread propaganda in our country. But still this was not enough. Mr. Ivan Golovin, the knowledgeable economist and distinguished statesman who had fled to Nice, was also sought by the police in order to be exiled. And what was the crime of this illustrious writer, this exile from Russia? He had never been involved in Piedmontese politics, but while writing in a Parisian newspaper, he had let flow from his pen an innocent epigram on the name of the Imperial Russian Minister of Justice who was staying at that time in Nice. In an article, Mr. Ivan Golovin had dared say that *Panin,* the Russian minister, was not a dwarf *(Pas nain).* And this was his sin! He had dared express innocent sarcasm about a minister of the autocracy, and immediately the police were on his tracks! Yet Mr. Ivan Golovin had lived so tranquilly and studiously in Nice that for the past month he had been in Turin and the police had been unaware of the fact that this very dangerous man had left Nice a month before and had been quietly living in Turin. Now I ask you, must we sanction such a system? . . . Must we become agents of the Russian police?[75]

In reply to Valerio, the minister of the interior, Galvagno, made meek and embarrassed declarations that were a prelude to a closing of the affair in favor of the expelled men. The main figure accused in the Nice agitations, J. Avigdor, had already been freed by the local magistrates. *L'Avenir de Nice* openly continued its campaign. As for Dameth and Mathieu, Galvagno said, "they had been expelled as agitators, not by the state, but by the city of Nice. As for Herzen and Golovin, he knew of their departure, but not the reasons, because the intendent general had not yet made his report." He declared that he "knew absolutely nothing about what had led the intendent general to exercise the authority given to him by the government under the urgent circumstances." In addition, *Il progresso* stressed the fact that Galvagno had also declared that "if the government had made a mistake, it would also make reparations." As for the *Gazzetta del popolo,* it was ironic about the "Minister who does not understand the reasons." *L'Avenir de Nice* insisted,

On the subject of the two Russians, M. Galvagno makes a strange admission: what are then the extraordinary powers delegated to the superintendent general that he can on his own initiative expel two foreigners of whom no complaint has been made and of whom, eleven days after this expulsion, the minister does not yet know why such a severe step has been taken? What was M. Herzen's crime, or the danger that he posed to the state, that made the intendent general wish (as we have been told) that he not be allowed to use a passport visaed for Switzerland two days earlier, seeing that the length of his voyage across Piedmont would delay by two days his leaving the state?

Finally, there is no doubt that Valerio's speech on the expulsions carried out by Radicati constituted a minor but significant success for the opposition. As Herzen wrote later in his memoirs, "As a result, *de facto* the expulsion order was removed. Although I wrote a letter to the minister, he did not reply."[76]

Meanwhile, Herzen was traveling. After having been in Paris and Switzerland, on his way back he decided to pass through Turin.

There I went to the Minister of the Interior. I was received not by him, but by a substitute, the head of the police, Count Ponza di San Martino, a man known in those districts; intelligent, clever, and devoted to the Catholic party. His welcome astonished me. He told me everything I had meant to tell him.... He was elderly, thin, sickly, and repugnant in appearance, with evil looking and sharp features. He also had a clerical appearance, with his straight gray hair. Before I could open my mouth about the reason for my request for an audience with the minister, he interrupted me saying, "But for goodness sake, how can you have any doubts? ... Go to Nice, or go to Genoa, or stay here, only without the slightest *rancune.* We will be pleased.... The superintendent arranged all this.... You see, we are still apprentices, we are not accustomed to legalities, to the constitutional regime. If you had done anything against the law, there would have been the court, and you would not have had cause to complain about injustice, is that not so?" "I agree entirely." "And one takes measures that arouse anger ... and that cause unnecessary shouting." After this speech against *himself,* he quickly took a sheet of paper with the Minister's letterhead and wrote: "Mr. A. Herzen has permission to return to Nice and stay there as long as is convenient for him. On behalf of the Minister: S. Martino, July 12, 1851." "Here you are, in case of need. But you can be sure you will not need this document. I am very pleased to have put an end to this affair with you." Since, *vulgariter,* this meant, "Go away," I left my Count Ponza, smiling at the prospect of the Nice superintendent's face. But God did not allow me to see him. He was transferred.[77]

Thus Herzen returned to Nice.[78] Naturally the situation was more difficult for the others who had been expelled with him. As we have seen, Dameth managed to persuade the authorities of his liberal and constitutional good will. On July 16, 1851, he again took up his work at *L'Avenir de Nice.* As for Golovin, he eventually concluded that he could more effectively carry out his work as a journalist in Turin.

Of the other Russian emigrés in Nice besides Herzen, there was one who was more peculiar than the rest. Vladimir Aristovich Engelson was born in 1821 and was educated in the secondary school of the capital. When he was about twenty, he began to frequent the Fourierist groups that Petrashevsky was creating in St. Petersburg. When these seeds of revolutionary ideas were repressed in 1848–49, Engelson left Russia to seek refuge abroad.[79] Herzen has given us a sketch of both Engelson and his wife. It is one of those extraordinary psychological portraits of which he was a master.[80]

Engelson declared himself to be a follower of both Petrashevsky and Speshnev (the man Dostoyevsky called his Mephistopheles). Thus he was part of the extremist wing of the Russian Fourierist movement.[81] As Herzen wrote, it was because of this that he felt as much sympathy as repulsion for him, as if he were an abnormal child of his ideas and of his propaganda, "a rather new type." "I saw only the seeds of his type in the forties. It developed in St. Petersburg at the end of

Belinsky's career and was fully formed after my departure for exile, before Cherny-shevsky appeared."[82] To use a general but not incorrect term, Engelson was the first "nihilist" Herzen ever met. Herzen maintained him at his house in Nice, listened to him, advised him, shared the suffering of those years with him, introduced him to the Italian circle which included Mordini, Pisacane, Orsini, Medici, Cosenz, and followed him in the slow and difficult maturation of his political ideas.

We can guess what concepts he brought from Russia when he moved to France by reading the article on the Petrashevsky circle that he wrote at Herzen's invitation and which Herzen sent to Michelet.[83] The head of the Russian Fourierists, Petrashevsky, was presented as an example of a gifted, ingenuous person.

If Barbier, speaking of the *sainte canaille,* meant grandiose simplicity, purity of motives, the courage of consequences, exemption from all roguery, the absence of any second thoughts arising from personal vanity—qualities that unhappily are only found these days among men of the people, and in the other classes of society only as rare exceptions—Petrashevsky can, without the slightest exaggeration, be considered a saint. The street urchin who goes to die on the barricade without regret if after his death someone will remember him, and who, victorious, forgets to claim any office or decoration for himself, that was Petrashevsky. He was an urchin, not by the system or by deliberate action, but because that was his nature.

Scorn for any "juste-milieu," polemic against religion, revolutionary spontaneity, yet at the same time conspiratory machiavellianism and a desire for enlightening propaganda—these are the main elements in the portrait he drew of the man who had inspired him in Russia. But this heroic ingenuousness and youthful primitivism were soon overshadowed, even for Engelson, by an increasing layer of German ideology and Proudhonian philosophy. From these diverse elements his political conception was born. It was a form of individualism and anarchism that seemed to affirm and solidify some of the features of Herzen's thought and even occasionally risked becoming a caricature of it.

In Nice, his main plan was to write a book on anarchy and socialism. Nothing came of it but a long introduction dedicated to Herzen, which Engelson sent to him from Genoa on July 13, 1852. It is a work that somehow summarizes the experiences the two men had undergone in Italy.[84] Engelson confesses to Herzen that on one occasion in Russia one of Herzen's philosophical works had saved him from suicide. ("The pistol was loaded, his soul was black as night. There was a snowstorm, it was half-dark, windy, stormy . . .") And now he too wants to begin his career as a publicist, as a "red Russian." It was in their country that reality surrounded them and drove them toward a radical view of political and social relationships. "If we recognize better than others the worthlessness of written rights, this is explained by the fact that our government shows us more clearly than others that the law, in simple terms, is nothing but blue smoke, that is, the vapor of ink. . . . The czar does not want to give us any rights . . ."

It is this antilegalistic and overlogical spirit that has driven him to expose his own ideas. "It is customary to think that socially the Russians are communists; instead I will preach absolute individualism." There is a complete contrast between the Russians and the state which prevents them from settling on any form of constitutionalism modeled on that existing in feudal Roman Europe. The risk of being ridiculed for his position, by either the aristocrats or the democrats, matters little to him. "Both parties are in equal measure foreign and enemies to me." The privileges of the aristocrats and of the wealthy are morally bad. "And, moreover, you drew the following fact to my attention: the so-called aristocratic party today is composed not of aristocrats but of the bourgeoisie." As for the democrats, he adds, "The means by which they hope to achieve their goals frighten me. It seems to me that now, just as at the time of the convention, in the final analysis they increasingly simplify and centralize what they intend to destroy. For example, what sense do these incessant speeches on nationality and national independence have?"

For the Russians, this last problem could never be the most important one. "Basically, it makes no difference to a Russian whether the man who exploits him is called Baron von Stockprügel or General Kulakov. Often, in fact, a master of one's own nationality is a worse despot than a foreigner." Neither laws nor national pride nor desire for conquests and privileges were dear to Russia. And the very absence of these concepts constituted the greatness of the country, therein lay its future. Engelson closes his dedication by inviting Herzen to continue his work, to take up the themes he treated in his letter to Michelet, to make his voice heard again after the misfortunes that have struck him and his family.[85]

He went about discussing and spreading these ideas in his current circle, among the Italian immigrants gathered in Genoa. The polemic against the nationalism and traditionalism of the democrats of 1848 was naturally tinged with hostility toward Mazzini. Engelson well remembered a little later, when he had left Italy, how the state of mind of some of his Italian friends had not been different from his own. For example, he had heard the violent words of Medici against the useless sacrifices that Mazzini had always imposed and continued to impose on his followers.[86]

Engelson's close involvement in Herzen's family situation had also drawn him closer to the Italian exiles, including Orsini, Medici,[87] and Mordini,[88] and the other signers of the declaration of solidarity with Herzen. In addition to the men mentioned, the signers included Cosenz, Pisacane, Mezzocapo, Bertani, and Boldoni.[89] In his memoirs, Herzen remembers Medici, Pisacane, Cosenz, and Mordini as the men who surrounded Engelson during his stay in Genoa.[90] Engelson even wanted to perfect his knowledge of his friends' language, and in a letter of that period we find his Italian teacher mentioned.[91] When he had to leave the Mediterranean coast, he had pleasant recollections of the world he left, and from Geneva he wrote to Herzen on October 20, 1852: "We often remember Nice, which has now become uninhabitable for you not only because of your personal affairs but also for another reason: you probably know from the newspapers (exempli gratia, "Débats,"

"Galignani") that Dameth was expelled to Malta and that the other Frenchmen are *internés.*"[92]

In Switzerland and in France he read, he reflected on what surrounded him, and he returned to the ideas that had dominated him in Nice and Genoa. The third volume of Haxthausen's work, which he studied in Paris, had led him to write a long letter on November 4. The German baron's study of the life of Russian peasants led him to wonder if some of Herzen's fundamental ideas on Russia's future could be supported by facts or if they were contradictory to reality. The conflict that Herzen postulated between the peasant communities and the state certainly existed, but it was greatly minimized by religion and by the meekness, the lack of rebellious spirit, among the peasant masses. The Russian myth that Herzen had used to overcome the disillusionment of 1848 was thus beginning to be corroded by this precursor of "nihilism."

But if Engelson's vision of Russia was discouraging, his opinions on the West were even more pessimistic. The 1848 revolt was not a prologue, as Herzen had written, but a full tragicomic act in which the bourgeoisie had shown its true nature. "The bourgeoisie is falling because of the contradictions that are arising in its own womb," he wrote to Herzen on November 30, 1852. Universal suffrage had aroused hopes and expectations to which the bourgeoisie did not know how to respond.

The bourgeoisie, who are generally the liberals (since the people are mainly concerned with economic problems), are now overcome, not only in France but in all other parts of the European continent. Who conquered them? To put it simply, one cannot confirm that entire classes are ever conquered by isolated individuals. The bourgeois, those who raised their heads in 1848, were beaten by the people's class directly below them. In Hungary the revolutionaries depended only on the citizens, on the cities; this was confirmed by Kossuth himself in the speeches he gave in England. That the Austrian emperor is restraining the bourgeoisie, that he supports the agricultural tenants, that he makes them favorable to his own side with a distinct decrease in *redevances,* and that as a result of this he was given a warm welcome by them last autumn, this too is not fantasy. In Lombardy, Radetzky depends on the *contadini* [in Italian in the text] against the *cittadini.* In Prussia, the recent elections brought the victory of the monarchic powers over the liberal party. Again this is only because the agricultural tenants were allowed to vote. There remains England, the privileged country of capitalists. There the problem of free trade is resolved in their favor. Now, naturally, dictatorships dominate the entire European continent. Not long ago the Reds said that dictatorship was indispensable for revolution. And now it exists, but it is not in the hands of those who spoke of it but in the hands of others. I confess that individual personalities do not interest me at all, and if one must discuss personalities, one can certainly prefer those now in power to Ledru-Rollin and Louis Blanc, who were not visibly clever and who did not reveal strength of character, but from whom one could expect endless self-praise and senseless bloodshed, as they demonstrated in those June days. It is more than likely that these people feel they are in an extremely difficult position, not knowing how to get away from the scene. In ancient times there was a custom (if history does not lie) that vanquished captains, if they had not left their bodies on the battlefield, would make an effort after the defeat to save the remains of their troops, and thus they carried out retreats like that described by Xenophon. Present-day generals seem to have a different view, to judge by what is happening in Lombardy. A consequence of war was always that people moved to new lands. It is thanks especially to this that the terrestrial globe has become populated, since the time of Moses, who led the Jews from Egypt, and of Aeneas who navigated with the Trojans toward Italy. To be the founder of a colony was the sole function that remained for defeated generals who wished to leave the European political scene without disgrace. If there were a repetition in the 19th century of what the Roman plebes attempted but failed to do—that is, to leave Rome to ascend the Monte Sacro, if Osip [that is, Mazzini] and Kossuth (to whom they had already mentioned this in America) used the money they collected through loans for this purpose, history would not reproach them, whereas it will reproach them for their desire to break down walls with their foreheads. More than once, Medici said to me, "Believe me, it is not a sentimental attachment to mountains, lakes, and rivers of one's country, but ignorance that makes people stick to their homeland, an ignorance that makes them believe that nothing exists beyond the borders of their own country. If those who suffer because of inadequate pay for their work knew as I do (he was familiar with America) that is very easy to live, for example, in Montevideo, practically everyone would move there . . ."

Faced with this bitter view of the Europe of his time and this equally bitter recollection of the Italy he had known, Engelson could only counter with his absolute individualism, supported by a desire to express it in the form of Hegelian dialectics. For him traditional Russian communism was not the seed of the future but the starting point of a development that would produce an affirmation of true individuality. In his letter of November 4, 1852, he wrote,

All developments begin with the masses, that is, with the formless communist mixture. In the beginning, the masses are gray and nebulous like the Milky Way; nothing stands out except geometrically, locally, and quantitatively. But gradually the component parts become distinguishable from one another. This marks the first appearance of the life of the masses—in a form of fermentation. Groups are formed this way. As the qualitative differences gradually become clearer, better defined, and more distinct, as the groups in the heart of the mass extend their reach, they become increasingly exclusive. Thus the struggle between groups develops. With the formation of the groups within, the primitive masses disappear. *Von lauter Bäumen sieht man nicht mehr den Wald, vor lauter Völkern nicht die Menschheit* [before too many trees one no longer sees the forest; before too many people one no longer sees humanity]. Nevertheless, a limit to the subdivision of the group exists. It comes where the borders between groups coincide with unity, the monad and the indivisible. Then a great lament arises, they grit their teeth, they cry over the dissolution of each group and the fact that everyone is alone [*für sich*] , that there is egoism, individualism, in a word, the end of the world. But, just as when the groups in the heart of the masses developed the masses went on disappearing, so now, with the destruction of the groups, with the destruction of their distinctions, the masses reappear and become visible, not in their primitive form, but transformed, enlightened with many facets, like a ray of sunlight that contains all the colors of the rainbow. As soon as there are no more groups within the masses, but only (tangibly) individuals, the masses become a general concept. Thus the tendency toward generalization and the tendency toward individualization coincide and become the same thing. . . . At the very end, unity lies in individuals and not outside them. . . . There is only one flock, but it will not have only one shepherd on earth. . . . External unity only represents an *expédient,* a *faute de mieux.* Unity cannot be *constructed.* It would be useless to desire unity if it did not already exist within individuals; it would be useless to force it—the masses would not accept it, and would reject it if it were not already within. . . . Unity will manifest itself without Popes or Mazzini.[93]

His "monologue," as he called it, was long. But it revealed a considerable attempt to theorize on the differences between the socialists and the supporters of Mazzini in the post-1848 years. It is a great pity that we do not have Herzen's reply to this letter. The attempt to reduce to dialectical terms an idea that was not substantially different from his own must have convinced him again how dangerous was philosophy in general and Hegelian philosophy in particular. He certainly reproved Engelson for being too preoccupied with Hegel. "You are now disenchanted with him, and you scold me because I respect him," countered Engelson on November 30, 1852. And he added a long quotation from the philosopher to show the profundity of his works.[94] He continued thinking about Hegel's works as he traveled about in Switzerland and France before rejoining Herzen in England.

The projected book on anarchy and socialism was never written, but its main substance was published by Herzen in the first issue of his journal, *Polyarnaya Zvezda* ("Polar Star"), published in 1855; and this fragment was entitled *The Philosophy of Revolution and Socialism. What Is the State?*[95]

Herzen recommended these fifty pages to the readers, saying, "A writer of unusual talent and incisive dialectic sent us, as soon as we started 'Polar Star,' an excellent article entitled *What Is the State?* We have read it ten times over, amazed by the boldness and profundity of the revolutionary logic of the author."

It was daring, in fact, to try to unite in one discourse the varied and complex arguments about the socialism of 1848 and to gather in one essay the political, religious, philosophical, and scientific ideas arising from the great change in European culture of those years, from dialectics to positivism. Still in the background is Fourier, with his disturbing parallels between the development of all nature and the passions and ideas of man, with his ever-present 18th-century natural palingenesis. In the middle are Saint-Simon, Proudhon, and Cabet, with their awareness of the essential importance of economic and social problems. Ludwig Feuerbach, Bruno Bauer, Arthur Schopenhauer, and Max Stirner bring philosophical formulae, awareness of individualism and of nihilism. ("It may interest the Russians to know that Mr. Bauer considers them a predestined instrument for the reduction of all that exists to zero.")[96] Auguste Comte and Carl Vogt (Engelson had met Vogt at Herzen's house in Nice) brought the concerns of sociology and natural science.[97] The frame of this picture was provided by Engelson's varied and diverse culture, which ranged from Vico[98] to Rousseau, from Guizot to Edgard Bauer.

The result is a radical definition of the state as a secret society, a conspiracy of the haves against the have-nots.[99] From its very beginning, the state has kept its own goals and methods secret. Seen from the economic point of view, as a commercial and industrial society, it dealt in goods that had to be kept secret, or in hidden goods such as ability and intelligence, the work and effort of others. Born from war, conquest, and violence, the state established civil and penal laws as "conditions under which the victor will let the vanquished live."[100] Religion reconfirms this state of things with the thought that "what exists is as it should be and cannot be otherwise," as Bauer said.[101] Christ's revolt, which in so many ways is identical to that of modern socialists, was falsified by his followers and crushed by Roman society. In the ancient as in the modern world, property is transformed from real to personal by "auctoritas" creating "circulation." That is, it is transformed from the work of slaves for the lord to that of the worker for the master; eventually property becomes concentrated in an increasingly small number of hands and gives way to terrible struggles between patricians and plebeians, as happened in Rome and also in the June days in Paris.[102] The barbarians, the Middle Ages, and absolute monarchies slowly prepared the way for this recurrence of history that to Engelson seemed to be repeating the struggles of the ancient world and to have resulted in the revolution of 1789, "the last act of the struggle between personal and real property."[103] In the revolution there was talk of liberty, equality, and fraternity. But Babeuf's proposal to apply the passage from Rousseau's *Social Contract,* in which he spoke "of the equality of property, was sufficient for the republicans to execute Babeuf."[104] Nevertheless a new and fundamental element, that of industry, was now making historical progress more complex. Engelson devoted a chapter of his study to industry and concluded that there were profound internal contradictions in modern industry and that one in particular would bring about a decisive crisis. The contradiction was that one could not maintain mass production if one was not able to or did not desire to continuously increase the market. And at the end of this development he saw revolution. Already the economy was moving toward increasing difficulties that the state would try to avoid.

Capital will be increasingly removed from circulation and put into state loans. This placement is already greatly appreciated by financiers as secure and free from worry. On the other hand, governments always have a propensity toward loans, as evidenced by the increase in their debts since the end of the last century. In the final analysis, capital will be in the hands of the state, which will then become the machinery, or better, the organism, which by endosmosis and exosmosis will serve to absorb the taxes of the working classes and redistribute them, in the form of dividends, among shareholders and creditors.[105]

To this final fusion of capitalism and the state, Engelson opposes the vision of a revolution capable of shattering modern man's fate, capable of infusing life to a world that oppresses modern men and is foreign to them, a world in which the individual has lost his raison d'être. It is a revolution as much philosophical as political, as opposed to Schopenhauer's nihilism and to Max Stirner's individualism as to statism. Engelson's work was truly a final fruit of the socialism of 1848. We can consider his ultimate conclusions vague and generalized, and can easily understand how Herzen, after thinking about the work, later wrote, "Engelson's article came at the wrong time. Russia, which was just awaking then, needed practical advice, not a philosophical treatise based on Proudhon and Schopenhauer."[106] It is precisely because it was behind the times that Engelson's work provides us with interesting and final evidence of the debates of the era in Nice and Genoa. As for the political conclusions produced by these views, however, they showed themselves at the time of the Crimean War, reemerged in the period immediately after, and ended by leading to a final break between Engelson and Herzen. The criticism of the "coryphaeuses of the revolution," the bitter distrust of democracy and democrats, the newborn nihilism that could not find any promise in the distant hope of a peasant Russia, eventually led Engelson to a position that was parallel to that of the French government and drove him to seek any means, including mediation through the hated Mazzini, to make contact with the governments and states that were combating the Russia of Nicholas I. Unlike Herzen, who remained aloof during the conflict and refused to join the anti-Russian coalition, Engelson let himself go, formulating strange plans that foresaw the use of balloons to carry both revolutionary propaganda pamphlets and new weapons against Russia. Already in the letters that he had written to Herzen from Switzerland, Herzen had noted, not without reason, "a shade of fanaticism and bonapartism." Then Engelson's attitude become more evident and led to "surrendering all his weapons and ideas,"[107] as Herzen wrote in his memoirs. While Herzen was developing, transforming, and criticizing—but not denying—the ideas and delusions of the world of 1848, Engelson had let himself be swept into a purely negative and negating position.

The period between June 1851 and August 1852, between the order for Herzen's expulsion and its revocation and his departure for England, was one in which his relations with the Italian emigrés had been most intense. The family tragedy, his wife's death, the dramatic conflict with Herwegh, had brought men such as Pisacane, Orsini, Medici, and Cosenz into close touch with Herzen's private as well as his political life. The help they offered him left traces that are clear to anyone who has read *My Past and Thoughts*. But the mark of the political ideas discussed and exchanged among them in those two years is less obvious. Nevertheless, there is some evidence that is worth examining closely. Whatever conclusions one draws, it seems that these contacts, linked with what we have seen of the echo of the Slavic problems in post-1848 Piedmont, of the interweaving of social ideas and the information and knowledge about Eastern Europe, make it easier to understand at least some elements in the formation of the Mazzini left. They also help us understand the rise of an embryonic socialism after 1848 among that group of men and ideas whose beginnings and development has already been accurately traced by Franco della Peruta.

In those years, Herzen moved between Turin (where he was, as we have seen, at the beginning of July 1851), Genoa (where he was between June 10 and 21, 1852), and Nice. Restless and in turmoil, he planned to establish himself first in one, then in another of these cities. "If we do not settle in Nice, then we can settle in Turin or in Genoa," he wrote to his wife on June 9, 1851.[108] Palazzo Carignano in Turin, the roads of Piedmont and of Liguria, the landscape of Nice remained fixed in his memory and his heart.[109] These places reappear even in his most important narrative work of that period, *Povrezhdennyy* ("The Alienated Man"). In its pages, the interplay of the elements of normality and those of nihilistic negation, of interest and of disinterested devotion (it is impossible to read this story without thinking of Engelson) reach the point of self-destruction. For a moment there is also a fleeting view of Herzen himself in Genoa. He is alone, at the Stabilimento della Concordia—that is, as he explains, at the "most elegant and finest café in all Europe."[110] "There, wandering among the fountains and flowers, between the deafening music and the blinding light, going from the marble rooms to the garden and from the garden to the frescoed rooms, among the vigorous corvine hears of the Roman exiles, the interminable Savoyard mustaches, and the native Genovese beauties, I continued to think about the alienated man."[111] The "Roman" exiles were the exiles from the Roman republic, those friends of Osip Ivanovich (Mazzini) who "an hour after *his* arrival in Genoa" were already at his house.[112] Among them Herzen singled out Giacomo Medici, of whom he said, "A few weeks spent with him in Genoa did me a great deal of good."[113] He painted a romantic portrait of Medici in his memoirs, as he also did of Orsini and Pisacane. He may have already known Pisacane in Geneva, and undoubtedly saw him in Genoa in June 1852.[114] ("I met 'il bel capitano' and spoke to him more than once about the fate of his unfortunate country.")[115]

Herzen eventually summarized his impressions of these men in a very interesting paragraph.

The Italian exiles were not superior to others either in talent or culture. In fact, a large number of them did not know anything beyond their own poets and their own history, but they did not follow the usual stereotype of the typical French democrats, who judge, proclaim, show enthusiasm, and feel in a flock, and express their emotions similarly. Nor do the Italians have the rough, unhewn character of students and of taverngoers that is typical of the German exiles. The normal French democrat is a bourgeois *in spe,* the German revolutionary is similarly a German bourgeois, the same philistine but in another phase of development. The Italians are more genuine, more individual. The French are produced by the thousands on the same model. Their present regime has not created but has only discovered the secret of the elimination of personality. In true French spirit, it has organized public education, that is, all education, since education at home does not exist in France. In all the cities of the empire they teach the same thing on the same day at the same time using the same books. The same questions are asked on all the exams and the same examples are used. Teachers who stray from the text or change the curriculum are immediately eliminated. This mechanical desert of instruction has reduced the vague thoughts of the past to an obligatory and hereditary form. It is democratic leveling formally applied to mental development. There is nothing like it in Italy. As a federalist and artist by nature, the Italian flees with horror from anything that smacks of barracks, of uniformity, of geometric precision. The Frenchman is a born soldier, he likes to march in formation, he likes commands, uniforms, and he likes to inspire terror in others. When forced, an Italian is more a bandit than a soldier, and I do not mean anything negative by this. Even at the risk of being shot, he prefers to kill as he likes best, without any orders, without the responsibility of others. He prefers to live in poverty in the mountains and to hide smugglers rather than report them and live as an honorable gendarme. The cultured Italian is formed as educated men are in our country: alone, with the life, the passions, and the books that happen to fall his way, he reaches one concept or another in this manner. Thus, as in our country, there are many gaps and there is much immaturity. Like us, he is inferior to the Frenchman in specialization and precision, inferior to the German in doctrine and theory, but despite this, in our country as among the Italians, the colors are clearer. We also have common defects. The Italian has the same tendency toward laziness that we have. He does not find work a pleasure; he does not like the anxiety, fatigue, and uneasiness that accompany it. Industry in Italy is almost as backward as it is in our country. In both countries, treasures lie at our feet, but they are not cultivated. Customs in Italy have not changed in the modern and bourgeois sense, as they have in France and England. The history of the Italian bourgeoisie is quite different from that of the other two countries. The rich bourgeois heirs of the artisans were often rivals of the feudal aristocracy, and dominated the cities. Because of this they were closer to the plebeians and peasants than to the wealthy men of other countries. The bourgeoisie in the French sense is really represented by a special branch in Italy, formed at the time of the first revolution, and which we can call, using geological terms, the *Piedmontese stratum.* It is distinguished in Italy, as throughout the European continent, by the fact that it is liberal in *many* matters and in *all* matters it fears the populace, as it fears indiscreet discussions of work and salaries, and always makes concessions to enemies from above without doing the same to *its own* members from below.[116]

Herzen also shared with the refugees his uncertainty, his suspicion about the measures taken by the Turin government. On November 11, 1851, he wrote,

"They say here, loosely speaking, that soon they will handcuff the refugees and send them all to the island of Sardinia to be classified...."[117] But despite the expulsions and the nuisance, it was true even for him that Piedmont maintained considerable elements of liberty. Thus, for example, contrary to what was happening in France and elsewhere, letters were not opened by the Sardinian censors. Herzen was quick to point this out to his correspondents, especially to the Russians.[118] On November 15, 1851, he wrote to Michelet, "As for Piedmont, letters are not unsealed here. The Chamber refused that right to the minister. But the letters that come to me from Paris often bear suspicious traces...."[119]

When the news of the December 2 coup d'état reached him, a new disillusionment and new pain were added to the tragedies that his family had repeatedly suffered. "It's time to think of England," he observed melancholically.[120] As for France, now he only thought of it as land to be crossed over to go somewhere farther away, but even this simple move was denied him.[121] In June 1851 he wrote to his wife from Paris, "Living in France is terrible. I repeat, either England or Piedmont."[122]

When he returned to the Kingdom of Sardinia, he concluded that for him it would be not only a refuge but also a center of cosmopolitan life, a corner that was still free in a world that was increasingly oppressed by reaction and tyranny. Around him he saw arrive not only the Italian and French exiles but also some Germans and Poles. Carl Vogt, the famous naturalist, after having been head of the Frankfurt parliament, had sought refuge in Nice to take up his zoological studies again and wait for the storm to pass. He had known the two Russians, Bakunin and Ogarev, for some time and had sympathized with them. Now he also established an enduring friendship with Herzen.[123]

In the summer of 1851 a Pole, Edmund Chojecki, stopped in Nice on his way back from Egypt. He was barely thirty (he was born in 1822), but he had already led a life of adventure. He was an emigré, had collaborated in G. Sand's and P. Leroux's *Revue indépendante,* and in 1848 had participated in the Slavic Congress in Prague along with Bakunin. He had then become one of the most active journalists in the Proudhon group, and it was there that he had met Herzen. Their relationship remained close even when Herzen had to leave Paris.[124] Charles Edmond (his French pseudonym, which eventually became, so to speak, his true name when he became more involved in the world of journalism, politics, and theater in France) maintained a close epistolary contact with Proudhon even from Nice. Proudhon wrote him from the prison of the Conciergerie, where he was being detained on August 28, 1851. "My dear prodigal son, we have all received your letters from Nice; your adventures have proven to us that which it is only too easy to see: that the policies of the different governments are now joined against universal democracy...." Thus it was useless to stay outside France without even being safe from the blows of reaction. It was better to return to Paris as soon as possible, "and, if possible, with our friends H(erzen), whose excellent work on Russia I have read,

and V(ogt), who slumbers, *ma foi,* more than Tyrtée and Homer were allowed to."
Great editorial projects awaited them, even a history of modern democracy. They
must prepare for the moment when he too would be released from prison. Only
nine months—then they would all again take up the life that they had led together
at the time of *La Voix du peuple.* No other hope existed. It was useless to think
of emigrating to London where the presence and influence of Ruge, Marx, Grün,
and Mazzini promised nothing good. "Their manifestos to Europe are always as
empty, as crack-brained, as the famous *circulaires.* I mistrust above all the ability
of Mazzini, in whom I see only a dreamer on the order of Sylvio Pellico: it is not
there, it seems to me, that what Italy needs will be found." Nor were the Hungarian exiles, with Kossuth at their head, any better. By now he considered Kossuth
and Mazzini, "whom I admired at first, like two plagues for their country and for
the revolution."[125] Charles Edmond (we can now call Chojecki by the name Proudhon used) did not respond negatively to this appeal; in fact, he tried to make his
rights to live in France known. Already on July 1, he, a "Polish refugee expelled
from France," had asked to be able to return there for a few days.[126] Now he
insisted that Proudhon should support him in his approach to the Chamber of
Deputies. Proudhon answered on November 25, a few days before the coup d'état,
describing the painful situation in France but still hoping that it would be possible
for them to continue their work together, even if not political, at least "philoso-
phique."[127] And at the end of his letter, he took up the theme that he had already
touched on when speaking of Herzen's Nice publications. Now, after *Du développement des idées révolutionnaires en Russie,* he had read the letter addressed
to Michelet: "It is very good; it is better, it is cleaner, more categorical than all
that he has done up to the present. We French only like things that are precise
and articulated. One has to dot the *i*'s for us; our method of reasoning, unlike
that of the Germans, is to proceed not by categories but by facts. One almost
knows the Slavic people, one feels them, one intuits them after having read these
pages."[128]

Proudhon's outburst was rendered both deeper and sadder by the pain that
united him with Herzen, who was then suffering from the tragic loss of his mother
and his son, Kolya. These terrible experiences created a new bond between the
two men.[129]

On December 19, Proudhon wrote again to Charles Edmond from the prison
of Sainte-Pélagie. "I come in my turn to clasp your hand and H(erzen)'s; to bind
more tightly, if that is possible, the links of our spiritual community, and to console myself, at this unhappy time, for the too well foreseen accidents of politics."
The Napoleonic coup d'état had inflicted a new wound on their fate and everyone's. "On December 2, 1851, a great outrage was committed, in circumstances
that left an indelible stain on the morality of our nation..."[130] Yet Proudhon,
relying on the passive optimism that is the natural defense of any imprisoned man,
searching with his paradoxical ingenuity for clear explanations that eventually

became justifications, finding in the intellectual life a refuge that could save him
from despair, began to sketch for his refugee friends in Nice that political vision
that soon led to the writing of his most discussed and discussible book, *La Révolution justifiée par le coup d'état.*

Herzen's reply on December 26 is one of the most impressive documents to
come from his pen. He offers, not explanations and justifications, but a complete
and integral fusion of his personal and public experiences. "I have no more tears.
It seems to me sometimes that the terrible catastrophe which took from me my
mother, my son, and a friend on the 16th of last month is already very far away.
Between the personal disaster and the present an entire world was wrecked..."
But Proudhon and he found different sources of support. "But we must let the
dead bury the dead. We do not belong to the past which has collapsed, we belong
to the future." One had to save oneself from disaster, to escape from it. Was
Proudhon not running the risk of becoming trapped in the ruins and the rubble?
One must emigrate, leave. Thus, at the height of the pain and suffering, a real
polemic developed between Herzen and Proudhon, a polemic that gained intensity
the longer it was pursued in its serious and subdued tone, yet by now, all rhetoric
on this theme was useless.

How happy we would be to know you outside of Paris and outside of France.—
Paris is Jerusalem after Jesus. Glory to her past, to her great revolution, but her
career is finished. The reign of the liberal, civilized, rebellious bourgeoisie is over....
She feared the excess of liberty—well, she shall have the excess of despotism;
she did not wish to give anything to the people—well, the people fold their arms
while she is fired on. She invented a red ghost, trembled before a barbarity coming
from below; the barbarity is from above. Is there a more impoverished idea in the
world than the idea of order; abstract order is mechanical; it is the negation of
initiative, of change....France fallen back into infancy, and Russia which has not
yet emerged from it—both under a degrading yoke—reach the same level. Russia
has gained nothing, France has lost everything. Despotism will prepare the way
for communism—and not for conservatism. Conservatism exists only in England,
and she alone will remain as a magnificent sketch of the civilized world, of the
Christian and feudal world...
Your work has been great. You have done everything to show the danger, you
have shown them the means to health, organic solutions, the need of the social
morphology, which cries out a demand for new forms. The civilized world from
New York to Moscow admires you...

And now what would he do? Herzen offered his hand in aid. "I am more obliged
to you than you think. Hegel and you have been the means of my philosophical
education, I would be happy to be able to work with you or to be useful to you..."[131]
Thus was born the plan to invite Proudhon to emigrate to the Kingdom of Sardinia and share the life of exile with Herzen and Charles Edmond. We know little
about his strange attempt, or perhaps we should say dream. But we have more in-

formation about Proudhon's plan to emigrate immediately after the Napoleonic coup d'état, partly seeking a pretext for making contact with the new power, and partly to prove himself useful to those who were being persecuted and deported at the time.[132] However, the idea of Proudhon himself moving to the Kingdom of Savoy or even to the island of Sardinia is much more nebulous. Darimon mentions it in his memoirs: "A rich Englishman offered Proudhon to harbor us all on a vast estate that he possesses in Sardinia near Cagliari. This project pleased most of us. We dreamed of a great agricultural and industrial establishment, to which we would be able to add an unassailable propaganda center for our ideas."[133]

This is confirmed in Proudhon's correspondence with Charles Edmond. On January 10, 1852, Proudhon wrote him in Nice: "You propose, on the basis of a word which was spoken to us and which I have confided to you, to take refuge in Sardinia. It would please me greatly, to be sure, as a place of exile and in order to organize an industrial concern. But would I not be even more buried there than in France? How could one serve the revolution, act on Europe from the end of this Sardinia? Who in the depths of Europe waits for the light from Cagliari?"[134]

Thus the plan faded. Nevertheless, it momentarily provided an important element in the dialogue between the cosmopolitan exiles gathered in Nice and the French socialist who was imprisoned in the Conciergerie. They feared that Proudhon would remain in France and adapt to the new regime, while Proudhon tried to convince them of his paradoxical idea that, objectively, Napoleon would eventually bring grist to the revolutionary mill. The question of emigrating or remaining in France was nothing but a practical consequence of different opinions about a France that was rapidly moving toward the Second Empire.

In fact, Proudhon insisted that Charles Edmond and Herzen return to Paris. Together they would work on some publishing enterprises that he was creating to reaffirm his "science nouvelle." "Other great works could follow, undertaken with all our friends, and you would be there, I hope, as well as H(erzen), there will be, for example, a *Biographie universelle,* fifty volumes in octavo, in two columns, providing work for twenty persons and a monument to the glory of the revolution."[135] But as the days passed (their correspondence was particularly intense during the first months of 1852), the broader and more grandiose Proudhon's plans became, the more frequent his insistence and the more adventurous his views about the politics of the times. "My dear Edmond," he wrote on March 6, 1852, "your last letter proves to me once again that exile, like prison, derails the judgment. Thus I draw from it one conclusion, that instead of following you to Sardinia, to America, to Holland, I should occupy myself with only one thing, and that is to cure you, and for that, to make you come back here near to me." "My dear Edmond," he wrote again on June 2, 1852, "you are a good and brave heart, but your imagination is ever exalted, always delirious and unhappy..."[136]

Herzen continued to compare these appeals, and this perhaps paradoxical desire to understand the new reality of France, with his own increasingly bitter and profound condemnation of all that was happening in Paris. The choice in favor of countries with organized liberty became clearer to him; it was a choice that influenced him to remain in Piedmont for the moment and which would soon lead him to England. "Up until now we have lived quietly under the protection of the Cross of Savoy—but I am thinking of leaving Nice in two, three months..."[137]

When he left for London, looking back, he felt all the anguish of what he was leaving. "It pains me greatly to leave Nice," he wrote the day before his departure, on June 7, 1852.[138] Traveling through Switzerland, in Bellinzona, he felt a violent urge to turn back. "I am longing to go back toward Italy. I have no other country. I have become one with that landscape and those people. What a beautiful landscape! How extraordinary was the time I spent in Genoa (besides, the blessing of Osip Ivanovich [Mazzini] accompanies me into Ticino). As for Medici, I have a tender fondness for him.... In Genoa, in Nice, at the cemetery, at the sea, which for me is also a cemetery. Perhaps I will return to Italy..."[139]

He thought back to those months, those years, when not only he but also little Alexander, his son, had been all involved in the Italian life. "The Italians in Genoa had had an extraordinary influence on him. Childishly, yet caring, he imagined himself to be a defender of Italy, and not of cold politics.... Here is one episode. One of his Italian friends gave him a little sword, saying it was 'for the Croats and the Cossacks.' Sasha was extraordinarily happy with the sword, but he answered very seriously, 'And why not for the Italians, who are against us, *contre notre cause*?' He was no fool. The Italian embraced him."[140]

But by now, for Herzen, the figures of Italian patriots he had met and loved in Nice and Genoa were only memories. When he had left, they had charged him with the task of being their spokesman to Mazzini, to tell him the reasons for their discontent and their opposition. They could no longer accept the Mazzinian idea of insurrection. They wanted to take military factors more into account. They talked of General Ulloa. Herzen carried out the mission that had been entrusted to him, but without result, as he had to restrict himself to uselessly affirming to Mazzini that he could personally confirm many of the things that his Genoese friends had said.[141] Many of those friends he never saw again. Others, like Orsini, remembered him and Engelson even when they were imprisoned.[142] Still others were profoundly changed when their paths crossed again. In these Russian, French, and Italian men, the fruits of the 1848 revolution were maturing.

Notes

1. "I have made inquires about Nice, even about Florence," he wrote to Herwegh on February 19, 1850. "Ah, to go to Nice...," he said on February 25. "I have talked with many people about Nice—they say that they bother foreigners there..." he added, nevertheless, on March 20. And on May 12, "But who told you that Nice is the freest city in the world...?" (E. H. Carr, "Some Unpublished Letters

of Alexander Herzen," *Oxford Slavonic Papers* 3 (1952): 106 ff., now in "Pisma k Georgy i Emme Gervegam" [Letters to George and Emma Herwegh] published by L. R. Lansky and Ya. E. Elsberg, in *Literaturnoye nasledstvo* [Literary legacy], no. 64, pp. 110, 117, 141, 182; and A. I. Herzen, *Sobranie sochineniy v tridtsati tomakh* [Complete works in thirty volumes] (Moscow, 1961), 23:274 ff., 24:45.

2. French translation by Herzen, carried out in Lugano on July 2, 1852, of the twelfth of his "Letters from France and Italy," in *Sobranie sochineniy,* 5:391 ff.

3. Carr, pp. 119 and 120, letters to Herwegh dated May 30 and June 27, 1850; also see *Literaturnoye nasledstvo,* pp. 203, 225; and *Sobranie sochineniy,* 24:97.

4. A detailed account of these events can be found in E. H. Carr, *The Romantic Exiles* (London, 1933), as well as in the impressive autobiographical documents of Herzen's wife published in *Literaturnoye nasledstvo,* no. 63, pp. 365 ff. On his intellectual evolution, see Raul Labry, *Alexander Ivanovich Herzen. 1812-1870. Essai sur la formation et le développement de ses idées* (Paris, 1928), chap. 10, "Le Retour à la Russie" (pp. 345 ff.), in which, however, the Russian aspect of his polemic against the West is stressed to the neglect of the revolutionary and socialist element which was prevalent in Herzen's works, even during this period.

5. *Sobranie sochineniy,* 5:190. Alfieri's name is already mentioned in Herzen's diary during the period of his Moscow sojourn before his emigration, and it reappears here and there in later pages. See, e.g., the recollection (dated July 25, 1863; in *Sobranie sochineniy,* 18:229), of the Alfieri dedication "to the free Italian people of the future."

6. He wrote from Nice on January 22, 1851, to Fasy, the well-known head of the radical party in Geneva: "Certainly you remember my dreams of naturalization in Geneva and the goodness with which you encouraged them. Now they propose to take the same step here; but you will understand very well the reasons that make me prefer Genevan naturalization.... You would place me, dear President, beyond the czar's reach and the city would lose nothing by having one more do-nothing. I will await your response with impatience. Give me your opinion frankly; if it is impossible, I will lose no more time and shall accept the proposal they make me here" (*Sobranie sochineniy,* 24:158).

7. Letter 13, *Letters from France and Italy,* in *Sobranie sochineniy,* 5:201.

8. *Byloye i dumy* [My past and thoughts], chap. 40, in *Sobranie sochineniy,* 10:152. Herzen relates these facts with some errors in chronology which are nevertheless easy to correct by referring to the letters and documents of the period. On Orsini's life in Nice, see *Lettere di Felice Orsini,* ed. Alberto M. Ghisalberti (Rome, 1936), p. 127; and especially the study by Alberto M. Ghisalberti, *Orsini minore* (Rome, 1955), pp. 148 ff. I. Imbert, in his article "Garibaldi et garibaldiens à Nice après l'annexion," in *Nice historique* (October–December 1950), p. 81, indicates a letter of Orsini's from this period, which seems not to have been published.

9. *Sobranie sochineniy,* 24:35, letter dated April 24, 1850.

10. *Byloye i dumy,* chap. 39, in *Sobranie sochineniy,* 10:152.

11. *Sobranie sochineniy,* 24:139 ff., letter dated September 13, 1850. See F. Della Peruta, *I democratici e la rivoluzione italiana* (Milan, 1958), in which the relationship between Mazzini and Herzen during this period is discussed in detail.

178   Russians, French, and Italians

In later pages, the importance of the concept of "formalism" in the arguments between Mazzini and the socialists of the Risorgimento is also stressed.

12. *Byloye i dumy*, in *Sobranie sochineniy*, 10:155–56.

13. One copy of this edition can be found in the State Archives of Turin and another at the Academy of Sciences of the same city. The latter copy is marked "Deposited on May 12, 1851." On the influence of this work outside revolutionary circles of the left, we note only one indication: it was read at the beginning of 1852 by the poet Zhukovsky and by future Foreign Minister A. M. Gorchakov, then ambassador at the court of Würtemberg (see *Literaturnoye nasledstvo* 63:661). For the history of the publication of this work in German, see the careful and interesting study by Gerhard Ziegengeist, "Die Erst Fassung von Alexander Herzens Schrift *Von der Endwicklung der revolutionären Ideen in Russland* in der *Deutschen Monatschrift*," in *Vorträge auf der Berliner Slawistentagung (11–13. November 1954)* (Berlin, 1956), pp. 312 ff.; and the volume by Eberhard Reissner, *Alexander Herzen in Deutschland* (Berlin, 1963).

14. *Sobranie sochineniy*, 24:180.

15. In the copy of *Progresso* preserved in the Museum of the Risorgimento in Milan the handwritten mark "C." is missing at the bottom of the page in these two *feuilletons*, whereas it is found in other articles of his. But this is insufficient argument for doubting the authorship of these pages.

16. *Le panslawisme. Son histoire, ses véritables éléments: Religieux, sociaux, philosophiques et politiques* (Florence, 1848). Count Adam Gurowsky, born in a village near Kalisch, had studied in Leipzig, Gottingen, and Heidelberg. He had participated actively in the 1830–31 Polish insurrection, but then he had come into contact with the Russian governor in Poland, Paskevich, and became a fanatic defender of Russian ideas, politics, and spirituality. It is certainly significant that in the years immediately preceding 1848 there was a particularly enthusiastic representative of Russian Slavophilic ideas living and writing in Italy. In the midst of strange religious, ethnographic, and linguistic fantasies, the work he published in Florence contained some interesting elements about the lack of social classes in Russian society; on *grazhdanstvo* (p. 219), which was mentioned by C. Correnti in his article on *Progresso;* on the relationship between Moscow and St. Petersburg (p. 234); and on the advantages to be gained by backward countries (p. 219). Here we read: "As if to compensate for their tardy appearance, for their long wait, and for the evils suffered or yet to be suffered, Providence has endowed them (the Panslavic people) richly, guided them onto the world's stage at the beginning of an era as rich in beneficial discoveries as in harmful errors. The Panslavic people could thus without hurry appropriate and assimilate the first, avoid and reject the second. The sun which rises higher and higher on their horizon, which darts, shining, on their future, will make them see the highlights and shadows of the inventions, ways, and systems followed by others." There is also (pp. 280–81) the classic comparison between the situation of the Russian peasants and that of Western workers. "The imagination as well as the coldest, calmest reason takes fright on reading these tales of the misery which preys upon the worker population of England and France." And he concluded (p. 312), "More than any other, the Russian Slavic people are apt to march under the banner of labor. More than to

any other, association is an innate sentiment to them." He foresaw that the nobility too would be able to support the evolution of the Russian economy (p. 312): "The Russian nobility, mingling more and more, associating themselves with the industrial movement of their country, will teach themselves in fact that the exclusive ownership of the land by the state will henceforth be advantageous. Mingling itself with industry by a combination of work, interest, and organization, they will sense that agricultural exploitation, becoming industrial in turn, to be successful should take place under the aegis of conditions resembling those that regulate industry." It is interesting that in this book Gurowsky showed his sympathy for Gioberti, whom he called "one of the most remarkable thinkers and wise men of the age." He quotes a sentence (p. 170) from Gioberti as his motto for chapter 2: "The Slavs are perhaps destined to infuse a new spirit of life into the exhausted veins of old Europe." It is strange evidence of an affinity that can be found between Slavophilia and neo-Guelfism. And one result of both trends will be to prepare the ground for the rise of Populist and Proudhonian socialism.

17. *Sobranie sochineniy*, 7:271. "The French government not only prohibited the first edition, but also stole it at the Nice customs office," said Herzen, remembering his "friendly polemic with Michelet" in the first issue of the *Polar Star* in 1855 (2d ed. [1858], p. 208, n. 2). The English translation, which appeared in the *English Republic*, W. J. Linton's journal (1855, pp. 75 ff.), bore the note: "Published in Piedmont, in 1852, and *the whole edition* seized at Marseilles, stolen by the reigning Order." In fact, the French government continued to bear a grudge against this pamphlet. On November 15, 1852, Carl Vogt wrote to Herzen from Geneva that it was impossible to send it to him through France because the censors would not allow it, and he added, "This damn pamphlet moreover has already cost me some disagreements. . . . Because of it they ransacked a case of books coming to me from Nice, tore the books, damaged the planks. . ." (*Autour d'Alexandre Herzen. Documents inedits*, ed. Marc Wuilleumier, Michel Aucouturier, Sven Stelling-Michaud, and Michel Cadot [Geneva, 1973], p. 98).

18. It is partly reproduced, for example, in *Libertà* (published in Genoa; 1, no. 1 [October 1, 1851 ff.]). *Il progresso* had already reported Michelet's ideas on Russia and Poland, taking them from *L'Evénement* and from *L'Avènement du peuple* on September 21 and October 24, 1851.

19. Gabriel Monod, "Deux Révolutionnaires russes. Pétrachevsky et Bakounine. Notices biographiques, par Alexandre Herzen," in *Revue bleue* (September 26, 1908); Monod, "Jules Michelet et Alexandre Herzen d'après leur correspondance intime (1851–1869)," in *La Revue* (May 10 and June 1, 1980); M. O. Gershenzon, "Pisma Gercena i Mishle" [The letters of Herzen and Michelet], in *Byloye* [The past] (July 1907); Z. L. Zaleski, "Michelet, Mickiewicz et la Pologne," in *Séances et travaux de l'Académie des sciences morales et politiques*, Paris (July–August 1928); and the excellent edition of Jules Michelet's *Légende démocratique du Nord, nouvelle édition, augmenté de fragments inédits*, ed. with introduction, notes, and index by Michel Cadot (Paris, 1968).

20. For an incisive interpretation of Herzen's works from this period, see Isaiah Berlin's introduction to A. Herzen, *From the Other Shore, and The Russian People and Socialism* (London, 1956).

21. This article is cited and quoted by G. Berti, *Russia e stati italiani nel Risorgimento* (Turin, 1957), p. 608, but Berti does not indicate the Herzenian origins of the ideas expressed in it.

22. In a letter to J. Weydemeyer dated April 12, 1853, Engels defined this period of Herzen's activity, basing his judgment mainly on a reading of *Du développement des idées révolutionnaires en Russie:* "Mr. Herzen has made the task easy, assuring himself against failure by constructing a Russian republic both democratic-social and communist-Proudhonian, directed by the triumvirate Bakunin-Herzen-Golovin" (Russian edition of the works of Marx and Engels, 25: 184; and K. Marx and F. Engels, *Letters to Americans, 1848–1895: A Selection* [New York, 1953], p. 54).

23. *Sobranie sochineniy*, 24:200. The interesting letters of A. A. Chumikov to Herzen are published by M. Ia. Poliakov in *Literaturnoye nasledstvo*, 62:710 ff. Chumikov proved skeptical about the possibilities of emigration in order to free Russia. In general, he put his trust solely in an internal process within the country: "Europe will not overcome the colossus, but the monster will fall because of its internal ills, and thus it is not very useful to collaborate through immigration. In addition, our emigration becomes estranged from anything native and it loses its support and becomes incomprehensible for the masses (more so if one begins to lie, like Golovin and also N. Turgenev). *A propos*, I would be interested in knowing your opinion and in general some details on those few Russian emigrés of your acquaintance, for example, Sazonov—we have heard nothing about him, yet they are worthy of note or even of fame..." (p. 725).

24. *Sobranie sochineniy*, 7:404.

25. *Byloye i dumy*, chap. 42, in *Sobranie sochineniy*, 10:213.

26. Ch. Dupont, *Les Republicains et les monarchistes dans le Var en décembre 1851* (Paris, 1883), p. 252. See Eugène Ténot, *La Province en décembre 1851. Etude historique sur le coup d'état* (Paris, 1869), p. 131: "La Garde-Freynet, a large borough situated in the Maure mountains not far from the sea... center of the cork-oak industry, it has a large worker population. A major, a veteran of February, recently condemned for political reasons, was an ardent propagator of republican ideas there." See also the very important book by Maurice Agulhon, *La Republique au village. Les populations du Var de la Révolution à la Seconde République* (Paris, 1970).

27. *L'Avenir de Nice* announced the publication of this leaflet on January 24, 1851, and recommended it highly to its readers.

28. *Dettagli inediti ecc.*, p. 44.

29. Ibid., p. 45.

30. *Le Vol et la tyrannie*, p. 2.

31. Ibid., p. 18.

32. Ibid., p. 17.

33. Ibid., p. 18.

34. Ibid., p. 186.

35. Ibid., p. 125.

36. Ibid., p. 126.

37. Ibid., p. 39.

38. Ibid., pp. 127–28.

39. Ibid., p. 128.

40. Ibid., p. 129.

41. Ibid., p. 126.

42. Ibid., p. 206. This problem of direct government and these theories of Ledru-Rollin, Rittinghausen, etc., were also discussed by H. Dameth in *L'Avenir de Nice* on September 1, 8, and 22. Mathieu was alluding to Alexandre-Auguste Ledru-Rollin, *Plus de présidents, plus de représentants* (Paris, 1851), and to two works by Carl Rittinghausen, who was a member of the Frankfurt parliament, *La Législation directe par le peuple ou la véritable démocratie* (Paris, 1851), and *Gouvernement direct. Organisation communale et centrale de la République* (Paris, 1851). On the cover of the first of these interesting pamphlets, published in December 1850, there is the announcement of a work by V. Considerant, *La Solution, ou le gouvernement direct du peuple universel.*

43. *Le Vol et la tyrannie,* p. 210.

44. Ibid., p. 211.

45. Ibid.

46. Nice, archives départementales, consulat de France à Nice, 1814–60.

47. I. Z. 44, Correspondance avec l'ambassade de France à Turin, fol. 193, report of January 25, 1852.

48. Archivio di Stato di Torino. Gabinetto Ministero Interni, Mazzo 6 bis. Fascicolo: Rifugiati francesi a Nizza. Among the worries of the Turin authorities at that time was the fear that Victor Hugo might come to live in Piedmont. According to information of May 31, 1852, Hugo "certainly would not come to Piedmont to live here in inaction and obscurity."

49. *Sobranie sochineniy,* 25:41.

50. Dupont, *Les Républicains et les monarchistes dans le Var,* p. 252.

51. See André Compan, "Les Réfugiés politiques provençaux dans la Comtée de Nice après le coup d'état du 2 décembre 1851," in *Provence historique* (January–March 1957), pp. 61 ff.

52. G. Vapereau, *Dictionnaire universel des contemporains* (Paris, 1880), s.v. "Dameth."

53. He recalls his imprisonment, and the encounter he had there with the German revolutionary K. Blind, in a letter to Carl Vogt dated November 4, 1859, published in William Vogt, *La Vie d'un homme. Carl Vogt* (Paris-Stuttgart, 1896), p. 127, n. 1.

54. Nice, archives départementales, consulat de France à Nice, 1814–60. I. Z. 20*, direction politique 1841–52, fol. 279, report of May 26, 1851.

55. *L'Avenir de Nice,* January 24 (program of the course), January 27 (beginning of the lectures).

56. Nice, archives départementales, consulat de France à Nice, 1814–60, I. Z. 20*, direction politique 1841–52, report of May 26, 1851.

57. June 6, 1851.

58. Nice, archives départementales, consulat de France à Nice, 1814–60, I. Z. 48, lettres de la légation française à Turin au consul de Nice, 1851.

59. Ibid., 1852.

182   Russians, French, and Italians

60. Archivio di Stato di Torino, Gabinetto Ministero Interni, Mazzo 6 bis. Fascicolo: Rifugiati francesi a Nizza.

61. Nice, archives départementales, consulat de France à Nice, 1814–60, I. Z. 48, lettres de la légation française à Turin au consul de Nice, 1854.

62. Op. cit., pp. 83–84.

63. *Histoire de l'Université de Genève. L'Académie et l'Université au XIXe siècle. Annexes* (Geneva, 1934), pp. 43–45. In Geneva Dameth had been recommended by Carl Vogt, and Dameth remained there as a professor until his death in 1884.

64. Nice, archives départementales, consulat de France à Nice, 1814–60, I. Z. 20*, direction politique 1841–52.

65. In print we have his: *Discours de M. l'Intendant général de la division de Nice, prononcé à la distribution des prix de l'Ecole de commerce, d'arts et manufactures et d'Agriculture de Nice le 24 août 1851.* Given in Italian, it was typical of the government economic policy.

66. On May 20 the French consul wrote, "After some words that the Intendant General said to me this morning, I would not be surprised that he asked the minister for the authorization to expel... H. Dameth... and J. Mathieu from Nice."

67. The destruction of the Ministry of the Interior papers from this period during the Second World War has made research on Turin documents impossible. Nor are Radicati's reports preserved in the Nice archives among the many administrative papers of his located there. The expulsion of the two Frenchmen and the two Russians (Herzen and Golovin) are indicated in the newspapers of the period. See *La campana* dated June 2 (H. Dameth and J. Mathieu) and the *Gazzetta del popolo* dated June 9 (defense of J. Mathieu).

68. The French consul at Nice communicated to the Foreign Ministry on March 24, 1851 that Herzen had requested authorization to go to Paris, "where he is called by the necessity of overseeing the repair of a house he owns there." On May 10 the Var prefect communicated to the consul that permission had been granted but that he was awaiting direct confirmation from the ministry. Herzen "comes every day to ask if the notification has arrived" (May 24, 1851). But he finally gave him the visa, and on June 4 he communicated that Herzen had left. Nice, archives départementales, consulat de France à Nice, 1814–60, I. Z. 20*, direction politique 1841–52. The permit for a three-month stay, dated May 21, is located in I. Z. 33 (Direction politique 1851–53).

69. *Literaturnoye nasledstvo*, 63:407.

70. In a copy in my possession, purchased in an antiquarian book shop in Genoa, of *Aus den Memorien eines Russen* (Hamburg, 1855), one can read in Herzen's handwriting, "M. Pinto wrote me that you wish to read my memoirs—dear Monsieur Valerio—I offer them to you with friendship and sympathy. London 2 Nov. 1856." On the cover where it was printed "Im Staatsgefängeniss und in Sibirien," Herzen had written the correction, "I protested against this title, I was never in Siberia."

71. *Sobranie sochineniy*, 27:177–78, letter to V. N. Kashperov dated September 15, 1861.

72. Ibid., p. 379, letter to V. N. Kashperov dated November 23, 1863.

73. *Literaturnoye nasledstvo,* 62:151. Even a letter of Herzen's wife, dated July 19, 1851 refers to Valerio. It is published in *Zvenya* (Anelli), issue 8 (1950), pp. 29–40.

74. "As soon as I received the news of what happened I asked Deputy Valerio to put a question to the Minister of the Interior," as he relates in his book *Der russische Nihilismus. Meine Beziehungen zu Herzen und Bakunin* (Leipzig, n.d. [but 1880]), p. 67.

75. Atti del Parlamento subalpino, sessione del 1851, vol. 6 (Florence, 1866), p. 2616.

76. *L'opinione* of June 11 reported this passage from the speech referring "to the departure of the two Russians" without naming them. *Il progresso* spoke of the banishment of "four foreigners, two Frenchmen and two Russians, upright and distinguished in all respects except in complying with the desires of their reactionary governments." On June 13, *L'Avenir de Nice* referred to them in more detail, mentioning Herzen and Golovin. On June 15, Herzen wrote to his wife from Paris that he had just received from Golovin the cutting from the *Gazzetta piemontese* containing Valerio's speech, and he requested that the newspaper be sent to him (*Sobranie sochineniy,* 24:180).

77. *Sobranie sochineniy,* 10:177.

78. Ibid., pp. 177–78.

79. This was announced by *L'Avenir de Nice* on July 18.

80. The article on the Russian Fourierist group, first published in *La Revue bleue,* nos. 13–14 (1908), is Engelson's, though it was originally attributed to Herzen. It is reproduced in the edition of Herzen's works edited by M. K. Lemke, 6:502 ff. Compare with *Sobranie sochineniy,* 7:411.

81. *Sobranie sochineniy,* 10:334 ff.

82. F. Venturi, *Il populismo russo,* 2 vols. (Turin, 1972), 1:154 ff.

83. *Sobranie sochineniy,* 10:343.

84. See n. 80.

85. Like all the other letters from Engelson to Herzen, this is published in the first (and last) issue of Petr Struve's journal, *Osvobozhdenie* [Liberation] (Stuttgart, 1903), pp. 102 ff.

86. Ibid., pp. 108–9.

87. Ibid., p. 104.

88. On June 29, 1852 he wrote to Herzen, "Come, come with Tessier [Marie Edmond Tessié du Motay, a French chemist and emigré and great friend of Herzen at that time] here, at Albaro, we will chat, we will drink champagne with the Engelsons, we will organize together democracy's revenge and yours..." (A. I. Herzen, *Polnoye sobranie sochineniy i pisem,* 7:69). Medici wrote to Engelson when the latter was in Geneva and, surprised by the lack of news, asked Herzen about him (ibid., p. 60).

89. Ibid., p. 70. Pisacane wrote to Mordini from Genoa on July 13, 1852: "I saw Medici at Angelson's yesterday and I gave him your letter...I sent your regards to the Angelson's" (Carlo Pisacane, *Epistolario,* ed. Aldo Romano [Milan, 1937], pp. 141–42).

90. A. I. Herzen, *Polnoye sobranie sochineniy i pisem,* 7:351.

91. *Sobranie sochineniy,* 10:351.

92. A. I. Herzen, *Polnoye sobranie sochineniy i pisem,* 7:67.

93. *Osvobozhdenie,* p. 112.

94. Ibid., p. 116.

95. We have used the second edition of this journal, procured by Herzen in 1858, pp. 15 ff. It is interesting to note that this essay by Engelson was reprinted in the form of a pamphlet in Geneva in 1870 by Nechaev's organization.

96. *Polarnaya Zvezda,* pp. 51–52, where the work, by Bruno Bauer, *Russland und Germanenthum,* is quoted.

97. Ibid., pp. 45–46, 49.

98. He quotes Vico at pp. 46–47 because of his affirmation that "proprietas" and "auctoritas" coincided for the ancient Romans.

99. Ibid., p. 55.

100. Ibid., p. 22.

101. Ibid., p. 26.

102. Ibid., p. 36.

103. Ibid., p. 41.

104. Ibid., p. 42.

105. Ibid., p. 55.

106. *Sobranie sochineniy,* 10:362.

107. Ibid., pp. 358–59.

108. *Sobranie sochineniy,* 24:175.

109. Ibid., 10:271 ff.

110. Ibid., 7:363 ff.

111. Ibid., p. 379. See Istituto per la storia del Risorgimento italiano, Comitato di Genova, *L'emigrazione politica in Genova ed in Liguria dal 1848 al 1857. Fonti e memorie,* 3 vols. (Modena, 1957). The correspondence on the emigrés in Genoa published in *Il progresso* of May 24, 1851 is interesting and strange. There is a vivid description of their daily meetings in Piazza della Porta and long excerpts from a letter that Louis Blanc wrote to one of them are quoted.

112. A. I. Herzen, *Polnoye sobranie sochineniy,* 7:54.

113. *Sobranie sochineniy,* 10:77. On the relationship that developed between Medici and Herzen, see the letter from Medici to Herzen dated November 6, 1852. After having urged him not to leave Europe, and to remain in the battlefield and finally to return to Genoa, he added, "Cosenz, Pisacane, Mezzocapo, etc., have asked me to send their regards, we all love you like a brother" (A. I. Herzen, *Polnoye sobranie sochineniy*).

114. *Sobranie sochineniy,* 10:464.

115. Ibid., p. 68, n. 1.

116. Ibid., pp. 69–71.

117. Ibid., 24:205 (letter to M. K. Reichel).

118. Ibid., pp. 197–98 (letter to A. A. Chumikov, dated July 25, 1851).

119. Ibid., p. 206.

120. Ibid., 24:213 (letter to M. K. Reichel, ca. December 5, 1851).

121. The French consul in Nice, Aladenize, communicated to the ministry on March 4 that Herzen had asked for permission to cross France, stopping for a few

days in Paris "to meet with his family in Belgium or Holland where he is planning to take up residence." And he supported this request: "In fact his political conduct, be it after or before the events of December, has not given rise to any unfavorable remarks." But the reply was negative. "After the information received on this individual, who was one of the principal members of the Paris revolutionary committee, it is not possible to give him the authorization that he solicits" (April 6, 1852). Nice, archives départementales, Consulat de France à Nice, 1814–60, I. Z. 20*, Direction politique 1841–52; and I. Z. 33, Direction politique 1851–53.

122. *Sobranie sochineniy,* 24:185, letter dated June 20, 1851.

123. Villiam Vogt, *La Vie d'un homme. Carl Vogt* (Paris-Stuttgart, 1896), pp. 81 ff.

124. *Autour d'Alexandre Herzen,* index.

125. P.-J. Proudhon, *Correspondance* (Paris, 1875), 4:89–93.

126. Nice, archives départementales, Consulat de France, Direction politique 1841–52, I. Z. 20*, fol. 392.

127. Proudhon, *Correspondance,* pp. 127–30.

128. This letter, already published in a Russian translation in *Polyarnaya Zvezda* (1859), pp. 222–24, and in the edition of M. K. Lemke, 6:536–38, was published in its exact text by Raul Labry, *Herzen et Proudhon* (Paris, 1928), p. 122.

129. R. Labry particularly stressed this aspect in chap. 5 of the book quoted. The chapter is entitled "Les Relations de Proudhon et de Herzen depuis la suppression de *La Voix du peuple* jusqu'à l'installation définitive de Herzen à Londres en septembre 1852. L'amitié dans le malheur."

130. Proudhon, *Correspondance,* pp. 144 ff.

131. *Sobranie sochineniy,* 24:216.

132. See the introduction by E. Dolléans and G. Duveau to their edition of *La Révolution sociale démontrée par le coup d'état du deux décembre,* in P.-J. Proudhon, *Oeuvres complètes* (Paris, 1936), 13:60.

133. Alfred Darimon, *A travers une révolution (1847–1855)* (Paris, 1884), p. 283. This may have referred to Benjamin Peircy, a large British agricultural landlord who at that time owned a concern in the area between Cagliari and Oristano, or it may refer to Lord Craig, who was living in Oristano between 1850 and 1855 and owned some land on the island, or it may be Augustus Henry Vernon, a member of the Agrarian and Economic Society of Cagliari.

134. Proudhon, *Correspondance,* 4:184.

135. Ibid., p. 185.

136. Ibid., pp. 230, 287.

137. *Sobranie sochineniy,* 24:217, letter dated December 21, 1851. On August 7, 1852, Proudhon wrote to Herzen, who was by then in London, sending him his book, *La Révolution sociale démontrée par le coup d'état du deux décembre,* and saying, "We march onward to empire; the humbling which the nation suffered will not interfere. The chaos of ideas is the primary cause of it; the popular cult of the emperor, warmed over and fostered by any means that will affect the people, is its instrument. However, I dare say that the Revolution still progresses, making use of all these mannequins, the ridiculous as well as the sublime to reach its goal . . ." And he announced that he was working to end the persecution of their mutual friends.

"I shall add your name to my request, my dear Herzen, and that of Charles Edmond; count on my discretion to do things to our convenience and entire satisfaction. The interdiction of France is useless to your glory and your cause; continue your travels; but it is necessary that you push to come to Paris, because when all is said and done, only there is one free, does one think" (*Correspondance,* pp. 316–17). On December 17, 1852, in a letter to M. K. Reichel, Herzen explained the reasons for his choice of England: "Today it is only possible to live in London" (*Sobranie sochineniy,* 24:373).

138. *Sobranie sochineniy,* 24:279.

139. Ibid., p. 286, letter to M. K. Reichel from Lugano dated June 26, 1852.

140. Ibid., p. 293, letter to M. K. Reichel from Lugano dated July 2, 1852.

141. *Byloye i dumy,* in *Sobranie sochineniy,* 9:16–17.

142. *Lettere di Felice Orsini,* ed. Alberto M. Ghisalberti (Rome, 1936), p. 184.

Six   Sazonov and Italian Culture

Nikolai Ivanovich Sazonov was not yet twenty when he first saw Italy and was exposed to Italian culture. He had sought refuge on the peninsula in 1835, at his mother's invitation, when the storm had broken over the heads of his Muscovite friends Herzen, Ogarev, and Satin, who had been accused of having Saint-Simonian ideas and of having philosophical and political ideas that were too liberal.[1] A quarter of a century later, recalling his own enthusiasm and hopes as well as those of his young companions, Sazonov wrote that "everything, starting with our clothing, denoted the most singular confusion: we wore black velvet bonnets in winter, à la Karl Sand, and mufflers of the French tricolors. In our meetings we recited the forbidden verses of Ryleev and Pushkin and we sang the Napoleonian couplets of Béranger alongside the anti-French songs of Arndt, Uhland, and Korner."

Their reading was even more varied and contradictory, including "the documents, still rare then, concerning the French Revolution," as well as the works of Schelling and Oken on the philosophy of nature. "From the mystical lucubrations of 'Jakob Boehme to the *Jambes* of Barbier and the *Peau de chagrin* of Balzac, everything moved us, interested us, and involved us in enthusiasm, sometimes a bit monotonous and sterile, but always sincere."

The social situation of these young men was also starting to seem strange and paradoxical to them. "Most of us were freed by the fortunes of our families from all worry about the future, and in consequence we studied only for the love of learning, with no particular goal." But when they returned home after having spent their days "in the middle of the abstractions of learning and of the poetic enchantment of comradeship," they could not help noticing the "reality of their native soil," of the "life of the people who surrounded us," as well as the "artificial and often parasitic life of the privileged classes. In Russia, serfdom gives something savage to this existence which can only be appreciated if you have seen it." "Between abstractions and barbarism, the intelligent minority of the Russian youth, sustained by love of the fatherland and of liberty, sought with indefatigable ardor the outcome which would reconcile it with the common people."[2]

The youthful figure of Sazonov is depicted in the midst of this intellectual enthusiasm and social repugnance in the philosophical and literary fragments that Herzen wrote in the 1830s, first during his incarceration in a Moscow prison and later on his long, romantic pilgrimage from one place of exile to another. In Herzen's writings we see Sazonov in a lively conversation, over a bowl of flaming punch, with Alexei Nikolaevich Savich, astronomer and scientist and "a man of 18th-century materialism." With his "swollen eyes" and "expressive face," the young Sazonov argues to Savich that "the tide that is beginning to rise will not recede; materialism has fulfilled its function and has died. Its funeral monument is the Vendôme column. German ideas ... are now penetrating into France ..."

Thus Herzen puts his own ideas into his friend's mouth, but he stops when faced with the lack of deep conviction which he seems to sense in Sazonov's heart. Herzen writes, with extraordinary psychological insight, that Sazonov is "one of those eccentric men who would be full of faith if his century had had any beliefs; but the restless demon in these men's souls breaks them, marking them with a strong sign of originality."[3] Many, many years later, in one of the more bitter and disenchanted parts of his memoirs, *Russian Shadows,* Herzen again recalls the time when he met Sazonov during his second year at the university. "We were young and fanatic; everything was subjected to only one idea, to one religion, everything: science, art, friendship, paternal home, social situation." Everything vanished when confronted with the idea of creating a group, a society inspired by Romantic doctrines. "Sazonov possessed incisive qualities and great self-love.... As a result, his companions had more respect than love for him. But there was also a deep urge that moved him." Together they went "to preach liberty and the struggle in the four corners of our young university.... We were always preaching everywhere. It is difficult to say precisely what we preached. Our ideas were confused; we preached about the Decembrists and the French Revolution, then about Saint-Simonism and its revolution, about the constitution and the republic, about reading political books and uniting in groups. But above all, we preached hatred for all violence, for all absolute power in government."[4]

When Herzen was imprisoned, and later in exile, his thoughts often turned to his distant friend Sazonov, who between 1835 and 1836 was traveling in Italy, Germany, and Switzerland. On July 18, 1835, Herzen replied to a letter in which Sazonov said he "felt he was blossoming" in Italy. He reminded Sazonov and Ketcher, those of the Muscovite group who had survived, of the isolation, of the frost in the midst of which he was condemned to live in Perm, far from everything and everyone. Nevertheless Herzen added, "You know all I expect from your trip, and on this I need write nothing. Farewell, my friend. Over there, in front of the Church of St. Peter, remember the unhappy Herzen, remember that he never doubted you or himself..." He suggested Sazonov read canto 25 of the *Purgatorio,* where he felt one could see a surprising prototype of modern theories of natural palingenesis.[5]

Herzen also dedicated the first of his imaginary *Encounters* to Sazonov. This was the episode in which a German traveler evokes Goethe during the Valmy campaign in 1792. In those pages he returned to the problem of faith, of belief, resolutely denying Goethian detachment, confirming the ethical and political significance of all literary expression in every culture. Thinking of his far-away friend he spoke of Italy, of how it had still been outside the revolutionary storm when Goethe had visited it, and now, half a century later, of Italy disturbed by the awareness of its own humiliation and decadence. "A year ago I was living in Venice," Herzen's German traveler says.

There are so many lands and cities in the world, but there is only one Italy, and only one Venice. I was at a ball given by an archduke, I remember, to celebrate the taking of Warsaw. Court balls are always tedious, the deceptive candlelight and the false joy of the people threw me into an extraordinary melancholy, and I left. What a night! ... The lion of Saint Mark had been slain, but his widow, beautiful Venice, *Sara la baigneuse,* is still as marvelous as before and is voluptuously mirrored in the waters of the Adriatic. I set off toward the lagoons in a gondola. You probably know that in Venice one can still find gondoliers who recite stanzas from Tasso and Ariosto. ... It used to happen frequently, now Italy is beginning to forget her poets. But that night fortune smiled on me. From a distance, a simple refrain could be heard, becoming louder, and I heard the last three lines; they remained in my memory:

"Dormi, Italia imbriaca, e non ti pesa
ch'ora di questa gente, ora di quella
che già serva ti fu, sei fatta ancella." [6]

The image of romantic Italy thus constituted one more link between Herzen and Sazonov, and when Sazonov, during his voyage in 1835, wrote a letter about his experiences, his exiled friend said that the letter "had a great influence on him." He replied saying that the year 1834, the year when he had been arrested, "had marked the end of our *Lehrjahre.*" Now it was no longer time for dreams but for a passionate investigation of reality.[7] As Sazonov had said when reading the story dedicated to him, the first *Encounter,* "these pages made one dream of the future."[8]

About ten years later, in 1847, Herzen and Sazonov met again in Paris. "His eyes too filled with tears at the recollection of the dreams of our university days."[9] But pride and the inability to concentrate fully on thought and reflection nearly made Sazonov's life, on the eve of the revolution, a vacant and passive wait, barely tinged by great hopes about the function that he thought he could soon carry out, once his country was liberated. As Herzen wrote to Ogarev, "Sazonov, in his way, is a romantic—fertile infertility."[10]

It was the fate of Herzen and Sazonov never to see their country again. Soon the revolution involved them more deeply in the events and hopes of Western Europe. And there they also rediscovered Italy. In the winter of 1847–48, Herzen made Italy his second home, when he discovered and felt the sense of liberty that was growing throughout the peninsula. Sazonov rediscovered Italy in 1849 when, with the defeat of the French left wing, the problems of nationality emerged again and hopes were focused on Hungary, Germany, Poland, and Italy. As an active member of the international club "La Fraternité des peuples," in the spring of 1849 Sazonov became one of the main editors of the *Tribune des peuples*, the newspaper founded by Mickiewicz.[11] As he wrote in the very first issue, the absence of a "solidarité des peuples" seemed one of the greatest obstacles in the development of the revolution in Europe. "No doubt," he added, some progress has been made since 1789, "but this progress has been slow and has come about by chance." For many decades during the early part of the 19th century, "brotherhood had vanished for a long time. Italy was barely known as a younger sister, Spain despised, Germany considered a natural prey, England a mortal enemy, and the rest of Europe relegated to the realm of diplomacy." It was only with the 1848 revolution that a different view had begun to emerge. "Actually the club of European solidarity ... comprises nearly all of Western Europe, but the Eastern part, Russia, remains still enveloped in Cimmerian darkness."

It was time now to explain to Western Europeans what autocracy and the peasant revolts had been like in Russia, and it was particularly time to affirm that "throughout these divers oppressions and successive revolts, under the Asiatic yoke of iron, as under the European yoke of rules, the Russian people knew how to keep their communal organization intact." Thus, for Sazonov too the hope for peasant socialism, rooted in Russian land, began to brighten the ruins and debris of the defeated Western revolutions. "One more effort, and the Russian people will throw off the yoke of an old and false order and reveal themselve to Europe, young, strong, and free ..."[12]

A few weeks later, on April 6, in commemoration of Good Friday, Sazonov recalled how the revolution had been oppressed and crushed. "The martyrs are the people ..." "May I be permitted to begin this litany with the people the farthest distant, reputed the most barbarous, who have suffered long ... the Russian people." Then naturally he turned to France and Italy:

Hail to Italy! Fertile land, vivacious people! Three times she has known how to place herself at the head of humanity as a conqueror, as the propagator of the Christian faith, and as the master of sciences, arts, and commerce. In creating a new unity for herself, in binding one to another all the forces that move the world in separate directions, she takes once more the place that is her due in the ranks of the nations marching toward the future. The martyrdom she suffers cannot last, and it is not for the phantom of Austria to dominate this powerful mother of nations, which after her time of slumber is awakening, more powerful than ever.[13]

The hope for the Russian peasants and the renewal of the Italian movement (this was the time of Novara, of the insurrection in Genoa, and of the revolutionary party turning its attention toward Rome) were growing together in Sazonov's heart.

But the spring and summer of 1849 brought nothing but disillusionment and disaster. With more scorn than anger, more skepticism than revolt, Sazonov was obliged to take note of the French intervention against the Roman republic and of the vain efforts of the Montagnards to oppose the policies of Thiers and Louis Napoleon. For Herzen and for many other French and European revolutionaries, the abortive insurrection on June 13 marked the time for exile and dispersion in Switzerland, Belgium, and England. Sazonov, who had taken part with Herzen in the demonstration that day, nevertheless was able at first to remain in Paris, and in the autumn and winter he tried to collaborate in the revival of the socialist press. From Geneva, Herzen did all he could to support him in his plans to work on Proudhon's *Voix du peuple,* thus hoping to contribute towards "cosmopolitizing" this newspaper that seemed too pettily Parisian to him.[14] "With his knowledge of four languages, of literature, of politics, of the history of all European populations, with his knowledge about the party, he could cause miracles in the international section of this paper," he wrote later.[15] Herzen also asked him to find some financial support for the *Voix du peuple.*

Thus Sazonov seemed to find a useful position in the difficult struggle that was taking place in Paris against the mounting reactionary and Bonapartist tide. The memory of a Mazzinian Rome still seemd to shine like an auspicious star over the common man's France which was now overwhelmed and defeated. "Today, re-turning to the *bureau* at one o'clock," Sazonov related to Herzen on July 3, 1849, "I saw a great mass of people on the *boulevard.* Everyone was standing still looking at the sky. The sky was bright and clear; the sun was shining. I asked what they were looking at. They answered: at a star that is visible despite the sunlight. What star, monsieur? *L'étoile de Rome...* Such are the people..."[16] But discontent soon gripped Sazonov again. As he wrote to Ogarev, "At the beginning I worked eagerly, but it is difficult to submit to the master [Proudhon] and his Darimon, and I believe it will be necessary to abandon this company."[17] When Herzen pub-lished his fundamental essay *De La Russie* in the *Voix du peuple* of November and December (nos. 50, 57, and 71), again opening the whole discussion on the past and present of his country, Sazonov left the Proudhonian paper and his post was filled by a Pole, Charles-Edmond Chojecki.

Sazonov had moved to the *Réforme,* that is, to the latest incarnation of this paper that had been so important during the decade of republican and socialist France. At the beginning of October 1849, Ribeyrolles had been forced to go into exile. At Ledru-Rollin's suggestion, the old but indefatigable Lamennais had been put in charge of the paper.[18] It seems that the money necessary for the continued publication of the paper, 25,000 francs, had come from supporters of Mazzini.[19] There is no doubt that the problem of nationalities and of Europe had an impor-tance in its pages that was rare in Parisian papers of the time. Sazonov was head of the paper's foreign section. On December 6, 1849, he reported this with pride in a letter to Karl Marx, with whose help he hoped to organize a "democratic correspondence for German papers." But "the citizens propose and the police dispose." Now the plan could no longer be realized, since Wolff, the instigator, had had to leave Paris. Meanwhile Sazonov asked Marx to report on his own work. "If you publish something, send it to me as soon as possible and I will include it in the 'Réforme.' If you have time, write something especially for us [on German problems] and we will be pleased to publish it. You can also send something about socialism or on the situation of the working class in England. I know how deeply you have studied these problems and I would be glad to acquaint the readers of the 'Réforme' with English social problems through your pen. But naturally, you will understand that if you wish to write for the 'Réforme' you will have to avoid doctrines and personality as much as possible. The newspaper's position requires this."[20] He did not fail to add a gibe against Proudhon, who according to Sazonov was no longer capable of attracting new followers.

Perusal of the *Réforme* of the last months of 1849 gives evidence of the atmosphere of oppression, censure, suspicion, and fear through which the paper was forced to navigate and which Sazonov indicated to Karl Marx. The polemic against the government was becoming vague and often lacked any sting. But Lamennais's *animus* was still strong, and the section of the paper entitled *Revue de l'étranger*, apparently headed by Sazonov, also continued to be of interest. By now, France was powerless in Europe. Far away, and to the east, Russia dominated: "We will survey its actions and political intentions with particular care." As for Italy, it "has not lost, in the eyes of the democrats, the interest that its sufferings and its heroic spirit of liberty and independence inspire; but for the moment its political life is in retirement and its destiny is not being decided upon its own ground.... With the exile of Mazzini and Garibaldi, the very spirit of Italy has been exiled..."[21] Two days later, on October 3, it is noted with evident satisfaction that "the noble exiles from Italy receive evidence of the sympathy of the people at every turn," and on October 4 the importance of the "solidarity of the people" is stressed.

There is a continuing polemic against Thiers's national egoism, and all signs of the new union between France and Italy, symbolized by the alliance between Ledru-Rollin and Mazzini, are stressed. On October 16, the newspaper rushed to publish "the noble and touching address which Mazzini made to the accused of June 13 in his journal, 'L'Italia del popolo.' Honor to the illustrious founder of the Italian republic; he knew how to see, through the miseries of the present, the splendors of the future; he knew how to understand the French people, when their government seems to act only to make them misunderstood and cursed by the people of Europe."

On October 23 there is a long discussion about Hungary and Italy, and on October 28 there are protests against the persecution to which *Italia del popolo* is subjected. The topic is raised in a discussion about the "magnificent article" that Mazzini had published in it "on the holy alliance of the people," an article that was then widely translated in subsequent issues. Italian life is often mentioned. On November 29, 1849, a letter from Giacinto Carini, written in Paris on November 27, defends the Sicilian revolution, and Italy is not neglected in an editorial on November 30 defending the struggle for liberty and independence in the great historical nations, Poland, Hungary, and Italy. Shortly before ceasing publication (the final issue is dated January 6, 1850), in the editorial on December 28, 1849, *La Réforme* concludes its international campaign saying, "The mission of France is to unite all the free forces of the people of Europe into an indestructible force and, relying on America . . . , to undertake the civilization and pacification of the globe."

But, according to Herzen, by that date Sazonov had already broken with Lamennais and been expelled from France.[22] The January 8, 1850, issue of *National* said, in its "faits divers," "We have learned that one of the principal staff members of 'La Réforme,' Russian by birth, naturalized Swiss, and residing in France for many years, has been ordered to leave Paris immediately and to leave the territory where he had been so hospitably received. It is with great difficulty, they say, that this foreigner obtained a two-day respite to put his affairs in order." Belgium showed great solidarity toward Sazonov, and on January 2, 1859, a new *Réforme* was created there. In the industrial and working-class center of Verviers, the Liège publicist Joseph Goffin, with collaboration from Paris and from French immigrants whose identity would be of interest to us, had created a lively daily paper that lasted until 1854.[23] "We have just replaced a journal which described itself, since its appearance, as the energetic defender of the rights of all, the untiring propagator of the immortal principles of justice and equality which ought to preside over the development of society. This journal has fallen, having failed in the beautiful and holy mission it had undertaken. We take up its work once again, adding important modifications that the flow of ideas has introduced into the domain of politics and social economy."

In other words, Lamennais was accused of having been too moderate and insufficiently socialistic. Was there perhaps an echo in Goffin's words of the discontent of Pierre Joigneaux, who had thought he might succeed Ribeyrolles? Joigneaux had not approved of the choice of Ledru-Rollin, and he later emigrated to Belgium after the December 3 coup d'état.[24] Or do we recognize in Goffin's polemic the mark of Nikolai Sazonov's designs? There is no doubt that in issue number 8, dated January 10, 1850, Sazonov was presented to the readers with particular benevolence, and it would have been difficult for the details regarding him not to have come from his own pen. The article said that *Le National* had announced the exile "of a Russian refugee, one of the principal staff members of the 'Réforme,'" but he was not named.

This refugee is Citizen Sazonov, who in fact has published, in the last three months, some remarkable articles on foreign affairs in the "Réforme." Though he has not been informed of the reasons for his expulsion, the writ ordering him to leave

France was sent to the offices of the "Réforme," and he leaves in France all those who had been his friends. Citizen Sazonov is one of the most erudite men in Europe. He is thoroughly at home in and writes all the continental languages. But neither his industrious habits nor his peaceful ways have been able to find favor for him with the men who have made it their business to proscribe, without pity, republican sentiments. Citizen Sazonov has gone to mingle himself with the phalange of noble exiles in Switzerland who are pursued by the violence of government and who will be protected, we hope, by the traditional Swiss hospitality.

This was a minor episode in the publication of the Verviers *Réforme,* but it was characteristic of the internal quarrels in the democratic and socialist party. With the polemic between Mazzini and George Sand, between Ledru-Rollin and Louis Blanc, these quarrels soon led to the formation of the Mazzinian trend on one hand and an incipient socialist party on the other. Despite the Belgian paper's interest in Italy and Mazzini in 1850 and 1851, it is evident that its main purpose was to become reassociated with socialist and Proudhonian trends, and to discuss economic and workers' problems. From the first issues, these struggles are illustrated in a distant and seductive light, in an unexpected and surprising view from the East. In the second issue on January 3, 1850, we read, "Today we commence publication of two letters written by a Russian about his country. This remarkable work will give our readers an idea of the social and political state of a people who are teaching themselves to play an important role in Europe . . ." It refers to the pages from Herzen's "De La Russie" taken from *Voix du peuple,* where it was published the previous autumn. *L'Italia del popolo* published an Italian translation, and a German version soon appeared; but this Belgian reprinting was forgotten and was not even cited in the most recent edition of Herzen's works.[25] Yet these pages form a link that cannot be neglected in the discussions on Russia that soon culminated, in Belgium, in the writings of Ernest Coeurderoy. He became a violent adversary of Mazzini when the latter took his stand against socialism. Coeurderoy put his hope in the barbarian East, saying it was the only force capable of overcoming the bourgeois organization of the West and of bringing to the West the seeds of the libertarian collectivism that Herzen had taught him to seek and find in the villages and people of distant Russia.[26]

In 1850, having found refuge in Switzerland, Sazonov too placed all his hopes in a socialist revolution. On January 4, 1851, he wrote to Moses Hess, "the future, a near future, will belong to communism."[27] In writing to Marx on May 2, 1850, he said he had reached Switzerland "irritated, ill-humored, and angry, but without having lost his spirit." As for his ideas, by now they were those of Wolff and "therefore yours." A careful examination of Proudhon's last work (that is, his *Confessions d'un révolutionnaire*) and a reading of his conciliatory articles in *Voix du peuple,* "took me a further step in your direction, and since I do not believe you have changed your opinions, you will be pleased to know that I agree on all the basic points about which you have written in the *Manifesto* which you published in

Brussels. Yes, my friend, in following a natural development, driven by irrefutable logic, by love for liberty as well as by a love of order, I reached the conclusion that a serious revolutionary can only be communist, and now I am a communist." He explained that by now "European civilization was only progressing in the field of industry, and that in all other fields, it was atrophying." He spoke of brutality that had some justification against such a civilization and of the exploitation that was innate in any modern economy. Regarding such conclusions, he said, "Mazzini, in whom I initially believed more than in anyone else, has proved to be a man of the past, simply retrograde." How could he write that the contemporary world was longing for authority! The French too promised little ("you know that the only communist is Cabet, and he is hardly attractive to the practical imagination"). Then he spoke of his grandiose plans, of a central printing organization of all socialists. It was a plan he had had to abandon after having recognized the lack of revolutionary conviction among those he would have liked to call upon. "For a new cause one needs new people; it is indispensable to have strong young men with a serious knowledge and deep convictions to undertake the task of unifying Europe in the name of the great idea of communism." There were two new men, Sazonov and Frapolli, "who had been the representative of Lombardy, of Tuscany and of Rome in Paris." When he wrote for the *Réforme* he had always supported the Italian cause. Now "the strong organization of Italians" would serve as a base for this European effort. Herzen, the French, and the Hungarians would join this nucleus. It was left to Marx to give the theoretical orientation to the movement. He was the only one capable of doing so.[28]

In the autumn of 1851, Sazonov was again in Paris, evidently to pursue the action that he, like so many others in those months, hoped would lead to a renewal of the revolution in France. He wrote to Marx that everything seemed to confirm his conviction about the increasingly rapid approach of the "ruin of the old society." The population was freeing itself from the prejudices of the past. "Worker's associations" contributed toward people's political education and they were now more progressive than one might expect on the basis of their original statutes. Cabet, Leroux, Louis Blanc, all tended to unify the communists.[29]

The expectant atmosphere was stifled a few months later with the Bonapartist coup. Sazonov had to leave Paris again and return to Switzerland. His economic situation was precarious. Nor was he able to work as a solitary thinker, as Herzen had done in those years, first in Geneva and then in Nice.[30] In addition, the conflict that separated him further from his old friend, a conflict that arose from Herzen's tragic family situation, demonstrated that Sazonov was incapable of living, not only intellectually but also morally, at the level of tension and unity between words and deeds, between ideas and daily existence at which Herzen was setting such an extraordinary and painful example. Sazonov's destiny was very different. By then, the emigrés had dispersed from Geneva. In 1852 he returned to Paris in the hope of finding work. He was embroiled in difficulties, debts, and troubles of all kinds. He made a vain attempt to revive his relationship with

Herzen, who had been mortally wounded by his old friend's indifference and weakness during the most tragic moments of Herzen's life. But once again it was from Herzen and from Italy that Sazonov took the symbol of his generation's deep despair after the failure of all revolutionary hopes. He wrote to Herzen from Paris on March 24, 1852,

Recently, I have thought more than I have acted, and I believe all sincere people would do likewise in these times. I have been thinking, and therefore I have read a great deal. Guess what I have read above all. Your beloved Leopardi. I do not know if you have read his correspondence. I have read and reread it, along with all his works, in order to get a complete and clear idea of the man, and I have fallen in love with him. He has all the elements that attract me: originality and novelty in the highest and best sense of the word, an incomparable beauty of form and a profound goodness of heart, and, finally, those few small defects that endear people to us. He has become an even better friend in that I approached him very gradually; a more interesting friend in that for the first time I have become attached to a man with different ideas from my own. My friendship with Leopardi, I hope will draw me closer to you.[31]

He was reminding Herzen of his more intimate life. The last book that his wife Natasha had looked at before dying had been by Leopardi, and Herzen always remained attached to this bound copy.[32] In Herzen's letter to Michelet on *Le Peuple russe et le socialisme,* only Leopardi seemed worthy of mention in his discussion of the moral situation in which Russian intellectuals and writers found themselves under the tyranny of Nicholas I. "Sadness, skepticism, irony, those are the three strings of the Russian lyre.... Life tires us like a long journey without end.... We hurl ourselves toward the tomb, without happiness, without glory, and before death we throw a glance of bitter disdain on our past. We pass unnoticed on this earth, a mournful, silent, and soon forgotten crowd. I know only one modern poet who has made the somber strings of the human soul vibrate with so much force. This poet too was born a slave, and he died before the awakening of his country. This was the apologist for death, the famous Leopardi, he who presented the world as a league of evildoers making relentless war on a few virtuous fools."[33]

In London, Herzen stoutly defended Leopardi against Mazzini. "Men of action, agitators, those who move the masses, do not understand such poisoned hesitations, such destructive doubts. They only see a fruitless lament and the discouragement of the weak. Mazzini could not understand Leopardi, this I knew from the start, and therefore I attack him rather roughly." Were Mazzini's opinions like those of Frederick II, who was said to get angry at Mozart's music because it was not suitable for his guards? Or did he expect Leopardi to take part in the Roman republic? In this clash, Aurelio Saffi defended the poet: "From this conversation, and from similar ones, I understood that in reality they were on different paths. For one man thought was searching for its own means, concentrating on them alone, and in one way this is an escape from doubts, while seeking an applied activity, and in another way this is laziness. For the other man, objective truth was dear; his thoughts labored; for an artistic nature, art above all is loved for itself, above and beyond any link with reality."[34]

Sazonov's passion for Leopardi, even though it corresponded to the same needs that moved Herzen, is less clear and direct. But his passion is certainly not without historical acumen and real critical comprehension. In 1855 he devoted one of his most important articles to Leopardi. It was published in the Parisian journal *Athenaeum français,* a periodical that in its erudition and elegance, in its affected and careful manner, fully reflects the tired and cold intellectual atmosphere of the first years of the Second Empire. In the journal Sazonov's writings stand out by contrast, if for no other reason than for the interest of the problems with which he deals.[35] Using as a pretext two modest books, *Silvio Pellico e il suo tempo* by Pietro Giuria (Voghera, 1854) and *La filosofia di Giacomo Leopardi* by D. Solimani (Imola, 1854), Sazonov underlines all that was of interest in Italian cultural life in those years. Naturally, his criticism of these two volumes could only be severe. But he said it would have been unjust to judge from them what was being written and taught on the other side of the Alps. "At this time, Italian literature, by a sudden effort—or rather, without any effort other than bringing up to date and reuniting its hitherto latent and dispersed forces into a luminous focus, has taken an honorable and uncontested place among the other modern literatures. There are not yet great works to point to, but, for those who love the beautiful land *dove il si suona,* there are tendencies both serious and progressive, a true rebirth of the Italian genius, to be noticed with joy." Fortunately, the "ambitious affirmations" of Gioberti and the pallid romanticism of Silvio Pellico had faded. A new light was clearing the scene of such "ghosts of the past." The symbol of this renewal, of this new modern and European awareness of Italy, was Leopardi. "Both Pellico, who died in 1854, and Leopardi, who died in 1838, belonged to the past, but with this difference, that one was the precursor of a future which we do not yet touch, while the other was, in our time, only the echo of ideas long since dead." Pellico represented the romantic idea of the regeneration, the rebirth, the revival of the past. It was born from the "bad side of romanticism, that movement that had the pretension of regenerating everything—religion, art, society—and which resulted only in imitations more or less pleasing in form, but equally lacking in real knowledge and serious inspiration. . . . Romanticism, confusion in religious, literary, and political ideas, the whole expressed in very fine style and resulting in an abstract resignation which in practice manages to destroy even hope; such, in our opinion, is the *caracteristique* of Silvio Pellico."

Leopardi was entirely different: "The ratification of the popular voice is still lacking for Leopardi's glory; it may even be lacking for a long time, but it will not always be so. Italy, which is accomplishing the national restoration of learning and of poetry, which studies with love its great philosopher Giordano Bruno, will not forget to raise a noble monument in its pantheon to one of the worthiest of its children." Only those who had never read his works could consider him to be a skeptic, a follower of Voltaire, a nonbeliever. In reality, he was "one of the most convinced spirits, one of the warmest and most believing hearts that has ever existed." How could Terenzio Mamiani have been so mistaken about him? To discover the truth one had only to read and reread his works, and let oneself be caught up by him, thus becoming not only an admirer of Leopardi, but also a friend. Undoubtedly his philosophy was "at first difficult and repulsive, as much from the severe simplicity of its method as by the frightful monotony of its principal theme. Unhappiness and death, these are the only two subjects of the meditations of Leopardi the philosopher, the two sources of Leopardi the poet.... He has not only written, he has lived his poetry and he has died of his thought." He was certainly not a man and an artist whom a critic like Sainte-Beuve could call "elegant and spiritual." He was a poet and thinker for a few, but these few were bound to him forever. In an effort to bring the French public closer to Leopardi, Sazonov translated "La Ginestra" and a part of the introduction to the *Manual of Epictetus*.[36]

Thus Leopardi opened Sazonov's eyes to a view of Italy that was both deeply wounded and disillusioned, but was also capable of drawing on its experience and starting a profound intellectual and moral renewal. One had only to glance at the Piedmontese periodicals of the time to recognize this. Consider the *Rivista contemporanea*, the *Rivista enciclopedica italiana*, and especially *Il cimento*. The editors of the latter "intend to renew Italian learning by applying to it both the national genius and the progress of foreigners. The principal contributors are: Bertrando Spaventa, a young philosopher who has studied Hegel extensively and who is preparing to publish a considerable work on Giordano Bruno; Antonio Gallenga, member of the Chamber of Deputies, who lived in England for a long time and who knows the politics and literature of that country well; Constantino Nigro *[sic]*, a remarkable poet, who at this time is collecting the national songs of Piedmont."

Nor did Sazonov forget Ausonio Franchi's *La ragione*, "an organ devoted exclusively to the high questions of philosophical learning."[37] The spectacle of the Milanese press was sadder, but still significant. The *Annali di statistica* had closed. The *Giornale dell'Istituto* was worth remembering in its role as a continuation of of the *Biblioteca italiana*. "Ugo Foscolo had to exile himself after refusing to write in it." "The only journal in Milan which represents serious studies and noble beliefs, always well supported and expressed, is the weekly review called 'Il crepuscolo,' under Carlo Tenca. Its young editors, after all the unhappiness suffered by their country, do not despair of the future, and to hasten its coming, they have chosen the better way, that of the persistent and always fruitful efforts of science and industry." "We wish that the 'Crepuscolo' may pursue its success until it is obliged to change its name."[38]

The publication of the third volume of the *Storia degli italiani* by Cantù (Turin, 1854), cheered Sazonov and seemed a new and important sign. "Up to the present time the history of Italy in its entirety was treated more by foreigners than by Italians." It was enough to think of Sismondi and Heinrich Leo. The material was rich and of extraordinary interest. "One can dispute with justice the *prééminence italienne* (Italy's primacy), but what is beyond dispute is the fact that the history of Italy is the most interesting of all those that one could write about."[39] Even the unpublished letters of Muratori attracted Sazonov's attention. The facility with polemics demonstrated by the historian from Modena reminded him of Voltaire, and Sazonov also admired the sensitivity he showed for the difficulties and the disasters in his own country.[40] Undoubtedly, the sense of isolation, the fear of being disregarded, and the compensating insistence on the superiority of their country—those sentiments that had so often dominated the Italians in the early 19th century—had neither been overcome nor disappeared. In the *Rivista europea,* on the occasion of Le Monnier's publication of Vittorio Alfieri's *Tragedie,* why did Coppino have to write that "France does not understand Italy"? "Although some noble souls from there like this country in general, an awareness of our spirit has not penetrated," he had added. And he wrote this just when Alfieri received "a resounding homage from learned Germany" in the *History of the 19th Century* by Gervinius and when it was becoming more evident that, a "lover of the beautiful, of the fatherland, and of liberty, Alfieri is assuredly a great poet, even more than a national poet. In recognition of his great qualities, we should know how to pardon some too famous epigrams, wherein there is more of spite than of hatred. It is time for his great shade to be reconciled with the land he loved so much in his youth, and for vain recriminations no longer to assail the poet who knew how to make the principles and sentiments which the French 18th century gave to mankind flourish in his country."[41]

Sazonov developed a similar reinterpretation of the Italian classics on the occasion of the publication of Lamennais's version of the *Divine Comedy.* Long past are the political struggles of 1850. Sazonov admires Lamennais's magnificent presentation of Dante. Before looking at the volume, he had been afraid that once again Dante would serve as a pretext for a repetitious statement about the Middle Ages and romanticism. He had wondered,

Are we going to make again the errors of Schlegel, Gorres, and Novalis, to walk in the steps of de Maistre and de Bonald? One could ask oneself that, and not without concern. . . . The publication of this posthumous and supreme work by one of the greatest writers of our time solves the problem in a different way. No one would ever have believed that love of the institutions and attitudes of the Middle Ages had led M. Lamennais to dedicate the last years of a life filled with glorious labors to the study and reproduction in French of the Dantean poem. It is quite the opposite. One of the most illustrious adversaries of the feudal spirit and of the social organization that derived from it has been unable to help becoming infatu-

ated with a deep and sympathetic love for the sublime poem which epitomizes
the life of the Middle Ages, even though that age itself was dead, vanished, even to
most of its social or moral consequences, dead without hope of resurrection. He
understood then that one could deliver oneself, without fear and without reproach, to the admiration inspired by the genius of the *ghibelline* poet.[42]

Now this great work by Lamennais, Sazonov continues, is taken up, pursued, transformed by the younger generation of Italian critics, and by one writer in particular,
Francesco De Sanctis. He

belongs to the army of young thinkers who have set themselves the task of initi-
ating their compatriots into German scholarship. After the works of Schlosser,
Karl Witte, and Tommaseo, he had the courage to undertake once again the ex-
plication of the *Divine Comedy*, to carry into the middle of the shadows of this
gigantic work the torch of modern criticism, and to seek to clarify the mystery
of the epic of the Middle Ages by means of the luminous methods of Hegel. The
work of De Sanctis is not yet published; it was done during two years when it was
the subject of a course he taught at Turin, and we know only fragments of it, that
is, what was published in "Il cimento," but these fragments bear witness to a deep
study of Dante, along with an original and gripping appreciation of the laws of
poetic conception.[43]

The words quoted above, the concluding words in Sazonov's contribution to the
Athenaeum français, should convince us of his sensitivity and of the exceptional
breadth of his knowledge about everything regarding Italian culture in the 1850s.
As in the past, his curiosity about Italy was accompanied by a broad discussion of
German themes and of the problems of Central and Eastern Europe. He was also
attempting to make Russian history and culture a little better known and less distorted than it had been in those years, a time still close to the polemics that had
accompanied the beginning of the Crimean War. In that period, Sazonov had begun a somewhat detached and cool collaboration with Herzen, announcing in the
Athenaeum français, "among the curiosities of our time" the publication of *Polyarnaya zvezda* (Polar Star), "a Russian review in London," paying tribute to its
director, to Herzen, "one of the most distinguished writers of Russia."[44] In the
changed climate, Sazonov had undertaken the task of "cosmopolitizing" the
French press, the job that Herzen had hoped he would carry out in the months
and years of the revolution.

But what contacts and ties did Sazonov have with Italians? Aside from his reading of journals and books, where did he obtain his information, which, as we have
seen, was unquestionably well-founded and up to date? As there is no direct evidence, we can only guess. It would be difficult not to place Sazonov near that
group of Italians who gathered around Giacinto Carini and the *Revue franco-
italienne.* They were exiles who had remained in France when, after 1851, Mazzini's
supporters, the republicans, had abandoned French soil, which had become im-

possible territory for them after the December 2 coup d'état and the imperial
dictatorship. Mazzini, Saffi, and many others had gone to London. Pisacane,
Medici, and Orsini were operating in Italy, trying to take maximum advantage of
the possibility of action offered by constitutional Piedmont. But an active and
intelligent group had remained in Paris. They decided to present Italy in a light
that was considerably different from that of the romantic decades, and which was
in clear contrast with the errors and the faults that had led to the ruined hopes of
1848. They wanted to show Italy as a country that was beginning to work again,
that was rebuilding its industrial and commercial framework, that needed technical assistance and loans, and that had now abandoned the vain dreams of the
past. These men were Francophiles, though they were distant and detached from
the Empire. They presented themselves as businessmen rather than as political
figures or warriors. They wanted to be realistic, they used statistics eagerly, and
they supported technical and industrial progress, convinced that this was the way
by which Italy would again be able to assert itself in Europe. In November 1854
they had created the *Revue franco-italienne* which, in obedience to the French
laws of censorship, carefully avoided discussing politics, but took advantage of
any economic or cultural topic to try to demonstrate that things were changing
on the other side of the Alps and that it was pointless to look at Italy in the light
of old prejudices. "Journal hebdomadaire non politique: sciences, industrie, commerce, littérature, beaux-arts, théatre," read the subheading of the *Revue franco-
italienne.*[45] "It has for its goal and ambition," we read in Giacinto Carini's presentation on November 16, 1854, "to activate the exchange of ideas and to strengthen
the solidarity of interests between France and Italy. We will apply to the accom-
plishment of this task our filial love of Italy and our admiration for this beautiful
France, whose destinies occupy and interest the whole world, and who preside
over the development of modern civilization."
    As one of the main French contributors to the *Revue* said,

We are, in France, the organ of thinking and acting Italy. This noble land, which
has such a rich patrimony of remembrances and traditions, has long remained outside the industrial movement which is the distinctive sign of the 19th century....
Behind the historic and poetic Italy which all the world knows, behind the pic-
turesque Italy which everyone has visited, there is a young, active, industrial Italy,
full of emulation and ardor, which makes use of the most useful and recent modern inventions, which covers its soil with a network of railways, which weaves
cloth, makes machines, implements, furniture, pottery, glassware, digs mines and
quarries, lays out electric telegraphs, founds loan societies; in a word, augments
its production, mobilizes and multiplies its capital.[46]

    Along with this periodical, an "Office franco-italien" was created and directed
by Carini. "This establishment is designed to serve as an industrial, artistic, and
commercial center between France and Italy, and *vice-versa.*" It was intended to
serve as a communications channel between Italian producers and the organizers

of the 1855 World Exhibition in Paris, and thus it would also help introduce manufacturing, industrial, and artisan Italy. The first broad and intelligent view of this aspect of Italy was provided by Pietro Maestri in the early issues of the *Revue franco-italienne*. He wrote a series of articles which he later revised and completed, but even in their first version they are a document of great interest for anyone wishing to learn about the economic history of that decade.[47] The cultural articles in the *Revue franco-italienne* are generally less outstanding, although books and journals that came out in Turin and elsewhere were carefully discussed. Here we also find expressed the delighted surprise about periodicals that "augmentent a vue d'oeil dans les Etats sardes," as well as warm praise for Ausonio Franchi's *La ragione*.[48] Carini dealt systematically with music, and when *Il Trovatore* was performed, he wrote with joy that "it was the definitive consecration of the glory of Verdi."[49] There is a clear liking for Michelet, especially for what the French historian writes about Italy.[50]

Going through the pages of the periodical, from articles on industry to ideas, from statistics to literature, suddenly starting on May 10, 1855, in issues number 18, 20, and 23, we come across a full study on Leopardi in which there seems to be an echo of or at least a reply to the same problems that had moved Nikolai Sazonov to write his article in the *Athenaeum français* on March 31 of the same year. Incidentally, the articles by F. Bourbon Del Monte, which as far as I know are completely unknown to historians of Italian literature, are worthy of remark. This author, too, tries first of all to clear the terrain of the traditional differences between France and Italy. He also tries to stress "the literary, philosophical, and political resurrection" of the peninsula during the age of Foscolo, Manzoni, Alfieri, and Romagnosi, and he concludes by affirming that "in the middle of this renaissance of Italian thought a man arose, who seems to us to outshine all his contemporaries ...a man who surpasses perhaps all the classics of Italy by the profound logic of his ideas...." The man is Leopardi, who "is still unknown." "An article by Sainte-Beuve ... has restored a portion of the brilliance that is due him, but the ingenious writer did not appear to suspect the philosophic importance of this great poet." Only by going back to the origins of modern skepticism, by understanding the break with the world of medieval faith brought about by Descartes, by the men of the Enlightenment, and by German philosophy, was it possible truly to understand the significance of the works of Leopardi.[51] The poet's torment is contemporary with and parallel to what lies in the center of modern thought: "In Germany, philosophy passed through many phases; it stopped itself at many stages before arriving at the complete negation of all belief. That is the characteristic difference between the Italian genius and the German genius. The Italian, more poetic than the German, gets by intuition to the place where the other comes only through an arduous series of logical deductions."

The German thinkers included Kant, Fichte, Schelling, and Hegel. But all these ideas continued to lend themselves to a religious interpretation. It was only Feuerbach who had achieved the final step, arriving at the "complete negation of belief." "Leopardi had arrived at this same point long before him, but, far from resigning himself, he cried out bitterly, and this plaint of an inconsolable soul is found in each line of his philosophical works."

Del Monte becomes involved in a detailed and passionate comparison between Feuerbach's and Leopardi's ideas on death and love, finding "an astonishing coincidence" as well as a profound difference in the psychological and moral consequences of their common ideas. Feuerbach, in accepting fate, is "more positive," "wishes to use this desolate doctrine to the profit of humanity," and thus reaches stoic conclusions. Leopardi is more logical: "If nature's laws are blind, if she creates and destroys with the same facility, it is not given to man to master his feelings; if his aspirations fall so far short of the power that he has to realize them, he must inevitably be unhappy. In occupying himself with the things of this world, he could, it is true, feel a certain enjoyment, a certain material well-being that will satisfy in part the vulgar, but no happiness for the intelligent, no enjoyment for the thinker; on the contrary, a void, an eternal unhappiness."[52]

These are concepts that Del Monte uses and exemplifies in a series of Leopardian texts that he translated. He concludes that only negatively, and through "an unbounded despair" derived from the absence of all political and religious faith, Leopardi had reached "the same conclusions as the author of the *Imitation*," and without wanting to, he had thus given "a new force to religion, sole refuge of humanity against a limitless sadness. Hegel, who had understood the sublimity of this divine power, had at least the merit of having raised the spirits to a grander and vaster level, and of having achieved the rout of the encyclopedic sensualism, the philosophic materialism of the 18th century.... This side escaped Leopardi entirely...."[53] But Leopardi had gone farther, to the very depths of his desperation.

Sazonov's continued interest in Italian life was for him one element, one note, in his continuous comparison between Russia and the West, a comparison that for him, as for Herzen, had become the central theme of the years immediately following the defeat of 1848. Soon, the Crimean War urgently presented a similar problem. Sazonov had contributed a vivid and well-informed pamphlet to the propaganda directed against the empire of the czars. It was called *La Verité sur l'empereur Nicolas par un Russe,* and it came out in Paris in 1854 along with a pamphlet addressed to prisoners of war, *Rodnoy golos na chuzhbine* (A fellow countryman's voice in a foreign land). Its purpose was to convince the prisoners that their true enemy was the government that maintained the slavery of peasants and denied civil and political liberties to all. (It was published by Herzen in London at the beginning of 1855.)[54]

Another of his contributions to the anticzarist propaganda was an article published a year later in issue number 2 of *Polyarnaya zvezda* (The Polar Star), Herzen's periodical, entitled "Mesto Rossii na vsemirnoy vystavke (Russia's position in the World Exhibition).[55] In fact, the war had prevented Russia's participation in the Exhibition. Thus Sazonov's article acquires an entirely hypothetical and paradoxical aspect, and its aim is to shed light from the inside on the differences and the uniqueness of the czarist empire as compared with bourgeois France and England. This work is precariously balanced between Sazonov's socialist ideas, influenced by Marx, and his evaluation and acceptance of Russia's unique and promising destiny. He is openly in favor of science, technology, and industry, but considers them to be distorted by Western social structure. Particularly in France, the state, the military, the police, the judiciary, the laws, everything tended to favor bourgeois profits, to transform all work into exploitation, to place all modern civilization into the hands of an increasingly small and increasingly powerful group of wealthy people. Sazonov seems to accept this concentration of economic power as an innate necessity in a bourgeois economy, but when he is faced with the concrete forms that this phenomenon takes, when he observes the products lined up in the World Exposition, he withdraws, horrified by the moral and social insensitivity that they show, before the useless and shameless luxury, before the oppressive atmosphere, including the economic atmosphere, of Second Empire Paris. "At present, France strikes the observer because of the uninterrupted shrinking, shriveling of her life. . . . In Paris, life is made of oppression and pain."[56] Technology itself is not advancing, but is becoming more exclusively an instrument for social exploitation. Railways serve to make the workers into slaves for the capitalists, and the minor capitalists are slaves of the bigger ones. Universal education has done nothing but provide monopolists with new means for action and oppression. The stock market and speculation prevent the expansion of scientific research. The poor, under the influence of industry, lose their appreciation for simplicity and their appreciation in general. Private property becomes an instrument of illiberality. The middle classes are systematically destroyed and society tends to become polarized between the big capitalists and the mass of slaves. Workers are increasingly subjected to a paternalistic regime that concedes life to them on the sole condition that they do not rebel. Criticism, irony, open discussion disappear. Public opinion becomes more and more humble, vulgar, and vile. Economic gain becomes a universal measure. Compared with a France like this, Russia, absent and distant, the Russia that could not display its products because of the war, seems to show the possibility and the hope of a different development. It is a country where a centralized state, the indispensable instrument of modern economic progress, exists; it is a land where the peasants, the artisans, the populace have maintained a strong collective mentality; it is a nation that was able to give life to the literature of protest that bears the name of Gogol. Chaadaev and many others seemed destined to benefit from the two great advantages that Russia has over the West: the lack of a bourgeoisie and the lack of a judicial tradition based on Roman law.

    In conclusion, Sazonov recalls the figures of the great writers he knew, Mickewicz and Lamennais, so as to remind readers of their evaluation of Russia and of the intelligentsia (Chaadaev was the De Maistre of Russia, Lamennais used to say). The past centuries that Sazonov quickly covers with an enraptured view seem to indicate the promise of a great future for the descendents of those who learned to free themselves from the Tartars and to build a Russian state. Was this a panegyric? an apologia? No, says Sazonov. The paths of the West and of Russia will meet in the future, provided the West becomes free of the bourgeoisie and creates an economy that is advantageous to all, and provided Russia avoids the errors and suffering of other populations, achieving the same goal by other paths.

The great wave of hope and enthusiasm that moved through Russia after the death of Nicholas I carried Nikolai Sazonov far. But he lacked the moral and intellectual strength of Herzen, who always managed to remain free during the years of preparation before Alexander II's reforms. The more Herzen showed his independence from the Western as well as the Russian governments, the more effective he became in his London exile. Instead, Sazonov's hopes, as well as his political weakness, led him to try to become part of the internal movement of Alexander II's reforms, trying to influence them from within, trying to be both their illustrator and their leading spirit. By 1857, he asked for a pardon and permission to return to Russia.[57] The diplomatic rapprochement between Russia and France following the Crimean War, the changes in Napoleon III's foreign policy, the preparation of the Empire for action in Italy drew Sazonov closer to those who placed growing hopes in France's actions in Europe. On March 4, 1858, Sazonov became a member of the Paris Lodge "Henri IV," and on August 5 of the same year, he became a master.[58] Thus he was also drawing closer to the group of German emigrés, gathered around Moses Hess, who supported the 1859 campaign. Like the men of the *Revue franco-italienne,* they had contributed to the preparation of what became Cavour's policies. Thus, Sazonov, whose great hopes, sustained during the Crimean War, had fallen flat, tried in the years immediately after to work for a new intellectual and political bond between Paris and St. Petersburg.

In August 1859, the first issue of the *Gazette du Nord* appeared. It was a "revue hebdomadaire internationale" that planned to deal with "littérature, moeurs, voyages, beaux-arts, commerce, industrie." The director was Gabriel de Rumine (Riumin), and its chief editor was Nikolai Sazonov. It would be interesting to know more about this paper. It probably expressed the views of those men in St. Petersburg who were turning to Archduke Constantine, the czar's brother, known for his tendencies for reform. It was also the most interesting attempt made in those years to acquaint the French world with Russia's problems. The empire of the czars was no longer presented as a warring force but as the land of Pushkin, Gogol, Turgenev, and Herzen. The paper no longer hid the fact that in the heart of Russia a sizable struggle was taking place between those who wanted reforms and those who supported "le vieux parti russe."[59] It recalled with pleasure the old tradition of Catherine II, the empress who was able to listen to French philosophers and economists.[60] It was vocal about the difficulties that interfered with the reforms, "rude and immense task! What abuse to root out! ... Yes, such is the goal of the Gazette du Nord, to play an active, resolute part in this movement of regeneration that stirs Russia, and to aid in its success." It did not hide the fact that the Crimean War and past wars in general had created a gap that now needed to be filled, a gap between the West and Russia. "Russia has entered the European family by a blind door.... Fateful error!"[61] Now Russia had to prove itself to be especially open to international cultural and political life.

Sazonov's first article in this paper was a full account of the *Jubilé séculaire de Schiller* celebrated in Germany as a symbol of a revival everywhere in Europe of the progressive and liberal forces.[62] As Luigi Kalisch said on this occasion in a speech that was translated into French and published independently by Sazonov, all populations could feel united in Schiller's name: "All of us, Russians, Poles, Italians, citizens of the ancient and of the new world, we salute your precious presence with joyous gratitude. It ornaments our feast and gives it its true consecration, because it bears witness that *our* Schiller is also yours. It offers us a beautiful and living image of the brotherhood of the people."[63]

The fundamental problem of the new Russia that was thus presented to the Parisians in 1859 was, naturally, the problem of the emancipation of the peasants. In issue number 10, dated December 10, Gabriel de Rumine introduced a series of articles that Sazonov was to publish on this topic. He challenged the idea, shared by many Russians, that it was an insoluble problem. "They are making of it a sort of bogey: to hear them, revolution, and a frightful revolution, would be the result. This is not our opinion; we believe that despite the interests which are at stake, emancipation will be accomplished without upset."[64] Sazonov's essays on this subject are a powerful exposition of the discussions that were taking place in Russia in those years about the procedure for liberation. He shows clear and evident sympathy for the solutions proposed by Herzen and further elaborated by Chernyshevsky, "this publicist who is as ingenious as he is clairvoyant."[65] At the center lies the defense of the *obshchina,* "an organization of labor *sui generis.*"

"Russia had till now avoided a proletariat, that gaping wound of modern societies; with the abolition of serfdom would it be necessary to accept the inoculation of this new malady? That was the real question.... The trend of public opinion, as well as the work of local committees," had led to the conclusion "that in abolishing almost the last traces of serfdom and slavery, it should be necessary to conserve from the old organization of agricultural labor in Russia all that which assures the well-being and liberty of the cultivator as well as the forces of the State."[66]

In the countries that were "the most advanced in civilization," such as France, England, and the United States, it had been concluded "that society ought to assure, in one way or another, a minimum to the poorest of its members." In Great Britain they had resorted to workhouses. "It is a form of succour that is quite insufficient, almost barbarous." In France they had used hospitals, almshouses, and public works. "All this is much more rational, much more humane than that which is done in England." As for America, the right of every citizen "who wished, to cultivate the lands belonging to the State" constituted "an essentially humane law." If the peasant community in Russia were dissolved, "it would be necessary to establish workhouses. May God keep us from that!" Furthermore, the *obshchina* could provide an excellent system for teaching the Russian people "to govern themselves by themselves," leading them "quite naturally to the ideas of association to which the future of the world belongs. From now on it will be necessary to dream, to facilitate the associations and fusions between the little economic communes, to manage to create vast communes fit to receive the fecund germ of association. An idea is beginning to develop in Russia, still vaguely, but it seems to us full of promise: it is that the agricultural commune should not be composed only of peasants, but of all inhabitants, without class distinction, of nobles, ecclesiastics (even landowners) and in general of all those who possess a field or enclosure." On this basis, schools and almshouses could be established "and especially exploitations on a large scale, whether agricultural or industrial." The cities themselves would take on the communal form. Sazonov ended his series of articles with an enthusiastic appeal: "Dear compatriots! We are the latecomers in universal civilization....We have invented neither gunpowder like the Chinese, nor paper like the Arabs, nor printing like the Germans, nor steamboats like the Americans, nor railroads like the English, nor the *crédit mobilier* like the French; but if we are able to organize a free people, in which there will be no proletarians, all our sins of omission will be pardoned us, and perhaps our elders, so proud of their seniority, will consent to admit us to equality. Let us go forward, then, in the name of our national honor and in the interests of humanity."[67]

Next to land comes liberty. The *Gazette du Nord* emphasized the need to overcome the monster of censorship. "It is truly the masterpiece of the bureaucratic spirit...it is moreover a polyp, a formidable polyp: I include political censorship, religious censorship, military censorship...."[68] The slowness and difficulty of establishing reforms were clearly attributed to the existing spirit of bureaucracy and censorship: "It is the bureaucracy. There, in that shadowy den, or rather, in that inextricable labyrinth, questions are not studied, they drag along, they go astray....For great harvests, free air and blazing sun are required. So long as Russia has not seriously, radically undermined its bureaucratic system, it will fly the flag of reform in vain."[69]

Sazonov stressed that "the first meeting" had been held in St. Petersburg. It was a discussion of the societies of shareholders, like the societies for action "that one has seen in England and France at different times and that are multiplying in Russia with dizzying rapidity. It was the first time, in Russia, that a question touching on the private and the public interest had been debated and resolved in public."[70] The entire system of public education needed review.[71] It was equally necessary to make reparations for the injustice, the persecution to which the Jews had been subjected under the czars.

It is not only a duty imposed by humanity and civilization, it is a measure which will turn everything to the advantage of Russia. The economic transformation produced by the abolition of serfdom can have a happy outcome only if it is accompanied by a great movement of industrial and commercial production. No system of credit, no combination of tariffs or of commercial treaties can create such a movement if there are not men within the country capable of interpreting it and of taking it to the end. The middle class in Russia is too small and generally not educated enough; the people, despite their promise, are plunged in ignorance and routine, the nobility too busy elsewhere, unprepared by education and perhaps hampered by aristocratic prejudices.

Therefore it was necessary to undergo

a life-giving ferment that could quicken the inert mass of sleeping capital and of the millions of human beings who waste their lives suffering from hunger. This yeast is there before us, in the Israelite race. Open the door to them, admit them to civil equality, and at once you would have, as if by magic, at your disposal men who are industrial from birth, commercial by nature, and who have financial science in their blood. You would have chiefs of industry and foremen, bankers and commercial travelers, all the necessary personnel to operate an economic movement such as the world has not yet seen.[72]

   As we see, the reform fever struck Sazonov, as it did many other Russians at the beginning of the 1860s. It was a fever that penetrated to the core of Russian society and its economic and social structure more than it dealt with the political and juridical aspects. It was not the constitution but the problems of land and of industry that were on the agenda. Evidently Sazonov feared that what had happened in Berlin, Madrid, and Naples would happen in St. Petersburg. The threatened Bourbons had taken refuge behind a screen of constitutionalism—not that Sazonov disapproved of parliamentary government, "with which, for our part, we are in complete sympathy." But a parliamentary government could not be applied in Russia as it had been in Italy, not until the basic problems, the emancipation of the serfs and national unification, had been solved.[73] As we learn from letters written to his sister, Maria Poludenskaya, in 1860, Sazonov followed with particular interest what was taking place in Italy—Garibaldi's battles in Sicily and Naples, the conflicts with the Vatican, etc.[74] But his thoughts were fixed on Russia, on the problems accumulating there, and on the great intellectual tradition, the original source from which he had begun and which, despite his meanderings, had remained at the center of his inspiration and his life. The creation, in St. Petersburg, of the Society to Assist Literary Persons and Scholars took him back to Novikov, Radishchev, and Belinsky.[75] In one of the last issues of his journal, he was pleased to announce that his French friends Philoxène Boyer and Charles Asselineau had contributed to the cause of the Russian intellectuals.[76]

During the final period of the *Gazette du Nord,* Sazonov's major essays were two portraits, one of Ivan Turgenev and one of Alexander Herzen, written as if to show the finest sources of inspiration in his tormented life as a writer, and also to introduce the French to the purest fruits of modern Russia. His encounter with Turgenev before the 1848 revolution became a symbol of his whole existence. They had discussed the major problems. In this dialogue, the novelist undertook to "make known the depths of the Russian soul," to reveal "the word of this national genius which up till now has seemed only to employ its forces to crush all life, to kill all liberty," whereas he, the publicist, undertook the study of "the elements of Western civilization," discovering "the latest formulas, the purest and most widely applicable ideas," in order to present them to Russia "as soon as she is able to welcome them." Sazonov could not avoid feeling the smallness, the frailty of his own contribution when compared with such vast aims. The work of Turgenev seemed so much greater and more important.[77]

Sazonov's review of Herzen's life, based on *My Past and Thoughts,* naturally signified a return to the very roots of his own existence. "Russia, last to come to modern civilization, and hurled, rather at the mercy of fate, into the adventures of European thought, could and naturally should stop only at the end of the line, at the outer limit of the principles that she had confidently accepted." Only through Hegelianism and socialism had the Russian intelligentsia, in pursuit of an ideal logic, found a way to be Russian and at the same time to associate more closely with the West. "Hegelian philosophy and socialism alone could make Russia emerge from the series of sterile imitations in which she was engaged and show her the way to achieve originality of thought. Herzen had the rare merit of being one of the hardy pioneers who opened that road."

Thus, Herzen's influence proved more profound than that of men like Aksakov, Chaadaev, Belinsky, and Bakunin. In an admirable work written in 1847–48, Herzen was the first in Russia to speak of the "happy days when Italy sought for the first time to regain her liberty and independence and to achieve unification." It was Herzen, in *Du développement des idées révolutionnaires en Russie,* who gave "an exposition of the moral and intellectual history of Russia—incomplete, no doubt, but animated by an excellent wit and distinguished by a just appreciation of the elements of national life." As for *From the Other Shore,* the book was

singular, eloquent, impassioned, exalted, written in the midst of the sufferings that a sensitive soul feels at the destruction of its dearest hopes, the check of its more intimate beliefs; we think it should remain in the universal literature as the monument of a dark and sad time that ought to have pushed even the most generous spirits to the excesses of reason, if not to other excesses. . . . In the overexcitement of the thought and even in the sputterings of the style, there is something unhealthy that denotes a crisis, but a crisis in a powerful constitution, one where health could not fail to triumph.

Herzen had found sanity and salvation in his memoirs, *Byloye i Dumy,* where a new relationship between Russia and the West was finally revealed. "It is necessary for this to find oneself in immediate, living contact with Western Europe, to have lived one's life during a time of activity, agitation, transformation; only then can one feel free, as a Russian and as a man, to speak in this regard." Throughout 1848 and the revolution as Herzen experienced them, "one hears beating the generous heart of the man who, in the sunshine of civilization, made his own distinct place, national and personal."[78]

The sadness of one who failed to achieve this is apparent in the words Sazonov devotes to Herzen. Even his last attempt, the *Gazette du Nord,* was heading toward ruin. On June 30, 1860, G. de Rumine and the "redacteur en chef" had to announce that the journal would cease publication. They said they had established new cultural relations between Russia and France, but only if they had been able to deal directly with "economic and political questions" would they have been able to gain the prestige that they needed to continue their work. "We have not been able to take up these subjects, and it is this fact that leads us to discontinue publication for the time being." What had been the value of obtaining the collaboration of the finest writers in France? (In the very last issues they had printed as a *feuilleton* Charles Baudelaire's *Paradis artificiels*.) Only one consolation remained: "To our enemies we have only one thing to say: they have pretended that the *Gazette du Nord* was subversive—that is a lie. This journal has never used any money other than that of its founder and subscribers."[79]

If we were to judge by Sazonov's fate, we could say that those responsible for the *Gazette du Nord* were right. The Clichy debtor's prison awaited him at the end of his last journalistic experience. Freed by his sisters, he retired to Switzerland. There he died in 1862, forgotten, without even one Russian in his funeral procession.[80]

"Russian shadows," Herzen had said. If nothing else, Sazonov would remain to show what interest we can find even in those whom Herzen was tempted to consider the shadows of his own generation. And, as we have seen, tracing Sazonov's experiences is like tracing a secret and strange itinerary through the world of 19th-century socialism and nihilism.

Notes

1. Wiktoria Śliwowska, *W kręgu poprzedników Hercena* [In the group of Herzen's predecessors] (Wroclaw: Ossolineum, 1971), pp. 202 ff. (This is the most complete study on Sazonov, to which we refer also for bibliographical references.)

2. Sazonov, "La Littérature et les hommes de lettres en Russie, II, M. Alexandre Hertzen," in *La Gazette du Nord,* no. 21 (May 26, 1860).

3. A. I. Herzen, "O sebe" [On himself], in *Sobranie sochineniy v tridtsati tomakh* [Works in thirty volumes] (Moscow: Akademia Nauk SSSR, 1954), 1:171.

4. Ibid., 10:317 ff.

5. Ibid., 11:44 and 46.

6. A. I. Herzen, *Pervaya vstrecha* [First encounter], ibid., p. 122.

7. Letter from Herzen to N. G. Ketcher, from Viatka, dated 22–25 November 1835, ibid., 21:56.

8. Letter from Herzen to N. A. Zacharina, from Vladimir, dated 30 January 1838, ibid., p. 274. There is considerable evidence of the contact between Herzen and Sazonov from 1836 to 1835 (ibid., see index).

9. A. I. Herzen, *Russkie teni* [Russian shadows], ibid., 10:322. See Michel Cadot, *La Russie dans la vie intellectuelle française, 1839–1856* (Paris: Fayard, 1967), pp. 31 ff.

10. Letter from Paris dated August 3, 1847, in Herzen, ibid., 23:34.

11. Śliwowska, *W kręgu poprzedników Hercena*, pp. 218 ff. and the bibliography indicated. Of particular importance is the photostatic reprint of this work, published by Ossolineum in Wroclaw, ed. Henryk Jabłonski, Stefan Kieniewicz, and Władisław Floryan in 1963.

12. Iwan Woinoff [N. Sazonov], "De la Russie," in *La Tribune des peuples*, 1, no. 1 (March 15, 1849).

13. Iwan Woinoff [N. Sazonov], "Vendredi saint!" (editorial), in *La Tribune des peuples*, 1, no. 23 (April 6, 1849).

14. Letter to E. Herwegh from Geneva, dated 5 October 1849, ibid., 13:193.

15. A. I. Herzen, *Russkie teni*, ibid., 10:330.

16. The letter was published by N. E. Zastenker, in *Literaturnoye nasledstvo* 62, no. 2 (1955):536.

17. Quoted in Herzen, *Russkie teni*, 23:408.

18. Pierre Joigneaux, *Souvenirs historiques* (Paris: Marpon & Flammarion, n.d.), 1:288.

19. Herzen, *Russkie teni*, 10:497. When the paper was revived after the suppression following the events of June 13, Herzen refers to *La Réforme* as having been "baptized by the Mazzinians" (ibid., p. 330).

20. *K. Marks, F. Engel's i revolyutsionnaya Rossiya* [K. Marx, F. Engels, and revolutionary Russia] (Moscow: Izd. Pol. Lit., 1967), pp. 146–47.

21. *La Réforme* (October 1, 1849).

22. Herzen, *Russkie teni*, 10:330.

23. See A. Weber, *Essai de bibliographie vervietoise. Journaux et publications périodiques* (Verviers: Fréquenne, 1899–1921) 5:53; and Roman Vann Eenoo and Arthur Vermeersch, *Bibliographisch Repertorium van de belgische pers. 1789–1913* (Leuven and Paris: Nauwelaerts, 1962), p. 48.

24. Joigneaux, *Souvenirs historiques*, 1:288 ff. Cf. Roger William Magraw, "Pierre Joigneux and Socialist Propaganda in the French Countryside, 1849–1851," *French Historical Studies*, 10, no. 4 (Fall 1978): 559 ff.

25. Herzen, *Russkie teni*, 6:150 ff., and 514n.

26. Coeurderoy and O. Vauthier, *La Barrière du combat, ou dernier grand assaut qui vient de se livrer entre les citoyens Mazzini, Ledru-Rollin, Louis Blanc, Etienne Cabet, Pierre Leroux, Marin Nadau, Malarmet, A. Bianchi (de Lille) et d'autres Hercules du Nord* (Brussels: A. Labroue, 1852), in which Mazzini is described as "devoured by ambition, dry, yellow, and feverish—his forehead pleated by cares, his eye burning with a dark fire—his mien ascetic—his hand clenched on his pen or on the handle of a dagger: that is Mazzini the monk: man, pope, god; Italy,

Europe, humanity" (p. 5). It also invokes against Mazzini "that part of Europe inhabited by a society of the disinherited, who one day will be called the elder sons of socialism, and who still at this moment are oppressed by a boyar's fist," and concludes, "they are worse than barbarians!" (p. 27). This is an idea that E. Coeurderoy developed later in his book *Hurrah!!! ou la révolution par les cosaques* (London, October 1854), in which he appealed to the "proletarian cossacks" (p. 25), claimed to be convinced that "the West will do nothing by itself" (p. 51), and, referring back to Herzen, concluded that "the only foreign people who could invade and revolutionize is Russia" (p. 59).

27. Edmund Silberner, "Sazonoff et les réfugiés politiques en Suisse en 1851," in *Annali dell'Istituto Giangiacomo Feltrinelli* (1961), pp. 194, ff., and *Moses Hess. Geschichte seines Lebens* (Leyden: E. J. Brill, 1966), pp. 310 ff., in which he discusses Sazonov's influence on Fasy, his contacts with K. Krolikowski, with Marie-Alexandre Massol, etc.

28. *Karl Marks, F. Engel's i revolyutsionnaya Rossiya*, pp. 147 ff. See M. I. Mikhailov, *Istorya Soyuza kommunistov* [History of the League of Communists] (Moscow: "Nauka," 1968), p. 370, in which one sees Sazonov involved somehow in the internal conflicts of the League.

29. Ibid., pp. 153 ff., letter from Paris dated September 10, 1851.

30. Franco Venturi, *Esuli russi in Piemonte dopo il '48* (Turin: Einaudi, 1959).

31. *Literaturnoye nasledstvo*, vol. 62, p. 540.

32. Herzen, *Russki teni*, 26:230, letter to his son, Alexander, dated December 12, 1858.

33. Ibid., vol. 7, *Le Peuple russe et le socialisme*, pp. 295–96.

34. A. I. Herzen, *Byloye i Dumy* [My past and thoughts], ibid., 10:79–80. See the presentation of the correspondence between Saffi and Herzen, ed. N. D. Efros, in *Literaturnoye nasledstvo* 64 (1958): 319 ff.

35. *Histoire générale de la presse française,* published under the direction of Claude Bellanger, Jacques Godechot, Pierre Guiral, and Fernand Terrou (Paris: P.U.F., 1969), 2:306.

36. *L'Athénaeum français,* 4, no. 13 (March 31, 1855): 255 ff.

37. Ibid., 4, no. 5 (February 3, 1855): 111.

38. Ibid., 4, no. 31 (August 4, 1855): 664.

39. Ibid., 4, no. 15 (April 14, 1855): 298.

40. Ibid., 4, no. 21 (May 26, 1855): 450.

41. Ibid., 4, no. 34 (August 25, 1855): 723.

42. Ibid., 5, no. 23 (June 7, 1856): 480.

43. Ibid., p. 483.

44. Ibid., 4, no. 33 (August 18, 1855): 714. On his articles on Russia, see Śliwowska, *W kręgu poprzedników Hercena*, pp. 239 ff.

45. In his interesting article, "Giacinto Carini journaliste à Paris (1849–1860)," published in *La Sicilia e l'unità d'Italia. Atti del Congresso internazionale di studi storici sul Risorgimento italiano (Palermo, 15–20 April 1961)* (Milan: Feltrinelli, 1962), 2:359, Ferdinand Boyer rightly confirms that the *Revue franco-italienne* is not preserved in the Bibliothèque nationale in Paris. A copy exists in the Biblioteca di Storia Moderna in Rome, under the call number: Per. Ris. 128.

46. J. Paradis, "L'Italie à l'Exposition universelle de 1855," in *Revue franco-italienne*, no. 5 (February 1, 1855).

47. See all the issues of the journal starting from no. 11, dated November 23, 1854. As we read in the *Annuario statistico italiano*, year 1, 1857–58 (Turin: Tipografia letteraria; Milan: Canadelli, 1858), p. 592: "The best picture of Italian industry was provided by Dr. Pietro Maestri in the 'Revue franco-italienne'; it is a picture from which foreign and our own newspapers drew information, as well as Mr. C. De Cesare in his reprimand against idleness and weakness among the Italian people (*Il mondo civile e industriale del secolo diciannovesimo* [Naples, 1857]). Now Maestri is reprinting his revised and amplified studies (in the *Rivista contemporanea*, in an article dated May 1858, etc.)..." According to the author's express declaration, from these articles has come the interesting book by A. Escourrou-Milliago, *De l'Italie agricole, industrielle et artistique, à propos de l'Exposition universelle de suivie d'un essai sur l'exposition du Portugal* (Paris: Serrière, 1856), in which one reads, among other things: "We wanted to furnish more victoriously the proof that Italy was not disinherited, as some writers have wished to pretend, and that, if she was not perhaps as advanced as the other nations on the road of industrial progress, she has none the less kept this taste, this cult of beauty which has so greatly illuminated her past.... It is not false to say that Italy, surmounting the obstacles that have been able to nullify her development, has taken again the place among the nations that her natural genius has assigned her, and has caused her noble aptitude, in the sciences as in the arts, to shine anew" (p. 11).

48. A. Guerrieri, "La Presse scientifique et littéraire en Piémont," in *Revue franco-italienne*, vol. 1, no. 5 (December 14, 1854).

49. G. Carini, "Revue musicale," ibid., no. 7 (December 28, 1854).

50. The *bonnes feuilles* of *La Renaissance* are published in no. 4, vol. 2, and the review that Montanelli writes on this work forms the editorial of no. 12, dated March 22, 1855: "Michelet's last book is a magnificent glorification of the Italian genius.... We have often confounded the Italian genius with the Roman genius: there is an abyss between the two ... the Roman genius is an immense recollection, the Italian genius is an immense aspiration." A few issues later (no. 13, dated April 15, 1855), Francis Torrente, in a "Coup d'oeil sur l'histoire de la pensée italienne," wrote that "the Renaissance caused a movement in Italian thought equal to that which was accomplished elsewhere by the Reformation."

51. F. Bourbon Del Monte, "Giacomo Leopardi," in *Revue franco-italienne* 2, no. 18 (May 10, 1855): 137 ff.

52. Ibid., no. 20 (May 24, 1855), pp. 155 ff.

53. Ibid., no. 23 (June 14, 1855), pp. 179 ff. Bourbon Del Monte gives a much more sweetened and fideistic version of this interpretation of Leopardi in *Correspondant* 59, n.s. 23 (July 1863): 491 ff. This article, but not the one in the *Revue franco-italienne*, is cited by N. Serban, *Léopardi et la France. Essai de littérature comparée* (Paris: H. Champion, 1913), p. 344. The problems of modern philosophy continued to interest Bourbon Del Monte. He pursued his discussions with Kant, Fichte, Hegel, and Leopardi in his book *L'Homme et les animaux. Essai de psychologie positive, par le marquis J.-B. François Bourbon Del Monte* (Paris: Boillière, 1877), in which he proves to be harshly critical of religious conservatism

and openly in favor of the "modern doctrine of evolution." In the Gospels next to the "morale sublime" were the fables. Politically, Bourbon Del Monte had proclaimed himself wholly anti-Piedmontese in 1859 (*L'Indépendance de l'Italie et le Piémont* [Paris: Charles Douniol]), saying, among other things, that "if one wishes to glance at the Italian literature of our century, at this intellectual renaissance of Italy, one will see surging from all parts of the Peninsula men whose nature and genius are of a totally different temper, of completely opposite character. When one sees such writers as Joseph De Maistre, Ugo Foscolo, Romagnosi, Alfieri, Vincenzo Monti and a bit more recently Manzoni and Leopardi, appearing at the same time, it is difficult to conceive of a fusion of such heterogeneous elements" (p. 10). He concluded saying that "Italy is not and never will be one nation, if by that one means a single, uniform state ruled by the same laws and the same customs" (p. 21). He published a moving obituary of his great friend Montanelli in 1862 with the publisher Charles Douniol. "He threatened to fall into the bottomless skepticism that had tormented the great souls of Foscolo and Leopardi in Italy when, in 1842, he had the good fortune of meeting several French Catholics, notably Ozanem..." (p. 6). For the genealogy of this Marquis Giovanni Battista Francesco III Bourbon Del Monte, born in 1831, married to a Princess Davydova "and married a second time to a French woman," whose death date is not known exactly, see Ugo Barbere, *I marchesi Bourbon Del Monte Santa Maria di Petrella e di Sorbello* (Città di Castello, 1943), table 7a.

54. See B. Kozmin, "Iz literaturnogo nasledstva N. I. Sazonova" [From the literary legacy of N. I. Sazonov] in *Literaturnoye nasledstvo* [Literary legacy] 41–42 (1941): 178 ff.

55. *Polyarnaya zvezda,* facsimile ed., ed. by M. V. Nechkina and E. L. Rudnitskaya (Moscow, 1966), vol. 2 (1856), pp. 209 ff.

56. Ibid., pp. 211 and 213.

57. Śliwowska, *W kręgu poprzedników Hercena,* p. 245.

58. E. Silberner, "La Correspondance Moses Hess-Louis Krolikowski. 1850–1853," in *Annali dell'istituto G. G. Feltrinelli* (1960), p. 590, and *Moses Hess. Geschichte seines Lebens* (Leyden: E. J. Brill, 1966), p. 355.

59. H. Stouf, "France et Russie," in *Gazette du Nord,* no. 7 (October 8, 1859).

60. P. Gournay, "Un économiste français en Russie" (M. de la Rivière), ibid., no. 2 (October 15, 1859).

61. Gabriel de Rumine, "Bulletin de la semaine," ibid., no. 7 (November 19, 1859).

62. Sazonov, *Le Jubilé séculaire de Schiller,* ibid., no. 6 (November 12, 1859), and no. 7 (November 19, 1859).

63. *Discours prononcé au Festival de Schiller par Louis Kalisch,* traduit de l'allemand par M. N. Sasonoff (1859).

64. Gabriel de Rumine, "Bulletin de la semaine," in *Revue du Nord,* no. 10 (December 10, 1859).

65. Sazonov, "De l'émancipation des serfs en Russie," ibid., no. 7 (February 18, 1860).

66. Ibid., no. 10 (December 10, 1859).

67. Ibid., no. 9 (March 3, 1860).

68. Gabriel de Rumine, "Bulletin de la semaine," ibid., no. 10 (December 10, 1859).

69. Ibid., no. 1 (January 7, 1860).

70. Sazonov, "Le Premier Meeting en Russie," ibid., no. 2 (January 14, 1860).

71. Sazonov, "De l'instruction publique en Russie," ibid., no. 6 (February 11, 1860).

72. Sazonov, *Les Israélites en Russie,* ibid., no. 14 (April 7, 1860).

73. Review of the book by P. Dolgorukov, "La Vérité sur la Russie," ibid., no. 16 (April 21, 1860).

74. Śliwowska, *W kręgu poprzedników Hercena,* p. 252. The letters are preserved in the Central Literary Archive in Moscow.

75. Sazonov, "Société de secours des gens de lettres et des savants en Russie," in *Gazette du Nord,* no. 20 (May 19, 1860).

76. Sazonov, "A propos de la souscription en faveur de la Caisse des gens de lettres russes," ibid., no. 24 (June 16, 1860).

77. Sazonov, "La Littérature et les hommes de lettres en Russie," I, "M. Ivan Tourguéneff," ibid., no. 13 (March 31, 1860).

78. Sazonov, "La Littérature et les hommes de lettres en Russie," II, "M. Alexandre Hertzen," ibid., no. 21 (May 26, 1860).

79. G. de Rumine and Sazonov, *A nos abonnés,* ibid., no. 26 (June 30, 1860). Professor Jacob W. Kipp of Kansas State University, an expert on Konstantin Nikolaevich and his period, was kind enough (I should like to thank him here) to let me know that he has found nothing new in his research on the *Gazette du Nord,* on G. de Rumine, and on N. Sazonov. Only an investigation in the Central Soviet Archives will shed new light on these questions and on these personalities.

80. As Herzen said in his *Pisma k budushchemu drugu* [Letters to a future friend], "Two years ago a man died in a small town on the Rhône. I only heard details of his death six months later. No one walked in his funeral procession; no one was impressed by the news of his death. The sad existence of a man tossed onto foreign shores, had passed with hardly anyone noticing him, without the fulfillment of his own hopes or those of others. Like a man from the *fugitive* sects, but belonging to the Russia of educated men, he was one of those useless, empty beings who once were ceaselessly idolized and who now are senselessly stoned. I feel great sympathy for them. I have known many and liked them for a unique melancholy we share, which they failed to dominate as they went—some toward their tombs, others toward foreign lands, others toward alcohol" (*Russki teni,* 18: 87). Sazonov's unpaid bills still followed Ogarev in 1873. See *Gertsen i Ogarev. Novyye materialy* [Herzen and Ogarev. New material], ed. S. A. Pereselenkov and Ya. Z. Chernyak, in *Zvenya* [Rings], 6:402.

Seven   Russian Populism

My plan—or, better, my desire—to study the history of the 19th-century Russian revolutionary movement dates back to the 1930s. In Leningrad and Moscow, a long silence about populist and libertarian movements began with the death of Kirov. In the world outside Russia, everything invited or forced one to look for the roots of socialist ideas and of the nihilist revolts. They were roots that inevitably led back to those who generation after generation had fought against czarist autocracy, passionately trying to predict, interpret, and change the fate of their own country. After the war, an unforeseen opportunity—a three-year stay in Moscow between 1947 and 1950—opened the doors of the Lenin Library to me; that institution housed the documents and memoirs of Russian revolutionaries as well as the texts of the vast Russian historiography of the 1920s and early 1930s concerning the movement. The Lenin Library's door was a narrow one in those days; it did not lead to a catalog (as a result, one had to reconstruct the bibliography solely on the basis of reviews, journals, and notes on the books), or to the archives containing manuscripts and documents (which were completely inaccessible to me then).[1] But it would be in poor taste, in fact unjust, to complain about the narrowness of that door, which at that time was closed to so many scholars, to so many Russians, for whom it was also a vital necessity to study the true relationship between their past and their present, between the revolutionary movement and the Stalinist dictatorship. For them it was even more difficult than for me, a foreigner, to form their own ideas about this relationship, engulfed as they were in the silence, isolation, and monotony of official historiography.

Perhaps that solitude was not without some benefits. At that time a wide gulf separated the populists from the Marxists, social democrats, and revolutionary socialists. It was impossible to study the period that followed the end of *Narodnaya Volya* in Moscow in the forties, and the first years of the new century were even more inaccessible. The populist era was practically the last period in the history of the Russian revolutionary movement about which it was possible to obtain texts and documents—perhaps not all, but at least in sufficient number. Then began the silence, so deep and impenetrable that even today, almost thirty years after Stalin's death, it has not been definitively broken. Despite some interesting exceptions, in the Soviet Union the beginning of the 20th century remains one of the less investigated and discussed periods of Russian history.

Later, after reading Marc Bloch, I saw how this break between the 19th and 20th centuries could change into something positive. It is not the historical generation immediately following, not the children who will understand what their fathers wanted and did. Some detachment is necessary for one generation to understand another above and beyond the immediate legacy. Historic continuity is anything but uniform, and it requires that one stand back. Instead, in Russia, the social democrats starting with Plekhanov, then the Bolsheviks and Mensheviks from Lenin to Dan, as well as the revolutionary socialists—that is, all the movements that dominated Russia during the 20th-century revolutions—tended naturally to consider the populists as a legacy either to deny or to use, to spend or to hoard. The image of the generation of Herzen and Chernyshevsky, of Bakunin and of Zhelyabov, was profoundly. changed by this process of assimilation, which was not historical but was largely political. Then Stalin's dictatorship began, and broke this continuity of the Russian intelligentsia and the revolutionary movement. In 1950, passionate discussions had become strict erudition at best; the legacy had been reduced to a few sentences of Lenin's, perpetually repeated; and an absolute silence had fallen over those revolutionaries, like the men of the *Narodnaya Volya,* who had tried more intensely than others to unite and hold together thought and action.

It was time to try to find the historical reality, to return to the sources. The first thing to do, obviously, was to cut unhesitatingly the dead and formal bond that in Soviet historiography apparently still united these men with the age of great political discussions, of Plekhanov, Lenin, Martov, and Chernov. Only one of these men had remained; this was Lenin, of course, and he too had been reduced to a pure and simple symbol and guarantor of a political and ideological continuity that in reality was becoming exhausted. To understand the populists, the first thing to do was to leave Lenin aside. How Lenin understood Herzen, Chernyshevsky, and the *Narodnaya Volya* is an interesting topic, but it mainly serves to understand Lenin and the Bolsheviks. A generation later, in 1950, his ideas seemed removed from the context in which they were born, far from the era of the Russian revolutions, transformed into a pure symbol of a continuity that was rhetorically and artificially reaffirmed. In order to understand the populists, it was better to replace this political symbolism with simple silence, in the midst of which the true words and the echo of the facts behind the 19th-century Russian revolutionary movement could be heard. Thus, in the book I wrote then, I deliberately mentioned Lenin only once, to thank the library in Moscow that bears his name.

In another matter it was necessary to react to the enforced antihistorical situation that had been created in the Soviet Union. The entire 19th-century revolutionary movement after the Decembrists and before the Marxists—that is, the

Russian populist movement—was no longer seen as a whole. It was not seen as a trend that, despite all the internal differences and conflicts, had its own unity and continuity and could be regarded as a single human event in its birth, development, decline, and tragic end. As often happens, official ideology had replaced this view with a last judgment, placing the evil on one side and the good on the other, obscuring the former in darkness and silence and blending the latter in the strained and indistinct light of an ideological paradise. In this division, the good were called revolutionary democrats and included Herzen (with the usual reservations and distinctions) and especially Belinsky, Chernyshevsky, and Dobrolyubov, along with a certain number of followers and imitators. The bad were Bakunin, Lavrov (with the extenuating circumstances of his case), Mikhailovsky, and, above all, the men from the *Narodnaya Volya.* In this vast historical novel, the characters of the 1860s were the heroes, those of the 1870s the antiheroes.[2] The motivation for these verdicts is of little interest. But it is important to know why such judgments were made. Even today, after such a long time, it is not easy to find the reasons.

The discussion of the *Narodnaya Volya* which took place in 1930 and 1931, with I. A. Teodorovich and V. I. Nevsky as protagonists, is vivid and of great interest, and filled with elements that strongly reflected the tense political situation of those years. In fact, it was the most interesting historiographical and ideological debate provoked by the collectivization of the peasants, which was then taking place.[3] Teodorovich's ideas had been derived from the populist movement, but later he had become a Marxist. Nevsky had been part of the group of men who, with Lenin, had carried out and guided the October revolution. In the debate one could hear the voices of the survivors of the 19th-century revolutionary movement, of the populist members of the "Society of Those Condemned to Forced Labor and Deportation," as well as the hoarse and monotonous voices of cold-blooded builders of the new state ideologies of convenience. Even today, in looking over all their works, one is struck by the tragic, unreal air of the debate among the survivors, mere shadows on the brink of the abyss. A few years later, in 1935–36, all the men, institutions, journals, publishers, and ideas had vanished. The primary cause, or at least the most obvious one, was the will of Stalin. He did not want anyone, for any reason, to talk about revolutionaries who were capable of using bombs and revolvers, of carrying out partisan actions and coups de main. As Stalin explained to A. A. Zhdanov, who told the city committee of the Leningrad Communist Party on February 25, 1935, "If we bring up our young on the men of the *Narodnaya Volya,* we will bring up terrorists."[4] The security measures adopted by Stalin thus dealt with both the dead and the living, and were applied with equal ruthlessness against the memory of revolutionary populism and against the historians and scholars who had studied it. As a result, the editing of the works of Bakunin, Lavrov, Mikhailovsky, and Tkachev was stopped; the journal *Katorga i Ssylka* ceased publication; and Nevsky and Teodorovich, Steklov and

Gorev, accompanied and followed by a great many others, disappeared. The official theory was expressed by E. Yaroslavsky, who in 1937 addressed the new generations, saying that "the young members of the Party and of the Komsomal do not always know or sufficiently appreciate the significance of the struggle that for decades our party carried on against this, overcoming the influence of populism, annihilating it as the worst of the enemies of Marxism and of the whole cause of the proletariat."[5]

As we have seen, the burden of immediate political necessity had been decisive in the mid-1930s in bringing about the sharp tear that Stalin made in Russia's historical fabric. At the same time, as we find from Zhdanov's conversation quoted above, the dictator had decided to cut short any reconsideration of the origins of the Bolshevik party itself. In his eyes, the whole history of the party before 1917 was nothing but insignificant "prehistory" clearly unworthy of study.[6]

More than just making a clean cut, however, it was also necessary to know where to insert the knife and how to separate the good men from the bad. Considerations of security and public order were no longer adequate. Inevitably, the choice was ideological. By expunging the revolutionary element in the 19th century from Bakunin to the *Narodnaya Volya,* one risked showing only the more democratic and reformist elements, from Belinsky to Herzen, from Chernyshevsky to Dobrolyubov. Obviously baptizing them "democratic revolutionaries" was not enough to change their nature. For when these men were authentic revolutionaries, as they often managed to be, they were revolutionaries in a different sense, contrary to the "revolution from above" that Stalin was carrying out in those years. How could this contradiction be remedied?

The problem was solved for about twenty years, starting in 1935, by the most diverse methods, from pure and simple censorship of texts to forced interpretations, and by the continuous attempt to make the images of these men coincide with the icons that official ideology had established for them. This division between the "democratic revolutionaries" and the populists occasionally took ridiculous forms, as when there was an attempt to separate Herzen and Ogarev, two men who during their lifetimes had been inseparable friends and companions. But despite all the difficulties and uncertainties, by these methods the democratic revolutionaries were preserved from the silence and scorn that were destined to fall on their followers in the 1870s. The works of the populists were printed, occasionally in editions whose new research and additions made them quite valuable (consider the works of Chernyshevsky). Despite all the restrictions, their ideas continued to be expressed openly in Russia.

To what, in the final analysis, was their at least partial survival due? Clearly there are practical reasons: how could one rid Russian literature of men like them? Herzen, whose every page contradicted the dictatorship, was especially difficult to eliminate. Yet we must not forget that these were the years when Russian literature was deprived even of Dostoevsky. One would think that an operation even more difficult than the one that would have had to be carried out on Herzen's living body. In fact, the reasons for this choice were not purely those of opportunity and convenience. There was something in the democratic revolutionaries that resisted any attempt at annihilation. The national problem, the problem of the bond between the revolutionary movement and Russian history, was continually raised in their work. Socialists in a particular country could not help wondering about the origins of socialism in that country. The ossification of Marxism required the circulation of a different and perhaps older blood. Devoid of true populistic content and of the real problems that Herzen and Chernyshevsky had posed in discussing the peasants and the original economic and political development of Russia, often reduced to empty formulae, Russian socialism nevertheless emerged and took the place left by the declining internationalism of the twenties. Thus, Chernyshevsky replaced Marx as the putative father of socialism in Russia. It was an inconvenient position, but it responded to a real need, and created the first rough outline of a new relationship between Russian tradition and the Soviet state, a very different relationship from what the Marxists and internationalists thought they had achieved in the 1917 revolution.

In the 1930s and 1940s this reemergence of the past took a negative form, of jealous guardedness and petty nationalism. When not denied altogether, the international ties of the populists and of the Russian revolutionaries were greatly obscured. The intent was to defend their originality and their autonomy, but it was a useless, vain, and wrong defense on a historic plane, and it hampered or even prevented the investigation and understanding of the deep bonds that united the populists with 19th-century Europe.

In this case, I concluded, while trying to break this artificial and suffocating isolation, that perhaps the best way was to affirm unhesitatingly, right from the first lines of the book I was writing, that I was dealing with a page in the history of the European socialist movement, that at every opportunity I would try to tie up the historical threads that had been dropped or broken by the official Soviet historiography of those years.

Even in the isolation and silence of Moscow between 1948 and 1950, there was still a faint echo of the 1920s' interrupted dialogue on Russia's revolutionary past. Until 1935, that discussion had been too lively to prevent the recognition of a few but obvious signs of some people's silent desire to resume and pursue it. I was aware that B. P. Kozmin was continuing his work in Moscow. He had produced some of the most important books and articles that I had read in the Lenin Library. Research on the true situation of the peasants in the 19th century had not been entirely stopped. To realize this, one only had to read the works of Druzhinin. As much as possible, I followed the forthright and patient work of Levin, Valk, Oksman, and others, men who, despite the adverse circumstances, were trying to keep the true tradition of historical and philological studies alive in the Soviet Union. The situation in which these men were working became clearer to

me day by day, in all its tragedy: I gradually discovered the impossibility of finding a number of great books, I saw whole collections of writers, memorialists, and
historians with the names of the editors and annotators barbarically defaced and
erased. The truth was evident; Russian historiography had been devastated in the
1930s and 1940s.

It was equally clear to me what needed to be done: to report as fully as possible, quoting texts and documents as widely as possible, demonstrating their true
voice, freeing them from their later petrification and ideological incrustations; to
recount the events of populism. I was increasingly convinced that in populism lay
the roots, the deepest and truest origins, of contemporary Russia.

This conclusion aroused in me considerable admiration and enthusiasm for that
generation of revolutionaries, as well as a keen interest in the Soviet scholars of
the 1920s who had tried so vigorously to make known and bring to life the experiences of the thinkers and rebels of 19th-century Russia, and who, like the works
they studied, had been overcome by the dark storm of the 1930s. When I presented the completed book to Italian readers in 1952, I concluded in the *Notiziario
Einaudi* of June 30:

As I progressed in my work I was caught by an increasing sense of admiration for
those who, in extremely difficult circumstances, wished to pursue the "narrow
path" they had chosen to its very end. That consequential spirit, which one of
them claimed was the distinctive characteristic of Russian history, proved to be a
source of energy, a force that swept the weaker men uninterrupted toward absurdity, but led the best men to that complete dedication that is the dominant characteristic of all populism. Thus it is not, I hope, psychological complacency that
drove me to gather the details of the lives of so many obscure characters. It was
the only way I could reach the individual without being distracted by outlines,
could stress the truly original element of Russian populism. And I hope this will
excuse me for having written two overly lengthy volumes.

These volumes, entitled *Il populismo russo,* were published by Einaudi in 1952.
The discussion they aroused in Italy centered on the basic points and, because of
the esoteric nature of these themes, was more historiographic than historical, concentrating more on principles, methods, and conclusions than on facts, research,
and doubts. Was it proper to write the history of a movement like populism, while
subordinating all the elements of social, political, economic, literary, and ideological history of the era in which it took place? Or, above all, should one insert it
into a more complex reality until it simply became part of a global view of 19th-
century Russia? I clearly favored the first alternative over the second. Aldo Garosci, writing under the pseudonym of Aldo Magrini, said in the *Mondo* (September
20, 1952) that I was right, while Giuseppe Berti, in the May and July 1953 issues
of *Rinascita,* said that I was wrong. Garosci also mentioned the problem of what
of the great political tradition of the Russian intelligentsia had survived and what

had been buried. He concluded by asking (this was 1952, in the era of extreme Stalinism) why the ideals of the 19th-century revolutionaries had failed to transform Russia or had "ceased to operate effectively"—"even if they certainly remained as inspiring myths and as the ideal culmination of something that, in part, reminds us more of what the populists were combating than of what they liked." In the Russian silence, czarism seemed to reacquire its rights.

Berti, on the other hand, was convinced that only economic evolution, only facts and figures on the transformation of Russian life, could make a Western reader understand the reality of this country; these were more significant than interpretations given by the revolutionaries and more effective than the revolutionaries' stated desire to change or overturn that reality. "A history of populism without a deep examination of the profound economic and class distinctions that occurred in Russian campaigns *after* the reforms, from 1861 to 1881 (distinctions that were to determine the entire resulting evolution of the *narodnichestvo*), such a history lacks a basis for judgment." This is an affirmation to which many historians, even non-Marxists, would readily subscribe, perhaps modifying it in various degrees. Yet even Berti, one of the greatest and most acute experts on revolutionary events in the modern world, relied on the internal logic of the movements, the conflicts of ideas and desires, the tragedies that resulted, when he related the history of the Communist International and recounted the function and origins of the Italian Communist Party and its relationship with parties in other countries.

I do not wish to deny the possibility of writing the history of a society like that in Russia after the peasant reforms of 1861. But to understand a movement like populism, it was necessary to disentangle it completely from all the general, sociological explanations that, in Russia and elsewhere, had shrouded it, stifling its most active and creative elements.

The most powerful confirmation I have had of this approach came from Andrea Caffi, an Italian well known to Russia since the first decades of the century. He was a participant in and witness of the age of the Russian revolutions, a companion and friend of the survivors of 19th-century populism, and in 1952, in Paris, was living out the last years of a free and talented existence.[7] He wrote to me that complete detachment from the legends and traditions of the century was correct; that even if it was difficult, the attempt to establish a relationship between Russia and Europe was indispensable. He corrected me on many specific points (and naturally I paid scrupulous attention to his suggestions in the second edition); he said he had discussed my book with his friends from the publishing house of Gallimard, with A. Camus and especially with B. Parrain, and he made me feel how useful it could be to bring to light the great age of the 19th-century intelligentsia and make it more widely known.

The comments of some of the Italian readers of *Il populismo russo* convinced me—though little persuasion was needed—of how little this era was known. For example, Giovanni Spadolini wrote in the December 12, 1952, issue of the *Gazzetta del popolo*, "It is strange that the Populist movement—so genuinely Russian, so adherent to the conditions and mentality of the Russian proletariat, so completely traditional and nostalgic in spirit—should have Western philosophical origins and declare a clear derivation from Proudhon's and Blanc's classic themes (not to mention the influence of classical German philosophy on Bakunin)."

But Leo Valiani responded to such statements, defending the writing of the history of political movements without then being obliged to write a total history. He affirmed that

the spirit that moved the Russian populists is not a measure of the backwardness of an immense semifeudal country, but rather expresses the ideological assimilation of the more radical and restless tendencies of European society on the part of a rather thin stratum of revolutionary intellectuals who consider their country, Russia, as a prison to be transformed, through the removal of the bars, into a superior social community, conforming to the most generous ideals of Western socialism....Is this a spirit of disunity that leads to more extreme desires just because one is forced to remain in the dream world? No, on the contrary, the characteristic of populism is its unlimited faith in Russia's capacity to achieve more rapid and especially more direct progress than that allowed by the dominant skepticism of other European countries....Although it developed under political, social, and economic conditions that were far behind those in the West, the Russian revolutionary movement was no less socialistic in its ideology and in its plans than the movements that were expressed at the same time in the First International and in the Paris Commune itself....But while in the West socialism deliberately represented a class schism in the heart of the nation, in Russia populism spontaneously succeeded in detaching the active and educated forces of the country from the czars....Populism could be considered, both in thought and in the material struggle, as the conscience (even if it was not the authorized representative) of the great national aspirations. Herein lies the reason for its intimate resistance, for its resurrection with its forces multiplied many times, only twenty years after the tragic end of the Narodnaya Volya. [*Lo spettatore italiano*, no. 6, June 1953]

It was 1953, the year Stalin died and Beria was eliminated. The problem of determining the value of the moral and political tradition that the Russian intelligentsia had managed to create through so many struggles and so many difficulties returned. It went beyond the circle of scholars and, in Italy as elsewhere, became everyone's problem. The evidence gathered in *Il populismo russo* succeeded in persuading at least some people, as we have seen in the examples quoted above, of the clarity of the message that was emerging after the revolution, the war, the dictatorship. Armanda Guiducci then wrote:

The most painful thing to establish is how, for a large number of Western men of culture, most of the works of Dobrolyubov, devoted to showing the discrepancy between the intelligentsia's task and its real position, are not at all outdated. Nor are Tkachev's violent satires on the pride of intellectuals and his struggle to make

them acquire such a clear social conscience that any general praise of progress is repulsed as a means of hiding reality (optimism was then called "positivism").
Nor are Lavrov's ideas on the responsibility of the intellectual class and his conviction that every society, even tomorrow's, that lacked the active and critical participation of cultured men was destined to be tyrannical. [*Il pensiero critico*, nos. 7-8, December 1953]

These themes of the ethical purpose of populism were particularly strongly felt in Italy during those years. And, though there were significant differences, something similar could be said about Germany.[8] On the other hand, two attempts to place the history of the 19th-century revolutionary movement in an entirely political and economic context came from England and America. A review in the *Times Literary Supplement* (June 12, 1953) took up the problems of the formation and function of the educated elite in backward countries from a perspective presented by the English historian Hugh Seton-Watson in his well-known works *The Decline of Imperial Russia, 1854-1914, The East European Revolution,* and *The Russian Empire, 1801-1917.* It said, "The Russian revolutionary movement started from the *intelligentsia.* The word is Russian, and the phenomenon first appeared in Russia. But later developments in other countries of southern and eastern Europe and of Asia have shown that it is in no sense peculiarly Russian. The *intelligentsia* is a product of modern education....The educated Russian shared the most advanced culture of contemporary Europe. He could not fail to see the contrast between this culture and the state of his own country. Material backwardness, social oppression and lack of freedom filled him with shame." The students who came from nonprivileged classes; the children of the preachers; and those who came from oppressed nations such as the Poles, the Ukrainians, and the Jews, thus joined in the opposition movement. "Ideal and personal motives combined to place the majority of the *intelligentsia* in opposition to the régime and caused them to prefer the revolutionaries to the Government. Certain flowers and weeds grow only in certain soils. Had not the *intelligentsia* as a group been alienated from the régime, the professional revolutionary conspirators, a small minority drawn from its ranks, could never have appeared."

Thus, Seton-Watson viewed populism as a particularly significant example of the formation of modern revolutionary elites. The English historian was trying to observe objectively, in its final results and in its typical elements, a process that in the book he was reviewing had been studied from within, from the viewpoint of the consciences of those who had been faced with the dilemma of either forming a limited and active group or expanding into the masses. They were men who had hesitated over that choice, struggling with themselves and with the external conditions that alternately induced or forced them to withdraw into an elite group or to mix with the entire Russian population. It was not the dramatic element in this choice, nor the desperate attempt to find a way out of the dilemma in which their numbers, their condition, and their ideas enclosed them, but the fatal formation of an intelligentsia and of a party of professional revolutionaries that was at the center of Seton-Watson's analysis. He was too good a historian to stop at this purely sociological view; fundamentally, he was more interested in the political than in the ethical function of populism. He was especially attracted by the paradigm that the revolutionary movement seemed to establish even in countries like Yugoslavia and China. The article in the *Times Literary Supplement* concluded, "This is not to deny the specific features of the Russian movement. Indeed, because it was the first movement on this pattern, it greatly influenced the leaders of others. Chernyshevsky, Bakunin, Ishutin, Tkachev and A. D. Mikhailov are unquestionably Russian. Those who study them should ... examine both those features which unite them to the stream of European thought and action, and those which distinguish them."

One had to go far back in Russian history to find these specific traits, going back to the influence of religion, whether orthodox or of the schismatic sects. Thus one returned to those dilemmas and moral and ideological problems which the desire to reach the roots of modern revolutions had initially seemed to place in the background in the English historian's analysis. But the fundamental, inevitable question remained. What part had Russian populism played in the birth and development of modern theories of elites?

Equally important for those who were studying 19th-century revolutionary Russia from the perspective of the middle of the 20th century was the other problem, posed by Alexander Gerschenkron in the *American Historical Review* of October 1953: What was the relationship between populism and the economic backwardness of Russia? What was its value and its importance in the theory of economic development? "The populists clearly saw the advantages inherent in Russia's being a late-comer upon the modern historical scene. They saw and stressed the possibility of adopting the results of foreign experience without incurring the heavy cost of experimentation, of errors and detours. Both Herzen and Chernyshevski found very felicitous phrases to express the essence of this situation." Thus, according to the American scholar, the awareness of economic backwardness had been the starting point for the whole populist movement. But Gerschenkron added that the populists had quickly distorted their intuition and had soon affirmed paradoxically that "the preservation of the *old* rather than the easy adoption of the *new* constituted the 'advantages of backwardness.' The result was a tragic surrender of realism to utopia. Here is perhaps the main reason for the decline of populism. When the rate of industrial growth lept upward in the middle of the eighties, after the government had committed itself to a policy of rapid industrialization, the divorce between the populist utopia and the economic reality became too great and the movement proved unable to survive the repressions which followed Alexander the Third's advent to the throne."

Gerschenkron thought that from the political viewpoint, too, Russian backwardness was the key element for understanding the radicalism of the populists. Both "the absence of constitutional government and the late start of economic development" explained the rise of the intelligentsia and the contradictions in the

revolutionary movement that accompanied it, always oscillating between a spirit of dedication and conspiratorial machiavellianism, between anarchy and exultation of the Jacobin state. Populism could and should be seen, not as one chapter in the history of socialist movements, but "as a chapter in the history of ideologies in conditions of backwardness." Viewed from this angle, "the story of Russian populism may acquire a note of actuality and may serve better to emphasize the great dangers that are inherent in unduly prolonged periods of economic and political backwardness."[9] These were ideas that Gershenkron was then developing in that series of essays that have made him, as is well known, the most incisive historian of modern Russian economics, as well as one of the most inspired theorists on the problems of backwardness and development.[10]

After reading his works, the very problem of Russian populism was transformed for me and, I believe, for others. Gerschenkron's interpretation has become a starting point in the discussion that has taken place on this subject in the last fifteen years. His contribution to that discussion has been so rich and complex that it has persuaded me to postpone the debate until we examine more closely what has recently been written on the Slavophiles and Herzen, on Chernyshevsky and Mikhailovsky. The only general element that emerges from this very fruitful dialogue concerns the function of ideas and political ideals in the historical process that we are studying. Is an idea that seems to look back in time—that apparently goes back to the past, that seems to prefer what has been and to exclude what is to come—in itself destined to have a negative effect, does it really constitute a utopian brake on economic and social development? Or does it represent, at least occasionally, an attempt to *reculer pour mieux sauter,* a fruitful attempt to conserve what had been precious in the past to transmit it to the future? History is not made by only looking ahead, but, I would say, by looking both forward and back. Is not socialism itself—the idea of a community and of equality of goods, of an economy based on solidarity—a remnant from the past that has been conserved and transformed into an ideal for the future? And were not socialism and communism, not just populism, ideas that were originally consciously opposed to economic development? Let us open again the old and very basic book of Filippo Buonarroti, the book through which 18th-century communist ideas were transmitted to the 19th century and to, among others, the Russian populists. In fact, without opening it, let us look at the cover of this venerated book. Under the title, *Conspiration pour l'égalité dite de Babeuf,* is the author's motto: *Eas enim optimas esse leges putandum est quibus non divites sed honesti prudentesque homines fiant.* It is taken from Diodorus of Sicily, book 2, chapter 5. It would be difficult to find a more explicit declaration against economic development. The populists' idea of the *obshchina,* their desire for revolution and for peasant equality, were no less involved in the same direction. Because of this, I believe Russian populism should also be considered as a page in the history of European socialism. Along with the movement itself, one should consider and study the ideas of

the past that it transmitted to the future, the utopian elements that it undoubtedly contained (but how can one be detached from the past without projecting it
outside of time and space and making it timeless and utopian?), and the stimuli
toward a modern economy that were certainly not lacking (Chernyshevsky
thought about the use of machinery in his *obshchina,* which had been transformed
into an agrarian cooperative). Only such a union of past and future, like every
other socialist ideal, would have allowed the establishment of.deep contacts with
the masses in Russia and elsewhere. Only in this way could they be brought to live
and struggle in a modern industrial society (here, too, not liberalism but socialism
was to become the political ideal of the proletariat). When Marxism arrived, even
in St. Petersburg, it was attractive for the element of socialism that it contained,
not for its analysis of the development of capitalism or for its justification of
primitive accumulation or of free trade. The reason for all this seems evident: it
was only through socialism that the workers could see the defense of their own
interests, of their own way of being and living. And why deny this to the peasants? They saw in Russia, in populist socialism, a defense of their own interests as
well as of their own traditions. As for the internal history of populism, is it truly
possible to note, as Gerschenkron maintains, that as we gradually move through
the 1860s and 1870s there is a step backward, even a reversal of tendencies, an
obscuring of the consciousness that the populists originally had of the advantages
of economic backwardness, a fall to the pure and simple extolling of the past?
Is the *Narodnya Volya* really a regression compared to Herzen? Were not the
Narodnovolcy the most clear-sighted and lucid judges of Russia's economic structure, of the fundamental importance that the state had had in its development?
These debates and those years seemed to mark progress, not regression. Gerschenkron knows about these matters better than most, but it is still useful to recall
them in discussing his interpretation of Russian populism.

In the mid-1950s in the Soviet Union, the debate moved from less general questions to a discussion of these problems. There was no longer a forced silence in
response to questions from the West. Research on these themes was reappearing
even in Moscow and Leningrad. It would be useful to describe in detail how this
occurred. It is not easy to tell when the change arose from a political directive
from above, derived from the party's and the government's preparation for the
Twentieth Congress (February 1956), and when it was a matter of a persistent
drive on the part of Soviet scholars. Evidently both elements were present, but in
what amounts and with what timing? In any case, we cannot say that Sedov, one
of the most active promoters of this debate, was wrong when about ten years later
he wrote that "the process of liberation from the ideas and concepts that had
been fixed for two decades was long and difficult."[11]

It was quite natural that in 1956 the most comprehensive and recent bibliography of populism during the 1870s and 1880s received its impetus from this
discussion.[12] Also in 1956, a polemic on the origins and character of populism

began to appear in historical journals. It is particularly interesting to note that among the most active participants in this debate right from the start were a historian of the student movement, Tkachenko, and a scholar who had specialized in problems of youth in the Stalinist period, Sedov. Already in 1956, writings of men who in later years were among the most active scholars of populism, such as Itenberg and Pirumova, were being published. In 1957, after over twenty years during which he had restricted himself to detailed, erudite contributions, B. P. Kozmin published his first important work, *The Russian Section of the First International.* In January 1958, under the direction and initiative of M. V. Nechkina, the "Group for the Study of the Revolutionary Situation in Russia from 1859 to 1861" was established. And in the same year the first book since the 1930s on populism as a whole appeared. It was written by Sh. M. Levin,[13] who remarked in the introduction, "On the whole, this work was already completed several years ago."[14] Like other writings that appeared around that time, this book had not evolved through urging from above, after the Twentieth Congress. Nevertheless, it saw the light thanks to the fact that censorship had become somewhat more lenient.

But along with the old wood that came to life again, the first crop of populist historiography during the 1950s also contained some less sound and tasty fruit. There were attempts to present ideas and views of the Stalinist era in a new form, not without some appropriate concessions and "updating." In this area, it was often a matter, not of a complete break or of a profound renewal, but of a thaw that carried with it much mud and silt.

One of the first exercises in updating was carried out on *Il populismo russo,* my work. It was the year (1955) of the Tenth International Historical Congress, held in Rome, where for the first time Soviet historians were full participants. In issue number 8 of the journal *Vosprosy istorii,* which was distributed then, along with a summary in Italian, was a review of my book by S. A. Pokrovsky. It dealt with the problem of the relationship between the 19th-century revolutionary movements in Russia and the West. But it was not presented in order to invite further research in this area (this became Itenberg's task in an article in the same journal, no. 9, the next year). Rather, his purpose was to take pleasure in the fact that a Western scholar had "rejected the preconceived and widespread viewpoint in reactionary literature on the would-be contrast between Western and Eastern culture" (from the Italian summary). It was balm to the wound of the traditional Russian and Soviet sense of inferiority, not a clear and precise confirmation that Stalinist nationalism, extending even into the field of historical research, had cut the ties between the Soviet Union and the rest of the world. Similarly, Pokrovsky confirmed that in the book he was reviewing no gap had been created between the "revolutionary democrats" and the "populists," but he did not face the discussion on this essential element, on this crux of the historiographical period that was ending. Some other old themes were again being hammered in: the Slavophiles should be considered purely and simply as reactionaries; the ideas of the Russian liberals could all be explained according to their class situation; any true libertarian element was nonexistent in the ideas of Herzen, who would never have rejected the Jacobin tradition; Chernyshevsky never had illusions about reform, he had always demanded the confiscation of all land belonging to the nobles; populism of the 1870s had a "progressive function" (and this was the main concession made regarding concepts of the Stalinist era), but it could not be considered a socialist movement because of this; nor should one forget that Tkachev, Bakunin, and Lavrov had actually taken steps backward and not forward compared with Belinsky, Herzen, and Chernyshevsky. Their ideas were and remained "petit-bourgeois." Any attempt to establish a deep relationship between the revolutionary populists and 1917 was and remained profoundly wrong. "The Great October Socialist Revolution was carried out by the working class, allied with the poorest peasants, under the guidance of the Communist party that was fighting under the banner of Marxism." Simple and easy. This was why Pokrovsky expressed "his regret for the fact that the book lacked a critique of the theory and tactics of populism."

Nevertheless, his review was interesting not only for what it said but also for what it did not say. He did not quote any other Russian books; those of the 1920s still could not be mentioned, and the more recent ones did not yet exist. He let it be understood that a book on the history of populism was also needed in Russia, as it was no longer a forbidden topic, but he hastened to warn readers against the temptation of accepting the approach of the "essential work" he had examined.

The contradictions in such a controlled updating were even more evident when, in 1957, S. A. Pokrovsky himself published a little book called *Falsifiers of the History of Russian Political Thought in Contemporary Bourgeois Reactionary Literature* (published by the Academy of Sciences of the USSR Institute of Law). The tenth, and last, chapter was entitled "The Progressive Scholars of the West Study the History of Russian Revolutionary Thought." There were only a few of these progressive scholars: Vernell M. Oliver (for his article in *Journal of Negro History*, October 1953, on Russian radicals and the American Civil War), Armand Coquart (for his work on Pisarev which came out in Paris in 1946), and the author of *Il populismo russo*. According to Pokrovsky, the limited size of this group had an explanation: "The falsifying literature and the activity of the authors who serve the imperialist reaction are born partly from an attempt to paralyze the influence of progressive literature that arises in Western Europe and in America as a result of the profound interest that world progressive environments have in Soviet culture" (p. 173).

But before observing more closely this conspiracy of the imperialist falsifiers of history against one of the few progressive historians of Russian populism who flourished in the West (it must have been a very effective conspiracy since only three men had managed to evade it), one should again ask what drove even such reserved and conservative reviewers as Pokrovsky to deal with populism, to discuss its nature and its recurrent interest. In his book Pokrovsky concluded that "Franco Venturi's work was serious scientific research. One could and should debate much with the author, but one could not remain indifferent to his essential work [*opera capitale*]. Its appearance is clear evidence of a reawakening of interest in the traditions of Russian revolutionary thought" (p. 179).

This last allusion actually had little to do with Western historians, whether imperialist or progressive. The rediscovery of Russian revolutionary tradition at the end of the 1950s was mainly a Soviet phenomenon. In historiographical research, as in literary and artistic research, one referred back to the 1920s, and from there one moved further back. One did not look exclusively or particularly toward Marxism, which remained an area in which discussion was difficult, but toward populism and the great debate between Westerners and Slavophiles in the early 19th century. There was a predominantly moral element in this aspect of the anti-Stalinist revolt before the Khrushchev era. In the *narodniki* one found a model of purity and energy, a return to origins and to principles, beyond the machiavellianism, the drama, and the compromises of the 1930s and 1940s. From Herzen to the *Narodnaya Volya,* every historian sought a source of inspiration that could persuade him of the importance and justice of the struggle of the intelligentsia, who were decisive men capable of any sacrifice. The updating and the concessions of official historiography were only one external and more visible aspect of a deep current that was leading the Soviet intelligentsia to reconsider its own origins and its own values. And in this, an encounter with populism was inevitable. As a result, the discussion on this aspect of past life expanded extraordinarily in those years.[15]

On closer observation, one can see that in the West, too, a growing number of scholars and historians were inquiring into the moral roots and populist origins of the intelligentsia and of the Russian revolution. This was partly in response to the work in Russia and partly because of a kind of parallel in the situations on both sides of the Iron Curtain, which was gradually being lifted at that time. In 1955 an important collection edited by Ernest J. Simmons, entitled *Continuity and Change in Russian and Soviet Thought,* was published. Though it dealt with more general problems, it particularly discussed populism.[16] In 1958 James H. Billington's book on Mikhailovsky was published. Among the many figures in 19th-century Russia who anxiously inquired into the interdependence and contrasts between moral and material progress, Mikhailovsky was one of the most significant theoreticians.[17] In 1961 Martin Malia's book, *Alexander Herzen and the Birth of Russian Socialism, 1812–1855,* was published. Here the moral concerns took on more psychological forms.[18] A subdued but very perceptive comment on these reemerging ethical and philosophical concerns in those years came from George L. Kline.[19] A stronger voice was Isaiah Berlin's in an article called "Russian Populism" published in *Encounter* in July 1960, which, in an enlarged and more complete form, became the introduction to the English translation of *Il populismo russo* published in London the same year.[20] In his contribution to *Continuity and Change in Russian and Soviet Thought,* Berlin had already touched on a central problem in his discussion entitled "Herzen and Bakunin on Individual Liberty.[21] The libertarian seed at the core of Herzen's ideas, and from which so much of populism had derived its origin and its strength, was pointed out as one of the most original and forceful elements in 19th-century political thought, not only in Russia but in all of Europe. "As an acute and prophetic observer of his time he is comparable perhaps to Marx and Tocqueville, as a moralist he is more interesting and original than either" (p. 478). Herzen alone had managed to create and live a morality that did not depend on a tendency to consider all human actions in relation to their historical background, on messianism, on the abstractions and the nightmares of postrevolutionary Europe. In comparison, Bakunin's thought and action seemed to be profoundly immersed in the morass and dangers of his century. Herzen was seen as the creator of the ideas and modes of feeling of the intelligentsia. In Bakunin lay the seeds of all the contradictions of the revolutionary movement.

Thus, somewhat paradoxically and with deliberate, forced simplification, yet with great vigor, Berlin tried to return to the purest source of the revolt and of liberty in 19th-century Russia, after a century of tragic events, defeats, dictatorship, and oppression. In true Russian fashion, he was taking to their logical conclusion things that had been implicit in many of the attitudes and hopes of the intellectuals of the post-Stalinist period. In another essay on the 1840s, entitled "The Admirable Decade," Berlin may have risked being too pleased about this rediscovery of the values of tradition and the anecdotes and peculiarities of this reviving tradition of the intelligentsia, but when he was confronted with the problems of revolutionary populism, he faced them with strength, without hesitation. "In spite of the emphasis on economic and sociological arguments, the basic approach, the tone and outlook of Chernyshevsky and of the populists generally is moral, and at times indeed religious. These men believed in socialism not because it was inevitable, but because it was just."[22] The populists had been aware of the danger that their voluntary position, which always maintained the tension of utopia in their struggle, might lead to the formation of an elite or revolutionaries who would impose socialism from above, or of fanatics who might place a new yoke on the Russian peasants in place of the old one, "a despotic oligarchy of intellectuals in place of the nobility and bureaucracy of the czar" (p. xii). The whole debate, all the internal conflicts in the populist movement, testified to the depth of feeling about this central issue. The nihilistic as well as the anarchistic attitudes, the popular movement as well as the varied forms of the clandestine organization, had been attempts to respond to the question that every revolutionary felt was essential and central. Chernyshevsky's hard realism, his bleak but honest pragmatism, had been decisive in the orientation of the attitudes of revolutionary youth. "He was a man of unswerving integrity, immense industry and ·capacity, rare among Russians for concentration upon concrete detail." His practical energy, his social position (as we know, he was the son of a parish priest), his moral strength had made him "a natural leader of a disenchanted generation of socially mingled origins, no longer dominated by good birth, embittered by the failure of their own ideals, by government repression, by the humiliation of Russia in the Crimean War, by the weakness, heartlessness, hypocrisy and chaotic incompetence of the ruling class" (p. xx). A generation was thus turned into a movement that was deeply convinced that "Russia could leap over the capitalist stage of social development and transform the village communes and free cooperative groups of craftsmen into agricultural and industrial associations of producers who would constitute the embryo of the new socialist society" (p. xxii).

Twenty years of attempts and defeats, of struggles and sacrifices, from 1861 to 1881, during which these ideas were tested against reality, would profoundly mark the destiny of modern Russia, not only for what they succeeded in doing and creating (a party of professional revolutionaries, a new relationship between the intelligentsia and the revolution, a profound faith in socialism), but also because of what the defeat prevented them from accomplishing. The leap into the world of liberty and justice, above and beyond the long and painful road of capitalism and industrialization, was not realized. Yet, concludes Berlin, even after such a long time lag, after the victory and triumph of Marxist ideas in Russia, after the disdainful silence of the Stalinist era, it was still necessary to return to studying and understanding the populists. One should do so, not only because their vision of the evolution of a modern economy influenced events in 20th-century Russia, not only because populist concepts appeared in underdeveloped countries of the modern world, but above all because the fears and struggles of those first Russian revolutionaries with the problems of the relationship between the elite and the populace, between the revolutionary dictatorship and the mass of workers, had a worrying immediacy in the Soviet Union between the 1950s and 1960s. Thus Berlin did not hesitate to write,

The populists were convinced that the death of the peasant commune would mean death, or, at any rate, a vast setback, to freedom and equality in Russia; the Left Socialist-Revolutionaries, who were their direct descendants, transformed this into a demand for a form of decentralized, democratic self-government among the peasants, which Lenin adopted when he concluded his temporary alliance with them in October 1917. In due course the Bolsheviks repudiated this programme and transformed the cells of dedicated revolutionaries—perhaps the most original contribution of populism to revolutionary practice—into the hierarchy of centralized political power, which the Populists had steadily and fiercely denounced.... Communist practice owed much, as Lenin was always ready to admit, to the Populist movement; for it borrowed the technique of its rivals and adapted it with conspicuous success to serve the precise purpose which it had been invented to resist. [P. xxx]

The discussion that followed these words, and the presentation of the English version of *Il populismo russo,* failed to confirm Pokrovsky's prediction about the desires of the "falsifiers of history serving the imperialistic reaction" to "suffocate and paralyze" progressive Western historians with the intention of preventing a broader knowledge of the 19th-century Russian revolutionary movement. The discussion was long and animated. Why, asked many of the participants (and Berlin had noted the same in his introduction), had this book been accepted both by the Soviets and by people from the West? And this especially in the years of cold, or even cultural, war?[23] Did history really have the power to overcome the conflicts of differing ideology and politics and to offer a common ground on which the Russians, who were emerging from the Stalinist experience, could meet Westerners who were shedding the results of the Cold War? Despite everything, the author of this book was and is convinced that one should have and one must answer in the affirmative. Naturally the limitations of Clio's clarifying capacity are evident, but her work should not be considered ineffectual because of this. One cannot expect her to be the remedy to all ills. Nevertheless, she always serves and will serve to arouse energy, to recreate a desire for truth that is capable of going beyond any ideological and political barrier. A detailed account, as precise as possible, of the events of the 19th-century Russian revolutionary movement could serve as a reminder and a measure for the Soviets who were beginning to understand the principles and roots of the society in which they lived. At the same time, it could be an indispensable means of showing Westerners the decades of struggles, of sacrifices, of moral victories, and of practical defeats of Russia in the past. In the midst of so many economic explanations, of so many fatalistic and sociological interpretations, a historical account of a political movement once again demonstrated its effectiveness.

But on closer examination, was this Soviet and Western acceptance based on a misunderstanding? After Pokrovsky's comments came those of M. V. Nechkina, which were much more comprehensive and open.[24] In the numerous studies on populism that appeared in Russia at the beginning of the 1960s, there was never a lack of favorable comment on *Il populismo russo* and its English translation. The acknowledgments almost became a ritual. In the West, too, in the thinking and research that was developing at an extraordinary pace in those same 1960s, *Il populismo russo* had often appeared as a useful departure point. But was this not a purely formal and academic convergence in which the Soviets and Westerners often meant different things even when they used similar or identical words?

The point of rupture was indicated by Leonard Schapiro. Russia and the West differed less in their interpretation of populism than in the importance attributed to this movement in the formation of Bolshevism, in the preparation for the 1917 revolution. Schapiro, a well-known expert on modern Russian history, wrote in the July 28, 1960 issue of *The Listener,*

Professor Berlin notes that Venturi's work has been acclaimed both in the West and in the Soviet Union, and attributes this unusual fact to the "calm impartiality" with which the book is written. It would indeed be a remarkable thing if this were the reason, since impartial scholarship does not usually command Communist admiration if its conclusions disagree with party shibboleths. [In this Schapiro was both right and wrong: right if he was referring to the state organs of cultural politics and wrong if he was referring to the numerous Soviet scholars who were sensitive, because of their experiences, to the demands of philological and documentary rigor.] But Sir Isaiah is not quite right. Venturi has been criticized in the Soviet Union for hinting that the psychological type of the Bolshevik was engendered in the nineteenth century. Bolshevik kinship with such conspiratorial fanatics of revolution as Tkachev is indeed fairly obvious. But it is contrary to the aura of pure democracy with which modern Soviet convention demands that Lenin be surrounded. Moreover the fact that Venturi is more often than not praised by Soviet writers is due, in my opinion, not to his impartiality, but to his, quite incidental, acceptance of the current Soviet view of the liberals, which was also that of the populists—cowardly, selfish, indifferent to the suffering of the masses.... It is this blind spot which leads the Soviet critics to label his work as "progressive"—the highest term of praise.

Let us temporarily leave aside the problem of Russian liberalism; we shall return to it as it deserves more detailed discussion. What counts more, and what was becoming more evident from Schapiro's words as well as from all the discussion in the 1960s on Russian populism, was the desire of Soviet scholars as well as English ones to characterize the relationships, to understand the link between the Russian revolutionary movement and October 1917.

Every day in Russia it was becoming more evident that in order to exorcize and remove this problem, and in order to set one's conscience at rest with history, it no longer sufficed to repeat the traditional formulae of orthodoxy. Had the populists not been utopians, petit bourgeois? Had Lenin not been a scientific and Marxist revolutionary? This obviously meant the a priori denial of a problem that continually presented itself before anyone who attempted to reconstruct a biography of Lenin, or his formation, or who studied the establishment of a professional revolutionary party in St. Petersburg, or who discussed the formulae and the reality of Russian economic development in the 20th century. From biography to economics, everything seemed to pose the question of the relationship between populism and Bolshevism. The pure and simple methods of censorship and silence were no longer enough, even if the works of the Russian Jacobin, Tkachev, edited by B. P. Kozmin, which ceased to be published during the 1930s, had not been taken up again in the 1960s, or if the whole dispute between the Mensheviks and the Bolsheviks on this theme remained "off limits" for Soviet historiography. But how could one avoid reconsidering what Lenin had written on Chernyshevsky and on the revolutionaries of the *Narodnaya Volya?* How could one remain silent about Bakunin, how could one pretend that Nechaev had never existed? How could one not pose the question of how the worker's movement in St. Petersburg had really been born? And aside from the stereotyped formulae, what had the discussions between the populists and the Marxists at the end of the century signified? It was a discussion that was fundamental, as we know, for Lenin's formation and for all trends among the Russian intelligentsia in those years. Something similar was taking place on the other side of the ocean. There, too, the usual and current interpretation of the roots of Bolshevism appeared increasingly unsatisfactory and false. The interpretation was entirely pragmatic and political, based on the cynicism and revolutionary machiavellianism of conspiracies and plots, first of the Jacobins and then of the Leninists.

In the May 6, 1961 issue of *National Review,* Stefan F. Possony used *The Roots of Revolution,* as it is called in English, as a starting point for his revolutionary genealogy of communism, showing the prophets of the revolution as having almost biblical descent. But the fathers and grandfathers of Bolshevism ended up multiplying, so that for a genealogist like him, they included not only Nechaev and Tkachev, but also Filippo Buonarroti and Babeuf, the Carbonari and Mazzini. Nothing remained but the increasingly firmly rooted conviction that history, at least the history of revolutionary movements, drew its roots and its raison d'être from the techniques of the conspiracy and from the idea of a perpetually renewed plot of which the Russians (and perhaps the Italians) had for generations seemed to be masters. This was the ultimate limit of a conception that had reached the point of absurdity. On the other hand, A. J. P. Taylor stressed the fact that during the czarist empire, the spirit of 1848 had survived, while it had disappeared or been transformed in European countries. Thus he stressed a fact of undoubted importance, that is, the difference in the rhythm of development of revolutionary ideas in Russia and elsewhere (*Observer,* July 3, 1960).

James Joll emphasized the importance of not deviating from a rigorous historical view. Even the relationship between the *Narodnaya Volya* and Lenin, which undoubtedly existed and was important, could be understood, not by contriving derivations and genealogies, but only by studying each man and each era in itself for what each had thought, said, and done.

There is a great temptation for a historian writing about Russia in the nineteenth century to see everything in relation to the upheaval of 1917, which is still the more important historical influence of our times today. The movements of the past century tend to be judged by the extent to which they contributed to the October Revolution and their success or failure is assessed by many writers according to their role in ultimately helping or hindering the success of Lenin and Trotsky. So it is salutary and refreshing when a historian looks at Czarist Russia for its own sake and analyses its vivid and vigorous intellectual life without reference to what was to come after. [*Spectator,* July 8, 1960]

Yet another English commentator concluded that the dramatic, moral, and historical value of the populists would have been lost if these men had been placed in a pantheon of revolutionaries or if they had been transformed into examples and models of the excellence or inadequacy of one ideology or another. "The history of this movement is above all a record of individuals," W. S. Merwin concluded, "many of whom would have been remarkable in any circumstance, faced with confusion and injustice, surrounded by suffering, devoting themselves, always at considerable risk to an effort to discover what, in such a situation, is the duty of a man, what he can live for and, if necessary, die for, what he can really accomplish for those around him. In the main, the populists were struggling to create values in a world without them, and any such attempt, it seems, is quite likely to fail. But if the account of it is ever really irrelevant, then surely everything else is too" (*Nation,* September 23, 1961).

Thus, the figures of the Russian populists, freed from the outlines and formulae to which they had often been reduced by their followers and their enemies, gradually reached the concerns, the questioning of the subsequent later century; they offered their experience to anyone who was again faced with the problems of nihilism and liberty, of dictatorship and socialism. The 1960s were a decade of intense work in these areas. The burden of the past was heavy, as we have seen, and not only in Russia. But it is the task of historians to help bear this weight, and despite many difficulties and many restrictions they seem to have carried out their duty to a considerable extent. It is certainly worth observing their work closely.

The thaw in Russia had just begun, and the first shift needed was among the great frozen blocks of quotations from Lenin and Marx. These were in great disorder and confusion after the disappearance of the "great simplifier," who even in this corner of Soviet ideology had placed everything in rigid and elementary order with obsessive monotony. It was not difficult to discover that, in order to fabricate such a picture, it had been necessary to dismember Lenin's sentences, removing them from their political and chronological context, isolating them and thus making them say whatever was wanted. One example will suffice. In an essay written between 1901 and 1902, "What Is to Be Done?" Lenin had included a few very fundamental pages on the function of theory in all revolutionary movements. "Without revolutionary theory there cannot be a revolutionary movement." This affirmation was particularly important for a party such as the recently formed Russian social democratic one, which was faced with truly exceptional problems. With a full awareness of the dreadful task that lay before the Russian revolutionaries and of their responsibility toward the world socialist movement, and with poorly disguised pride arising from the exceptional situation, Lenin went on to say that "the tasks of the Russian social democracy are greater than any faced by other social democratic parties in the world." "Later we will discuss the political and organizational tasks that are imposed by the need to free the whole population from the yoke of czarism. Here we want to discuss the fact that the fighting function of the avant-garde can only be taken on by a party guided by avant-garde theory. To understand what this means in concrete terms, one need only recall the predecessors of Russian social democracy, Herzen, Belinsky, Chernyshevsky, and the extraordinary group of revolutionaries of the 1870s, one only need consider the universal function that Russian literature is now acquiring, one need only. . . . but we do not need other examples."[25] These words alone would be sufficient to show how the moral and ideological tension of populism was still alive in the young Lenin. In the Stalinist era these words were constantly subjected to the anthological method: some men cut Chernyshevsky's quotations, others removed the revolutionaries from the *Narodnaya Volya*. Each took the piece that served him best.

Is it worth recalling these sad events? It is essential, if no less sad, to recollect that in the 1960s in the Soviet Union, Lenin's deleted phrases, once returned to the world, often provided protection or cover for those who planned to study the populists. Behind the shield of Lenin, in whom the relationship with the 19th-century revolutionaries was still alive and personal, the Soviet scholars of the 1960s were able to return, though against the trend of the times, to "the predecessors of social democracy," to "Russian socialism," to the very origins of the revolutionary movement in their country. Lenin's words were made use of, as they had been in the Stalinist era. But at that time they had been used for suppression and prevention. Twenty years later, they were at least occasionally used to reestablish contacts with the past.

But the bust of Lenin remained Janus-faced in the Soviet Union. If one side encouraged and supported the historians in their effort to get away from Stalinism, the other hindered open discussion of the populists' ideas, of their conception of Russia's economic development, and of their vision of peasant socialism. Lenin's words were interpreted in a great variety of ways, as happens when one looks in old texts for support and proof of one's own ideas rather than seeking historical reality, and when one treats the words as an authority rather than as a stimulus for research. Those who wish to know this work of orientation (I do not think it is worth a detailed description, yet only in detailed exposition would it acquire value and significance) should see the bibliography already mentioned which accompanies the miscellany in honor of the eightieth birthday of B. P. Kozmin, and also the review by S. S. Volk and S. K. Mikhailova in *Sovetskaya istoriografiya revolyutsionnogo narodnichestva 70-kh-nachala 80-kh godov XIX veka* (Soviet historiography of revolutionary populism of the seventies and eighties in the 19th century).[26] The authors rightly concluded, after quoting numerous articles and scientific conferences on Lenin and populism, that "after having reestablished a comprehensive evaluation that is favorable to populism, scholars gradually moved to investigate it in detail and more deeply" (p. 147).

We too must follow the Soviet historians on this path, noting an important preliminary ideological readjustment, that is, along with and beyond Lenin, the return to Marx and his ideas about the 19th-century Russian revolutionary movement. In 1947, almost without any introduction or explicit justification, a precious little volume was published: *Perepiska K. Marksa i F. Engelsa a russkimi politicheskimi deyatelyami* (The correspondence of K. Marx and F. Engels with Russian political men). Twenty years later the Marxist-Leninist Institute collected notes, letters, and documents of any kind that gave evidence of the relationship between Marx and Engels and revolutionary Russia. These documents were published in a fundamental volume which provided a vivid picture of the great interest, doubts, and problems that Russian populism had evoked when Marx and Engels saw it arise at the same time as the revolution of 1848 and develop before their eyes during the 1860s and 1870s.[27] It is a pity that Soviet editors have not yet lost the habit of only providing translated texts without bothering to also provide the original French, German, and English. Above all, it is a pity that they did not want to be more complete in their collection. Why give only a fragment of the four outlines of the letter Marx sent to Vera Zasulich on March 8, 1881? These documents vividly demonstrated his hesitations, his doubts about the central problem of populism, that is, about the affirmation that Russia could have had, thanks to its backwardness and to the peasant *obshchina,* an economic development that was substantially different from that in Western Europe, avoiding capitalism and moving directly to socialist forms of life and production. In the definitive version of this letter, Marx admitted that this was possible provided that the *obshchina* freed itself from the social environment in which it was forced to exist and which prevented its development. Thus, Marx ended up accepting Chernyshevsky's ideas. Taking advantage of Western Europe's experience with capitalism, Russia could make the traditional peasant communities the basis for her socialism. This was 1881, and for twenty years the populist movement had posed the question of how to detach the *obshchina* from the czarist world in order to lead it to the socialist world. These were passionate questions to which Marx did not reply in 1881, despite the insistent and repeated inquiries from the most diverse trends of Russian populism.[28] The Gordian knot of the Russian revolution had not been cut. Some years earlier, discussing the problem with Mikhailovsky, Marx had already left the matter open, refusing to prophesy or to descend into an empty philosophy of history.[29] While preparing to write to Zasulich in 1881, in his notes and outlines, he continually returned to the idea that only a revolution in Russia could save the *obshchina.*[30] But in the letter that he actually sent, he did not go beyond the simple possibility of a socialist development in a country like

Russia, where capitalism had not yet broken the ancient peasant community traditions.

It was Engels, in discussion with N. F. Danielson, who in the 1890s affirmed with increasing clarity that capitalism had already won in Russia and that the country had already started on the road that the West had followed previously. Through a concise and very interesting discussion, the populist hypothesis was discarded. In the foreground, there emerged with increasing clarity the idea that Marx had seemed to accept in 1882 when he and Engels (who probably was the real author) signed the introduction to the second Russian edition of the *Communist Manifesto*. The idea was that the revolution, which alone could save the *obshchina*, could only be realized if the example and the initiative for social transformation that went beyond capitalism were to come from the West. Those who arrived late on the historical scene had the advantage of benefiting not only from the technical and economic experience of the more advanced capitalist countries but also and especially from the socialist revolution that had matured in the meantime. "If the Russian revolution serves as a sign for the proletariat revolution in the West, so that they complement each other, then the present Russian *obshchina* will be the starting point for socialist development."[31]

After 1882, Engels spent a decade developing this point of view. The Western European model became the center of his view of Russia's future as he further discarded the hypothesis, which Marx had accepted, of the possibility of socialist development in the world of the Russian peasants. There was a large element of historical fatalism, and full acceptance of the consequences that this triumph of the capitalist way must bring. As Engels wrote, "History is the most cruel of all the goddesses, and she drives her chariot through heaps of corpses, not only during wars but also in periods of 'peaceful' economic development. And we are fools enough not to find the courage in ourselves to make progress a reality unless we are forced to it by suffering that seems almost intolerable."[32] The populist ideas seemed more and more like illusions in Engels's polemic, which was not without a renewed sense of superiority mixed with scorn for those who sought a different road to economic and social development in Russia. "In a land like yours," Engels wrote to Plekhanov on February 26, 1895, "where modern large-scale industry is grafted onto the primitive peasant communities and where all the intermediate stages of civilization are present, in a land surrounded intellectually by a more or less effective Chinese wall desired by despotism, one should certainly not be surprised that ideas take shape in the most unexpected and extraordinary ways."[33] And, as Engels well knew, this situation was creating a new form of fanaticism and ideological superstition. As he said, "The works of Marx were being interpreted in the most diverse and contradictory ways, almost as if they were quotations of the classics or of the New Testament."[34] What for the populists had been a desire to fulfill their moral convictions through practical solutions now risked being changed into a total acceptance of Russia's development according to the capitalist and proletariat model. In vain, Danielson confronted Engels with the physical, biological, and demographic limits beyond which Russia could not go in its efforts to industrialize (and this limit will be a heavy burden on the rhythm of Russia's development in the subsequent decades, as Gerschenkron has stressed). In vain, faced with history which passed over heaps of corpses, the populists stressed everyone's right to rebel and protest (and this was an essential element of Russia's development in the 20th century). But with the great drive toward industrialization at the end of the 19th century, Marx's doubts seemed to vanish into the past momentarily, while a new and rigid view of bourgeois development was taking shape.

One cannot say that the recent Soviet discussions on this first encounter and clash between populism and Marxism, engaging though they are, went very far. The return to Marx has often dealt with his relationship with the Russian revolutionaries of the 1860s and 1870s, rather than with those who fought for his ideas.[35] The books of Reuel and Polevoy seemed to revive interest in the problems of grafting Marxism onto the trunk of the 19th-century Russian revolutionary movement. However, the clear separation between the history of populism and the history of Marxism, and the desire not to mix the two or even to juxtapose or compare them, again led to silence.[36] Not even the renewed interest in Plechanov seems to have led to a deeper investigation into these questions.[37] The important publication of a broad selection of populist economic texts, in 1958, can be considered a significant sign, but nevertheless it was not followed by the expected debates.[38]

In the last decade, more significant contributions have come from America and England. Studies by Salomon M. Schwarz, Leopold Haimson, D. W. Treadgold, Arthur P. Mendel, J. L. H. Keep, S. H. Baron, J. Frankel, and A. Walicki, to mention only a few, again discuss the question of the relationship between populism and Marxism.[39] Despite their considerable value, it must be said that these books often risk perpetuating the deep division and separation established in Russia between the history of social democracy and the history of the previous revolutionary movement. In the name of political formulae and ideological forms, they risk severing the profound psychological and political unity between the various phases of the struggle against czarist absolutism.

From the standpoint of our particular interests, the studies of Richard Pipes have special importance. Pipes reexamined the relationship between the young Lenin and the populist and Jacobin tradition. In a brilliant and penetrating investigation into the history of words and their rapid change in the last decades of the 19th century, he has presented the precise meaning of the terms *narodnik* and *narodnichestvo*.[40] In his "semantic inquiry," Pipes has confirmed that these terms were coined and became established only in the mid 1870s and that then they designated only a part, a trend, in the Russian revolutionary movement, the part that maintained that "the intellectuals should not lead the people in the name of abstract, bookish, imported ideas but adapt themselves to the people as it was, promoting resistances to the government in the name of real, everyday needs" (p. 445). The meaning of the term soon broadened, but there is no doubt—and it is to Pipes's credit that he stresses this—that the Russian Marxists were the first to give it a more general meaning, and to make it synonymous with all Russian revolutionary trends that did not accept their new ideas. Thus the semantic investigation leads to the same conclusions as the ideological one, and emphasizes the great importance of the discussions of Marx, Engels, and their followers which we have already mentioned. It is certainly not the first time in the history of ideas and political movements that a baptism comes from the adversaries. But why should one deduce from this, as Pipes does, that the use of the word *narodnichestvo* "had no historical justification"? Pipes probably does not take sufficient account of the weight that traditions, ideas, and sentiments formed in the 1850s and 1860s had during the 1870s. To me it seems impossible to maintain that in the mid 1870s the *narodniki* supported "the commune or artel' not so much because Herzen or Chernyshevsky had done so, but because they were the institution they actually encountered in the villages and therefore considered them 'popular'" (as Pipes asserts, p. 452).

The ideas and passions aroused by Herzen and Chernyshevsky in their followers who "went to the people" were too important for the young men to discover the *obshchina* by themselves and with their own eyes. In reality they saw it through the colors and the problems that their masters—not just Herzen and Chernyshevsky, but also Bakunin, Lavrov, and Tkachev—had taught them to look for. And it is this continuity and this tradition that constitute, beyond all internal differences, the character and the unity of the populist movement to which the Marxists and the social democrats contributed in the 1890s, leaving the mark of their definition. On closer observation, a return to the events of the 1860s and 1870s is not just legitimate, but essential. Among other things, the term *narodnichestvo* has the advantage of recalling how, through the discussions of the 1880s and 1890s, the existing great revolutionary hope was transformed. This was the hope that Russia would avoid passing through a capitalist phase, a hope that, despite many doubts, was upheld by Karl Marx himself.[41]

Like the Soviet scholars of the sixties, we too must set aside these "comprehensive evaluations" to begin to "investigate in detail and more deeply." First of all, how and when were the ideas born that later characterized the whole populist movement? How did that ideology start to crystallize? The most important answers do not come from historians of the political movements but from historians of the world of the Russian peasants, that is, from those who saw the problem from the viewpoint of the villages, not from the viewpoint of the intelligentsia. Pierre Pascal, the scholar whose investigations go back to the protopope Avvakum, Pugachev, and Dostoevsky, in collecting his articles (or *"esquisses,"* as he calls them), in a book entitled *Civilisation paysanne en Russie* has helped us understand the tragedy of the Russian peasants. He describes their conflict with the modern industrial world, their tenacious defense of their traditions, their forms of life, their interests as compared with those of the nobles, the bureaucrats, and the organizers from the cities.[42] In these pages we observe the intelligentsia's discovery, between the 18th and 19th centuries, of the autonomous existence of the Russian people. We can feel the peasant *obshchina* still pulsating and surviving tenaciously in the years immediately before Stalinist collectivization.[43] We live next to "la paysanne du nord" in her hard but productive and dignified labor (pp. 45 ff.). We are directly in touch with the traditional organization of solidarity in the village through his "Entr'aide paysanne en Russie" (pp. 63 ff.). We experience life in a small, isolated village in the province of Nizhni Novgorod in 1926-28 ("Mon village, il y a quarante ans," pp. 75 ff.). And in his last essay, "Esénine—poète de la campagne russe," we too are carried away in the frightful storm which momentarily seemed to exalt and give universal value to the Russian peasant world, only to crush its ancient traditions and deny its deepest and truest values. It is a tragedy that was expressed with the greatest purity and despair by the poet Esenine. Here he is, like the village within him, where he continues to live even when he takes part in the events of the city. He too is caught up

in this great turbulence of unanimity, with all the Russian people. Only those who, like them, have lived through it can understand their conduct and their works at this time. It is not merely a throne which crumbles, it is not a monarchy which is going to be replaced by a parliamentary regime, it is not such and such reforms which are going to be enacted: the jurists and professors can believe that if they like. The Russian people themselves feel otherwise, have other ambitions.... It is an immense revolt against all the iniquities, the oppressions, the cruelties, the hypocrisies, against the great scandal of the war, an immense aspiration toward the happiness of all men. The mighty will be cast down from their throne and the poor shall be exalted. Peace to all the universe! [Pp. 121 ff.]

Better than anyone else, Pierre Pascal has revealed to us what immense, explosive power lay at this time in Russia in the revolutionary encounter between secular peasant aspirations and the intelligentsia's profound desire for a moral renewal, in the populist charge that the 19th century had passed on to the 20th century.

More recent investigations into the history of the Russian village seem to confirm and add specifics to Pierre Pascal's view, from the detailed and accurate history by Jerome Blum[44] to the excellent collection of articles by Wayne S. Vucinich entitled *The Peasant in Nineteenth-Century Russia*.[45] The reality of peasant life in 19th-century Russia is described and studied from the social standpoint by Mary Matossian, while Terence Emmons has reexamined the question of the emancipation of 1861. Donald W. Treadgold raises the question of religion in Russian village life. Among other historians, John S. Curtiss has written about the military, Francis M. Watters about the *obshchina*, Reginald E. Zelnik about the transformation of the peasants into workers, Michael Petrovich about Russian historiography on peasant problems, and Donald Fanger about *The Peasant in Literature*. Nicholas V. Riasanovsky provides a conclusion in *The Problem of the Peasant;* it is a carefully arranged and precise little encyclopedia on what has been written and said about the Russian village from the age of Alexander I to that of Nicholas II. Of particular importance, on the other hand, are the studies on the permanence and the revival of the peasant *obshchina* after the 1917 revolution. In this area, it is enough to cite the works of Moshe Lewin and D. J. Male.[46]

It has been the task of Michael Confino, the Israeli historian, to create a new basis for discussing the results of the agronomic, economic, and social transformations, ordered from above, that came from the West and were imposed on the Russian peasant world by state machinery and world market demands. Confino's first work was *Domaines et seigneurs en Russie vers la fin du XVIIIe siècle. Etude de structures agraires et de mentalités économiques.*[47] In it he made a precise study of the rise and development of new methods of administration that seemed to promise a renewal of all noble estates during Catherine's reign. But these conflicted with the harsh realities of serfdom, of diffidence, of the resistance of a village threatened by a progress that might make the working and living conditions of a *muzhik* even harsher. The final phase of this development, which coincided with the beginning of the new century, was one of crushed hopes, disillusionment, and stasis. The Russian nobles, shaped by military discipline and by service to the absolute state, had brought to the villages, not a spirit of enterprise, but an aura of officialdom and bureaucracy, of being judges and tutors. The peasants had responded, exceptionally but dangerously, by revolting, and generally by the daily defense of the unwritten laws of their village community. In the long run, the nobles maintained and even aggravated the rule of serfdom, while the peasant ended up preserving and often imposing his own techniques, his own mentality, and his own traditional life-style on the landlord.

In his second work, *Systèmes agraires et progrès agricole. L'assolement triennal en Russie au XVIIIe–XIXe siècles,* Michael Confino used a technical investigation (the effects of triple crop rotation) to penetrate all aspects of peasant reality in modern Russia.[48] In his work, we see the Russian triangle—the landlord, the *obshchina,* and the state—being gradually modified and transformed, driven by technical reality and its requirements, by the search for new land, by the exhaustion of fields, by demographic changes, by the variation in market opportunities, but it still remains the immovable basis of social relationships both before and after the reforms of 1861. With great difficulty and only in part, the landlord manages to replace triple rotation with extensive agriculture. The *obshchina* continues to regulate, balance, and maintain stable village life, imposing its own techniques and its own mentality. The state, even when it manages to carry out reforms as fundamental as those of 1861, cannot avoid defending the interests of the nobles and trying to control the peasant *obshchina* without being able to break it down or change it. Only the industrialization of the late 19th and early 20th centuries provided a way out of this situation. However, industrialization was a weighty instrument, difficult to manage, burdensome for all Russian society, and was far from producing all the effects of which it was capable when Russia entered in the era of its modern revolutions.

It should not surprise us that, before industrialization, a movement was born that sought not only the breakdown of the Russian triangle but that wished to do this by supporting the peasant *obshchina*. The landlords had to be eliminated, and what about the state? Doubts about this past problem made some revolutionaries seek the complete destruction of the state while others wanted its transformation and utilization.

Thus, by following Michael Confino in his *étude d'économie et de sociologie rurales*, we seem to truly return to the terrain where populism was born. Observing the movement, so to speak, close to the ground, we see it arise when the ideas and technical knowledge imported from the West fail to transform local reality and seem to make life even more burdensome for the peasants, at first evoking a defensive and diffident reaction toward foreigners and hostility for anything that threatens traditions, and eventually, fairly quickly, bringing the belief that only by going to the peasant's side, only by accepting and making the village traditions one's own, would it be possible to introduce foreign ideas and techniques to everyone's advantage. Thus the justification of serfdom and of the landlord's control over the village was replaced by a defense of Russian agronomic traditions, of the *mir*, of the periodic redistribution of land, of the lack of enclosures, of the spirit of solidarity and equality that dominated the Russian village.[49]

This process was anything but linear. Rather, it was a continual regermination of similar ideas at the most varied times and in varied forms, from the age of Catherine to that of Nicholas I. It is a remarkable fact that as far back as 1789, a man like Radishchev, in a series of notes and sketches on the situation in the regions around St. Petersburg, could reach the conclusion that the periodic redistribution of land, with the intention of assuring every peasant plots of similar yield, "was a bad thing for agriculture, but good for equality."[50] In discussing annual redistribution, Radishchev remarked, "Who in our time would have thought that in Russia we are realizing what the finest legislators sought in ancient times and what more modern ones think of, and from which arises the great Russian agriculturalist's love for his own hearth?"[51]

Naturally such opinions were continually and vigorously contradicted by those who looked at the peasants in the West, the "farmers" or *fermiers*, as a model of what should be followed and imitated in Russia. Everything in the present agrarian system must be changed, they thought, and certainly the *obshchina* could not escape this total condemnation. But how was this change to be achieved? The *muzhik's* resistance was deep and invincible. Faced with this resistance, the ruling class had a persistent need to find the reason for the peasants' obstinate desire to maintain their traditional forms. At the same time there was a temptation to yield to

it, accepting reality and justifying it before the West. Even the famous statesman
P. D. Kiselev, talking about the state peasants who during the 1830s and 1840s
were the object of his activities as a reformer, concluded: "It is true that the
periodic redistributions are a nuisance, but one can only change this usage by in-
stituting individual ownership, which also has its inconveniences; it eliminates the
marvelous advantage of communal ownership, thanks to which there are no proletarians among the peasants of the state, and each family has its share in the village's assets."[52]

Nor could these landlords and state officials, wrestling with the Russian economic situation between the 18th and 19th centuries, avoid one question that was
continually posed by the reality surrounding them. Did the roots of backwardness
lie in the regime of peasant serfdom or in the collective responsibility of the *mir*,
in the *obshchina*, and in the redistribution of land? What were the relationships
between one aspect and the other of this single reality? All the discussion between
the economist Tengoborsky and the young Ogarev, Herzen's friend, was based on
this problem that was discussed in a variety of forms until 1861.[53] Even after his
detailed and lucid historical investigation, Confino seems to hesitate before such a
question. "Did the peasant neglect his work because of the fact that the plots pass
from hand to hand or was it because he was conscious of working for others, without being recompensed or rewarded for his labor?" And the "morcellement des
terres," the cause of poor yields, was it due to the communal regime of the village
or rather, as Confino maintains, to the "historical circumstances of the formation
of the *terroirs* and the evolution of seigneurial land ownership"? Undoubtedly
"this symbiosis of communal practices and of rules of organization was at the
heart of the ambivalence that one notices in the attitude of the landlords toward
the rural commune."[54]

That ambivalence and ambiguity were crystallized into an ideology of the *obshchina* and the *mir* as soon as these truths about peasant life were ideally detached
and isolated from the context of landlords and serfs in which they had been
placed, and were inserted into a more general historical, religious, political, and
social view. We have already found Radishchev regarding the *obshchina* as the
solution to the lengthy search for a more just society. In the Decembrists, and
especially in Pestel, there is a return and development of the desire to see the Russian village from the point of view of economic initiative and improvement, on one
hand, and security for all on the other. The liberation of the peasants, which the
provisional republican government would have assured, would rest on this double
principle. The recent excellent edition of Pestel's *Russkaya pravda* allows us
to follow closely the development of these ideas by the head of the Southern
Society.[55]

Other studies on the Decembrists allow us to observe other moments and
aspects of this discussion. For example, in the early 1820s, S. I. Turgenev tried to
raise the nobles' desire for agrarian modernization to a political and not just a
technical level, trying to explain to them that the abolition of slavery was the

foremost problem, that to achieve this it was even worth accepting and supporting the autocratic government, and that from this fundamental reform a more liberal and just regime would necessarily arise. Thus the reality of the Russian peasants forced an alliance between the tradition of enlightened despotism and the newer and more lively tradition of liberalism. Power and the state became the pivot point, the central element in the vision of those who were not resigned to conservatism and a standstill. There arose a "statist" view, in contrast with the "popular" view, of the past and the future of Russia.[56]

One function of the Slavophiles in the 1830s and 1840s was to insert the popular elements—the *obshchina,* the *mir,* the whole peasant world—into a vision that was no longer enlightened, statist, or liberal, but religious and romantic. This grafting was often contrived and imprecisely executed, and produced abundant but flaccid fruits on the communal spirit, on the innate Christianity of the Russians, and on the purity and health of the peasant community which was uncontaminated by egoism, violence, foreign influence, and by the city and the state. All these ideas led to a reactionary rhetoric, conservative and even nationalistic.[57] But the first generation of Slavophiles had a historical function that was far from such tasks of propaganda and the defense of czarism. Even the Soviet historians, after decades of massive and monotonous condemnation, began to discuss these opinions and to try to get a better idea of what really had been the function of men such as Kireevsky, Khomyakov, and Aksakov in the history of Russia. There is a particularly interesting discussion of this in the pages of *Voprosy literatury,* which began with a brilliant article by Aleksandr Yanov, published in issue number 5 in 1969. In the Slavophile movement he sees a first positive response to the sense of inferiority caused in the 18th century by contrast with the West, by the conviction that became crystallized in the early 19th century that a true culture and literature did not exist in Russia. The Slavophiles countered this negation with a real religion of the Russian people, the peasants. If the destiny of the Slavophiles was to become reactionaries, this was not because of their initial ideas, which were anything but reactionary, but because they did not understand that the roots of despotism in their country lay in the very Russian people they idealized. Despite this, it was the Slavophiles who posed the problem of what could and should be drawn from the national reality in order to achieve the more liberal world of which they dreamed. It was they who pointed the way, the hopes for Russia's liberation. Once despotism had been removed, all progress would be assured. Thus they were comparing Utopia with autocracy, and it was this utopian, religious attitude of theirs that led them away from liberty. Their reactionary fate did not derive from the feudal and aristocratic character of their ideas but from their abstract democratic attitude, their adoration of the Russian people.

Again in *Voprosy literatury,* through the words of S. A. Pokrovsky, the echo of the past years, of the Stalinist era, replied to Yanov, showing that the sense of inferiority and the fear of the West have not disappeared from present-day Russia, and that their present form is just the same: a feeling of bitter nationalistic vindication (no. 5 [1969], pp. 117 ff.). Others contributed to this debate, including B. Egorov (no. 5, pp. 128 ff.), A. Dementev (no. 7, pp. 116 ff.), and I. Ivanov (no. 7, pp. 129 ff.). Ivanov rightly emphasized the fact that the Slavophiles were so convinced of the meekness of the Russian peasant, so persuaded that he neither intended to nor knew how to rebel, that one could conclude that it was possible and desirable to introduce and establish the freedom of the press in Russia. Ivanov insisted that the Slavophiles were actually opposed to the savage methods of combating barbarity, to revolutions, and to despotism. It is in this attitude that the deepest root of the renewed Soviet interest in these figures lies. It is an interest in men who were distant from the Russia of today, 19th-century romantics who for decades seemed to have been scorned and left in oblivion. An extensive movement of return toward ancient Russia, to the religion of their fathers, leads men to see the past differently and to consider and again appreciate values that seemed to have been destroyed or buried. (To be convinced of this, one only need observe the new attitude toward medieval Russian art or read the works of Pasternak or of Solzhenitsyn, or just see Tarkovsky's film on Andrei Rublev.) But, more significantly, one can see how this profound and varied movement extant in Russia today, eventually turns, as in the 1830s and as in the period of the development of Slavophilism, against an adversary, an enemy who is both feared and loathed, that is, against the despotic and bureaucratic state.

Another contributor to this debate, L. Frizman, stresses that the Slavophiles were a very small minority amid a great sea of reactionary nobles in the age of Nicholas I (no. 7, p. 148). Did not the utopian element that undoubtedly existed in the Slavophiles' ideas derive from this unequal struggle against the reality that overwhelmed them? As utopias go, writes E. Maimin, was not the idea of giving Western political forms to Russia in 1905 and 1917 also utopian? It is evident that today some profound and unexpected echoes are responding to the revived and subdued voice of the 19th-century Slavophiles. In the early 1960s, *Vosprosy literatury* had included an impassioned discussion on revolutionary populism. At the end of the decade, in 1969, there was a return to the more distant first origins of the intelligentsia, to an aspect that had remained in the shadows for many years; there was a return to the relationship between Russian and the Western world, from where there reemerged the ever-present problem of the despotic and bureaucratic state.

The discussion we have examined has another remarkable aspect. It quite clearly admits that outside Russia the Slavophiles and their historical significance had been discussed at length, well before it was decided to reopen the debate in the Soviet Union. As in the case of populism, there had been approximately a fifteen-year delay. Therefore, naturally, N. V. Riasanovsky's book, *Russia and the West in the Teachings of the Slavofiles: A Study of Romantic Ideology,* was recalled.[58]

There was also mention, though perhaps not enough, of the work by Andrei Walicki, undoubtedly the most searching and intelligent investigation of these problems.[59] Other works named include the studies by Eberhard Müller, *Russischer Intellekt in Europäischer Krise. Ivan Kireevskij, 1806-1856;* the work by Peter K. Christoff, *An Introduction to Nineteenth Century Russian Slavophilism: A Study in Ideas, Vol. 1: A. S. Xomjakof;* and the revised and enlarged second edition of Robert Stupperich's work, *Jurij Samarin und die Anfänge der Bauernbefreiung in Russland.*[60] If to these we add the works publihed in recent years on the ever fascinating problem of the continual reflection and intertwining of the Western image of Russia and of the idea that Russia had about herself (e.g., that of Dieter Groh, or the more restricted and specialized but very useful work by Karsten Goehrke), and if from the Soviet side we add the detailed and clear, though somewhat dull and handbookish, work by N. A. Cagolov, we have before us the main elements of the recent rich discussion on the formation, among the Slavophiles of the 1830s and 1840s, of the ideological terrain in which populism set down its roots.[61]

Despite all the uncertainty, contradictions, and romantic vagueness, there is no doubt about the function and importance of men such as Kiereevsky, Khomyakov, and Koshelev. The feelings of rivalry, envy, love, and hate that the Western world had aroused in the Russians for centuries grew deeper, causing a painful awareness of the cost, mainly on a moral plane, of the works of Peter, Catherine, and Alexander. It also brought an awareness of the effort required to build a strong and powerful state modeled on the Western pattern but at the same time responding to Russia's deep need for expansion and power. After a century in which Russia struggled to follow Western Europe, to imitate and use her, there developed a profound disillusionment, an insurmountable repulsion toward the Europe that had come out of the French Revolution. The forms and opinions through which this disillusionment was expressed were taken from the West itself, from Saint-Simon and Thierry, from Louis Blanc and Carlyle, from Schelling and from the German romantics. But Russia's withdrawal into herself, the return to Russian tradition, cannot be explained exclusively by cultural influences and a simple repetition of forms. It is something deeper and less clear that was mingled with a growing distrust in Russia's capacity to become completely European, to reach the West on an economic, political, technical, and intellectual plane, and the fear of still being too weak and young to be able to accept the examples coming from outside her borders. This movement resulted in Russia seeking refuge not so much in Christianity (too universal to serve as a protection or shelter) as in the church; after all, the church really was local and Russian. And if orthodoxy became the religious utopia of this disillusionment and isolation, the people, the *narodnost,* and the traditional forms of the Russian village became its political and social utopia. They, too, developed slowly and uncertainly at the end of the 1830s. Eberhard Müller is right in saying that for a long time the *narodnost* remained a very problematic concept, not a certainty and a faith.[62] The same applies to the *obshchina* and the *mir,* which in the writings of the first Slavophiles are not real elements to be observed, studied, and understood, but rather a possible incarnation of a religious and social community with a mystic and orthodox content. It was only when Haxthausen joined in that the debate among the Slavophiles about the *obshchina* deepened. What a strange fate for the German baron who came to be considered the discoverer of the Russian peasant community. He did observe and describe it, and in doing so made no small contribution to bringing down to earth the Russians' discussions in the 1840s about the origin and nature of the *mir.* (He never used the word *obshchina* and is responsible for the fact that in the West the structure of the Russian village is generally referred to by the first and not the second of these words.)

Haxthausen was well aware of the fact that he was not dealing with an exclusively or typically Russian reality. He had come from Westphalia and had studied the agrarian regimes of Western Germany before studying Prussia and Russia. At least since the age of von Möser the problem of the mark, the primitive Germanic community, had been the subject of lively discussion among historians and agronomists in those regions. In his eyes, the Russian situation demonstrated a particularly remarkable and perfect survival of forms that had disappeared elsewhere.[63]

It was Slavophiles who gave Haxthausen's "discovery" a national value, and by doing so assimilated it and made it their own. Their views of the *obshchina* were anything but unanimous. Some considered it an excellent element of Russian life, while others saw it as an obstacle to the country's economic improvement. These conflicting views reflected the debates on these subjects that had taken place earlier among the Russian nobility.[64] In the *obshchina* Khomyakov saw the expression of orthodoxy, the cornerstone of Russian society, the seed of a better world in the future. Koshelev replied that it really was a matter of the survival of the youth of the Russian people. Such youth had long since vanished in the West. Self-administration was an illusion, as personal experience had already proved (in elections the strongest and the richest win and the spirit of unanimity is soon destroyed). Land is worked more effectively if it belongs to the peasant. Furthermore, the community spirit was dangerous. Should artisans, too, place their income in a communal account? And the landlords, "should they join the *obshchina?* There would be nothing left to do but hand over our land, forests, fields, etc., to it. With the principle of the *obshchina* we will either reach the point of general collective property, that is, the end of all property, or we will do nothing but perpetuate the subdivision of the country into classes." It was not the *obshchina* but the soil's fertility and the amount of available labor that had always determined the fate of Russian agriculture. Only someone like Haxthausen who had not lived in Russia could speak enthusiastically about the peasant communities, concluded Koshelev.

Khomyakov countered these remarks with his historic, aesthetic, and above all moral and religious view of the *obshchina,* without confronting the economic and technical problems that his friend had raised.[65] It was in this contrast between ideology and technology, between the religious ideal and economic needs, that the vision of the Russian village became crystallized during the 1840s and 1850s and greatly influenced the reforms of 1861.[66]

If this is the terrain from which populism was born, the revolutionary seed was sowed there by Herzen. The value and significance of his words—in 1848 and during the years of disillusionment, despair, and difficult recovery that followed the revolutionary period—have naturally continued to attract attention and arouse discussion in Russia and abroad.[67] Even in the past decade it has been possible to observe how Herzen remains a sensitive index, a barometer of the Russian intelligentsia's position; they regard him not only as their founder but also as an ever present secret adviser in times of doubt, difficulty, and the tragedies of daily existence. The edition of Herzen's works, begun in 1954 and completed in 1965 (the dates somehow seem symbolic),[68] can be considered a true monument to him. In its pages, Herzen's lucid, penetrating thought seems to be continually freeing itself from the rigid academic forms in which it was edited, to continue an ongoing dialogue on the problems of revolution and liberty. Its publication was followed by the appearance of photocopied editions (rare in Russian editorial policy) of the periodicals Herzen published, *Polyarnaya zvezda* and *Kolokol.*[69] The Soviet scholars who participated in these publications collected their observations, *trouvailles*, and reflections in a miscellany.[70] The volume begins with one of Herzen's previously unpublished thoughts, edited and commented upon by Oksman; it shows extremely clearly how aware Herzen was on his own role and that of the Occidentalists. On May 24, 1862, he wrote:

Only the powerful thought of the West, the last expression of its long historical development, could have stirred to life the germ that slumbered in the breast of the patriarchal order of the Slavic people. The *artel* [the workers' association] and the rural commune, the division of products and of fields, the communal assembly and the union of villages in self-governing arrondissements, all this will serve to establish our future regime of national liberty. But these establishments are nothing more than scattered stones, and without Western thought the edifice of our future would never have more than its foundations.[71]

Herzen reached this conclusion after considerable hesitation and vacillation. For him, as for the Slavophiles, disillusionment with the West had been one of the most powerful forces driving him to seek a reason to live in and have hopes for Russia. Herzen's disillusionment was not rooted in the pettiness and meanness of the age of Louis Philippe. His wound was caused by the defeat of the Parisian workers in June 1848, the impossibility of France's becoming an active supporter of Poland and Italy, and the fact that France had become an open enemy of Mazzini's Roman republic. In Herzen's eyes the West had proved itself incapable of living up to the very ideals it had created. Would Russia be able to make them live again and to develop them on her own soil? Even in his worst moments of desperation, Herzen did not lose faith in the people and the intellectuals of his country.

The most important documents in this dialogue between Herzen and the West have been studied by Michel Cadot, an expert on the relationship between Russia and the West during the early 19th century. Cadot's edition of Jules Michelet's *Légendes democratiques du Nord,* which includes much previously unknown material, is a substantial contribution to the understanding of the world in which Herzen's ideas were maturing.[72] However, what has not been adequately discussed, either in Russia or abroad, is the political tangle in Herzen's ideas at the height of the revolution when, in a unique way, he tried to unite his admiration for Proudhon with his hope in Blanqui. The problems and contradictions of the populism and socialism of the 1860s and 1870s were already germinating during Herzen's intense experiences in Rome, Paris, Geneva, and then, when he was defeated, in Nice. The theme of his disillusionment is central to the work of Vera Pirosch-kow.[73] We can gather what Herzen's activities were in those years only indirectly from the first pages of Eberhard Reissner's work.[74] Lampert, who has provided us with a vivid portrait of Herzen, does not treat the burning political and social issues of the 1848 revolution or Herzen's participation in it.[75] So let us look at the most important book on Herzen published in some time, by Martin Malia. In its pages there is certainly at least a partial answer to the questions we have asked.[76] It is only partial because the author's perspective is psychological rather than historical. The title promises *The Birth of Russian Socialism.* But to understand Russian socialism we are taken through the young Herzen's rebellion against his father and his family, the stress under which he developed—in effect, a kind of historical psychoanalysis. This is always a difficult, uncertain, and unreliable method to apply, even to a man like Herzen, who wrote so much and so confessionally. Would it not be better to understand the political problems of the 1848 revolution, observing and comprehending the meaning and significance of the replies Herzen tried to give day by day, month by month? Naturally, Malia tries to do this, but his psychological method leads him to explain Herzen through Herzen rather than to see his concrete actions. There is a grave risk of imprisoning a character in a closed, individual, and often impenetrable existence. The biographical method—used very effectively by Malia in following an individual's activity in his world—is as fruitful as the psychological method is uncertain; the latter fatally detaches the individual from his own actions and from his own environment. Thus, for Malia, Herzen's "crucial year" is 1847, when Herzen left Russia for good, rather than 1848 or 1849 when he was seeking a way out of the contradictions of the European and Parisian revolution. Malia concentrates more on Herzen's travels and adventures than on his books and pamphlets, his discussions and ideas, which really were what Herzen lived for in those years. The relationship between the revolution of 1848 and those of 1789 and 1793, the problem of the French state, the profound influence of Proudhon, and Herzen's understanding of Blanqui's will to insurrection, these were at the "birth of Russian socialism" more than Herzen's personal drama and his extraordinary psychology. Moreover, we can taste the fruits of that psychology directly in every page of Herzen's marvelous writings which give us immediate contact with his moral, political, and intellectual experiences. But the historian must look for the political experiences through the political and social logic of Herzen's era.

Herzen wrote with a mastery and originality unequaled by any of his contemporaries and friends who, in those decisive years, were creating the new populist, radical, and socialist ideas of the Russian intelligentsia. He surpassed Bakunin, whose letters from his youth are nevertheless so vivid as to make us regret that they have not been published again in the Soviet Union. He was unequaled by Belinsky, who along with Herzen was the greatest contributor to the formation of the intelligentsia's mentality. It is interesting to observe how political and academic bias and censorship in the Soviet Union have often divided this group of friends in recent historical research. Belinsky, entrusted to historians of literature, is separated from Bakunin, who has only recently and partially emerged from the shadows where his later anarchic ideas had placed him, and from Herzen, who has ascended to the heavens of the great men and thus is often prevented from continuing the very human dialogue that he had held with these and other friends in St. Petersburg and Moscow.[77]

If we want to relive and participate in the intensity of the feelings that bore the seed of later populist protests and revolt, we must open the works of Julian Gregorovich Oksman. For example, let us consider his work devoted to the famous letter Belinsky wrote to Gogol on July 3, 1847, or his essay on the continuity and detachment between Belinsky and the political traditions of the Decembrists.[78] Here a psychological incentive is certainly not lacking, even if it is restricted by the rigid integrity of philological and historical research. In these pages we find the authentic tradition of the intelligentsia, where liberty is conquered with difficulty, is always threatened, and is worth defending by any means, including a double or aesopian language. For both Oksman and Herzen, Belinsky's letter to Gogol is, in Herzen's words, not only "something ingenious" but also "his testament." Oksman recognizes its power and its historical importance through the effect it had on his friends, on Bakunin (who used the letter as a starting point for a speech in Paris on November 29, 1847, which caused him to be exiled from France), on Herzen who spoke of it in an unforgettable way in *My Past and Thoughts* ("I felt a lump in my throat and remained silent for a long time..."), on I. S. Turgenev ("Belinsky's letter to Gogol is my whole religion"), on N. I. Sazonov, and on P. V. Annenkov. Not only is Belinsky's political position with respect to his contemporaries established, but it is also defined in comparison with his predecessors, like the Decembrist exile N. I. Turgenev whose book *La*

Russie et les russes, published in early 1847, had no small influence on the formulation of Belinsky's "minimal program."

This is a theme that Oksman takes up again and develops in his essay "Belinsky and the Political Traditions of the Decembrists." Here too the problem is both difficult and subtle. How and to what extent did the echo of an ill-fated and defeated struggle for liberty, like that of the Decembrists, reach a new generation during Nicholas I's age of repression and tyranny? How did it reach people like the young Belinksy, who continued on the road without daring to look back or to question those who had preceded them, and who, like Belinsky, sometimes ended up condemning them for their past failures, for their historical deficiencies? When Oksman talks about Gogol, and also when he follows the difficult legacy of the Decembrists, in both cases the conclusion he suggests seems evident. The message of liberty, he tells us, does not let itself be submerged, and the request for democracy, even if limited or partial, and even if it is smothered, still forms the seed for a deep renewal of revolutionary will.

Outside the Soviet Union such problems were certainly less pressing, even in the 1960s. In the West the door was opened wider (and a sacred text assures us that this is not always an advantage). There was a broader perspective in placing these distant and hidden conflicts, which were emerging from underground in the Russia of Nicholas I, into their correct historical place in the midst of a Europe that was undergoing the 1848 revolution. If Edward J. Brown's book on Stankevich suffers from too much political and ideological detachment, others by Scheibert, Lampert, Schapiro, and Pomper managed to achieve a sounder historical reconstruction.[79]

The first years of Alexander II's reign, the liberation of the peasants, and the beginning of the age of reform substantially confirmed Herzen's and Belinsky's intuition. Liberty was revolutionary in Russia. Each reform would raise the problem of a complete transformation of Russian society. In one decade, conventionally called the 1860s, though it was actually the period from 1854 to 1864, there was a movement from a timid emergence of liberalism and Slavophilism in the early part of the century to the formation of a socialist and revolutionary movement which in later decades could not be eradicated from Russian lands. What was the reason for such an important change?

For decades, people had continued to look back at the 1860s in times of crisis, in periods of uncertainty in Russian society. It was natural, too, that even a century later, between 1954 and 1964, Soviet writers (consider Pasternak) and historians emerging from the despotism of the Stalinist era should look back to the age of reform, the end of peasant servitude, the development of the student movement and of the first *Zemlya i Volya,* and this tempestuous dawn of liberty. What could they tell us about such an important period in their country?

One must admit that on the level of economic and social history the answer has been inadequate. It has been tirelessly repeated that capitalism had developed sufficiently in Russia to lead fatally to the dissolution of feudal bonds. This was just repetition of an ancient chorus, and did not restate the problems of Russian society in the middle of the last century. It did not bring an understanding of the details of the process of industrialization in Russia. Nor did it ask what the real situation was at the beginning of the reign of Alexander II. The answers in this area did not come from Soviet historians but from across the ocean, from American scholars such as Emmons and especially from Alexander Gerschenkron, in the pages of his economic history of Russia written for the *Cambridge Economic History* (vol. 6, 1965) and later included in his volume *Continuity in History and Other Essays*.[80] Halfway, so to speak, between the Americans and the Russians are the French scholars, with a *Recueil d'articles et de documents*, organized by R. Portal and entitled *Le Statut des paysans libérés du servage. 1861-1961*.[81] The traditional interpretation has not been expressly questioned, but in itself the material presented in this work is so rich, especially Confino's contribution, as to cause one to seriously reconsider the very bases of the problem.

The Russians too have contributed to the debate, and not insignificantly. Among communist historians, the idea of the passage from feudalism to capitalism had generally been accompanied by the affirmation that this transformation, even if required by the changed economic situation, had to find its own driving force in the revolt of the peasant masses, in the revolutionary drive of the *muzhiki,* who rebeled against the burden of their lords and masters. This brought about the studies, including some very valuable ones, on the peasant movements, uprisings, and repression by the state. But in the 1930s and 1940s a significant obstacle evidently arose in the Soviet Union. Even the finest scholars (like Ignatovich, for example) who came from the prerevolutionary period, or who carried on the great tradition of peasant history which is one of the cornerstones of Russian historiography, evidently had to mark time. In those Stalinist years one could still study and investigate the revolts of the *muzhiki* in the archives. But a reinterpretation of the facts or reflection on the nature, character, and value of these obscure rebellions was certainly not encouraged. Stalin, convinced as he was that the populists should be abandoned in silence, was equally convinced that the only acceptable peasant revolts were those that had come from above. The situation in rural Russia after the collectivization in 1929 certainly did not invite close study of the rebellions and revolts that had accompanied the reforms of 1861. Soon there developed one of those dissociated and contradictory situations so common in the intellectual life of the Soviet Union. On one hand, the moving force behind the reforms had been the rebellious peasants; on the other, it was better not to look too closely at these village movements. The revolutionary myth was hovering over reality without illuminating it or penetrating it.

The situation was even more peculiar if we recall that Alexander II, too, had preferred revolutions from above rather than from below. It was he who had promulgated this expressive and typical formula. In fact, the process through which the 1861 reforms were carried out, their consequences in later decades, and their function in the development of industrialization in the country all seemed to confirm what the men of the *Narodnaya Volya* had clearly foreseen. The state had played a decisive role in this process. The revolution from above not only represented a defensive reaction by the emperor and the nobles, it responded to a profound need of the whole social life in Russia, where transformation could only come from above, through the machinery of the state. This was simply because the classes and groups that were capable of moving the Russian giant toward the modern world were too weak economically and too impotent socially. Thus in a historiographical plan, it is natural that the best and most careful research was directed, not at the buried truths of the 19th-century Russian villages, but rather at understanding the plans and reality that had preceded or accompanied the first ten years of Alexander II's reign. One only need consider the now classic works of Druzhinin and Zayonchkovsky. The latter undertook to explode the myths of the peasant revolt, which in the Soviet Union had often fallen into a pattern of retrospective revolutionary rhetoric, and to clear the field of the grave methodological errors that had spoiled these studies. But, above all, he faced a task that could no longer be deferred, that of providing a history of the politics of the Russian state during the second half of the 19th century.

Some of Zayonchkovsky's battles have been won, and he can even allow himself some irony, for example, when he describes the methods by which statistics on the 19th-century peasant movements were, and, we fear, are, constructed.

Unfortunately, we do not have precise data on the breadth of the peasant movement. The method for their computation has not been given in detail, and the figures concerning it recall the "statistical" method which consists of summing two phenomena of completely different dimensions (following the principle: "one camel plus one chicken"). Thus a peasant uprising in which thousands of people took part is considered as one unit, and at the same time the refusal to do forced labor by a handful of peasants also counts as one unit....The second defect found in the historiography of the peasant movement lies in the constant effort to augment the dimensions of the uprisings (letting oneself be guided by the principle: "the more uprisings, and more important the research"). Unfortunately, this tendency became very widespread, especially in the work of minor historians, but not only among them.[82]

In reading these statistics and skimming the numerous documents published recently on the peasant movement in Russia (a collection under this very title and composed of large and basic volumes was published about twenty years ago under the direction of Druzhinin[83]), we are faced with the thought of what the French historians of the *Annales* school might make of it. Meanwhile, some advances have been made toward the use of the tools of anthropology in the interpretation of the dreams, hopes, and utopias of the *muzhiki*.[84] But this line of inquiry, though suggestive, is obviously not the road to understanding of the age of reform under Alexander II. In the center of the picture, even in Soviet historiography, lies the political problem.

Here is the standard form, repeated thousands of times, used in the Soviet Union to define the problem: "revolutionary situation in Russia between 1859 and 1861." A group of historians, following the initiative of the Academy of Sciences of the USSR and directed by M. V. Nechkina, undertook a study of this theme. With great care they collected an impressive amount of material, debates, and conclusions published, at least in part, in five volumes in a large and important miscellany which came out between 1960 and 1970.[85] Every aspect of these three years was examined, from the problems of the czar's government to the peasant movement, from the development of the first clandestine organization to the mood of the intelligentsia. All this was held together by the idea of the "revolutionary situation" which Russia had experienced on the eve of and at the time of the application of the manifesto for the liberation of the serfs. Naturally, the formula comes from Lenin, who long since had matured it and expressed it in its clearest and most definitive form in his article, "Failure of the Second International," published in the journal *Kommunist* in June 1915:

What are the signs of a revolutionary situation? We will not be mistaken if we point them out in these three elements: 1) the impossibility of the dominant classes maintaining their dominion unchanged, one crisis or another among those who are in high positions, a crisis in the politics of the dominant class that creates a division through which the discontent and wrath of the oppressed classes erupts. For the revolution to take place, it is usually not enough for "those who are on the bottom not to accept it anymore," but it is necessary that those who are above "can no longer live as before"; 2) the intensification beyond the normal level of the needs and the difficulties among the oppressed classes; 3) an increase, due to the causes mentioned, of the activity of the masses, who in peaceful times let themselves be preyed upon without protesting, and who in times of turmoil, as in any crisis situation, are driven to make their own protests, as much as "those who are above."[86]

As an example of such a revolutionary situation, Lenin mentions Germany in the 1860s and "the years 1859–61 and 1879–80 in Russia."

Soviet superstition had transformed this simple example into a true procrustean bed. How could one make the revolutionary situation terminate in 1861 when it was evident that the crises of the ruling class and popular discontent had augmented and deepened after 1861, all through 1862, and in 1863? (As we know, that was the year when a revolution actually did occur, though it was not the revolution of the Russian peasants, but of the most important nation oppressed by czarism, that is, Poland.) The distortion caused by this erroneous chronology became even more serious if one considered what, from the revolutionary point of view, was the most important element and the one that left the biggest mark in the future. This was the emergence and the consolidation of a true party intent on interpreting and leading the peasant revolt and defeating the Russian autocracy. The more closely one observed this process of the formation of the first *Zemlya i Volya,* the more evident it was that it had not reached a point of consolidation and did not become a true secret society until the final months of 1861. The height of its operation was in 1862 and continued into 1863. The numerous attempts to make it exist and function before the manifesto of February 19, 1861 merely created a series of hypotheses and suppositions that could not stand up to a critical examination of the facts. The book by Ya. I. Linkov, which came out in 1964, marked the end of these vain attempts to make Herzen and Chernyshevsky the heads of a mysterious conspiracy, when in fact their function was to be the creators of the revolutionary and populist animus in 19th-century Russia. Linkov put an end to the conspiratorial theory that had been superimposed on a historic reality, made, in fact, of free initiative, profound revolts, and desperate individual research in the midst of the contradictions in the situation created in Russia in the decade between 1854 and 1864.[87]

Naturally, this end was precarious and provisional, so that there was no lack of backsliding. The temptation to replace the free creation of new ideas and new political forces with organizations, plots, and conspiracies continued even in the most recent Soviet historiography. A hard, dry, gray cement still tends to imprison and immobilize men as free as Herzen, or those young men who created the customs, morality, and psychology of the Russian revolutionary. What they left within the solidified Soviet ideology seems like fossil remains. To find them alive one first has to crack the enveloping rock. It is necessary to do so, for example, in reading the volume by N. N. Novikova called *Revolyutsionery 1861 goda* (The revolutionaries of 1861). Even this very obvious title is taken from Lenin. And a real Leninist obsession induces the author, in discussing the relationship between the Velikoruss group and the developing *Zemlya i Volya,* to use arguments of the following kind against the historian Linkov: "In this case Ya. I. Linkov does not contradict our opinion but that of V. I. Lenin, who called the members of the Velikoruss 'leaders of the democratic movement' and linked them to the names of Chernyshevsky, Dobrolyubov, and their companions."[88] And to think that Novikova carried out considerable research even—and this is rare in the Soviet Union—in private archives. But nothing stands up, everything gives way before a generic definition, a journalistic mention, a simple list of examples which Lenin compiled by chance.

An overall view of the work carried out in Russia on the period of the first "revolutionary situation" (naturally shifting its chronology, as many, in fact most, Soviet scholars did more or less silently) establishes first of all that the new material gathered is important. One need only consider the academic edition of Herzen's works, completed in 1965; or the editions of the works of Dobrolyubov, of N. A. Serno-Solovevich, of Ogarev; or the patient reprinting of the recollections and memoirs of Panteleyev, Sleptsov, Shelgunov, Mikhailov, and many others; or the very complete research that has been done on the Polish revolution of 1863 and the participation in it by the men of the *Zemlya i Volya*. One need only list the titles from the veritable library created in the past fifteen years about the first decade of Alexander II's reign to realize how much interest and what results have come from work on these problems. Men and facts put so much pressure on the preconceived outlines, deforming them, distorting them until one would expect to see them broken down. Is the monotonous repetition of the classic quotations in the introductions and conclusions of so much of this research really any guarantee that these traditional outlines have not been broken down in the minds of those who confronted them with the problems and results of their own research? It remains a formal compliance with an ideological ritual which already is devoid of substance.

The main problem of the 1860s had been the relationship between the reviving desire for liberty and the need that was developing for equality and then for social revolution. These two ideas and these two aspirations had arisen together during the Crimean War and after the death of Nicholas I. They took on dozens of different forms in the debates between Herzen and Chicherin, Herzen and Kavelin, Chernyshevsky and Turgenev, Herzen and Chernyshevsky, Herzen and Dobrolyubov, Ogarev and Serno-Solovevich, Bakunin and the Polish revolutionaries, and others in every aspect of that period. If that era were to be judged solely on the fervor with which liberty and equality were experienced and discussed, it undoubtedly would merit the Leninist definition of the "revolutionary situation."

In the Soviet Union, the greatest temptation was to date the split between the liberals and socialists further back than it had actually occurred. There was a further temptation to establish a much deeper and wider division between them than had actually existed. By contrast, in the West the greatest temptation was often to try to establish a Russian liberal tradition quite separate from the populist and revolutionary tradition and to set it apart from the revolutionary tradition as distinctly as possible. In 1957, Victor Leontovitsch began this trend with his *Geschichte des Liberalismus in Russland*.[89] The next year George Fischer continued it with his study, *Russian Liberalism: From Gentry to Intelligentsia*.[90] The historiographic and juridical aspect, a very important element of Russian liberalism, was examined by Klaus Detlev Grothusen in *Die historische Rechtsschule Russlands. Ein Beitrag zur russichen Geistesgeschichte in der zweiten Hälfte des 19. Jahrhunderts*.[91] This trend reached its culmination in a brilliant little book by Leonard Schapiro, *Rationalism and Nationalism in Russian Nineteenth-Century Political Thought*.

The result of all these efforts, which have brought to light a whole world that had been buried under the ruins of the Russian revolutions, seems very clear: once an insurmountable gap had been established between the liberals and the Russian revolutionaries (that is, between Chicherin and Herzen), the liberalism of the czar-ist era increasingly clearly revealed its conservative character, and it seemed better suited to the renewed attempt at enlightened despotism that was one of the main aspects of the reign of Alexander II. In fact, these liberals desired a state of law more than political liberty. They believed more in the state machinery, in laws, and in the courts than in a constitution or an open political struggle. They empha-sized judicial guarantees more than freedom of the press. And we must not forget that they too lived, not only in the age of Alexander II, but also in the age of Napoleon III and Bismarck. Thus, to use again the particularly important and characteristic example of Chicherin, if Chizhevsky had been able to consider him a "classical liberal"[92] and Leontovitsch could speak of him as a man of "liberaler Konservatismus,"[93] it was not by chance that George Fischer found in the German but not in the British tradition the suitable word to express his thoughts and called him a "Rechtsstaat liberal."[94] Schapiro concluded by saying that Chicherin, "one of the most outstanding intellects of the Russian nineteenth cen-tury," had been "too liberal to be welcomed by the conservatives, and too con-servative to be accepted by the liberals. The unity and consistency of his thought justify the application to him of the epithet which Viasemsky chose for Pushkin—liberal conservative."[95] One can understand, after reading such opinions, why Richard Pipes concluded that the theme to be studied in 19th-century Russia was the conservative trend rather than the liberal.[96]

Fortunately, this historical separation between liberty and revolution, between liberalism and populism (of which both Westerners and Russians are guilty), was made unreal by the life of the 1860s, by the incontrovertible fact that liberalism, Slavophilism, radicalism, and populism were born in the same social world, the world of the intelligentsia. The men of both tendencies were not cold adversaries and enemies, but passionate friends who suffered deeply in the conflicts, clashes, and differences that arose between them. This is made abundantly clear in the relationship between Herzen, Chicherin, Chernyshevsky, and Dobrolyubov. It is not just by chance that their differences have been so thoroughly studied in recent years. Against every forced division between those who live and suffer together there is always a man of genius, Alexander Ivanovich Herzen, who evades all aca-demic labels or classification related to party politics. To anyone who opens the new and accurate edition of his complete works, the explanations, often repeated in Soviet literature, of his "liberal illusions" must seem weak and vain. Herzen is the last man in the world to become an icon or a portrait of "socialist realism." In every page, he repeatedly poses the question of the relationship between liberty and revolution.

Something similar could be said although on a different level, of Ogarev, who finally emerged from the limbo where he had been left for years, or of Dobroly-ubov, who with his deep and passionate moralism played an important part in separating the liberals from the radicals. The same could also be said of Cherny-

shevsky, the key figure for understanding the birth of the revolutionary movement in Russia, who is finally, though slowly, being freed from the icon where he
too had been placed. He speaks to us especially in his *Letters without an Address,*
about his last hope and that of his companions, about their last effort to show a
democratic and liberal way out of the crisis caused by the emancipation of the
peasants. In his young friends and followers, Nikolai and Alexander Serno-Solovevich, we already see the consolidation of the revolutionary party when the
doors were closed to all other developments. (And for them, and for Chernyshevsky, the doors were prison doors.) These young men, also, were too strong to
remain perpetually deformed and mutilated by the reaction. Their desire for liberty (even in a liberal and constitutional form, as with Nikolai Serno-Solovivich, for
example) stands out clearly in their writing, even when the Soviet presenters wish
to see it as little as possible.

Despite all these rediscoveries, and despite the need for a general view of this
whole period, a history of the ten years from 1854 to 1864, of the great drama of
the reform and the birth of the revolutionary movement, has still not appeared in
Russia. Clearly, this period must have attracted the passionate attention of the
Soviets. It contained a crisis after a long period of dictatorship; reforms imposed
from above; a desire to give life to a *Rechtsstaat,* without arriving at liberty and
democracy; repeated attempts to use old tools to confront new problems; and a
new sense of futility and fatigue deriving from this policy of administering the reforms just as absolutism had been administered before. Finally came the explosion
of rage, of nihilism, of bile, as Herzen called it, before the doors that had opened
briefly but were now closed, the disappointed hopes. How could all this drama of
the 1860s not have interested the Russians a century later? They were undergoing
a crisis that, though certainly different, had many points in common with the
19th-century one. It was not a matter of taking the passions of the present back
to the past; that had already been overdone in Soviet historiography during the
Stalinist age. One should not yield to the temptation of again painting Herzen and
Chernyshevsky, Dobrolyubov and Serno-Solovevich in one's own image. One had
to achieve more complete and objective historical research. There had been a step
in this direction, and it had produced good results. Nevertheless, if a more integral
historical view did not develop, it was because the basic problem was not solved.
On the political level, liberty had not won, and on the historical level the interweaving in the relationship between liberalism, socialism, and populism had not
been examined and fully unraveled. The outlines of the "revolutionary democracy" of the 1860s, of the "revolutionary situation" of 1859–61, were weakened, stretched, and deformed, but they were not abandoned. A historical view in
which Herzen and Kavelin, Chernyshevsky and Chicherin, Alexander II and Zaich-
nevsky each had his own function (no longer classed as elect or reprobate) seemed
to emerge slowly, but it did not achieve the required clarity and firmness.

Both inside and outside the Soviet Union, what has remained vivid and poignant is the sense of bitterness and disappointment caused by the destruction of so many hopes, of so many illusions born in the years of preparation for Alexander II's reforms, of so many sacrifices engulfed and annihilated by the great Russian state machine. The "revolutionary situation," seen as a whole and in its development, again took on the appearance that it had had in the eyes of the most sensitive and passionate of its contemporaries, that is, the form of a failed revolution. It was no great consolation to affirm that there had been figures like Chernyshevsky, who had had the intelligence and the lucidity to foresee such a failure. What was more important historically was to observe, in a case as interesting as this one, whether disappointment had aroused the revolt, and whether a new revolutionary will had emerged from the failure. The men of the first *Zemlya i Volya* had briefly hoped that a *jacquerie* would arise from the disappointment experienced by the great peasant masses once they had recognized the injustices and the deception that existed to their own detriment, when they had understood that liberty obtained from above was that of the lords and of the state, not that of the people and of the villages. Yet it was the revolutionaries of those first clandestine organizations who were forced to acknowledge that the peasant movements diminished between 1861 and 1863 and that this last date had not marked, as they had hoped, the beginning of a general revolt.

Then, in 1863, the revolutionary intellectuals, ready for any sacrifice just in order to stand with the Poles in their revolt against the czarist state, had to recognize that the Polish insurrection had only served to unleash the most violent forms of nationalism and reaction in Russia. The students of those years who had hoped for a life in an entirely new culture soon had to accept the only path that seemed open to them: they had to abandon the lecture halls, cultivate individual detachment, and deny all culture. This was the situation, the terrain in which the Russian nihilism of the 1860s took root. The first person to realize its importance and its danger was Herzen ("Very dangerous!!!" was the title of his first call of alarm). It then spread, taking on the most diverse and contradictory forms, absorbing elements of Schopenhauer's philosophy, of French radicalism from the last years of the Second Empire, and of Darwinism and positivist science. Yet deep down, from the first *Zemlya i Volya* to the tragic failure of Nechaev's *Narodnaya Rasprava,* it preserved an element of powerless rage, of disillusioned protest when confronted with the failed revolution from which this nihilism had been born and had developed.

In order to truly understand the bitter ferment, the first thing to do, as Vittorio Strada has suggested, is to reconsider Herzen's writings, which after a hundred years are still extraordinarily vivid and penetrating in their analysis of the state of mind of the protesters of a century ago.[97] The other way, followed more frequently in the past decade, leads to a close examination of the writings of the major nihilists of those times, of Pisarev as well as of the most important journal of that tendency, the *Russkoe slovo*. Again, the international situation in which this ferment developed has not been sufficiently considered in Russia. The results of A. Coquart's research, published in Paris in 1946, have not been sufficiently appreciated in Moscow and Leningrad (for example, in matters regarding the relationship between Pisarev's and Carl Vogt's ideas). One parallel in particular—that is, the simultaneous discussion of Darwin's ideas in America and in Europe—has been omitted. Regarding the social effects of this debate, and the elitist and racist consequences it may have produced, Robert Hofstadter's *Social Darwinism in American Thought* seems essential. Only in this way can B. P. Kozmin's valuable ideas and observations on Pisarev and his era have a less restricted and esoteric meaning, and almost become symbols or signs of an internal dialogue in the Russian and Soviet intelligentsia which has continued uninterrupted for a century.

Already in 1929, Kozmin had opened a wide path to an intelligent reconsideration of these problems in his article "D. I. Pisarev and Socialism," recently reprinted in a posthumous collection of his essays.[98] From the suffocating sense of the impossibility of achieving the revolution, which dominated the Russian intellectuals of the 1860s, Kozmin had gone back to the results of the failure of the 1848 revolution, thus expanding the Russian drama of the age of reforms to all of Europe. In this light, the function of the intellectuals—of the "proletariat of thought," as Pisarev called them—had seemed all the more essential. This was not an exclusively Russian concept, and naturally it could be found in the West. But while in the West the proletariat of thought had turned its attention to the working class, in Russia the situation had soon proved profoundly different. In Russia, the proletariat of thought was poorer and less powerful than anywhere else. It tried futilely to open the way to cooperatives, to mutual aid, to any kind of defense organization, as it was even more defenseless than the peasants themselves. "The peasant had his house, a little plot of land"; the proletariat of thought had none of this.[99] All attempts to impose itself, to make itself indispensable, seemed to fail. Before the young intelligentsia lay an abyss. *Hic Rhodus, hic salta.* In fact, having exhausted efforts to save itself alone, or to dream of systems as a ruling class, to regard itself as an elite, in the early 1870s the proletariat of thought ended up carrying out its "go to the people" movement. As Kozmin concluded, "This was why that trend in our social thought, represented by Pisarev, really had only one short-lived victory, despite the brilliant victories recorded in the second half of the 1860s. Then they had to give the initiative to the adversary, to populism, which looked to the peasants. After this date, Pisarev had many attentive readers, but he no longer had anyone to exalt him and follow him with enthusiasm."[100]

In an essay written in 1941 but not published before it was included in the collection mentioned, Kozmin had tried to find a reconfirmation of his interpretation of nihilism in the reactions and polemics of the populist writer Saltykov-

Shchedrin.[101] The true enemies of the proletariat of thought, of the young Russian revolutionaries of the 1860s, he said, were not the liberals but the absolutism and the despotism of the czar. Chernyshevsky had said so in his *Letters without an Address*. Herzen had not tired of repeating this. But these truths could not be stated in the Stalinist era. Nevertheless, as the recent publisher of his works points out, Kozmin had not accepted the Stalinist interpretation which had become an axiom of Soviet historiography in the 1940s and which on close examination was nothing but "a transposition to the field of study of the thesis that considered social democracy in Western Europe as the basic enemy of communism."[102] For Kozmin, deep inside every phase of the whole Russian revolutionary movement, including nihilism, lay the problem of the relationship between liberty and revolution.

In recent years, studies on the nihilist period and on Pisarev have multiplied. This is evident from the two books by F. Kuznetsov and by L. E. Varustin on the *Russkoe slovo,* the main journal of this trend. We also see that, though the time since the 1920s has not passed in vain, the mark of the Stalinist period has not disappeared. In these two books, but especially in the first, there is a striking element of naiveté. The authors seem to rediscover the men and the Europe of the 19th century, almost as if they were very distant and unusual people and lands. They are carried away by the radicalism, the drive, the extremism of their compatriots of a hundred years before, without sufficiently investigating the side of them that is darker, stranger, and more disquieting. The division—or, as it was then called, the "schism"—between "nihilists," that is, between the readers of Pisarev and those of Saltykov-Shchedrin, is extenuated by the effort to reconcile posthumously the contenders of a common progressive faith.

Something of this too normal, too positive view also remains perhaps in works that are nevertheless considered among the best recent books on the Russian revolutionary movement between the end of the Polish insurrection and the 1866 assassination attempt. These works are R. V. Filippov's *The Populist Revolutionary Organization of N. A. Ishutin and I. A. Khudyakov (1863-66),* published in Petrozavodsk in 1964, and the book by E. S. Vilenskaya, *The Revolutionary Underground in Russia (The 1860s),* published in Moscow in 1965. The authors' research is in depth, and they have clarified numerous complicated questions, exploding long-standing myths and retrieving men and facts that had fallen into oblivion. What does not reappear is the atmosphere of the "underground." One wonders if the authors, especially Vilenskaya, actually asked themselves what might have been the ideas that drove Khudyakov to the people and what put a revolver in Karakozov's hand. Filippov speaks of 1865 as a "phase of tormented uncertainty and tactical research."[103] Was it really only tactical? The author adds, "One need only imagine the political atmosphere in Russia in 1864-65 to understand how natural was the fact that some leaders of Ishutin's group began to develop a conspiratorial mentality."[104] Natural? The desire to create a close group of revo-

lutionaries and terrorism are not so easily explained. The conspiracy's choice of
the name "Inferno" and expectation of completely abnormal behavior from its
members were facts that stirred the imagination of contemporaries and became a
basis for wild tales, but it must not be rejected and set aside.

Soviet scholars in the 1960s tried to explain the explosion of the conspiratorial
mentality not only through the depressed situation in the 1860s but also by
attributing particular weight and value to political elements that were foreign to
the world of the populists and which then penetrated their movement, adding
"liberal" elements or even reviving clandestine Polish groups. Filippov and Vilenskaya and especially T. F. Fedosova have turned their attention to the existence
of contact between Ishutin and Khudaykov's organization and elements of the ruling class who were dissatisfied with the policies of Alexander II, and also with
Polish conspirators who were trying to pursue the conflict after the defeat of the
1863 insurrection.[105] The alleged witnesses are undoubtedly important. Vilenskaya has shown that Karakozov's trial was greatly distorted by internal quarrels
within the emperor's entourage. Fedosova has stressed the importance of the clandestine Polish Committee and of its Siberian ramifications during this whole
period of the Russian "underground." But still, these historians do not manage to
find the meeting point between the tactical and organizational elements and the
evolution of the ideas inside the revolutionary movement in those years.

Filippov is certainly correct in emphasizing the populist and socialist character
of Ishutin and Khudyakov's organization. He is also right in pointing out how the
need for liberty was deeply rooted in these young men's feelings. In fact, liberty
was potentially anarchical, Proudhonian, and federalistic, since, as Filippov rightly indicates, the spread of Bakunin's ideas seemed to begin with the Muscovite ferment in the 1860s. Nevertheless, another liberty existed, a constitutional or democratic one. It reached the young men from outside, like the remains of the liberal
ideas or linked with the Polish desire for independence. Ishutin and Khudyakov
tended to solve the problems that were urgently put to them on a tactical and
practical plane, not an ideological one. They were and remained socialists, and together they soon were prepared to use any means (conspiracy, assassination attempts, a conquest of power, an alliance with the liberals or with national movements) just to realize an ideal that the whole world around them seemed to negate
and repudiate. The situation made them have doubts about the peasant revolt. Yet
the people were the only social force capable of giving life to socialism. All means
began to seem good as long as they destroyed this contradiction. "This was the
tragedy of populism," concludes Vilenskaya. "In fact, the idea of creating a 'party'
that would undertake the functions that the previous revolutionary generation
had attributed to the popular masses contained the intuition, as yet unconscious,
that the peasant could not win the struggle against autocracy without the
guidance and organizational power of another class. And since this other class did
not exist in Russia in the 1860s, there was nothing left for the revolutionaries but

to shift the people's task to a 'party' and add considerable conspiratorial tactics to the idea of the peasant socialist revolution."[106]

As we can see, the Marxist scheme provides the deus ex machina of this populist tragedy. But we must concentrate on this drama, which actually had no hope or faith in the proletarian messiah, if we want to understand the deep conflicts that lay in the hearts of these young men. Were the tensions and contradictions not deeply scarred by the corrosive acid of the nihilistic ideas and atmosphere of those years, as Filippov seems to maintain? There is explicit evidence of the hostility against Pisarev, of the polemic against the model of Bazarov presented by Turgenev in *Fathers and Sons.* Yet in Ishutin and Khudyakov's organization there was no lack of the cynicism, violence, and desperation against which Herzen had reacted and which led to the tragic events of Nechaev's life.

In the Soviet Union, after so many discussions and polemics in the 1920s, silence has fallen on Nechaev. It is the embarrassed silence of one who, having set out to look for the most genuine sources of the thoughts and inspiration of the Russian revolutionary movements, suddenly finds himself face to face with a monstrous product of that source. *Toute proportion gardée,* Soviet historians sometimes react to Nechaev as they do to Stalin, repeating rituals of condemnation with varying degrees of vigor, thus trying to ward off his possible reappearance, without really trying to investigate the nature of and reasons for his actions and his power. And, unlike Stalin's case, one actually could let silence fall on Nechaev who was studied so much in the past and on whom an entire curious little library of books has been written. Like those who have sinned and suffered much, he too could be accorded the oblivion applied to cases that are considered closed.

This could have happened if two men, Tkachev and Bakunin, whose intellectual and political background were very different from Nechaev's and whose lives crossed his, had not appeared to keep his memory alive. For both these revolutionaries, the episode of the young workman who became the violent, arrogant organizer of the *Narodnaya Rasprava,* the People's Summary Justice, did not pass without leaving deep marks. The history of their relationship still remains one of the most basic and revealing elements in the more intimate life of the Russian revolutionary movement between the 1860s and 1870s. If one adds that Nechaev left his mark on the entire evolution of the student movement during that period, as well as on events in Russian emigration, on Herzen's environment, on Herzen's daughter Natalia, and on Ogarev, one must conclude that it is impossible to try to reconstruct the development from Nechaev's conspiracy to the "go to the people" movement without recalling this disturbing figure. This was the first example of an element coming from the common people and penetrating the revolutionary intelligentsia, bringing a profound desire for action and at the same time momentarily breaking down moral and political bases. Nechaev is a *revenant* who cannot be exorcised.

The previously unknown documents on Nechaev published by Michael Confino are impressive. They confirm the criminal and abnormal characteristics that Nechaev was known to have and that were inextricably linked with an exceptional capacity for action and an even greater gift of making people listen to him and follow him. Above all, they are impressive because of the political and moral problems they pose. Here is Bakunin, one of the most famous revolutionaries of his times, a man who had seen the 1848 revolution and Siberia, who had literally gone around the world. And he let himself be conquered by an uncultured and violent boy, so much so as to see in him the incarnation of the Russian revolution that he was then theorizing and preaching about. Confino identifies the psychological and personal reasons for this attitude: Bakunin's incipient and premature old age, the vulnerability of his revolutionary passion in a time of historic calm, on the very eve of the tempest of the Franco-Prussian war and of the Commune. More significant are the roots and moral and ideological conclusions of this encounter and these clashes. No one has expressed them more clearly than Bakunin himself in a letter to Nechaev dated June 2, 1870, at a time when his enthusiasm was waning and a break between the two men began to emerge as the only logical outcome of their increasingly deep disagreements. This long letter deserves to remain one of the fundamental documents of the whole history of the Russian revolutionary movement.[107]

Ten years later, Bakunin was in the same situation in which Herzen had found himself before the first manifestations of nihilism. There was the additional aggravation that now the new Nechaevian incarnation of nihilism also seemed a consequence of his own thought, of his own weaknesses and hopes.

The *Revolutionary Catechism* that Bakunin had circulated along with his own written appeals, and which so many historians (including myself) attributed to him, now seem to be the fruit of Nechaev's despair, resentment, and desire for revenge and abuse. "Votre catéchisme—un catéchisme d'*abrek*" (that is, a Georgian bandit's catechism), he writes in a phrase that seems to attribute the paternity and all the responsibility for the famous document to the young Russian. Whatever Bakunin's part in the writing, if there was any (and perhaps the question will always remain unresolved), the important fact is that now Bakunin repudiated the work, considering it foreign and unacceptable. In it, he had finally recognized a terrible urge for fanaticism and violence that was not even enlightened by a vision of a free and better world, but rather was darkened by a fiercely close and cruel concept of society. "Your cruelty full of abnegation, [the Russian text is more expressive and profound: *samootverzhennoe izuverstvo*], your extreme fanaticism—you wish to make them ... the rule of life for the community." It was a desire for "the total negation of the nature of man, and of society."

Only religious fanatics and ascetics can dream of conquering nature; that is why I was astonished—but not too much so and not for long, to find in you a sort of mystic, pantheistic idealism. . . . Yes, my dear friend, you are not a materialist like the rest of us poor sinners, but an idealist, a prophet, a sort of monk of the revolution; your hero should not be Babeuf, nor even Marat, but one such as Savonarola. . . . In your way of thinking you are more like a Jesuit than like us. . . . You are a fanatic—therein lies your enormous and characteristic force, and there too is the cause of your blindness; but blindness is a great and deadly weakness, blind energy wanders and stumbles and, the more powerful it is, the greater and more inexorable its failures."[108]

The foundations of Bakunin's thought were the Enlightenment and Rousseau, and reacted against Nechaev's fanaticism and machiavellianism; once the monstrous plant that had overgrown them had been painfully torn out and discarded, the bare foundations reappeared. Bakunin knew he had nourished the plant, but now he wanted to be freed from it. It was not just a matter of the more conspicuous aspects of Nechaev's mind, his continual deception, his indifference to evil and to crime itself. Bakunin wanted to deny, to shake off Nechaev's political substance. He reaffirms that only a "spontaneous, popular, and social" revolution is admissible and desirable. "It is my profound conviction that any other revolution is dishonest, harmful, and fatal to liberty and to the people." The single goal of the revolutionary movement must be "to awaken the spontaneous forces of the people, to make them cohere and to organize them." Any attempt to replace them, to act in their name, to deceive them was damaging and futile. In Russia, only *l'idéal populaire* (we could call it populism) had the right to call itself revolutionary. Any conspiracy, any plot, any artificial device would only falsify and distort the profound movement of the country.

Yet, a few months earlier, Bakunin had seen in Nechaev an incarnation of this *révolution populaire (narodnaya revolyutsya)*. In addition to recognizing him for his energy and his violence, he had accepted not only his positive aspects but also his negative ones. Was it not perhaps Bakunin himself who for decades had wanted the unleashing of the "evil passions," the only ones capable of overturning the present society and of destroying the modern state? Had he not looked hopefully at the great and the petty bandits in the Russian popular world? And now, why protest against this *abrek,* this Russian boy who, in his eyes, had become a desperate Georgian bandit? Like Herzen ten years earlier, Bakunin had recognized in the first exponents of the Russian revolution, not only a spirit of dedication and a willingness for sacrifice, but also those profound distortions, those inevitable wounds that society and the Russian state had inflicted on their personalities. Now, faced with the figure of Nechaev, Bakunin too was faced with the reality of his country. Here fanaticism and cruelty were born and grew side by side, along with dedication and sacrifice. The people's revolution in Russia would be terrible, the explosion of the desire for liberty and of the dreadful passions would be tragic. Like Herzen, Bakunin eventually envisioned Russia pervaded with and soaked in mud "from the infinite and multiform Russian mire. The Russian world —state, privileged class, and people at the same time—is a horrible world. The Russian revolution will be horrible certainly. He who fears the horrors and the slime, let him distance himself from this world and from this revolution, but he who wishes to serve it, let that one, knowing where he is going, strengthen his nerves and be ready for everything" (pp. 651–53). For everything? Was this not precisely what Nechaev had said and done? In the final analysis, the problem became a moral one.

The Russian revolution would have been aroused and helped by the "proletariat of thought." Bakunin does not use this expression, but he alludes to the phenomenon, describing it as "an enormous mass of educated and thinking people who are at the same time deprived of every job, of every career, of every way out...three-fourths at least of the university youth, the seminarians, the sons of peasants and bourgeois, the sons of petty functionaries and of ruined nobles...." The people were "the revolutionary army." From the proletariat of thought would come the general staff. But what guarantee would they give of truly desiring the liberation of the people? This guarantee could only come from the morality of those dedicated to it. "It is necessary to organize and truly *moralize* this world." In itself, the proletariat of thought was no better than the society around it. "There is in this world little enough of moral sense, with the exception of a small number of iron natures, eminently moral, formed according to Darwinian law in the midst of filthy oppression and infinite misery." It was not difficult to imagine what the vast majority would have done if they had found themselves "in a situation which permits them to exploit and oppress the people. One can affirm with certainty that they would exploit and oppress them in all tranquility" (p. 657). Only virtue, only morality could enable them to avoid the danger of falling into the surrounding mud. Adopting jesuitical means in the revolutionary movement meant preparing them to become "excellent spies and lackeys of power." Only the struggle against the state, only the ideal of liberty could help them avoid fatally substituting themselves for the government that the revolution was to defeat. Thus, in the heart of every action one had to insert "the self-determination of the people on a base of absolute equality, of complete and multiform human liberty." Only such a high and true ideal could dominate the harsh reality of the future revolution.

"Imagine yourself in the middle of the triumph of the spontaneous revolution in Russia." By now every barrier, every obstacle has been overcome. "It is general anarchy." And it really is not an idyll. "The horrible mud that has accumulated in enormous quantities in the depths of the people mounts to the surface." The competition among the new men who have just come from the heart of the country is unleashed. "Audacious, intelligent, dishonest, and ambitious...they confront, struggle with, and destroy one another." The only ones who can give meaning to this spontaneous anarchy are the revolutionaries. "Strong in their thought which expresses the essence of the instincts, desires and needs of the people; strong in their clearly understood goal amidst the crowd of men struggling with no goal and no plan," these men would eventually establish the "collective dictatorship" of their secret organization. "This dictatorship is not tainted by cupidity, vanity, or ambition, because it is impersonal and imperceptible and because it does not procure for the men who belong to its groups, nor for any groups, any advantages, or honors, or any official recognition of power." In reality, such men are only strong in their energy and in their mind (pp. 661-63). Thus, right from the start they must be the best, the most lucid, and invariably the most ready to sacrifice themselves for the people, "the strongest, the most passionate, inflexibly and invariably devoted" (p. 665). Fatally, such men were few, but what counted was their excellence and their total dedication.

Yet how could such a nucleus, such a secret society, have arisen if it adopted trickery and deceit? Undoubtedly, the terrible struggle that was taking place in Russia and the struggle that would have to be faced on the day of the revolution did not allow them to spare any means or blows—provided, as Bakunin says, they were directed solely against the enemy. Inside the secret society, principles of the purest equality and the most perfect liberty had to prevail. "Equal rights among all the members and unconditional and absolute solidarity...absolute sincerity... mutual fraternal confidence.... The nervous, fearful, vain, and ambitious are excluded from the society.... In adhering to the society, each member condemns himself forever to public anonymity and insignificance.... Each decision of the general meeting is absolute law.... Each member has the right to know everything..." (pp. 669-71). Thus Bakunin made a definitive break with Nechaev's hierarchical conception, with any Carbonaro-type secrecy, with any centralization of Jacobin origin. He was the first of the Russian revolutionaries to base everything on democracy and on internal fraternity, both elements united and joined with the maximum energy and decision in the external struggle. Everything was permitted against the enemy—secrecy, violence, assassination attempts, and conspiracies. But within the fraternity of those dedicated to bringing about a different and better world, rights were sacred and duties absolute.

This solution often recurs in the history of the Russian revolutions. In 1870, it had at least one great and inestimable merit, that of arousing the energies of the revolutionaries and taxing them to the utmost. Everything would depend on them. All political and moral responsibility fell on their shoulders. Anyone who accepted such a terrible challenge was certainly an exceptional man, as Bakunin had foreseen. In reality, as he had said, few responded to the appeal. But from those men came the populism of the 1870s, from the followers of Natanson and of Chaikovsky to the second *Zemlya i Volya* and to the *Narodnaya Volya*. It was on the basis of morality that they recruited supporters, reacting with the strength and purity of youth against the machiavellianism, the aberrations, the hidden and overt fears, and the nihilism of Nechaev. At the beginning of the 1870s a few dozen youths were able to recreate a limpid atmosphere in a world (they too were aware of it) floundering in slime. Though slowly and from afar, Bakunin's appeals reached them. Some of the pages of his *Statism and Anarchism* became the fundamental documents of their movement. They felt that these pages corresponded closely to their deepest needs.[109]

Initially they were unaffected by the ideas of men like Tkachev, who had briefly been allied with Nechaev and who later, with great lucidity and intelligence, had criticized the ideas of Bakunin and the populists. Tkachev and others had observed these ideas from a viewpoint that was machiavellian, not in the negative sense, but in that it reminded everyone of the inevitable problem of power and the state. They said that the secret and omnipresent dictatorship in which Bakunin saw the future of the revolution would lead to the development of a sort of church with a power similar to that of a party or government, and affirmed that the internal organization of the revolutionary movement would not remain free and egalitarian but would fatally change into a conspiracy and a plot. Tkachev, the Jacobin and supporter of Blanqui, was thus going against the current, and in some ways he remains in that position in the Soviet Union, where his ideas have been surrounded by a preoccupied silence which was broken only briefly in the 1920s with the publications of scholars who saw in him an element of the internal debate of the revolutionary movement that could not be ignored.

Thus, it was not in Tkachev that the young men of the "go to the people" movement found what they were seeking. Rather, they found it in the populist theorists and writers, in the theories of progress that were then being elaborated, in a view of history that fully expressed their rejection of the world around them and their hope for a profound socialist transformation. They found it in minor writers such as D. A. Sleptsov who now continued writing, on a different and enduing level, the "literature of denunciation" which had flourished ten years before, providing continuous sustenance for the young men as they drew closer to the people and explored the villages. They found it in men like Nekrasov and Saltykov-Shchedrin. But, above all, their guides were the ethnographers, who opened the Russian peasant world to them, and thinkers such as Lavrov and Mikhailovsky who were able to enlarge on the meaning of the debt that these young men felt they owed to the people, opposing positivism and scientism of the nihilistic sort, to create a new morality founded on the desire for a free and pluralistic society.

Even the minor writers of this populist trend have continued to attract the attention of Soviet scholars. In some recent works on the poetry and literature of populism, one finds the same enthusiasm for the rediscovery of this movement that we already observed in the research on its political aspects. However, not much work has been done on the thinkers, philosophers, and economists of the 1870s.[110] The collection of Lavrov's works that appeared in 1965 is certainly useful, but its new sociological covering conceals a return to traditional themes and interpretations.[111] Sedov's article on Mikhailovsky and B. S. Itenberg's contribution on him in his essay on revolutionary populism are important symptoms of a rebirth of interest in Mikhailovsky, who had seemed buried under the old party condemnations. But we still must look outside Russia to find a real discussion of his ideas.[112]

Undoubtedly, recent Soviet research on the revolutionary populists of the 1870s, from the "go to the people" movement to the *Narodnaya Volya,* has been fuller and more important. In fact, this is one of the brightest chapters in recent Soviet historiography. After a hiatus of many years, the documents published in the past were taken up again and unknown ones were sought in the archives. Even a complete and valuable review of the archive sources regarding revolutionary populism was published, a rare thing in the USSR, which it would be futile to seek for other political trends of the 19th and 20th centuries.[113] Some syntheses that re-examine all the fundamental aspects of the movement have been published.[114] In the second edition of *Il populismo russo* the reader can find many additions and corrections that I have been led to make in the thirty-year-old text after reading numerous Soviet articles and studies that are impossible to list here, but from which there is much to be drawn and to learn.

What historical nourishment can we gain from this rich harvest? Apart from enthusiasm for the rediscovery of the past that had been obliterated in the Stalinist era, apart from admiration for the heroism of the revolutionary populists, what fruits have Soviet historians reaped from this research?

First of all, it seems evident that they were more able to insert populism into the history of Russia than they had been earlier. In this, P. A. Zayonchkovsky has been very effective, doing as much to clarify the second revolutionary crisis of the late 1870s as he did to explain the first one during Alexander II's reforms. His book·on this subject is one of the best to have come out of Russia in recent years. In his introduction to the text he successfully breached party interpretations of this crisis, clearing the field of nonexistent major peasant movements and reestablishing a true perspective on the final duel fought between the government and the revolutionaries of the *Narodnaya Volya* at the end of the czar's reign, a duel that seems even more tragic as we realize that it was not accompanied or aroused by mass movements.[115] Zayonchkovsky, in extending his research in the archives and reconstructing the day-to-day government policies, has definitely demonstrated how extraordinarily effective the populist revolutionaries were, what their influence was on the evolution of the czarist situation at that time. Of course the *Narodnaya Volya* was defeated, but the desire for liberty and justice that it had brought to the very heart of the Russian state could not be cast aside. Historians such as N. Troitsky and B. V. Vilensky have illustrated other aspects of the Russian state structure of that period, especially the character and function of lawyers and the judiciary. There still remains a wide area for investigation, that of the liberal, moderate, and reactionary movements and their effective weight in the "revolutionary situation" at the end of Alexander II's reign. But Soviet scholars seem to be well on their way to an understanding of the political value, the actual force of revolutionary populism during that period in Russian history.

We cannot say the same about the relationship between the second *Zemlya i Volya* and the *Narodnaya Volya* and the world revolutionary movement of that time. It was the epoch of the great historical development of socialism toward politics, from Proudhonian and Bakuninist anarchism, through the Paris Commune, toward the creation of great social democratic movements and parties, and toward the constitution of the Second International. Leo Valiani has presented this development, in which the Russian movement was one of the most significant elements, with special thoroughness.[116] But there are still too many obstacles in the Soviet Union that prevent a historical view such as the one Valiani has presented. The conflicts between Bakunin and Marx are still too much part of the local mythology to permit a broader and more detached perspective. The recent interest in Bakunin that has been shown in Russia is certainly a positive sign, but for now we must admit that the study of the passage from the First to the Second International lies mainly in non-Russian hands (consider the Institute of Social History in Amsterdam). It is not that Soviet writings do not discuss the links between the Russian, English, German, French, Italian, and Polish movements. (The books of Itenberg, who was one of the first to publicize this internationalization of the history of populism, are sufficient evidence.) But they treat only the links, relationships, and influences, all of which are useful and require study but do not pose or solve the problem of the European role in what happened in Russia, or of the Russian contribution to in the more general evolution and configuration of socialism in the 1870s and 1880s.

In less than a decade, the young revolutionary populists rejected without difficulty, almost naturally, the calls of the constitutionalists and the liberals. Having vigorously condemned Jacobin and conspiratorial ideas as well, they plunged into direct social action, without intermediaries, among the peasant masses and the workers in the cities. Through the "go to the people" movement, through the formation of the first groups in the villages and factories, above all through their experience in the clandestine struggle—the blows that fell on them, the arrests, the succession of defeats, the trials—after a few years, and faced with the problem of politics, they more or less completely abandoned the anarchic ideal and recognized the need for a centralized organization. At the end of this development the *Narodnaya Volya* gave a particularly deep and thoughtful form to these conclusions, pointing out the exceptional and specific function of the state in the evolution of the economy and of modern Russian society. They formed a real clandestine party, capable of gathering and directing the most efficient and active forces of the revolutionary generation of the 1870s.

Did they represent a step backward, then? Or a continuous pendulum motion between the anarchic ideal and the reality of the struggle? The history of populism itself seems to demonstrate how superficial and inadequate such explanations are. There was no return to Nechaev and to Tkachev. The Executive Committee of the *Narodnaya Volya* no longer had anything in common with Ishutin's Hell. In fact, through the "go to the people" movement and the organizations that came out of it, Russia found a road toward democratic thought and action, at the same time reconfirming the socialist ideal that lay at the root of the whole populist movement. The needs of politics and liberty were felt in the very heart of populism, and by now they were far from and different from the aspirations of the age of reform. The anarchic ideal increasingly became a desire for autonomy in the villages and in the workers' organizations. Slowly and with difficulty, Proudhonian federalism gave way to an ideal of liberty, of local self-administration as opposed to a centralized and bureaucratic state. Protest became an organized and conscious struggle against autocracy. Internally, the need for clandestine action and terrorism imposed an extraordinary discipline on the populist party, but this did not prevent struggles between trends based on clear and explicit ideas and desires. The moral ferment that had moved the young populists in the early 1870s brought exceptional loyalty and frankness to their organizations. For a moment it seemed that what Bakunin had hoped for, that is, a free party, was truly realized even in the midst of the harshest battles and the greatest oppression.

This germination of a democratic will in Russian populism has particularly attracted the attention of Soviet historians in recent years. Let us take only one example, and one of the best, that of the book by G. G. Vodolazov, *Ot Chernyshevskogo k Plekhanovu* (From Chernyshevsky to Plekhanov), published by the University of Moscow in 1969. According to Vodolazov, what distinguishes Russia is the fusion between revolutionary democracy and socialism. Economic backwardness explains this brief unification of two political elements that elsewhere had manifested themselves at different chronological times. The best expressions of Russian populism and socialism were those in which both elements were present. However, when they appeared separately, decadence and corruption followed. The supreme expression of Chernyshevsky's thought came in *Letter without an Address*, "a last attempt to improve the life of the people while avoiding bloodshed...an attempt by an intelligent and wise revolutionary leader. He always sought a way to avoid the peasant revolution. He called for an end to serfdom because it was an obstacle to economic life."[117] He was not listened to, and his politics of authentic and thorough reform were rejected. Nevertheless, a great debate emerged in the 1860s and left deep traces in Russia's later history. Chernyshevsky knew how to combat liberalism. Though its optimism eventually prevented access to the root of the problem, Chernyshevsky never failed to take advantage of all the legal possibilities. Vodolazov adds that one must not exaggerate the repressive character of the censorship of those days, "if only because in the years after Chernyshevsky's death the concept of the possibilities of censorship expanded considerably" (p. 53). The creator of populist policies was really "neither a liberal nor an unreasonable revolutionary" (p. 41). His ideas conflicted entirely with those of men like Tkachev and Nechaev, who intended to "drive the people to paradise with a stick" (p. 79). Russian socialism was not born of such despotic dreams as theirs, but from the germination of a new popular awareness. Dobrolyubov represented the beginning of the reawakening in the darkness. Pisarev indicated what science and knowledge could bring to this democratic process. For him "self-education" was "liberation" (p. 116). Of course, he started from disillusionment; reform and revolution seemed to lead to nothing and to evil. Where had the French Revolution led? But this sense of disillusionment had to be overcome. When did revolutions ever lead where one intended? From the republic of virtue had come Bonapartism (p. 85). The Russian revolutionary movement was able to go beyond this disillusionment and these defeats. Populism maintained faith in the socialist ideal that had been maturing. The discussions of the 1870s dealt with the means, not the ultimate goals of the whole movement (p. 128). From the polemics of that era, from the experience of the revolutionaries in this decisive period, it became increasingly apparent that "a socialism that is not democratic is not socialism." Russian Jacobinism seemed increasingly clearly like a "communism for the barracks, as Marx and Engels called it" (p. 146). Lavrov's followers, in contributing to the criticism of Tkachev, drew closer to the central line of the development of socialism as a whole.

What were the roots of the fanaticism, of the voluntarism that played such a large role in the history of Russian socialism? Vodolazov looks for the answer to this fundamental question in the very heart of the populist idea, that is, in the hope and the possibility of skipping the capitalist phase of economic development. "The objective possibility of accelerating the development process of certain countries (using the results from more developed countries) made the function of the conscious element more important."[118] This was the function of the parties, of the intelligentsia. The intelligentsia occasionally ended up presenting itself as truly providential for the Russian people. Nevertheless the history of revolutionary populism demonstrated how it wanted and knew how to keep the "conscious element" and its own fundamental democratic will united. According to Vodolazov, the union of the two was the essential element in all of Russian socialism.

Following this route, Vodolazov saw in Plekhanov the logical and natural outcome of all populism. This era, too, in the history of European socialism flowed into the age and life of the Second International. Such a Marxist conclusion nevertheless seems too simple among so many internal differences; it offers a too conventional and easy unravelling of the drama of Chernyshevsky, Bakunin, Tkachev, and of the *Zemlya i Volya* and the *Narodnaya Volya*.

A sense of dissatisfaction with the explanations given about populism in the past seems to pervade the most recent historiography both in Russia and in America. In the United States, Richard Wortman especially has stressed the moral and psychological questions.[119] In the USSR, in an introduction for V. A. Tvardovskaya's book *Socialist Thought in Russia between the 1870s and 1880s*, M. Ya.

Gefter, one of the most lively scholars studying this problem, has expressed similar doubts and has urged research on something new, though still clearly stating the problem in terms of political history. "One of the greatest difficulties of the Marxists lies in the need to explain why the utopianism [of the populists] that had undergone serious defeats in the ideological duel with proletarian socialism, not only did not die an obscure and quiet death...but was transformed in 1905 into the ideal of millions of peasants who were reawakening, and became the direct ideology of peasant democracy in Russia."[120] In more ideological and less directly political forms, others in the Soviet Union have expressed a need to discuss again the history of Russian socialism, that is, of the socialism that developed in Russia before, alongside, and in a different way from Marxist socialism.[121] As we have seen, twenty or thirty years ago, this interest in the local roots of socialism arose from the nationalistic end of the Stalinist era and brought upon itself all the crude contradictions of that period. At present the experience of revolutionary populism is often observed because in it one can see a democratic experience, because there is a search for a relationship between the popular masses and the intelligentsia.

The inevitable problem, the obligatory conclusion of this renewed interest is always the same: a historical confrontation with Marxism. As Soviet historiography gradually advances, taking up and reconsidering, one hopes, the relationship between the Mensheviks, the Bolsheviks, and the revolutionary socialists, it will be faced with the questions that are already *in nuce,* as we have seen, in the history of populism and of the whole revolutionary movement, from Herzen to the *Narodnaya Volya.* I am personally convinced that there is only one way out of the Marxist difficulty. One must understand that for the past two centuries socialist thought and movements in all Europe have been too rich and varied to be monopolized by only one trend, even if the trend is Marxism. Every attempt to establish in the context of socialism a so-called scientific trend that is considered authentic, and opposed to other utopian and false trends, is not only historically wrong but eventually leads to a voluntary mutilation and distortion of all socialist thought. By now, Soviet historians are also faced with a similar problem. Democracy and socialism, intelligentsia and the people, backward or advanced economic development, these are some of the many points one cannot escape if one wants to understand what populism was historically and how it affected modern Russian history.

Notes

1. In an article entitled "Recent Soviet Historiography of Russian Revolutionary Populism," John E. Bachman writes: "Venturi's post-war research was based on extensive materials from Soviet archives, and he received considerable aid from Soviet historians" (*Slavic Review* [December 1970], p. 602, n. 10). *Utinam,* as the ancients said, or "wishful thinking," as we say.

2. A lively and critical description of the situation, especially from the standpoint of literary history, can be found in A. Belkin, "Narodniki i revolyutsionnoye demokraty" [Revolutionary populists and democrats], in *Vosprosy literatury*, 1960, no. 2, pp. 116 ff. In response, in the same issue of the journal, p. 142, Ya. Elsberg pointed out that the position of the Stalinist age had had "the great merit" of having fought "against the socialist revolutionary critics (V. Chernov, Ivanov-Razumnik and others)." A few issues later, B. Meilach also praised such merits (no. 10, p. 87). On the fate of one of the two adversaries indicated, see *The Memoirs of Ivanov-Razumnik,* with a short introduction by G. Janovsky, trans. from the Russian and annotated by P. S. Squire (London: Oxford University Press, 1965).

3. See V. I. Chesnokov, "V. I. Nevsky kak istorik revolyutsionnogo dvizheniya v Rossii" [V. I. Nevsky as historian of the revolutionary movement in Russia], report on a doctoral thesis (Voronezh: Izdatelstvo voronezhskogo universiteta, 1966).

4. These words are taken from the archives and quoted by M. G. Sedov, "Sovetskaya literatura o teoretikakh narodnichestva" [Soviet literature on the theoreticians of populism], in *Istoriya i istoriki. Sbornik statey* [History and historians, a collection of articles] (Moscow: Nauka, 1965), p. 257.

5. E. M. Yaroslavsky, *Razgrom narodnichestva* [The downfall of populism] (Moscow, 1937), pp. 79–80; quoted in Sedov, pp. 256–57.

6. Sedov, "Sovetskaya literatura," p. 257.

7. See Andrea Caffi, *Critica della violenza* (Milan: Bompiani, 1966), and *Scritti politici* (Florence: La Nuova Italia, 1970).

8. See Peter Scheibert, "Wurzeln der Revolution," *Jahrbücher für Geschichte Osteuropas,* no. 3 (October 1962), pp. 323 ff.

9. This review is reproduced in Alexander Gerschenkron, *Continuity in History and Other Essays* (Cambridge, Mass.: Harvard University Press, 1968), pp. 454 ff.

10. In addition to the volume cited, see Alexander Gerschenkron, *Economic Backwardness in Historical Perspective* (Cambridge, Mass.: Harvard University Press, 1962).

11. M. G. Sedov, *Geroichesky period revolyutsionnogo narodnichestva* [The heroic period of revolutionary populism] (Moscow: Mysl, 1966), p. 38.

12. "Literatura po istorii revolyutsionnogo narodnichestva 70–80 godov XIX veka vyshedshaya v 1956–1964" [Literature on the history of revolutionary populism in the 1870s–1880s which appeared between 1956 and 1964], in *Obshchestvennoe dvizhenie v poreformennoy Rossii. Sbornik statey k 80-letiyu so dnya rozhdeniya B. P. Kozmina* [The social movement in Russia in the years following the reform of 1861. A collection of articles commemorating the 80th birthday of B. P. Kozmin] (Moscow: Nauka, 1966), pp. 370 ff.

13. Sh. M. Levin, *Obshchestvennoe dvizhenie v Rossii (60–70-e gody XIX veka)* [The social movement in Russia in the 1860s–1870s] (Moscow: Soc. Ek.-Lit., 1958).

14. Ibid., p. 11.

15. For an initial and partial orientation, see N. Ja. Kraineva and P. V. Pronina, *Trudy Instituta istorii Akademii Nauk SSSR, 1936–1965* [The work of the Insti-

tute of History of the Academy of Sciences of the USSR, 1936-1965] , 4 vols. (Moscow, 1965). However, a considerable part of the discussion can be found in the publications of the different universities of the USSR, as well as in a variety of journals. A mechanical and simplified view of the relationship between intellectuals and the state in the Soviet Union makes Bachman's informative article, "Recent Soviet Historiography" (see n. 1 above), unpersuasive.

16. Ernest J. Simmons, ed., *Continuity and Change in Russian and Soviet Thought* (Cambridge, Mass.: Harvard University Press, 1955). The volumes of the *Harvard Slavic Studies* (1953 ff.) of those same years are also characteristic.

17. James H. Billington, *Mikhailovsky and Russian Populism* (Oxford: Oxford University Press, 1958).

18. Martin Malia, *Alexander Herzen and the Birth of Russian Socialism, 1812-1855* (Cambridge, Mass.: Harvard University Press, 1961).

19. See the three-volume anthology inspired by him, *Russian Philosophy,* ed. J. M. Edie, J. L. Scanlan, and M.-B. Zeldin, with the collaboration of George L. Kline (Chicago: Quadrangle Books, 1965). (Vol. 1 is devoted to the beginnings of philosophy in Russia, to the Slavophiles and to the occidentalists; vol. 2 is devoted to the nihilists, populists, and critics of religion and culture; vol. 3 deals with prerevolutionary philosophy and theology, philosophers in exile, Marxists, and communists); see also George L. Kline, *Religious and Anti-Religious Thought in Russia* (Chicago: University of Chicago Press, 1968).

20. *The Roots of Revolution: A History of the Populist and Socialist Movements in Nineteenth Century Russia,* trans. from the Italian by Francis Haskell, with an introduction by Isaiah Berlin (London: Weidenfeld & Nicolson, 1960). The American edition was published by Alfred E. Knopf. In 1966 a paperback edition was published by Grosset & Dunlap, in New York.

21. In Simmons, *Continuity and Change,* pp. 473 ff.

22. Berlin, "Introduction," *Roots of Revolution,* p. xxiv.

23. "One of the few recent historical works that have been favorably received both in the Soviet Union and the West," wrote Geoffry Barraclough in the *Manchester Guardian* of July 1, 1960.

24. Regarding the book *Il movimento decabrista e i fratelli Poggio* [The Decembrist movement and the Poggio brothers] (Turin: Einaudi, 1971). The review appeared in *Voprosy istorii,* no. 3, pp. 156 ff.

25. *Chto delat?* [What is to be done?] *Complete Works,* 4th ed. (Moscow, 1946), 5:342. I cite Lenin's works in this edition because it was typical of the Stalinist era. See the fine edition of *What Is to Be Done?* edited by Vittorio Strada (Turin: Einaudi, 1971).

26. *Sovetskaya istoriografiya klassovoy borby i revolyutsionnogo dvizheniya* [Soviet historiography of the class struggle and the revolutionary movement in Russia], ed. A. L. Shapiro (Leningrad: LGU, 1967), 1:142 ff.

27. *K. Marks, F. Engels i revolyutsionnaya Rossiya* [K. Marx, F. Engels and revolutionary Russia] (Moscow: Izd. politicheskoy literatury, 1967).

28. Ibid., pp. 433-34.

29. Letter to the editor of *Otechestvennye zapiski* (1877), in ibid., pp. 77 ff.

30. The Russian translation of Marx's sketches can be found in K. Marx and F.

278 Russian Populism

Engels, *Sochineniya* [Works] (Moscow: Gos. Izd. politicheskoy literatury, 1961), 19:400 ff.

31. K. *Marks, F. Engels i revolyutsionnaya Rossiya*, p. 89. The preface is dated January 21, 1882.

32. Ibid., p. 646, letter to Danielson on February 24, 1893.

33. Ibid., p. 723.

34. Ibid., p. 656, letter to I. A. Gurvich, dated May 24, 1893.

35. See, for example, S. S. Volk, *Karl Marks i russkie obshchestvennye deyateli* [Karl Marx and the political men of Russia] (Leningrad: Nauka, 1969).

36. A. L. Reuel, *Russkaya ekonomicheskaya mysl 60-70-kh godov XIX veka i marksizm* [Russian economic thought of the 1860's–1870's and Marxism] (Moscow: Gos. Izd. politicheskoy literatury, 1956). Yu. Z. Polevoy, *Zarozhdenie marksizma v Rossii* [The rise of Marxism in Russia] (Moscow: Akademiya nauk SSSR, Institut istorii, 1959).

37. On this, see the bibliography in V. V. Micurov and Yu. M. Kritsky, *Rossiyskiye rabochiye i social-demokraticheskoye dvizhenie 70-ch-nachala 90-ch gg. XIX v. v sovetskoy istoriograficheskoy literature* [The Russian worker's and social democratic movement from the seventies to the beginning of the nineties of the 19th century in Soviet historiography], in *Sovetskaya istoriografiia klassovoy borby*, pp. 200 ff.

38. *Narodnicheskaya ekonomicheskaya literatura. Izbrannye proizvedeniya* [Populist economic literature: selected works], ed. N. K. Karataev (Moscow: Izd. soc.-ekon. literatury, 1958).

39. Salomon M. Schwarz, "Populism and Early Russian Marxism on Ways of Economic Development of Russia (The 1880s and 1890s)," in *Continuity and Change in Russian and Soviet Thought*, pp. 40 ff.; Leopold Haimson, *The Russian Marxists and the Origins of Bolshevism* (Cambridge, Mass.: Harvard University Press, 1955); Donald Treadgold, *Lenin and His Rivals: The Struggle for Russia's Future, 1898-1906* (London, 1955); Arthur P. Mendel, *Dilemmas of Progress in Zarist Russia: Legal Marxism and Legal Populism* (Cambridge, Mass.: Harvard University Press, 1961); J. L. H. Keep, *The Rise of the Social Democracy in Russia* (Oxford: Clarendon Press, 1963); S. H. Baron, *Plekhanov, the Father of Russian Marxism* (London: Routledge & Kegan Paul, 1963); Jonathan Frankel, *Vladimir Akimov, or the Dilemmas of Russian Marxism: 1895-1903* (Cambridge: Cambridge University Press, 1969); and Andrzei Walicki, *The Controversy over Capitalism: Studies in the Social Philosophy of the Russian Populists* (Oxford: Clarendon Press, 1969).

40. Richard Pipes, "The Origins of Bolshevism: The Intellectual Evolution of the Young Lenin," in *Revolutionary Russia* (Cambridge, Mass.: Harvard University Press, 1968), and "Narodnichestov: A Semantic Inquiry," in *Slavic Review* 23, no. 3 (September 1964): 441 ff.

41. See Andrzei Walicki, "Russia," in *Populism: Its Meanings and National Characteristics*, ed. Ghita Ionescu and Ernest Gellnern (London: Weidenfeld & Nicolson, 1969), pp. 62 ff. See now the first volume of the fundamental biography by Richard Pipes, *Struve: Liberal on the Left, 1870-1905* (Cambridge, Mass.: Harvard University Press, 1970), certainly the most important book on the

relationship between populism and Marxism in Russia at the turn of the century. Of great interest is Vittoria Strada's discussion of the relationship between populism and Marxism in the introduction of his edition of Lenin's *What Is to Be Done?* (see n. 25 above).

42. Pierre Pascal, *Civilisation paysanne en Russie. Six esquisses* (Lausanne: Editions de l'Age d'Homme, 1969).

43. "La Commune paysanne après la révolution," an article published in *La Révolution prolétarienne* (November 1, 1928), and collected in ibid., pp. 29 ff.

44. Jerome Blum, *Lord and Peasant in Russia from the Ninth to the Nineteenth-Century* (Princeton, N.J.: Princeton University Press, 1961), esp. pp. 277 ff., "The Last 150 Years of Serfdom."

45. Wayne S. Vucinich, *The Peasant in Nineteenth-Century Russia* (Stanford, Calif.: Stanford University Press, 1968).

46. Moshe Lewin, *La Paysannerie et le pouvoir soviètique. 1928-1930* (Paris and The Hague: Mouton, 1966); and D. J. Male, *Russian Peasant Organization before Collectivization* (Cambridge: Cambridge University Press, 1971).

47. Michael Confino, *Domaines et seigneurs en Russie vers la fin du XVIIIe siècle. Etudes de structures agraires et de mentalité économiques* (Paris: Institut d'ètudes slaves de l'Université de Paris, 1963).

48. Michael Confino, *Systèmes agraires et progrès agricole* (Paris and The Hague: Mouton, 1969).

49. Ibid., pp. 295 ff. For a similar and parallel shift from the defense of slavery in the English colonies, based on the affirmation of its superiority over the peasant and the modern worker in general, to the use, by liberals and socialists, of a similar criticism of the capitalist world, see the interesting article by E. Bickerman, "Pouchkine, Marx et l'Internationale exclavagiste," in *La Nouvelle Clio,* no. 8 (September 1950), pp. 416 ff.

50. Confino, *Systèmes agraires,* p. 296. See A. L. Shapiro, "Zapiski o peterburgskoy guberniy A. N. Radishcheva" [Notes on the governorship of St. Petersburg of A. N. Radishchev], in *Istoricheskiy archiv* 5 (1950): 253, n.d. See A. N. Radishchev, *Polnoye sobranie sochineniy* [Complete works] (Moscow and Leningrad: Akademiya nauk, 1952), 3:549, n. 4.

51. Shapiro, "Zapiski," p. 273; and Radishchev, *Polnoye sobranie sochineniy,* p. 132.

52. Quoted by Confino, *Systèmes agraires,* p. 300.

53. Ibid., pp. 331 ff. and 355 ff.

54. Ibid., p. 356.

55. *"Russkaya pravda" P. I. Pestelya i sochineniya ey predshestvuyushchiya* ["Russian Law" by P. I. Pestel and the writings that precede it], ed. M. V. Nechkina (Moscow: Glavnoye archivnoye upravleniye, 1958). See S. S. Volk, *Istoricheskiye vzglyady dekabristov* [The historical conceptions of the Decembrists] (Moscow and Leningrad: Akademiya nauk SSSR, 1958), pp. 347 ff.; Hans Lemberg, *Die nationale Gedankenwelt der Dekabristen* (Köln and Graz: Böhlau, 1963); B. E. Syroechkovsky, *Iz istoriy dvizheniya dekabristov* [From the history of the Decembrists] (Moscow: MGU, 1969), pp. 14 ff.

56. V. V. Pugachev, "Sergei Ivanovich Turgenev," in *Uchenye zapiski,* of the

State University of Gorky, no. 58, Historical-Philosophical Series, 1963, pp. 299 ff.

57. Nicholas V. Riasanovsky, *Nicholas I and Official Nationality in Russia: 1825-1855* (Berkeley and Los Angeles: University of California Press, 1959); and Edward C. Thaden, *Conservative Nationalism in Nineteenth Century Russia* (Seattle: University of Washington Press, 1964).

58. N. V. Riasanovsky, *Russia and the West in the Teachings of the Slavofiles: A Study of Romantic Ideology* (Cambridge, Mass.: Harvard University Press, 1952).

59. Andrei Walicki, *W kręgu konserwatywnej utopii. Struktura i przemiany rosyjskiego słowianofilstwa* [In the world of conservative utopias. Structure and development of Russian Slavophilism] (Warsaw: Państwowe wydawnictwo naukowe, 1964). An Italian translation of this work has been published by Einaudi.

60. Eberhard Müller, *Russischer Intellekt in Europäischer Krise. Ivan Kireevskij, 1806-1856* (Cologne: Böhlau, 1966); Peter K. Christoff, *An Introduction to Nineteenth Century Russian Slavophilism: A Study in Ideas,* vol. 1, *A. S. Xomjakof* ('s-Gravenhage: Mouton, 1961); Robert Stupperich, *Jurij Samarin und die Anfänge der Bauernbefreiung in Russland* (Wiesbaden: O. Harrassowitz, 1969).

61. Alexander Von Schelting, *Russland und Europa im russischen Geschichtsdenken* (Bern: A. Frank, 1948); Dieter Groh, *Russland und Europa. Ein Beitrag zur europäischen Geistesgeschichte* (Neuwier: Herman Lucherhand, 1961); Karsten Goehrke, *Die Theorie über Entstehung und Entwicklung des Mir* (Wiesbaden: O. Harrassowitz, 1964); N. A. Cagolov, *Ocherki russkoy ekonomicheskoy mysli perioda padeniya krepostnogo prava* [Essays on Russian economic thought during the final period of the servitude of the serfs] (Moscow: Akademiya nauk SSSR, Institut ekonomiki, 1956). To these works one can add the anthology edited by Dmitrij Tschizewskij and Dieter Groh, *Europe und Russland. Teste zum Problem des westeuropäischen und russischen Selbstverständnisses* (Darmstadt: Wissenschaftliche Buchgesellschaft, 1959).

62. Muller, *Russischer Intellekt,* p. 31.

63. Goehrke, *Theorie über Entstehung und Entwicklung des Mir,* pp. 14 ff. See what Haxthausen wrote later (not without being influenced, in turn, by the Slavophile ideologies of the fifties) in the pamphlet *De l'abolition par voie législative du partage égal et temporaire des terres dans les communes russes* (Paris: A. Frank, 1858), p. 11: "For my part, I know the communal constitution of several countries in Europe, either by having seen them close at hand or having made them the object of study, but I never knew a single one that was worth those of the Russian countryside," and on p. 14 he added that "one must not imagine this communal organization of the equal division of arable land to be something particular or unique to Russia." For Germany, one had only to recall what Tacitus had written, and he adds: "I found even in 1834, in the Hochwald of Treves, communes *[Geherberschaftsgemeinden]* where they divided the land anew among the members of the communes every thirteen years. The land taxes and the ordinance survey have made this state of things impossible to maintain. One can imagine the complaints and resistance of these folk when they are obliged to a final definitive division of the common property." For Haxthausen's interpretation of Tacitus, see his study, *Über die Agrarverfassung in den Fürstenthümern Paderborn und*

Corvey und deren Conflicte in der gegenwärtigen Zeit (Berlin: G. Reimer, 1828), pp. 95 ff.

64. The fundamental documents of this debate (it is too bad they are not more accessible and easily available for consultation) are: the letter of A. I. Koshelev to A. S. Khomyakov, dated March 16, 1848, published in N. Kolyupanov, *Biografiya Aleksandra Ivanovicha Kosheleva* [The biography of A. I. Koshelev], ed. O. F. Kosheleva (Moscow: Kushnerev, 1889–92), vol. 2, app., pp. 103 ff.; the reply of A. S. Khomyakov, published in *Russkiy arkhiv* (1878); and the response of Koshelev, inserted in the book cited here, by Kolyupanov, pp. 106 ff.

65. See Christoff, *An Introduction*, pp. 202 ff., and "A. S. Khomiakov on the Agricultural and Industrial Problem in Russia," in *Essays in Russian History: A Collection Dedicated to George Vernadsky* (Hamden, Conn.: Archon Books, 1964), pp. 131 ff.

66. N. M. Druzhinin, "Krestyanskaya obshchina v ocenke A. Gakstgauzena i ego russkikh sovremennikov" [The peasant community in the opinion of A. Haxthausen and his Russian contemporaries], in *Ezhegodnik germanskoi istorii* (Moscow: Nauka, 1969), pp. 28 ff.; and Druzhinin, "A. Gakstgauzen i russkie revolyutsionnye demokraty" [A. Haxthausen and the Russian democratic revolutionaries], *Istoriya SSSR*, 1967, no. 3, pp. 69 ff.

67. For what was published in the fifties, see F. Venturi, "Testi e studi herzeniani," *Rivista storica italiana*, 1959, no. 4, pp. 395 ff. More recently, of particular note is the little volume by A. I. Volodin, *Gertsen* (Moscow: Mysl, 1970).

68. A. I. Herzen, *Sobranie sochineniy v tridstati tomakh* [Works in thirty volumes] (Moscow: Akademiya nauk SSSR, 1954–55).

69. *Polyarnaya zvezda* [Polar star], 9 vols. including nn., indexes, ed. M. V. Nechkina and E. L. Rudnitskaya (1966–68); and *Kolokol* [The bell], 10 vols., ed. M. V. Nechkina (Moscow: Akademiya nauk SSSR, 1963).

70. *Problemy izuchenya Gertsena* [Problems in the study of Herzen] (Moscow: Akademiya nauk SSSR, 1963).

71. Ibid.

72. Jules Michelet, *Légendes démocratiques du Nord, nouvelle édition augmentée de fragments inédits, avec introduction, notes et index par Michel Cadot*, Faculté des lettres et sciences humaines de l'University de Clermont Ferrand, 2d ser., no. 28 (Paris: Presses Universitaires de France, 1968), esp. pp. 387 ff. See also the vast study by Cadot, *La Russie dans la vie intellectuelle française. 1839-1856* (Paris: Fayard, 1967), esp. pp. 330 ff., in which Cadot discusses the ideas about Russian peasants commonly held in France during that period, and pp. 381 ff., about Russia's past. Above all, see pp. 461 ff., the chapters entitled, "La Pologne, la Russie et le panslavisme" and "La Russie, l'Europe et la révolution."

73. Vera Piroschkow, *Alexander Herzen. Der Zusammenbruch einer Utopie* (Munich: Anton Pustet, 1961).

74. Eberhard Reissner, *Alexander Herzen in Deutschland* (Berlin: Akademie-Verlag, 1963), chap. 1, "Alexander Herzen in der Kritik der deutschen Offentlichkeit der 50er Jahre."

75. E. Lampert, *Studies in Rebellion* (London: Routledge & Kegan Paul, 1957).

76. See Malia, *Alexander Herzen and the Birth of Russian Socialism* (see n. 18 above), pp. 335 ff., "The Crucial Year, 1847," and pp. 369 ff., "The Revolution of 1848."

77. The collection of Bakunin's letters edited by Yu. M. Steklov, broken off in 1935, has become a bibliographic rarity and is not to be found. The Soviet reader has not been offered any choice of the youthful works of Bakunin, contrary to what has occurred for considerably less significant writers of the thirties and forties. Nevertheless, on the renewal of interest in Bakunin in Russia, see here pp. lxxxii ff. As for Belinsky, the most characteristic work to have appeared in Russia is by V. S. Nechaeva, *V. G. Belinsky, zhizn i tvorchestvo* [V. G. Belinsky. Life and works], in 4 vols. The first appeared in 1949, the second in 1954, the third (concerning the years 1836–41) in 1961, and the fourth (1842–48) in 1967, in Moscow, edited by the Academy of Sciences of the USSR. Unquestionably competent and useful, this biography is often weak in presenting the moral and political problems in the life and activities of Belinsky. On the vast literature on him, as on his writer friends, we refer the reader to K. D. Muratova, *Istoriya russkoy literatury XIX veka. Bibliograficheskii ukazatel* [History of Russian literature of the 19th century. Bibliographical indicator] (Moscow and Leningrad: Akademiya nauk SSSR, 1962).

78. Yu. G. Oksman, *Pismo Belinskogo k Gogolyu kak istoricheskiy dokument* [The letter from Belinsky to Gogol as an historical document], in *Ot "Kapitanskoy dochki" k "Zapiskam okhotnika." Pushkin. Ryleev. Kolcov. Belinsky. Turgenev. Issledovnaiya i materialy* [From "The Captain's Daughter" to "A Sportsman's Notebook." Pushkin, Ryleev. Koltsov. Belinsky. Turgenev. Research and materials] (Saratov: Knizhnoye Izdatelstvo, 1959), pp. 203 ff; Oksman, "Belinsky i politicheskiye traditsiy dekabristov" [Belinsky and the political traditions of the Decembrists], in *Dekabristy v Moskve. Sbornik Statey* [The Decembrists in Moscow. A collection of articles] (Moscow: Moskovsky rabochii, 1963), pp. 185 ff.

79. Peter Scheibert, *Vom Bakunin zu Lenin. Geschichte der Russischen revolutionären Ideologien. 1840–1895*, vol. 1, *Die Formung des radikalen Denkens in der Auseinandersetzung mit Deutschem Idealismus und Französischem Bürgertum* (Leiden: E. J. Brill, 1956); Edward J. Brown, *Stanchievich and His Moscow Circle, 1830–1840* (Stanford, Calif.: Stanford University Press, 1966); Lampert (n. 75 above); L. Schapiro, *Rationalism and Nationalism in Russian Nineteenth-Century Political Thought* (New Haven, Conn.: Yale University Press, 1967); and Philip Pomper, *The Russian Revolutionary Intelligentsia* (New York: Thomas Y. Crowell, 1970). On the problem of the intelligentsia, see the collection of articles edited by Richard Pipes, *The Russian Intelligentsia* (New York: Columbia University Press, 1961); Allen McConnel, "The Origin of Russian Intelligentsia," *South and East European Journal* 8, no. 1 (1964): 1 ff.; Daniel F. Brower, "The Problem of Intelligentsia," *Slavic Review* 26 (December 1967): 1163 ff. An English version of Belinsky's letter to Gogol can be found in Marc Raeff, *Russian Intellectual History: An Anthology, with an Introduction by Isaiah Berlin* (New York: Harcourt, Brace & World, 1966), pp. 252 ff.

80. Gerschenkron, *Continuity in History*, pp. 140 ff.

81. R. Portal, *Le Statut des paysans liberés du servage. 1861–1961* (Paris and The Hague: Mouton, 1963).

82. P. A. Zayonchkovsky, *Otmena krepostnogo prava v Rossiy. Izdaniye trete pererabotannoye i dopolnennoye* [The abolition of peasant serfdom in Russia. Third edition revised and completed](Moscow, 1968). The first two editions of this work appeared in 1954 and 1960. A comparison between them is very instructive for understanding the evolution of Soviet historiography in the last fifteen years. A still classic work is that by P. A. Zayonchkovsky, *Provedenie v zhizn krestyanskoy reformy 1861 g.* [The application of the peasant reform of 1861] (Moscow, 1958).

83. N. M. Druzhinin, ed., *Krestyanskoye dvizhenie v Rossii v XIX-nachale XX veka* [The peasant movement in Russia in the 19th century and at the beginning of the 20th century] (Moscow: Mysl). Here is how it is divided, with indication of the date of publication: 1796-1825 (1961), 1826–49 (1961), 1850-56 (1962), 1857–May 1861 (1963), June 1861–69 (1964), 1870–80 (1968), 1881–89 (1960), 1890–1900 (1959), 1901–May 1907 (not published), June 1907–July 1914 (1966). See also the recent investigation by N. M. Druzhinin, *Byvshie udelnye krestyane posle reformy 1863 g. (1863-1883)* [The ex-peasants of the appanage after the reforms of 1863 (1863-1883)], in *"Istoricheskiye zapiski,"* no. 85 (1970), pp. 159 ff.

84. Kirill Vasilevich Chistov, *Russkiye narodnye socialno-utopicheskiye legendy XVII-XIX vv.* [The popular social-utopian legends of Russia in the 17th to 19th centuries] (Moscow: Nauka, 1967).

85. *Revolyutsionnaya situaciya v Rossiy v 1859-1861 gg.* [The revolutionary situation in Russia between 1859 and 1861] (Moscow: Akademiya nauk SSSR, Institut istoriy, 1960–).

86. Lenin, *Sochineniy* [Works], 4th ed. (Moscow, 1948), 21:189–90.

87. Ja. I. Linkov, *Revolyutsionnaya borba A. I. Gercena i N. P. Ogareva i taynoe obshchestvo "Zemlya i Volya" 1860-ch gg.* [The revolutionary struggle of A. I. Herzen and N. P. Ogarev and the secret society "Land and Liberty" in the 1860s] (Moscow: Nauka, 1964).

88. N. N. Novikova, *Revolyutsionery 1861 goda* [The revolutionaries of 1861] (Moscow: Nauka, 1968).

89. Victor Leontovitch, *Geschichte des Liberalismus in Russland* (Frankfurt am Main: Vittorio Klostermaan, 1957). See especially pt. 3, *Entwicklung der politischen Freiheit. 1856-1914,* pp. 233 ff. The author himself explains how the inspiration came to him from *Storia del liberalismo europeo* by Guido De Ruggiero, even if he then admits immediately that the tasks facing Russian liberalism were very different from those that this political trend had to face in the West.

90. George Fischer, *Russian Liberalism: From Gentry to Intelligentsia* (Cambridge, Mass.: Harvard University Press, 1958).

91. Klaus Detlev Grothusen, *Die historische Rechtsschule Russlands. Ein Beitrag zur russischen Geistesgeschichte in der zweiten Hälfte des 19. Jahrhunderts* (Giessen: Justus Liebig-Universität, 1962). See esp. the two chapters devoted to Kavelin (pp. 90 ff.) and to Chicherin (pp. 120 ff.). From a sociological standpoint, one can add Klaus Von Beyme, *Politische Soziologie im Zaristischen Russland* (Wiesbaden: Otto Harrassowitz, 1965) (the pages on Chicherin, Mikhailovsky, etc., are of interest).

92. D. Tschizewskij, *Hegel bei den Slaven* (Darmstadt, 1961), p. 311.

93. Leontovitsch, p. 246.

94. Fischer, *Russian Liberalism*, p. 67.

95. Schapiro, *Rationalism and Nationalism*, p. 90 (see n. 79 above).

96. Richard Pipes, "Russian Conservatism in the Second Part of the Nineteenth Century" (paper presented at the XIIIth International Congress of Historical Sciences, Moscow, 1970).

97. Vittorio Strada, *Leggendo "Padri e figli,"* in *Tradizione e rivoluzione nella letteratura russa* (Turin: Einaudi, 1969), pp. 14 ff.

98. B. P. Kozmin, *Literatura i istoriya. Sbornik statey* [Literature and history. A collection of articles], ed. E. S. Vilenskaya (Moscow: Khudozhestvennaya literatura, 1969), pp. 243 ff.

99. Ibid., p. 326.

100. Ibid., p. 327.

101. "Politicheskaya napravlennost ocherka Shchedrina Kapluny" [The political significance of Shchedrin's essay "The Capons"], in ibid., pp. 328 ff.

102. Ibid., p. 357, and see p. 510n.

103. R. V. Filippov, *Revolyutsionnaya narodnicheskaya organizatsiya N. A. Ishutina-I. A. Khudyakova (1863-1866)* [The populist revolutionary organization of N. A. Ishutin and I. A. Khudyakov (1863-1866)] (Petrozavodsk: Karelskoye knizhnoye izdatelstvo, 1964), p. 40.

104. Ibid., p. 71.

105. T. F. Fedosova, "Polsky Komitet v Moskve i revolyutsionnoye podpole 1863-1866" [The Polish Committee in Moscow and the revolutionary underground, 1863-1866], in *Revolyutsionnaya rossiya i revolyutsionnaya Polska (Vtoraya polovina XIX veka). Sbornik statey pod red. V. A. Dyakova, I. S. Millera, N. P. Mitinoi* [Revolutionary Russia and revolutionary Poland (second half of the 19th century), a collection of articles edited by V. A. Dyakov, I. S. Miller, N. P. Mitina] (Moscow: Nauka, 1967), pp. 125 ff.

106. Ibid., pp. 464-65.

107. Michael Confino, "Bakunin et Nečaev. Les débuts de la rupture. Introduction à deux lettres inédites de Michel Bakunin. 2 et 9 juin 1870," in *Cahiers du monde russe et soviétique*, 7, no. 4 (1966): 625 ff. See now the definitive edition of all the documentation in *Michel Bakounine et ses relations avec Sergej Nečaev. 1870-72. Ecrits et matériaux. Introduction et annotations de Arthur Lehning* (1971), in *Archives Bakounine,* ed. A. Lehning, A. J. C. Rüter, and P. Scheibert (Leyden: E. J. Brill, for the International Institute of Social History of Amsterdam, 1961 ff).

108. Confino, "Bakunin et Nečaev," pp. 633-35.

109. *Gosudarstvennost i anarchiya* [Statism and anarchism] was included in the definitive edition of the *Archives Bakounine.* Needless to say, this whole collection is indispensable also for the history of the Russian revolutionary movement from the sixties to the seventies.

110. Purely as an example, see vol. 32 of *Literaturnoye nasledstvo,* which came out in 1963, devoted entirely to D. A. Sleptsov, with an introductory article by K. I. Chukovsky; the numerous and important articles by E. Bushkanec in *Russk-*

aya literatura; the discussion on populism that took place in the pages of *Voprosy literatury* in 1960 and 1961; the book by N. V. Osmakov, *Poeziya revolyutsionnogo narodnichestva* [The poetry of revolutionary populism] (Moscow: Akademiya nauk SSSR, 1961); the interesting studies by E. Taratuta on Stepnyak-Kravchinsky; the article by V. F. Zacharina, "Revolyutsionnaya propagandistskaya literatura 70-ch godov XIX veka" [The literature of propaganda of the 1870s], *Istoricheskiye zapiski,* vol. 71 (1962); the ed. of V. G. Bazanov and O. B. Alexseeva of the *Agitatsionnaya literatura russkikh revolyutsionnykh narodnikov* [The propaganda literature of the Russian revolutionary populists] (Leningrad: Nauka, 1970); M. S. Goryachkina, *Khudozhestvennaya proza narodnichestva* [The literature of populism] (Moscow: Nauka, 1970), and *Russkaya literatura i narodnichestvo* [Russian literature and populism] (Leningrad: LGU, 1971); and V. F. Zacharina, *Golos revolyutsionnoy Rossiy. Literatura revolyutsionnogo podpolia 70-kh godov. "Izdaniya dlya naroda"* [The voice of revolutionary Russia. The literature of the revolutionary underground of the 1870s. "The editions for the people"] (Moscow, 1971).

111. P. L. Lavrov, *Filosofiya i sociologiya* [Philosophy and sociology], 2 vols., ed. by I. S. Knizhnik-Vetrov and A. F. Okulov (Moscow: Mysl, 1965). See the definitive edition of the Lavrov documents collected by Boris Sapir, *Vpered: 1873-1877. From the Archives of Valerian Nikolaevich Smirnov,* 2 vols. (Dordrecht: D. Reidel, 1970).

112. M. G. Sedov, *K. voprosu ob obshchestvenno-politicheskikh vzglyadakh N. K. Mikhailovskogo* [On the question of the social and political ideas of N. K. Mikhailovsky], in *Obshchevstvennoye dvizhenie v poreformennoy Rossii. Sbornik statey k 80-letiyu so dnya rozhdeniya B. P. Kozmina* [The social movement in Russia after the reform of 1861. A collection of articles for the 80th birthday of B. P. Kozmin] (Moscow: Nauka, 1965), pp. 179 ff.; and B. S. Itenberg, *Dvizhenie revolyutsionnogo narodnichestva. Narodnicheskiye kruzhki i "khozdenie v narod" v 70-ch godakh XIX v.* [The movement of revolutionary populism. The populist groups and the "go to the people" movement of the seventies of the 19th century] (Moscow: Nauka, 1965), pp. 104 ff.; Billington (see n. 17 above); Mendel (see n. 39 above); F. B. Randall, "N. K. Mikhailovskij's What Is Progress?" in *Essays in Russian and Soviet History in Honor of Geroid Tanquary Robinson, Edited by John Shelton Curtiss* (Leyden: E. J. Brill, 1963); Pomper, pp. 107 ff., contains a particularly clear and persuasive exposition on the contrast between nihilism and Mikhailovsky's ideas between 1861 and 1870. This vast bibliography, though it does not pretend to be complete, will to some extent make up for a weakness of which *Il populismo russo (The Roots of Revolution)* has often been accused, that is, the lack of a specific discussion of Mikhailovsky's ideas. In fact, Mikhailovsky always refused to participate in the revolutionary movement and organization and therefore can legitimately be excluded from a book that discusses only revolutionary populism. Nevertheless, there is no doubt about his influence on young men who were preparing to go to the people, and on the whole movement of the seventies. (But then why not discuss Saltykov-Shchedrin and many others?) I had to resist the temptation to make this book into a history of

Russian culture and society in the latter half of the 19th century, even if, admittedly, it is particularly difficult to make a division between revolutionary populism and the general movement of thought of that era and one easily runs the risk of being unjust when dealing specifically with Mikhailovsky. See the discussion of this in R. V. Filippov, *Iz istorii narodnicheskogo dvizheniya v pervom etape "khozhdeniya v narod" (1863-1864)* [From the history of the populist movement in the first stage of the "go to the people" movement (1863-1864)] (Petrozavodsk: Karelskoe knizhnoe izdatelstvo, 1967), pp. 99 ff. On problems that are parallel and related to those posed by the figure of Mikhailovsky, see the interesting studies of E. L. Rudnitskaya, "Nikolai Nozhin," in *Revolyutsionnaya situaciya v Rossiy v 1859-1861 gg.* [The revolutionary situation in Russia between 1859 and 1861] (Moscow: Akademiya nauk SSSR, Institut istoriy, 1962), 2:444 ff.; V. I. Taneev, *Detstvo, yunost, mysli o budushchem* [Childhood, youth, thoughts on the future], ed. M. P. Bastin (Moscow: Akademiya nauk SSSR, Institut filologiy, 1959); P. S. Skurinov, *Kritika pozitivizma V. I. Taneevym* [The criticism of V. I. Taneev of positivism] (Moscow: MGU, 1965); and A. P. Kazakov, *Teoriya progressa v russkoy sociologii kontsa XIX veka (P.L. Lavrov, N. K. Mikhailovsky, M. M. Kovalevsky)* [The theory of progress in Russian sociology at the end of the 19th century (P. L. Lavrov, N. K. Mikhailovsky, M. M. Kovalevsky)] (Leningrad: LGU, 1969); and Walicki, *The Controversy over Capitalism.*

113. *Revolyutsionnoye narodnichestvo 70-ch godov XIX veka. Sbornik dokumentov i materialov v dvuch tomakh* [Revolutionary populism of the 1870s. A collection of documents and materials in two volumes], ed. S. N. Valk, S. S. Volk, B. S. Itenberg, and S. M. Levin (Moscow: Nauka, 1964-65), 2:391-444.

114. R. V. Filippov, *Iz istoriy revolyutsionno-demokraticheskogo dvizheniya v Rossiy v kontse 60-kh—nachale 70-kh godov XIX veka* [The history of the democratic revolutionary movement in Russia at the end of the 1860s and at the beginning of the 1870s] (Petrozavodsk: Gosudarstvennoye Izdatelstvo Karelskoy SSSR, 1962); "Ideologiya Bolshogo obshchestva propagandy (1869-1874)" [The ideology of the great society of propaganda (1869-1874)], in ibid., 1963; N. A. Troitsky, *Bolshoe obshchestvo propagandy (1871-1874). (Tak nazyvaemye "Chaikovsky")* [The great society of propaganda (1871-1874). The so-called followers of Chaikovsky] (Saratov: Izdatelstvo saratovskogo universiteta, 1963); Itenberg; S. S. Volk, *Narodnaya Volya. 1879-1882* [The will of the people. 1879-1882] (Moscow: Nauka, 1966); Sedov, *Geroichesky period revolyutsionnogo narodnichestva;* Filippov, *Iz istoriy narodnicheskogo dvizheniya;* and N. A. Troitsky, "Nekotorye voprosy istoriografiy revolyutsionnogo narodnichestva 70-kh godov" [Some historiographical problems on the populist revolutionary movement in the seventies], *Istoriograficheskiy sbornik,* 1971, no. 3, pp. 70 ff.

115. P. A. Zayonchkovsky, *Kriziz samoderzhaviya na rubezhe 1870-1880 godov* [The crisis of autocracy between the seventies and eighties of the 19th century] (Moscow: MGU, 1964). See M. I. Kheyfec, *Vtoraya revolyutsionnaya situaciya v Rossiy (konets 70-kh i nachalo 80-kh godov XIX v.). Krizis pravitelstvennoy politiki* [The second revolutionary situation in Russia (end of the 1870s and beginning of the 1880s). The crisis in government policy] (Moscow: MGU, 1963).

116. Leo Valiani, "Dalla I alla II Internazionale," in *Questioni di storia del socialismo* (Turin: Einaudi, 1958), pp. 168–263.

117. G. G. Vodolazov, *Ot Chernyshevskogo k Plekhanovu* [From Chernyshevsky to Plekhanov] (Moscow: MGU, 1969), p. 39; following quotations are also from this volume.

118. G. G. Vodolazov, "Osobennosti razvitiya socialisticheskoy mysli v Rossii v otrazhenii russkoy zhurnalistiki 60-70-ch godov XIX v. Aztoreferat dissertacii na soiskaniye uchenoy stepeni kandidata istoricheskikh nauk" [Details on the development of socialist thought reflected in the Russian pampleteering of the 1860s and 1870s. Author's report on the dissertation for the title of candidate in historical sciences] (Moscow: MGU, Fakultet zhurnalistiki, 1967), p. 19.

119. Richard Wortman, *The Crisis of Russian Populism* (Cambridge: Cambridge University Press, 1967).

120. M. Ya. Gefter, preface to V. A. Tvardovskaya, *Sotsialisticheskaya mysl Rossiy na rubezhe 1870-1880-kh godov* [Russian socialist thought between the 1870s and 1880s] (Moscow: Nauka, 1969), p. 6.

121. See, for example, *Idei sotsializma v russkoy klassicheskiy literature* [The ideas of socialism in classical Russian literature], ed. N. I. Prutskov (Leningrad: Nauka, 1969).

AUTHOR'S NOTE: While correcting the proofs of this second edition, I received the valuable bibliography compiled for the Institute of History of the Academy of Sciences of the USSR by N. Ya. Krayneva and P. V. Pronina, under the editorship of B. S. Itenberg. It is entitled *Narodnichestvo v rabotach sovetskikh issledovateley* [Populism in the studies of Soviet researchers between 1953 and 1970] (Moscow, 1971). I also received an interesting essay by M. G. Vandalkovskaya, *M. K. Lemke—istorik russkogo revolyutsionnogo dvizheniya* [M. K. Lemke —historian of the Russian revolutionary movement] (Moscow: Nauka, 1972).

Eight

In Memory of Lev Semenovich Gordon

When, in 1948, the slender, nervous figure of Lev S. Gordon appeared on the wide landing of the Saltykov-Shchedrin Library in Leningrad, he declared that I could speak to him in any language I chose, including Italian. I was struck by his manner. On one hand he showed deliberate detachment and hardness, typical of many Russians, but this was mixed with a passionate interest in culture and lively curiosity, characteristic of the intelligentsia. Gordon was curator of Voltaire's library which, as is known, is housed in Leningrad along with numerous other documents of the Age of Enlightenment, including works of Diderot and Catherine II. Our dialogue was of the kind that was possible in those years: a courteous request to see the annotations that Voltaire had written in the margins of the works of Nicolas-Antoine Boulanger and of Adalberto Radicati di Passerano, followed by an equally polite refusal. Almost as if to soften this official rejection, Gordon took me to visit the Voltaire library, to see the books lined up on the shelves. He allowed me to admire a few volumes that had just been taken from the shelves and were on his desk. He was looking for even the slightest sign that they had been read or considered by "le philosophe."

He was working on the catalogue of Voltaire's books that every 18th-century scholar knows, edited by V. S. Liublinsky and published in 1961 by the Academy of Sciences of the USSR. From his research, in 1947 Gordon produced a valuable and curious article, "Voltaire and the Government of Jesuits in Paraguay," that was included in a miscellany called *Voltaire: Articles and Materials*. This had been published under the direction of M. P. Alexseev by the University of Leningrad (not yet bearing the heavy name of Zhdanov) in commemoration of the 250th anniversary of the philosopher's birth (the commemoration actually fell in 1944, during the war, and was therefore celebrated a little late). This small book of research was one of the first signs of the revival of 18th-century studies in the Soviet Union. It represented a reaffirmation of faith in reason, in philological precision, and in scientific honesty. Gordon's contribution was one of the finest in the book, a little heap of coals from Voltaire's fire.

At the time, I did not know that *Candide*, a work thoroughly treated in this article, had been the subject of Gordon's doctoral thesis, completed in 1946 but never published. However, from the brief dialogue that we had managed to have in the Leningrad library, and especially from the way he held the volumes of the Age of Enlightenment, I could recognize Gordon's sincerity and true passion as a historian and scholar. For this reason I tried to maintain what relationship was possible between a foreigner and a Russian during the Stalin era. I sent him a few books without expecting or receiving any reply. I had so fully anticipated this response that it seemed natural for the silence to continue for months or years. I certainly did not expect a Russian scholar to correspond with a colleague in Russia, much less in Italy.

But I was mistaken. Gordon's silence, at first attributable to the restrictions in a totalitarian state, had had more serious causes since 1949, deriving from the more tragic aspects of Stalinist despotism. I was distressed to discover this on February 17, 1957, the day Gordon answered a letter of mine concerning the library. Now that the dictator was dead, I was renewing my ten-year-old request to see Voltaire's volumes. Gordon did not answer from Leningrad where I had written. He was in Molotov in the Urals, in the far north, and said he was only a reader at the Saltykov-Shchedrin library, when he was allowed to go there, twice a year. He was now at the University and Pedagogical Institute of Molotov. "This is already fortunate," he said in his pathetic and invented Italian mixed with French, "for during a period beginning in 1949, I completely forgot the existence of the library, I who had worked there, and I could only recall the line from Dante, 'Lasciat'ogni speranza...'" He had been exiled to Siberia (naturally, he did not write this), his library had been sacked and scattered (this he did say). He had barely survived the forced labor, the abuse, the humiliation, and like so many of his companions, day after day he, too, had opposed tyranny with dignity, angry shouts with silence, and organized bestiality with the strength of thought and perhaps irony. He paid dearly for his survival. He came out of the concentration camp with tuberculosis and died of it in 1973. As he wrote on January 4, 1963, "We must pay for the trips we made at the expense of *il Baffutissimo* (I've taken three and Faina one)." He showed energy and irony in such a tragic situation. "I thought we had already paid with our work, but it is not enough. We pay with our precarious health. Last year and this year I have had three (3!) operations. I hope I have paid off these debts by now, but who knows."

A decade had passed. It truly seemed possible to regard the Stalinist period as the irreversible past. After the words I have reported, Gordon added, "This is not an expression of discouragement. On the contrary, last year was a year of great joy for us, both personal and impersonal.... You must already know the story by Solzhenitsyn, *One Day in the Life of Ivan Denisovich*. The appearance and publication of this work is an act of redemption for the past. Our generation, the generation to whom the 'cult' is not a forgotten tale, is celebrating. Let us hope we will be able to read other books in the same vein."

He had two compensations for his long resistance. First of all there was his wife, Faina, his companion in exile, who was even more fragile physically than himself. She was a scholar of Russian philology, a refined lover of the poetic tradition of her country, but was so deeply disturbed by the life in the camps that she still bore the psychological wounds of those years. His second compensation was a renewed desire to study, understand, and dedicate himself to the Age of Reason. In the Enlightenment he found the germs of democratic and communist ideas, of libertarian and revolutionary passions, that formed the foundations of the society in which he had to live and struggle. He returned to the sources, using great philological care. He showed the interest of one who finds his youth again, the lost freshness, and the fundamental reasons for work and suffering.

Gordon was born in 1901, and had fought in the ranks of the Red Army at a very young age. He had been taken prisoner by the Poles, and with a smile, remembered his adventures as a soldier, when "wounded, defeated, anticipating the gallows that evening," he had met a "Catholic priest, a chaplain of the Polish army. And while he fought for his life he remembered his Latin lessons and asked, "*'Pater reverendissime; qui agit Polonia hostibus captatis?'* I am not sure of my Latin even today, but the chaplain looked at me (I was wounded in August 1920) marveling—and then said I would be saved . . . *'quod erat demonstrandum!'*" From 1921 to 1923 he had studied at the University of St. Petersburg under great masters in history and literature, V. F. Shishmarev, V. M. Zhirmunsky, and N. N. Sretensky. He had then gone abroad, mainly to London, studying, among other things, Italian literature. Now, released from the concentration camps, he still clung to his initial hopes. He still believed in scientific rigor in research without allowing concessions. His approach was a singular mixture of utopian ideals and philological methods, not unusual among Russian scholars. It was as if the long decades of Stalinist isolation had frozen and preserved faiths and beliefs which had been dissolved and transformed elsewhere by more dynamic experiences. "Today," he wrote in that same first letter to me on February 17, 1957, "after my resurrection, I am working with great pleasure and renewed energy. This shows me that, as the French say, 'A quelque chose malheur est bon.'"

Gordon drew the following conclusion one day after having read, with fear and pain, the book by Primo Levi, *La tregua*. "In general, it seems to me that medieval squires had to keep a vigil before being knighted and twentieth century knights had to endure the test of the camps (but this duty lasts too long), and I (and Faina, too) divide my acquaintances into two groups: those who endured (the noble ones) and those who do not understand (the remainder). It is very difficult not to canonize oneself; I have always fought against this victim's prejudice . . ." All the more to his credit, since for Gordon the modern concentration camps affected not only himself, his wife, and friends, but also his father and mother, who died in the Drancy concentration camp in France under the Nazis.

Even when Gordon was finally free, it took his strength of character to overcome the innumerable obstacles that confronted him. The teaching post at Molotov was a kind of forced residence. On November 27, 1957 he was able to write with evident satisfaction that he had "changed address without moving." The city where he lived had reacquired its old name of Perm. Since the days of Herzen it had more or less been a place of internment, and it retained this function even when it was no longer called Molotov. The local authorities, academics, and others considered Gordon an inconvenient person. The anti-Semitism of the Stalinist era had become less virulent but had certainly not ceased. Gordon, of Jewish origin but not practicing, suffered along with so many others. The worst aspect was the atmosphere of ambition and arrogance which had grown rather than dissipated after Stalin's death. This ever-present attitude was courageously denounced by Sakharov recently.

It took ten years for Gordon to be transferred. He had to apply directly to Moscow; the ministry of education characteristically showed more understanding and more intelligence than the academic and local authorities. On August 25, 1968 he wrote, "*Alea iacta est* ... as Julius Caesar said when changing residence. And now we are shouting it with great joy. From the first of September I will be a professor in the history department at the University of Saransk, in Mordovia." His appointment in an area known for its high number of concentration camps ends up being considered good fortune. "Compared to Perm it is a small city, but the climatic conditions are much more favorable." In another letter he adds that it is not only a matter of climate, but the whole psychological atmosphere is better. His wife, Faina, would be able to pursue her studies and finish her doctorate.

Meanwhile, in those ten years, Gordon had had the strength to plan and continue with his research. He had always refused to regard the French Enlightenment as a unique movement. He was trying to trace clear indications within it of the Classicists, the Optimists, the major dominant figures from Montesquieu to Helvétius, from Voltaire to Diderot. On the other side, he was searching for the rebellious figures, the refractory ones, the pessimists and the persecuted ones. On one side were the bourgeois, on the other were the representatives of the plebeian wing of the Enlightenment. The former would be precursors of the winners in the revolution at the end of the century, and the latter would be precursors of the vanquished "enragés" of Babeuf. It is a class and psychological distinction, Marxist and existentialist—and certainly disputable, but Gordon always used it with great sensitivity and finesse, without ever transforming it into an empty sociological classification. This was because there were strong and deep personal roots in his research. In each of those rebellious and offended personalities he recognized elements of his own drama and that of his generation.

The history of the Russian intelligentsia, on the other hand, offered him continuous incitement and confrontation. From the 18th century to the present there had been a long series of writers of popular origins or passions who had brought rebellious and original accents to Russian culture and literature. Naturally, Gordon greatly admired Herzen, the father of the modern intelligentsia.

He says, "There are some historical personalities who we like from our first encounter in youth. Herzen is one of them. His independence of thought always
seemed an example to follow—forgive me such emphasis!" Even in minor figures,
Gordon only needed to see a spark of independence and originality to forgive a
thousand other sins. He did his utmost to explain the reason for the development
of this "plebeian" trend in France in the middle of the 18th century, offering
evidence from the spread of literacy to the increase in number of schools, from
the dispersion of forbidden books to the crumbling of the borders of the old
regime, from the increased discontent to the growing protests. He was especially
successful in creating vivid portraits of little-known characters, each of whom
revealed an element, an aspect of this world on the verge of the Age of Enlightenment: Dulaurens, Ange Goudar, La Beaumelle, Coyer, Tiphagne de la Roche,
Augustin Rouillé. But was it really a current? Gordon was convinced it was. He
certainly managed to underline the common denominators which, even in their
diversity, existed in these many, varied, and unusual figures.

Gordon encountered every kind of obstacle in his work. It was the kind of
research which should be carried out in Paris and in the French provinces, with
access to archives, legal documents, and pamphlets. Gordon never had an opportunity to leave the USSR, not even when he was invited to participate in meetings and other international gatherings. The isolation of the Stalin era was diminished, but far from overcome. It was not easy to keep up to date with studies
being carried out in the rest of the world. With what pleasure, for example, he
had read Moravia's article on the ideologists in *Rivista storica italiana.* It "contains a wealth of information for me: the history of thought does not end after
the fall of Robespierre or Babeuf; we forget this all too often" (December 21,
1966). And how disappointed he was not to be familiar with the works of Elie
Halévy!

There were difficulties within his country as well. Academic traditions are
certainly no less rigid in Russia than elsewhere. Literary scholars objected, saying
that he should concentrate on major writers without getting lost in research on
minor ones. Historians, after the tragic experiences of the previous decades, were
hardly disposed to reopen debates about the Jacobin left, the "enragés" and their
origins, distant or near. Yet on April 19, 1964, Gordon said, "I have found more
audacity and more understanding among the historians than in the circle of my
own colleagues [linguists]."

In spite of everything, Gordon's articles appeared here and there in various
journals and miscellanies, often published in distant centers such as Ufa, Perm,
and Sverdlovsk, but also in Odessa and Moscow. One collection of these works
appeared shortly before his death, not in Russian, but in German, edited by the
great expert on 18th-century Europe, Werner Krauss. It is entitled, "Studien
zur plebejisch-demokratischen Tradition in der französischen Aufklärung," published by Rütten & Loening in Berlin in 1972. It is an excellent edition, in which,

among other things, the quotations are left in the original French whereas previously they had been translated into Russian, according to the enduring Russian tradition. This edition lacks a complete bibliography by Gordon. However, the essentials are there and a Western reader can get a more than adequate idea of what this Russian historian wanted to do and succeeded in doing. An excerpt from Werner Krauss's biographical note makes a worthy conclusion to this volume. "Gordon, that superb Voltaire scholar, dedicated all his passion to studying the generally unknown, neglected writers of the French Enlightenment, who were largely of plebian origin. In this field Gordon showed himself to be a *maximus in minimis*.... Though a specialist, Gordon never dissipated his energies in fragmentary and barren research, but remained open, within this specialty, to the broad currents of Enlightenment and revolution."

Gordon is no longer with us. He died, consumed by tuberculosis. He was often prevented from doing his work and endured this restriction patiently. His circumstances did not always allow him to reach the standard he felt he could achieve. The frustration caused by these limitations must certainly also have contributed to his death. Until the very end he maintained clarity of mind and freshness of soul. He once said he had lived during an epoch of "epidemics" or "pandemics"; that is, he was closed in a world where it was an achievement merely to retain one's sanity. He died reciting some lines of Gumilev, an ultimate confirmation of his profound dedication to the values of the intelligentsia.

Index

DATE DUE

DEMCO 38-297